The
Socialization
Of
Emotions

Genesis of Behavior

Series Editors: MICHAEL LEWIS
Rutgers Medical School
University of Medicine and Dentistry of New Jersey
New Brunswick, New Jersey

and LEONARD A. ROSENBLUM
Downstate Medical Center
Brooklyn, New York

Volume 1   The Development of Affect

Volume 2   The Child and Its Family

Volume 3   The Uncommon Child

Volume 4   Beyond the Dyad

Volume 5   The Socialization of Emotions

The
Socialization
Of
Emotions

Edited by
Michael Lewis
Rutgers Medical School
University of Medicine and Dentistry of New Jersey
New Brunswick, New Jersey

and

Carolyn Saarni
Sonoma State University
Rohnert Park, California

PLENUM PRESS • NEW YORK AND LONDON

Library of Congress Cataloging in Publication Data

Main entry under title:

The Socialization of emotions.

(Genesis of behavior; v. 5)
Includes bibliographies and index.
1. Emotions in children. 2. Emotions in children—Social aspects. I. Lewis, Michael,
1937 Jan 10–   . II. Saarni, Carolyn. III. Series.
BF723.E6S63   1985   155.4′12   85-3701
ISBN 0-306-41851-7

Contributors

DAPHNE BLUNT BUGENTAL, *Psychology Department, University of California, Santa Barbara, California*

LINDA A. CAMRAS, *Psychology Department, DePaul University, 2323 North Seminary, Chicago, Illinois*

AIMÉE DORR, *Graduate School of Education, University of California, Los Angeles, California*

MARGOT L. GREEN, *Department of Psychology, Temple University, Philadelphia, Pennsylvania*

SARA HARKNESS, *Department of Maternal and Child Health and Aging, Harvard School of Public Health, Boston, Massachusetts*

PAUL L. HARRIS, *Department of Experimental Psychology, Oxford University, South Parks Road, Oxford, England*

JEANNETTE M. HAVILAND, *Department of Psychology, Rutgers University, New Brunswick, New Jersey*

MICHAEL LEWIS, *Department of Pediatrics, UMDNJ-Rutgers Medical School, Institute for the Study of Child Development, New Brunswick, New Jersey*

CATHERINE LUTZ, *Department of Anthropology, State University of New York at Binghamton, Binghamton, New York*

Carol Zander Malatesta, *Graduate Faculty, New School for Social Research, New York, New York*

Linda Michalson, *Department of Pediatrics, UMDNJ-Rutgers Medical School, Institute for the Study of Child Development, New Brunswick, New Jersey*

Suzanne M. Miller, *Department of Psychology, Temple University, Philadelphia, Pennsylvania*

Bert S. Moore, *Department of Psychology, University of Texas at Dallas, Richardson, Texas*

Carolyn Saarni, *Department of Counseling, Sonoma State University, Rohnert Park, California*

Charles M. Super, *Judge Baker Guidance Center, Boston, Massachusetts*

Preface

How are we to understand the complex forces that shape human behavior? A variety of diverse perspectives, drawing on studies of human behavioral ontogeny, as well as on humanity's evolutionary heritage, seem to provide the best likelihood of success. It is in an attempt to synthesize such potentially disparate approaches to human development into an integrated whole that we undertake this series on the genesis of behavior.

In many respects, the incredible burgeoning of research in child development over the last decade or two seems like a thousand lines of inquiry spreading outward in an incoherent starburst of effort. The need exists to provide, on an ongoing basis, an arena of discourse within which the threads of continuity between those diverse lines of research on human development can be woven into a fabric of meaning and understanding. Scientists, scholars, and those who attempt to translate their efforts into the practical realities of the care and guidance of infants and children are the audience that we seek to reach. Each requires the opportunity to see—to the degree that our knowledge in given areas permits—various aspects of development in a coherent, integrated fashion. It is hoped that this series—which will bring together research on infant biology, developing infant capacities, animal models, the impact of social, cultural, and familial forces on development, and the distorted products of such forces under certain circumstances—will serve these important social and scientific needs.

Each volume in this series will deal with a single topic that has broad significance for our understanding of human development. Into its focus on a specific area, each volume will bring both empirical and theoretical perspectives and analysis at the many levels of investigation necessary to a balanced appreciation of the complexity of the problem at hand. Thus, each volume will consider the confluence of the genetic, psychological, and neurophysiological factors that influence the individual infant and the dyadic, familial, and societal contexts within which development occurs. Moreover, each volume will bring together the vantage points provided by studies of human infants and pertinent aspects of animal behavior, with particular emphasis on nonhuman primates.

Just as this series will draw on the special expertise and viewpoints of workers in many disciplines, it is our hope that the product of these labors will speak to the needs and interests of a diverse audience, including physiologists, ethologists, sociologists, psychologists, pediatricians, obstetricians, and clinicians and scientists in many related fields. As in years past, we hold to our original objectives in this series of volumes to provide both stimulation and guidance to all among us who are concerned with humans, their past, their present, and their future.

The chapters in this volume are derived from papers presented and discussed at a conference, "The Socialization of Affect," held under the auspices and with the support of the Educational Testing Service in Princeton, New Jersey. The participants in the conference were Daphne Blunt Bugental, Joseph Campos, Linda A. Camras, Aimée Dorr, Sara Harkness, Michael Lewis, Catherine Lutz, Carol Zander Malatesta, Linda Michalson, Suzanne M. Miller, Bert S. Moore, Leonard Rosenblum, Carolyn Saarni, Richard Schweder, Craig Stenberg, and Charles M. Super.

MICHAEL LEWIS
CAROLYN SAARNI

Contents

1 Culture and Emotions

MICHAEL LEWIS AND CAROLYN SAARNI   1

I. CULTURE

2 Child–Environment Interactions in the Socialization of Affect

SARA HARKNESS AND CHARLES M. SUPER   21

3 Cultural Patterns and Individual Differences in the Child's Emotional Meaning System

CATHERINE LUTZ   37

4 Contexts for Experience with Emotion, with Special Attention to Television

AIMÉE DORR   55

II. PROCESSES OF SOCIALIZATION

5 Signals, Symbols, and Socialization: The Modification of Emotional Expression in Human Development

CAROL ZANDER MALATESTA AND JEANNETTE M. HAVILAND   89

6 What Do Children Know about Emotions and When Do They Know It?

LINDA MICHALSON AND MICHAEL LEWIS   117

7 Socialization of Affect Communication
LINDA A. CAMRAS   141

8 What Children Know about the Situations That Provoke Emotion
PAUL L. HARRIS   161

9 Indirect Processes in Affect Socialization
CAROLYN SAARNI   187

III. REGULATION OF BEHAVIOR AND EMOTIONAL STATES

10 Behavioral Consequences of Affect
BERT S. MOORE   213

11 Unresponsive Children and Powerless Adults: Cocreators of Affectively Uncertain Caregiving Environments
DAPHNE BLUNT BUGENTAL   239

12 Coping with Stress and Frustration: Origins, Nature, and Development
SUZANNE M. MILLER AND MARGOT L. GREEN   263

Author Index   315

Subject Index   321

Culture and Emotions

MICHAEL LEWIS AND CAROLYN SAARNI

Emotions are undisputedly multifaceted and derived from an interaction of biological and environmental socializing influences. To date in the study of emotions among children, much effort has been expanded in measurement issues and tracing the measurement of facial expression across the opening months and years of life. In general, the guiding principle of this task has been the assumption of a strong biological model that posits a fixed and universal connection between emotional expression—in particular, facial expression—and emotion. Following Darwin, many have focused on infant facial expression and on the connection between stimuli and emotions as expressed in the face and the voice.

Although the measurement of the neuromusculature of facial expression and the relationship of emotional expression to a particular situation are important topics for study, for the most part the ways in which emotions are socialized have been neglected. This is especially true in the socialization of early emotional behavior. This topic, the socialization of emotion, particularly through the interaction of the child with its social environment, is the focus of this volume. Insofar as our interests lie with the socialization set of influences on emotional behavior, it is necessary that we ask (a) what it is about emotion that is socialized and (b) how emotions become socialized. In examining these two

MICHAEL LEWIS • Department of Pediatrics, UMDNJ-Rutgers Medical School, Institute for the Study of Child Development, New Brunswick, New Jersey 08903.   CAROLYN SAARNI • Department of Counseling, Sonoma State University, Rohnert Park, California 94928.

issues, individual and group differences in the socialization of emotion also need to be considered.

Before addressing these questions, it is necessary to consider the two general models of emotional development usually proposed, as well as what is meant by *emotion*. As we shall see, without a clear definition of what is meant by *emotion*, the discussion of the socialization of emotion is impossible.

THEORIES OF EMOTIONAL DEVELOPMENT

In the discussion of emotional development, two prototypical models of emotion have been used to contrast the various theories of emotional development. Hochschild (1979) discussed these and contrasted the biological model, as primarily concerned with the relationship of emotions to biological given instincts or impulses. Thus, for example, the measurement of emotion focuses mainly on the constant and universal aspects of expression rather than on individual differences in expression that may require socialization interpretations. Moreover, when they are recognized, socialization factors are usually considered only when questions are raised about how emotions are stimulated and expressed.

> The image that comes to mind in considering the biological view is that of a sudden automatic reflex syndrome, Darwin's instant snarl expression, Freud's tension discharge and a given breaking point of tension overload, James and Lang's notion of an instantaneously unmediated visceral reaction to perceived stimulus, the perception of which is also unmediated by social influences. (pp. 553–554)

In other words, emotions are viewed as analogous to knee jerks or sneezes. They are unlearned, biologically controlled, and subject to relatively little socialization influence.

In the socialization view, attention is focused on the ways in which social influences affect emotional development. In socialization models, emotions are not regarded as fixed or universal phenomena, nor is emotional development viewed as the unfolding of various and combinatorial maturational systems. Instead, the fundamental questions posed by any socialization model must be concerned with what it is about emotion that is influenced by social relations and how emotions become integrated within social structures and norms. This approach does not deny the importance of organismic functions; rather, it stresses the equally important role of socialization in learning and emotional development.

WHAT IS IT ABOUT EMOTION THAT IS SOCIALIZED?

In order to talk about the socialization of emotion, it is necessary to specify as carefully as possible what is meant when one uses the term *emotion*. Recently, Lewis and Michalson (1983) attempted to provide a common parlance for discussing what is meant by *emotion*. Briefly, we proposed five components as constituting aspects of emotion that are most often referred to. The first component consists of *emotional elicitors*, which are essentially stimulus events (internal or external to the individual) that can trigger particular biological changes. Some emotional elicitors do not have a developmental history (e.g., falling), whereas others do (e.g., separation-provoked anxiety). The second component is *emotional receptors*, which appear to be specific receptors or central nervous system pathways such as may be found with innate releasing mechanisms or possibly even facial muscle configuration. The third component is *emotional states*, general defined as changes in somatic and neurophysiological activity that occur when the emotional receptors are activated.

The fourth component is *emotional expression*, which consists of the observable and potentially communicative changes in facial, vocal, and kinesic behavior that occur with changes in emotional state. It is in this component that the interactive blending of socialization and biology is most evident in emotional development. Not only is maturational differentiation in the coordination of skeletal muscles involved in emotional expression, but one's social milieu contributes heavily to one's coming to know when to modify, inhibit, or substitute expressive behaviors for assorted emotions. The fifth and last component is *emotional experience*, which Lewis and Michalson defined as "the interpretation and evaluation by individuals of their perceived emotional state and expression" (p. 181). They suggested that emotional experience requires a sense of self (meaning self-permanence and self-as-object), and that therefore this last component is intimately linked to the social and cognitive factors that influence self-development.

Typically, the sequence of an emotion begins with an elicitor impacting on a receptor, continues with the initiation of a state change and an observable expression, and culminates in an emotional experience. However, it must be emphasized that this structural model is multidirectional; that is, an emotional experience that produces an intense evaluation of an emotion may function as a new elicitor (an internal one) and start a whole new cycling process of diverse affective responses. It is precisely this multidirectionality of the model that allows us to examine some of the more subtle effects of socializing influence. We shall now

take each component in turn and suggest some ways in which socialization influences the developmental course of each component. The
specific contributions to this volume are mentioned where relevant.

Emotional Elicitors

The first component to be considered from a socialization perspective is emotional elicitors. In discussions of emotions from a biological perspective, one often finds reference to a class of elicitors that
seem to have no cultural history nor any developmental pattern. Elicitors
such as loud noises, falling, and sudden stimulus onsets have a strong
and often immediate biological consequence. Although such examples
are important and require explanation and model building, most elicitors
in human life are not of this nature. In general, elicitors have differential
effects, which are due to cognitive changes, socialization rules, and
maturation. The classes of emotional elicitors that are often considered
include strange approach, separation from mother, or failure-to-achieve
situations. Each of these seems to have a developmental history and to
reflect particular cultural values. These elicitors are external. Emotional
elicitors that are internal—that is, those that precede emotional experience in a cycle of affect—are also likely to reveal these influences.

Illustrations of how these two sorts of elicitors may be socialized
are to be found in the chapters by Michalson and Lewis, by Moore, and
by Dorr. Michalson and Lewis point out how particular elicitors may
have an effect on particular emotional states through the influence of
others in the child's life. When presented with an eliciting situation,
some children believe that one emotion over another is likely to occur.
Moreover, these individual differences can be traced to the particular
socialization experiences of the child. Thus, for example, one child, when
told a story about a little girl lost in a grocery store, responds that this
child is likely to have a sad face, whereas another child presented with
the same story reports that the child in the grocery store is likely to have
a fear face. The difference in the children's beliefs appear to be related
to the beliefs of their parents.

Miller and Green's chapter on cognitive styles of coping with threat
or frustration also directs our attentions to the issue of elicitors. The
authors remind us that the nature of the stimulation is treated differently
by different children, the result being different emotional states. One
child turns off the cues and is not anxious, whereas another child monitors the cues carefully and becomes anxious. Such a demonstration
reminds us that socialization (or dispositional) factors, related to how
we interpret stimuli, affect the subsequent emotional process.

Although Moore emphasizes the behavioral consequences of affective states, such as altruistic actions stemming from the child interpreting his or her emotional experience as sadness, his review also discusses how the child's emerging self-concept moderates a number of these response consequences to his or her emotional experience, rendering them elicitors of new affect cycles. If one's self-concept represents the confluence of a number of social and cognitive factors, then we can begin to hypothesize how emotional experiences that result from affect cycle A might become transformed into internal emotional elicitors for affect cycle B. Conceivably, one's self-evaluation must be intimately linked to emotional experience A if it is to become the elicitor for a subsequent cycle. There may also be a developmental curve associated with this hypothesis that suggests an inverse U-shape: in early childhood, the self-concept would be too rudimentary to function in this fashion. By middle childhood and on into adolescence, this self-evaluation is conscious, and the links between emotional experience, self-evaluation, and internal emotional elicitors are most readily demonstrated. By adulthood, the cycles may have become so habitual that the awareness of oneself vis-à-vis one's emotional experience occurs typically thereafter only during periods of conflict or of psychological crisis and change. Needless to say, such speculation awaits further research.

Dorr's perspective emphasizes the impact of culture via the media (especially television) on the determination of emotion elicitors. She analyzes contexts in which affect socialization might be expected to occur, with special attention to what she calls the context of "framed experience," which refers to situations in which children observe emotional transactions but are precluded from participating directly in them. Television and radio programs, books, plays, and movies all fall within this context of framed experience. The power of television for focusing on classes of stimuli and rendering them emotional elicitors is discussed by Dorr. She traces how television can evoke emotion, stimulate learning about emotions, model conventional or normative affect-expressive displays, and provide reinforcing pleasure simply through providing entertainment.

Emotional Receptors

Emotional receptors have received the least attention when considered from a socialization perspective. It is generally assumed that, if these hypothetical structures exist, they resemble biological processes similar to those in the retina that are designed to detect certain visual stimuli. These emotional receptors, wherever they are located, do not appear to have a developmental course. Nevertheless, it is necessary to consider whether emotional receptors may not be present at birth and may, in fact, develop as the organism matures. Such a model of receptors may require the consideration of socialization factors in their acquisition. Perhaps the closest to a discussion of emotional receptors to be found in this volume is Bugental's chapter on unresponsive children commonly labeled *hyperactive*. This work suggests how difficult it is to modulate arousal-related emotional receptors (and perhaps states) via social influences. Bugental's chapter suggests that one way of considering individual differences in emotional behavior is through the consideration of individual differences in arousal. Such differences may be related to receptor and state changes and therefore may play an important role in determining individual differences in emotion.

Emotional States

Emotional states are defined as changes in bodily activity: somatic, biochemical, and neurological changes. It has generally been assumed that emotional states are biological givens and that any socialization of emotional states is in the modulation of these given states. Whether such a view is valid or not, it is necessary to consider in what way socialization may play a role in the production as well as in the transformation of given emotional states. One way among many in which emotional states themselves may be socialized has been suggested by the work of several investigators. For example, Buck and colleagues (Buck, Miller, & Caul, 1974), as well as Ekman (Ekman, Levenson, & Friesen, 1983) have claimed that emotional expressions through feedback mechanisms can alter emotional states. Thus, for example, it is argued that if I smile and act happy, it is likely that I can produce a happy state, even though I am not smiling because I am happy. Thus, expression and change in expression have been held to directly affect emotional state. If this hypothesis turns out to be true, it is possible that emotional states are socialized through the social world's effect on emotional expression. If a child is positively reinforced for making happy as opposed to frowning faces, and if making a happy face leads to a happy state, then one can postulate that the emotional state of happiness has been socialized. Although no claim is made that the state—that is, the particular constellation of somatic, neural, and hormonal changes—is itself produced through socialization, it is possible to elicit particular emotional states through socialization experiences. Any research that investigates the effects of socialization on emotional expression does, in fact, study the effects not only of socialization but of state as well. Michalson and Lewis and Camras, in arguing for strong socialization models related to emotional expression, provide, at the same time, information on and support for the socialization of emotional states.

Emotional Expression

Because emotional states and receptors are internal and are not readily available to socialization experiences *per se*, emotional expression (facial, vocal, and postural activity) appears to be the component of emotion that provides the most direct opportunity for socialization. When expressive behavior is socialized, what occurs is that the individual acquires beliefs, which are culture- or family-mediated, about "appropriate" ways to reveal internal states and feelings. Such mandated expressive behavior is guided by display rules that lead to the minimization, the inhibition, or the dissimulation of expressive behavior. Especially relevant contributions in this volume are the chapters by Malatesta and Haviland, by Camras, and by Harkness and Super.

Malatesta and Haviland's work with young infants (3–6 months) shows that, even at this early age, facial expression frequency and range appeared to be responsive to maternal imitative behavior and contingent responding. Thus, in their work, by 6 months of age, the frequency of expression changes had diminished somewhat, and there was a proportionately greater reduction in negative expressions, which were not responded to by mothers as often as positive expressions.

Camras reviews some of the research on the recognition of emotional expressions. One of her studies revealed that abused and neglected preschoolers were less accurate than nonabused children in identifying emotional expressions. Camras speculates that parents of abused children may not display appropriate or consistent expressive behaviors contingently, so that facial expressions do not become linked with emotion-eliciting situations. As a result, their children reveal deficits in their decoding of facial expressions, as well as in predicting what sort of feeling is likely to be experienced in common situations facing young children. Such children may acquire conventional cultural display rules either at later ages or in modified forms. Conceivably, emotional inhibition and minimization become their preferred expressive displays, although further research is needed to explore these possibilities.

Harkness and Super present fascinating data on the cultural pressures not to cry on the children and youth of the Kipsigis of western Kenya. Crying is viewed very negatively in the culture, and in particular at the time of circumcision and clitoridectomy (the puberty rites of passage), crying brings disgrace to the child as well as to his or her family. These authors analyzed interactive behavior samples of children at different ages and concluded that the culture/family provides systematic "cultural scripts" about the display of distress that the child internalizes and ultimately generalizes.

Emotional Experience

Emotional experience has a developmental course, as suggested by Lewis and Michalson (1983), in that, in order to experience emotional states or expressions, one needs first to develop a concept of oneself. Moreover, it is clear that emotional experience, the most cognitive of the five emotional components, requires that organisms possess a language of emotion. The impact of socialization on this aspect of emotion is seen as it affects the individual's knowledge about emotion, his or her knowledge of the language of emotion, and his or her cultural knowledge of what others feel under what circumstances. Moreover, the interpretation of or insights into one's own affective process must rest on the cultural acceptance of emotion as a valid and meaningful experience, one to which the lexicon is applied, and one in which socially acceptable behavior is expected. Thus, for example, in a culture in which anger is inappropriate, one should find a reduction in the individual experiential history related to the particular emotional state of anger.

Michalson and Lewis's chapter on very young children's knowledge of particular social situations that are likely to elicit particular expressions points to the fact that one of the earliest aspects of the socialization of a conspecific is to teach the child that particular situations are likely to be associated with particular emotional expressions. That 3-year-old children are able, often as well as adults, to point to the particular faces likely to go with particular situations suggests that the discriminative cues of situations and faces are available and are socialized quite early in the child's life.

Harris's chapter on children's conceptualization of links between situation and emotion suggests that younger children (6 years old) tend to think of emotions as stemming from situations. By age 11 or so, children were more likely to refer to "mental processes" as mediating between situation and emotional response. These mental processes appeared to be the older children's analyzing situations for their *implications* and not simply for their identity. Thus, older children were also more likely to conclude that a given situation could lead to one's experiencing multiple emotions, not just one. Other research described by Harris includes children's insight into the emotional experience of ambivalence and their beliefs about the duration of emotions.

Saarni's chapter also examines children's insight into their affective processes. She investigated children's beliefs around the topic of emotional expression, specifically (a) motives to reveal or not reveal one's genuine feelings; (b) expectations about interpersonal consequences when emotional expressiveness is dissimulated, and (c) beliefs about how to "balance" adaptively revealing or not revealing one's true feelings. In addition, parental attitudes toward emotional expressiveness were assessed and analyzed in conjunction with their children's beliefs. She concludes that the parents' expectations or attitudes do influence the children's complexity of insight into their effective processes.

Of particular import for the socialization of emotion in general and experience in particular is the acquisition of an emotional lexicon. In the chapters by Michalson and Lewis and by Lutz, consideration is given to developmental changes in the acquisition of the lexicon and to cultural differences in emotional terms. Michalson and Lewis present data on children's ability to produce as well as to comprehend emotional terms. By presenting children from 2 to 5 years of age with pictures reflecting six basic emotional expressions, the authors were able to demonstrate that the emotional lexicon is acquired relatively early and that there appears to be a sequence in which the production of the emotional lexicon occurs. As in other aspects of the acquisition of the lexicon, comprehension precedes the production of emotional terms.

Lutz undertakes a definition of cultural patterns and individual differences in children's emotional meaning systems. For her, culture is the carrier variable by which meaning is acquired, and any attempt to understand emotional development must be provided through observation of the cultural definition of particular emotional features. By focusing on children's emotional environment on the Ifaluk atoll, the author shows us that the assumption that specific emotional responses have universal application is not necessarily true. That children move from household to household and that children may be adopted by adults without children once again shows us the relative nature of emotional elicitors as well as of emotional states and experiences. More specific to the socialization of meaning is the children's acquisition of a particular word that has a unique meaning within the culture. For Lutz, the meaning of an emotional word for any particular child arises out of a sum of the contexts in which the child has heard the word used. The meaning of an emotional word, therefore, is not, as she says, inscribed in stone or a dictionary; rather, the meaning of the word is found in how the speaker uses the term to serve his or her purposes. Moreover, individual differences in the use of the word and in the meaning ascribed to it can readily be determined. Thus, for Lutz, the relativity of the acquisition of emotional meaning and, in particular, of words based on cultural specificity is a hallmark in understanding the socialization of emotion.

Overall, then, what is socialized about emotion is far ranging. Work exists that shows the impact of socialization in the areas of emotional expression and emotional experience (i.e., one's interpretation of one's affective processes). Less clear is the research on how socialization affects emotional elicitors, and very ambiguous is the research on the effects of socialization on emotional receptors and states.

HOW ARE EMOTIONS SOCIALIZED?

In any discussion focusing on the process of socialization, there is no reason to believe that the socialization of emotions proceeds through mechanisms very different from those of the socialization of any other set of behaviors. Thus, the socialization of emotion can be divided into two broad classes of processes. In the first, we refer to direct effects, and in the second, to indirect effects. Direct effects are those processes in which one or more agents of socialization act on the child. In indirect effects, the child is socialized through the observation of others' behavior. Lewis (Lewis & Feiring, 1981; Lewis & Weinraub, 1976) has referred to these two types of effects as they influence the socialization of social behavior, and they can be applied to emotional development as well. Saarni also addresses indirect processes, although from a somewhat different perspective.

Direct Effects

The direct effects of socialization include instrumental learning, classical conditioning, and didactic teaching. The reinforcement of emotional behavior includes the reinforcement of particular emotional expressions (see the Malatesta and Haviland chapter). Moreover, although unexplored recently, classical conditioning of emotional responses was reported as early as 1919 by Watson. Here, an emotional reponse of fear was classically conditioned from the original fearful object to an associated object. In similar fashion, one can address the conditioning of emotional states. As we have suggested, by reinforcing a particular emotional expression it is possible to condition a particular state in response to a stimulus not associated with that state before.

Didactic teaching is also a direct effect. The mother who says to her child, "Boys don't cry" or "girls don't get dirty" socializes particular emotional expressions as well as states by educating children to feel and to express feeling in one way or another. These direct forms of learning are processes that account for some of the socialization effects. They are particularly relevant when the socialization of expressions is considered.

Indirect Effects

The indirect effects that are associated with the socialization of emotion include identification, imitation, and social learning. Identification is a psychoanalytic concept in which the organism, in some undefined way, incorporates the values, goals, and behaviors of another. The child's identification with the parents results in the copying of the parents' behavior, including their emotional behavior. Imitation is an active process in which the imitator copies the model; for example, the child watches the way another person behaves when a toy is taken and, in turn, acts in a similar manner when her or his toy is taken. Social learning is another form of indirect learning that can be divided into two parts. In the first, the structure of the social environment of the child serves as information for the child's own hypothesis generation. Consider, for example, a child growing up in a home in which there is little or no laughing and smiling. Independent of the reinforcement principles associated with the child's smiling or laughing, this child is less likely to smile and laugh than a child raised in a setting in which there is much smiling and laughing. The structure of the environment in which the child is raised acts on and determines the child's behavior independent of its reinforcing value because it supplies information that can be used to generate hypotheses about how to behave.

The second process of social learning can also be used to explain how the behavior of parents, for example, affects the child. The child watches and listens to the behavior of one person directed toward another person. In this way, the child learns something about emotional behavior by watching. This is one way in which the child comes to learn about emotional expressions, emotional words, and even the appropriateness of particular behaviors in particular contexts. This type of social learning has been addressed by Lewis, Feinman, and Campos in their discussion of social referencing. For example, Feinman and Lewis (1983) showed that an 8-month-old infant's emotional behavior toward a stranger can be affected by the mother's emotional behavior toward that stranger. Social references or the use of others to affect one's own emotional behavior has received considerable attention recently and certainly can be shown to be an important indirect effect in modulating children's emotional learning.

One of us (Saarni, this volume) has proposed a variation on the theme of indirect processes in the socialization of emotion that emphasizes the individual's construction of expectancies about what to feel and how to express his or her feelings "appropriately." This focus leads to an analysis of how expectations held by others (i.e., socializing agents) about how one "should" feel and look are first accommodated to, are then gradually internalized as personal expectancies about how one anticipates feeling and looking, and finally, once the expectancies are firmly in place, function assimilatively via generalizability to novel, albeit similar, affect-eliciting situations.

Biological Effects

There is one further class of effects that does not fit neatly into either direct or indirect learning. Here, we refer to a particular biological process. Although the term *socialization processes* usually refers to learning, as opposed to biological processes, it is important to keep in mind that a culture or the gathering of groups of individuals itself constitutes a type of influence. In emotional behavior in particular, there are classes of activities that appear to have a biological concomitant. These we call *contagion*. There are many examples of contagious behavior within the emotional domain. There seems to be general agreement that the emotional expression of others serves as an elicitor. For example, the laughter of an audience in a theater serves to elicit more laughter in the individual than when the individual watches the same performance without others. Likewise, emotions such as sadness seem to be contagious, and even more dramatic, perhaps, is the emotion of passion. The expressed passion level of the partner serves as an elicitor and an enhancer of one's own emotional passion state.

Although not directly related to emotion, the current observation that women living together organize their menstruation cycle in accord with that of others suggests that such contagious mechanisms—whether they be based on communication, subtle behavioral shaping, some other effect—serve to organize and enhance an internal state of individuals through the influence of others. This kind of contagion process can be seen in smiling or yawning behavior, as well as in complex biological processes like menstruation. Such data support our contention that, in considering how emotions are socialized, it is necessary not only to take into account direct and indirect learning processes but to include a contagious effect, which appears to operate at some biological level.

INDIVIDUAL AND GROUP DIFFERENCES IN EMOTIONAL BEHAVIOR

Everyday observation supports the belief that there are individual and group differences in the socialization of emotion. Differences exist within a culture group, as well as across cultures. Of interest is the question of the origin of individual differences within a culture. Some differences are likely to be explained by such biological factors as differences in temperament, in facial neuromusculature, in arousal levels, and in perceptual discrimination ability. On the other hand, it seems likely that many more individual differences within a culture can be explained by differences in experiential factors and in socialization practices. For example, Michalson and Lewis have shown that, although parents and children, in geneal, assign the face of sadness to such a situation as the loss of a pet, and both parents and child show a happy face for a situation like a birthday party, there are idiosyncratic differences. When observed more carefully, these individual differences in choosing what expression is likely to go with what story are found to be related either to experiential factors or to particular socialization practices. An example of experiential factors would be one child's choosing a fright face instead of a happy face for the birthday party situation. On questioning the child, we discovered that, during the last birthday party, when the child was opening a present, the present exploded, showering the child and the company with an unexpected array of confetti. The memory of this event caused the child to choose an idiosyncratic response.

In terms of socialization factors, we have found, at least with a small number of mothers and children, a consistency in unusual responses. If mother and child are given the same task of choosing an expression that goes with a particular story, idiosyncratic responses on the part of the child are likely to be mirrored in the idiosyncratic response of the mother. It seems reasonable to assume that the particular socialization practices of particular families have an intergenerational effect.

Individual differences in the socialization of emotion can occur at any level of our analysis of emotion: which stimulus elicits what response, what is the nature of the expressive behavior, and which is the appropriate emotional state for a particular situation. Moreover, that individuals have differential self-reflection capacities suggests that emotional experiences have a strong individual component.

Individual differences in cognitive style represent still another aspect of important individual differences. In their review of the coping strategies used toward threat and frustration, Miller and Green remind us that how children choose to deal with stimuli determines, to a large degree what emotional state these stimuli will evoke. Children, as well as adults, have two ways of coping with aversive or frustrating events: (a) cognitive avoidance, or turning down or off incoming information as a means of reducing arousal, and (b) cognitive sensitization, monitoring or turning on cues. Individual differences in these styles can be demonstrated that may have a dispositional factor or may be learned.

Sex differences as well as social class and cultural differences also provide evidence of differences in the socialization of emotional behavior. Perhaps the most widely studied group differences are sex differences. Here, the evidence from a variety of sources indicates strong socialization pressures vis-à-vis sex differences in emotional expression, emotional states, and even the emotional lexicon. Thus, for example, Lewis and Michalson (1983) pointed out reinforcement differences in maternal responses to infant cries as a function of the sex of the infant. Mothers are significantly less responsive to male infant cries than they are to female infants when the children are 1 to 2 years of age, whereas there is no difference in their response when the children are 3 months old. Likewise, several of the chapters in this book report sex differences. Across chapters, one finds that, although sex differences are rarely found in children's knowledge about their affective processes (see, for example, the Harris and Saarni chapters), they are found when actual expressive displays are observed and analyzed (see, for example, the Malatesta and Haviland and the Camras chapters in this volume). Typically, the sex difference found is that females exceed males in frequency of positive affective display. Another sex difference that appears to emerge, especially in Saarni's research is between mothers' and fathers' attitudes. Permissive parental attitudes are associated by Saarni with greater complexity in the child's thinking about the interpersonal consequences of dissimulating expressive behavior. On the other hand, relatively more controlling maternal attitudes are associated with greater complexity in the child's insight into how to achieve an adaptive balance between showing and not showing genuine feelings. These sex differences in the parenting approach appear to be similar to some research conducted with much younger children (see summary by Gardner, 1982). That sex differences in maternal behavior and in child behavior can be seen in infancy should not be surprising, as early childhood differences in expressive emotional behavior have been widely reported.

Cultural differences have received much less study, although the chapters by Lutz and by Harkness and Super provide direct support for the generally accepted proposition that cultural differences occur in emotional expression as well as in emotional terms, and perhaps even in emotional states. Indeed, Lutz's insistence that the meaning of emotional terms is culturally determined should ensure that all phases of emotional behavior will have strong roots in cultural norms.

Although little studied, there are some data to suggest strong social-class differences in emotional behavior. It has been reported that lower-class children and adults are much more likely than are middle-class members to express anger in physical displays. Whether or not such findings can be validated today, social-class differences in maternal perceptions of infant behavior do exist. When mothers returned to a room after leaving their 1-year-olds alone for 2 minutes, significantly more lower-class mothers than middle-class mothers reported their children to be angry (Lewis & Michalson, 1983). Such findings support the proposition that class differences in the display of anger may exist and, if so, are a function of the early socialization differences between classes.

Group and individual differences in emotional behavior, including stimuli that are likely to elicit emotional behavior, and differences in emotional expressions, state, and experience all need further exploration. Well within the first year of life, individual and group differences in emotional behavior exist and suggest the importance of the early socialization of these behaviors.

Although some have argued that the primary role of socialization is to shape what has already been laid down by biological imperative, it seems clear that, except for a small class of events, the socialization of emotion is equal in importance in the creation of emotional life. Although the biology of human beings disposes us to emotional, as well as cognitive and social, behavior, the nature of that behavior, the situations that elicit it, the ways of thinking and speaking about it, the things we feel, and whether we feel or not are all dependent on an elaborate set of socialization rules. We have tried to suggest and present some of the more critical factors in the socialization of emotion. No single volume can, of course, do justice to such a complex and diverse task. Lewis and Michalson (1983) suggested at least five aspects of the socialization process that need attending to, and we include these to demonstrate the diverse studies possible: (a) how to express emotion and (b) when to express emotion. In addition, (c) how emotions are managed, (d) how emotions are labeled, and (e) how emotions are interpreted are all critical dimensions in understanding the socialization process.

How to express emotion is critical in understanding the use of display rules. When to express emotion refers to our knowledge of emotion by situation and to the cultural rules related to the appropriate emotion, given the context. Although simple biological models dictate that certain emotions go in some way with particular situations, it seems necessary to include socialization rules in that relationship. How emotions are managed addresses the social interplay among the individual's emotions. Here, the use of others, in terms of the display rules, is relevant. The use of others to enhance our emotional life or the use of others to inform us of what emotional behaviors are appropriate both fall within this aspect of socialization. The labeling of emotion as a socializing factor in and of itself needs additional attention. The lexicon of emotional life has been under study, but group, cultural, and individual differences in the labeling and the use of emotion terms are important to study. Finally, the interpretation of emotions by others and by the self needs consideration. Within the socialization of the interpretation of emotion, one must consider the individual's interpretation of her or his own emotion, or what we have addressed as emotional experience. The mental life of children continues to receive study as it relates to the individual child's feelings. Likewise, the interpretation of emotions from a parental as well as from a cultural point of view needs to be explored. The parents' interpretation of their children's behavior and its effect on the children's subsequent emotional life needs to be studied. Likewise, from a cultural point of view, differences in what emotions are likely to be elicited by what situations need interpretation. Is it true that, between cultures, there may be situations in which the same elicitor or stimulus event can be characterized as provoking different emotional states and experiences?

Although many more aspects of socialization can be discussed, our attempt within this book is to present the reader with the types of studies in the socialization of emotional life that are currently being conducted. The 12 chapters in this book address a variety of the problems that we have discussed. After this introductory chapter, the remaining 11 are divided into three groups. The first grouping, on "Culture," includes the chapters by Harkness and Super, by Lutz, and by Dorr. The second, on the "Processes of Socialization," includes chapters by Malatesta and Haviland, by Michalson and Lewis, by Camras, by Harris, and by Saarni; and the third, "Regulation of Behavior and Emotional States," includes chapters by Moore, by Bugental, and by Miller and Green.

REFERENCES

Buck, R. W., Miller, R. E., & Caul, W. F. Sex, personality, and physiological variables in the communication of affect via facial expression. *Journal of Personality and Social Psychology*, 1974, *30*, 587–596.

Ekman, P., Levenson, R. W., & Friesen, W. V. Autonomic nervous system activity distinguishes among emotions. *Science*, 1983, *221*, 1208–1210.

Feinman, S., & Lewis, M. Social referencing and second order effects in ten-month-old infants. *Child Development*, 1983, *54*, 878–887.

Gardner, H. *Developmental Psychology* (2nd ed.). Boston: Little, Brown, 1982.

Hochschild, A. R. Emotion work, feeling rules, and social structure. *American Journal of Sociology*, 1979, *85*, 551–575.

Lewis, M., & Feiring, C. Direct and indirect interactions in social relationships. In L. Lipsett (Ed.), *Advances in infancy research* (Vol. 1). New York: Ablex, 1981.

Lewis, M., & Michalson, L. *Children's emotions and moods: Developmental theory and measurement*. New York: Plenum Press, 1983.

Lewis, M., & Weinraub, M. The father's role in the infant's social network. In M. Lamb (Ed.), *The role of the father in child development* (Vol. 1). New York: Wiley, 1976.

Watson, J. B. *Psychology from the standpoint of a behaviorist*. Philadelphia: Lippincott, 1919.

I

Culture

2

Child–Environment Interactions in the Socialization of Affect

Sara Harkness and Charles M. Super

Research on the universality of facial expressions (Ekman, 1972) suggests that the socialization of affect involves interactions between situational variables and a finite repertoire of human emotions whose meanings are at least roughly synonymous among all members of the species. At the same time, Izard's formulation (1978) of "affective-cognitive structures" shows that emotions are in reality not separable from the particular circumstances that are associated with them. The fact that it is possible to construct a list of "basic," universally recognizable emotions derives not only from a species-specific repertoire of facial expressions, but perhaps more fundamentally from a larger set of human expressive behaviors, including laughter and crying as well as bodily movements and postures. These behaviors, for which a universal capacity exists, are also, without exception, carried out in particular circumstances. As elements in the human communicative function, they create the necessity of response from the environment while also being shaped by it. To use Lewis's terms the contextual reality of emotional expression transforms "state" into "experience."

Sara Harkness • Department of Maternal and Child Health and Aging, Harvard School of Public Health, Boston, Massachusetts 02115. Charles M. Super • Judge Baker Guidance Center, Boston, Massachusetts 02115. The research reported here was supported by the Carnegie Corporation of New York, the William T. Grant Foundation, the Spencer Foundation, and the National Institute of Mental Health (Grant 33281). All statements made and views expressed are the sole responsibility of the authors.

In this chapter, we are concerned with processes in the interplay between the universal and the particular in the shaping of emotional experience. The point of view to be developed is that these processes can best be seen as interactions between two dynamic structures: the developing individual and the environment as it is shaped for the individual by social and cultural factors. Although we recognize that the experience of each person is the unique product of his or her own life space, the idea of the *socialization of affect* would not be possible without the assumption of regularities in the environment as well as in developmental processes. An illustrative parallel can be drawn from child language socializaton. All normal children have the capacity to learn language, but the languages that they must learn vary around the globe. For each child, the language to be learned is not idiosyncratic; rather, it is an organized system that is shared by a community. The basic issue in describing the socialization of either language or affect is how the child and the environment interact with each other so that the regularities of the environment are assimilated in successive developmental stages.

THE "DEVELOPMENTAL NICHE"

The authors (Harkness & Super, 1983; Super & Harkness, 1981) have elaborated the idea of the *developmental niche* as a theoretical framework for culture transmission in normal human development. Briefly, the developmental niche is conceptualized in terms of three basic dimensions. The first consists of the physical and social settings that the child lives in, including, for example, aspects of daily routine such as where he or she spends different amounts of time, in whose company, and engaged in what kinds of activities. A second dimension consists of culturally regulated systems of child care and rearing, or the repertoire of strategies that parents and other caretakers call on in meeting the needs of children. The third dimension of the developmental niche is the psychology of the caretakers, or the beliefs and values that inform the ways in which parents and others both structure and respond to behavior in children. This structuring of the child's environment, we have suggested, provides the primary source of the child's acquisition of culture, including the experience, the encoding, and the expression of affect. The regularities of the physical, social, and psychological parameters of the niche, as well as the thematic continuities from one culturally defined developmental stage to the next, provide the material from which the child abstracts the rules of the culture.

CULTURAL SCRIPTS AND THE SOCIALIZATION OF AFFECT

Recent research in cognitive science has highlighted regularities in everyday communicative sequences as a source of understanding about social processes (Hutchins, 1980; Lakoff & Johnson, 1980; Lutz, 1982; Quinn, 1982; Schank & Abelson, 1977). A related development has been the study of speech between adults and young children in different cultures, which examines the ways in which parents teach cultural values as well as language to their children (e.g., Schieffelin, 1979). A similar approach can usefully be taken to the analysis of communicative sequences related to the expression of affect. Sequences of interactions surrounding affective behavior are selected so as to focus on the expression of affect itself as a target of socialization. As in studies of child language development, nonverbal as well as verbal behavior is seen as carrying communicative loading (see Greenfield, 1979, for an example of this approach to child language study). In taking the point of view that behaviors organized around a particular affective expression illustrate mechanisms of socialization, it is also useful to assume, as with child language socialization, that communications directed to the child are modulated in accordance with the child's developmental capacities.

In this chapter, we explore possible mechanisms for the socialization of affect in young children in a rural Kipsigis community of Kenya. Specifically, we focus on the communicative processes surrounding one particular kind of affective expression: crying. In order to interpret these processes, however, we must first review some general characteristics of these children's developmental niches, including their social and physical surroundings, their customary activities, and the lives of their parents. We then briefly describe how crying relates to other aspects of Kipsigis culture in infancy and adulthood. With this background, we then proceed to examine and interpret actual communicative sequences involving crying in young children. Finally, we use these ethnographic and observational data to make some inferences about the processes of internalization in the socialization of affect.

THE RESEARCH SETTING

The sample community, called Kokwet, is a Kipsigis settlement in the western highlands of Kenya. The Kipsigis are a Highland Nilotic people whose subsistence base is cattle herding and hoe agriculture. Like other nearby peoples, the Kipsigis are patrilineal and traditionally used age-sets as the basis of military organization; today, male and female circumcision ceremonies remain the focal point of cultural solidarity. Kokwet, where the authors carried out anthropological and psychological research for three years (from 1972 to 1975), consisted of 54 households established on land repatriated from the British in 1963. Although as a government-sponsored "settlement scheme" Kokwet was intentionally modern in some agricultural practices, the community remained traditional in many significant respects: most adults had little or no schooling, few men worked at salaried jobs away from the homesteads, cows were still used for the customery brideprice, and virtually all adolescents still chose to undergo the traditional circumcision ceremonies.

Many features of child life in Kokwet, as elsewhere, have been derived from the economic and social organization of adult life. The work of mothers in Kokwet included farming on the family fields, as well as gathering firewood and bringing water from the river, preparing food, and being responsible for the care of the children. Fathers were in charge of the cows, ploughing the fields, major repairs around the property, and the important political business of the community. Families were often polygynous, with each co-wife located in her own hut on the compound, sharing the tasks of the household while the children played together.

Children were also important contributors to the economic well-being of the family: they were used to help in taking care of younger siblings, in watching the cows, in weeding the gardens, in running errands and in general helping around the household. One striking aspect of these childhood tasks was the age at which children were expected to carry out important responsibilities. It was not unusual, for example, to see a child of three chasing a calf out of the garden. The children responsible for taking care of babies were usually about 8–10 years old and might be as young as 5 or 6.

The characteristic settings for child life in Kokwet were the homesteads and the surrounding fields, where the children spent their time alternating between play with groups of siblings, half-siblings, and close neighbors, and attending to their domestic responsibilities. The mothers were, if not actually present, at least within calling distance most of the time; but they were not available to engage in playful activities with the children. Rather, these "executive mothers" directed and organized their children while carrying out the many activities required for running a successful farm. The fathers, the titular heads of the families, were also usually nearby but were usually less closely involved in the children's activities. The children themselves, even while playing, were also responsible for each other—particularly the older siblings for the younger ones.

CRYING IN KIPSIGIS CULTURE

Crying is, so far as we know, a culturally universal form of affective display. It is present in people of both sexes and all ages. Crying is both an expression of an inner state (or various different inner states) and, when done in the presence of others, a form of social communication that demands a response. It is a salient form of affective display, readily recognized by others, though it may be done in various different styles (e.g., quiet, noisy, hysterical, or ritualized). Perhaps because of these characteristics, it is our impression that most if not all cultures have strongly held values related to crying and responses to it: when and where, and by whom, it is or is not appropraite, and even what style it should be done in. Thus, this kind of behavior may provide an especially available window on mechanisms for the socialization of affect in different cultures.

Among the Kipsigis, crying took on an important negative significance in the context of the culturally focal circumcision ceremonies. These ceremonies, involving circumcision for the boys and clitoridectomy for the girls, were, at the time of our research, still both the most important rite of passage for individuals during the life span and the most important social and ceremonial event of each year for the community. Preparations by the community included inviting an important *boiyot ab tumdo*, or master of the circumcision ceremonies, as well as preparations for feasting to last several days for all the kin, friends, and neighbors of the initiates. The preparations by the boys and girls to be initiated were psychological: they must be ready to withstand the pain of the ritual surgery without showing any sign of fear. Crying, on this occasion, would bring disgrace to both the child and his or her family for the rest of their lives. For the girls, it would cancel their chances of making a good marriage; for the boys, it would preclude their ever attaining a position of respect in the community. Thus, both the parents and the children themselves were careful in the years preceding the circumcision ceremonies to make sure that the child was really ready for the ordeal, waiting an extra year or two if necessary before making the commitment to undergo the ceremonies.

Kipsigis views on crying in relation to the circumcision ceremonies presented an interesting contrast to responses to crying by infants. In the infancy context, crying was perceived positively as an important signal that should be attended to immediately. As in other East African groups, adults responded rapidly to an infant's cry by picking the baby up and by feeding, comforting, and back carrying (Munroe & Munroe, 1971; Super & Harkness, 1981). The idea of leaving a baby to cry in order not to "spoil" it would be seen as bizarre, and the American practice of letting babies or toddlers cry for long periods at night in order to break them of the habit of getting up was strongly disapproved of by Kipsigis observers.

The Kipsigis views on crying in the context of the circumcision ceremonies and crying in infancy did not represent a cultural inconsistency; on the contrary, cultural values related to crying in infancy and during circumcision served to underscore the cultural contrast between childhood and adulthood. From a developmental perspective, however, this contrast raises the question of how socialization proceeds from infancy to adolescence. Whereas the circumcision ceremonies were seen by the Kipsigis as a discontinuous point in development, it was also clear that some kind of transition must have already been made in order for the initiates to comport themselves successfully—as well as to carry themselves with equal aplomb through the stresses of adult life.

The socialization of crying can be traced through the study of communicative sequences surrounding this behavior by young children in Kokwet. Responses to children's crying, in these sequences, reflected at least three different kinds of considerations. First, they can be interpreted as they related to the immediate demand characteristics of the situation, for example, the cast of characters present, their roles in relation to the child, their other activities, and the nature of the physical space in which all were living. Second, these sequences reflected the developing capacities of the child, both in the frequency and the causes of the children's crying, and in the ways in which others responded to this behavior. Third, of course, the communicative sequence around children's crying should be relevant to the larger cultural values that the Kipsigis people held about crying.

CRYING IN COMMUNICATIVE SEQUENCES

In this section, we first present a series of narratives drawn from the behavior observation protocols, in which a young child cried and others (especially the mother) responded. We then offer a preliminary analysis of these sequences as "scripts" in the sense used by Schank and Abelson (1977). An understanding of the basic components of these cultural scripts provides some insights into processes in the socialization of affect in this particular community.

The behavior observations were organized according to the system designed originally by Whiting (1968, 1980). A trained local observer went four times to the homesteads of 152 children from Kokwet, at 9, 11, 3, and 5 o'clock on different days. The children were selected from the community census to be representative of variation within the community and to be balanced in age and sex. They ranged in age from 18 months to 9 years. Each of the four observations lasted 30 minutes, and during this time, the children and the families were asked to carry out normal activities. Thus, the observer accompanied the child as he or she went to the river and the fields, as well as sitting unobtrusively in the house to observe the child's activities there. In the relatively fluid, mostly outdoor setting of family life in Kokwet, this procedure generally seemed comfortable for all concerned, and the activities recorded were consistent with casual observations throughout our fieldwork. During the formal observations, the research assistant kept a descriptive running record of all the selected child's acts and anyone else's behavior directed toward the child, along with general notes on the setting and the surrounding activities. The five observations used to construct the narratives here were chosen to illustrate a variety of characteristics of the sequences in which a young child cried:

CHEBET (AGED 2.1)

Chebet was in her yard playing with her older siblings. Her 5-year-old sister carried Chebet on her back to a cart, where Chebet sat with another little boy her age. It was five o'clock in the afternoon, and Chebet's mother arrived, perhaps returning from a nearby errand.

"Mummy's here," commented Chebet. The other children departed.

Chebet began to cry and followed her mother inside. Chebet's mother offered her the breast, and Chebet nursed briefly.

"Do you want to nurse?" asked her mother.

"Yes," said Chebet.

"That's bad," replied her mother. "Move off."

Chebet moved off her mother's lap, and her mother said, "Go pick up those maize kernels." Together Chebet and her mother picked up the kernels, Chebet getting a basket to put them in.

KIPROTICH (AGED 2.1)

Kiprotich and his 5-year-old sister were playing together near their house one morning. At Kiprotich's request, the sister had pushed him in a little cart. Now she teased, "Shall I push you into the cows?"

"No," he replied.

"Come with me," she urged.

"No, let's stay here," Kiprotich said. "Wait while I get a skin for us to sit on."

His sister refused, so the children sat down together on the ground and chatted. Kiprotich leaned over to see a piece of paper that his sister was holding and tried to take it.

"Don't tear the paper," she admonished, letting him have it.

"Let's go inside," said Kiprotich.

"What?" said his sister.

"Let's go to Mummy," he repeated.

"We'll go, be quiet," his sister answered.

Kiprotich began to cry, saying, "Mummy," and then calling to Chepkoech, an older girl nearby who paid no attention to him. He then sat and cried.

"Who beat you?" his 4-year-old brother asked rhetorically, as Kiprotich went on crying.

"Keep quiet," said the brother, to no effect.

Kiprotich got up and walked to his mother, who picked him up. She sent Kiprotich's brother to get some food for him, then held him in her lap while uttering soothing words.

Kiprotich's mother offered him some food and said, "You sit here and eat this, and I'll be back soon." Kiprotich sat eating with his brother and sister.

KIPKORIR (AGED 2.1)

Kipkorir had been in the yard with several of his older siblings while their mother was nearby. At a reprimand from a 5-year-old sister, Kipkorir ran to his mother.

"Come take Kipkorir for me," his mother called to her 7-year-old daughter. Kipkorir cried as the girl carried him away.

"Let your sister take you inside," his mother said; but Kipkorir sat and cried.

The mother chatted with Kipkorir to comfort him.

"Come with me, Kipkorir!" called his sister. Kipkorir climbed into his mother's lap and chatted with her as he handed her things.

"Why did you run away from Rosemary [the research assistant]?" asked his mother.

"I didn't run away," he replied.

"Who ran then?" she asked.

"My sister did," he said.

"Go over there and sit with your big brother," his mother suggested. Kipkorir refused, and his mother said cajolingly, "Why don't you go and ask your sister to carry you?"

"No," said Kipkorir.

"Shall I carry you then?" she asked. As Kipkorir climbed on her back, she said, "Let's go see if your oldest brother has arrived." "No," said Kipkorir. "Mummy, my sister is stepping on the flowers." His mother ignored this comment and carried Kipkorir into the house.

"Where's Daddy?" asked Kipkorir.

"Over there in that house," his mother replied, pointing to the nearby man's hut. "Don't cry, and I'll get you some food."

Kipkorir cried but stopped when his mother handed him some *kimiet*, the Kipsigis porridge.

KIPKEMOI (AGED 3.3)

Kipkemoi's mother was in the pyrethrum field, picking the daisylike flowers that are sold for use in making insecticide, while Kipkemoi dallied nearby. His father was ploughing in the next field, using the family oxen. Kipkemoi, being too young to help with this male task, watched his father, then nibbled on a pyrethrum stem as he turned to watch his mother bending over the rows of pyrethrum plants nearby. His mother moved steadily down the row picking flowers, and Kipkemoi, finding himself suddenly alone, struggled to his feet to follow his mother. On his way to catch up with his mother, he reached out to pick a plant.

The plant was poisonous. "Don't pick that plant!" shouted his mother, as she snatched the plant and tossed it away, then returned to where she had been picking.

Kipkemoi began to cry and ran after his mother. She straightened up and waited for him. Kipkemoi reached his mother and stood crying, pulling at her skirt to be picked up. His mother reached down and, with her fingers, wiped the little boy's runny nose, then slowly moved away to continue her picking.

Kipkemoi cried more loudly than before, and again his mother waited for him. As Kipkemoi stood and cried at his mother's legs, she leaned over and picked him up. Kipkemoi stopped crying and attended to his father's voice from the next field, talking to his mother.

"Hold my shoulders so you don't fall," his mother told him as she bent once more to her task among the flowers. "Why don't you get down now so I can pick these things?"

The communicative sequences presented above vary somewhat in setting and content, but all except one can be characterized as variations on one basic script, which consists of several basic segments. The beginning of the crying sequence consisted of a *precipitating incident* involving frustration of the child's desire to be with the mother. For all the 2-year-old sequences, this happened in the context of the child's being taken care of by older siblings. The next part of the sequence involved the *mother's response*. This segment was consistent in all the examples except the first one (where the mother nursed the child), a possible example of a transitional period where the mother was uncertain about how to respond. In the other examples, the mother's response consisted, first, of waiting for the child to come to her. The mother then offered comfort in three ways: holding the child, chatting with the child, and (for the 2-year-olds) offering food. The third segment in the script is *disengagement*, or return to the previous status quo. For the "transitional" script, this segment consisted of involving the child in an economic chore with the mother: a preview of the activities that would form the basis of their relationship in the years to come. In the other 2-year-old examples, the child was left again in the company of older siblings, but with something to eat. In the 3-year-old example, the child was simply asked by his mother to get down off her back so she could continue with her work.

Based on this preliminary analysis, we may offer some observations on how processes of affective communication between Kipsigis children and their caretakers developed with age. First, although the transition from infancy to early childhood was marked by rather abrupt transitions with regard to some caretaking practices, such as breast-feeding and back-carrying, these examples show evidence of continuity in the mother's repertoire of responses to crying. In general, the breast was not offered to 2-year-olds, but holding the child, being sociable, and offering food were still used in responding to the child's distress. At the same time, an important difference in the mother's response to these children was that she waited for the child to come to her, rather than hurrying to the child as she would to an infant. Although this difference may, in part, be attributed to the child's greater mobility, it also seems to have reflected the mother's attitude that crying in 2-year-olds was not the same kind of important signal that it was in infants. It is also clear that the mother's delegation of caretaking to her older children did not involve absenting herself completely, and that this issue had to be frequently negotiated with the child. Finally, it may be that, as the child grew older and became more independent, the mother's "executive" role became more dominant in contrast to her direct nurturing role, so that children's crying episodes (which were now in any case much less frequent) were dealt with more summarily. The following example, again drawn from the Kokwet behavior observations, illustrates this hypothesized trend:

KIPKIRUI (AGED 7)

Kipkirui was sitting on the path leading to his house, when his older sister came by carrying a tin of water to wash her hands for lunch.

"Let's both use that water together," suggested Kipkirui.

His sister refused, so Kipkirui grabbed the tin from her. His sister pushed him down, and Kipkirui began to cry.

"What happened?" called his mother.

"She pushed me down!" said Kipkirui.

"Don't push your brother!" the mother scolded her daughter. "And you," she added to Kipkirui, "keep quiet."

Kipkirui fell silent and occupied himself with removing kernels of roasted maize from the cob for his lunch.

The interpretation of these communicative sequences as related to the socialization of affect gains from cross-cultural as well as developmental comparisons, as an example of an American script indicates.

DOUGLAS (AGED 13 MONTHS) (from Lewis & Rosenblum, 1978, p. 1)

> Douglas, a 13-month-old, sits quietly playing with blocks. Carefully, with a rapt expression, he places one block on top of another until a tower of four blocks is made. As the last block reaches the top, he laughs out loud and claps his hands. His mother calls out, "Good, Doug, it's a ta-l-l-l tower. Don't you feel good!" Returning to the tower, Doug tries one more block, and as he places it on top, the tower falls. Doug bursts into tears and vigorously scatters the blocks before him. His crying brings his mother, who, while holding him on her lap and wiping his tears, says softly, "Don't feel bad. I know you're angry. It's frustrating trying to build such a tall tower. There, there, try again."

Taken as an example of an American script, the sequence of communications between Douglas and his mother can be contrasted with the Kipsigis examples in many ways. First, the setting is different: mother and child are in the house with no other people present. The ongoing activity is also different, as Douglas is involved in individual play with toys (a virtually nonexistent event in the Kokwet sample, where the children had almost no toys). The nature of the play is also different from what we find in Kokwet: in this case, an achievement activity. The precipitating event for Douglas's crying is related to this, as it involves the frustration of his attempts to build a taller tower.

The mother's response also differs from that of the Kipsigis mothers in most respects. First, she comes to her child instead of waiting for him to come to her (although Douglas is younger than the Kipsigis children in the examples above, a toddler's cry of frustration would not bring her or his mother in the Kipsigis setting). Like the Kipsigis mothers, Douglas's mother holds her child on her lap to provide comfort and talks to him. But herein lies the greatest contrast: whereas the Kipsigis mothers' talking took the form of "chatting," or distracting the child by talking sociably about other things, Douglas's mother directly addresses her son's crying. First, she labels the emotion that produced the crying ("I know you're angry"). Next, she offers an explanation of what made him feel that way and indicates that this is a natural way to feel ("It's frustrating trying to build such a tall tower").

Finally, the disengagement segment of the communicative sequence is also different: the mother in this case directs her son to return to the activity that led to his crying. Like the Kipsigis mothers, she ends the sequence by arranging a return to the status quo, but with an important difference. Whereas the Kipsigis mothers arranged to leave the distressed child again in the company of the older siblings, they provided a different activity (most commonly eating). Douglas's mother, on the other hand, redirects her son to return to his tower building, presumably in the hopes that he will end the next sequence on a more successful and therefore happier note. Yet, he will enter this activity with a new consciousness of his own emotions as he builds a tower: building a high tower makes him feel good, whereas having the tower fall is frustrating and makes him feel angry.

THE INTERNALIZATION OF SOCIAL COMMUNICATIONS

In the preceding section, we have presented a series of communicative sequences around the expression of one particular kind of affective expression (crying) as representing more generally shared cultural scripts. These scripts are modified somewhat in response to children at different developmental stages, but by contrast with the one American example presented, they have many features in common. In the Kipsigis scripts, the goal seems to be a quieting of the child's state, a redirecting of his or her attention to an external focus (whether food, doing a chore with the mother, or simply continuing to watch the mother at her chores) that will not be stressful. By contrast, the American mother redirects her child to confront again the task that brought on the episode of crying, while directing her child's attention to his inner experience through verbally labeling and interpreting it.

We suggest that the socialization of affect, like the learning of a first language, is based on the child's abstracting of regularities in these cultural scripts. The social communications between the child and others are internalized as communications with the self. The cognitive schemas that result from this learning, like schemas for correct speech, are not often the subject of conscious reflection, but they form the basis for behavior in many situations. It follows that processes in the socialization of affect must be consistent over the life span at some level. As in learning a language, different registers are appropriate in different situations, but the basic structure remains the same for people of all ages. In relation to the socialization of affect, it appears that the basic theme that carried over different developmental stages in the Kipsigis community was the theme of distraction and calming: in Miller's terms, emotional "blunting" (see Miller and Green's chapter in this book). The theme carried from infancy through middle childhood and was probably the strategy developed to deal with the stress of circumcision.

AFFECT AND COGNITION

Although possible mechanisms for the socialization of affect can be inferred from social interactions such as the above and can be related to both individual growth and cultural context, the actual process of learning cannot actually be seen. At the cultural level, differences in behavior could, in theory, be ascribed to situational variation rather than to differences in a more basic processing of affective elicitors. Although it is easy to document situational differences for people in different cultures, there is good evidence that children abstract internal structures from these differences. We suggest that the internalized responses that are generated by the developmental niche and its cultural scripts come to endow elicitors that might seem semantically similar with distinctive meanings. One kind of evidence to support this point of view comes from comparing Kipsigis and American responses to symbolic line drawings of emotions, particularly the term *happy*. *Happy* exists in Kipsigis, as in English, as a common, easily understood construct that conveys the idea of a positive state of being, opposed to being sad. Bilinguals have no confusion about the appropriate contexts for using the word to describe inner states. Kipsigis and American understanding of the meaning of that state, however, are the products of experience.

The use of line drawings to illustrate the transformation of physical stimuli to symbolic forms was developed by Werner and Kaplan (1963) as part of a larger theory of symbol formation. In their theory, the naming of linear forms involves the same physiognomic, "concrete-affective-dynamic" qualities that can be seen in early linguistic and other symbolic development. Drawing on the experimental work of Lundholm (1921), Kraus (1930), and Scheerer and Lyons (1957), Werner and Kaplan (1963) summarized evidence for consensus on the comprehension and production of generic similarities in the features of linear patterns and personal referents such as *happy, cruel, sad,* and *cheerful.* In general, large, smooth, graceful, upwardly oriented lines were chosen for the term *happy,* whereas sharp angles implied pain, moodiness, or strength. Despite the individual and contextual determinants of the labeling, the authors see in the German and American data the primordial development of "natural" symbols, ones in which the physiognomic properties capture significant aspects of the inner cognitive-affective-dynamic experience. Although Werner and Kaplan made no explicit claims of cross-cultural universality for the particular symbolizations involved, their general theory and discussion of the linear naming material lead naturally to the question of variation.

One hundred and forty-four Kipsigis from Kokwet (ages 3–10 years, and adults) and an equal number of Americans from a middle- and upper-middle-class neighborhood of Duxbury, Massachusetts, were presented two linear forms and asked which one was "happy" (in Kipsigis, *baibai*). One form was a large, graceful, looping line, the other a small but sharply undulating horizontal figure (see the illustrations in Figure 1). For the first few age points (starting at 3 years), the percentage of the respondents choosing the large curve as "happy" seems stable, but by 6 years the two samples have begun reliably to diverge. Among the adults, all the Americans labeled the large curved line as the "happy" one, whereas only 35% of the Kipsigis adults did so. By middle childhood, it seems, Kipsigis children learned to associate a relatively calm ("flat") state as positive, whereas the larger, swooping figure was interpreted as trouble. As one adult Kipsigis woman explained, in a separate context, "Being happy is when nothing is bothering you." In contrast, the American respondents saw happiness as containing an element of excitement and movement, whereas the relatively flat line was seen as tight and constrained, sometimes with simmering anger. A variety of cultural themes may be called out by this divergence, but the point here

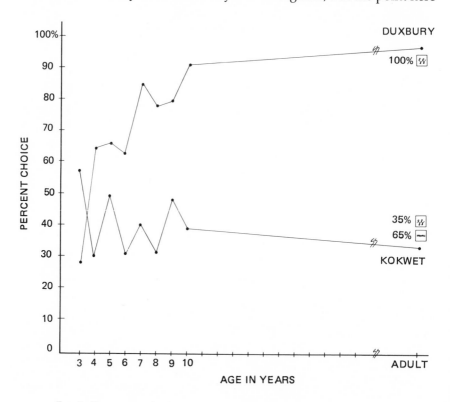

FIG. 1. Percentage of subjects choosing the large curved line as "happy."

is a simple one. Even though the Kipsigis and Americans were using a term with a common general meaning, the term seemed to elicit different cognitive-affective structures, based on the different kinds of emotional experience provided by the two cultures.

SUMMARY AND CONCLUSIONS

In this chapter, we have proposed and illustrated some possible processes in the socialization of affect. Our starting point is the assumption that the socialization of affect can best be viewed as an interactive process involving two entities: the developing individual and the culturally structured environment. The "developmental niche" is proposed as a framework for describing the regularities of the environment for the child at any given developmental stage. In order to represent the interactions between the child and the environment as related to the socialization of affect, we have described communicative sequences involving one particular form of affective expression, crying, in young children of a rural African community. We hypothesize that the "cultural scripts" common to these sequences, which contrast with an American sequence, were learned by the children much as the rules of grammar are abstracted from the regularities of the speech environment. Both the developmental niche and the cultural scripts in which children participate are shaped to the child's developmental capacities; at the same time, they represent more general thematic continuities in the culture. Finally, we propose that there is a process of internalization based on the niche and its scripts, so that differences in affective experience are not due simply to individual or situational variations.

It is clear that the kind of learning proposed by this model is not conscious and therefore is not available except perhaps on reflection. Like most aspects of language and culture, it consists of a body of assumptions that are rarely questioned. A challenge for future research in the socialization of affect will be to develop ways of observing and measuring these "cognitive-affective structures" in the individual. Analysis of cognitive data related to the representation of emotion terms, as in the example used here, may be a fruitful approach. Other methods, such as those used by Lutz (see the chapter in this book) in deriving meanings of emotion terms from situations, also provide interesting results. From the point of view of the culture, the creation of patterns of shared understanding is the goal of the socialization of affect, as it is for other domains of socialization. Scientific study of these patterns in the individual will, in turn, benefit from an understanding of their contextual derivation.

REFERENCES

Ekman, P. Universal and cultural differences in facial expression of emotion. In J. K. Cole (Ed.), *Nebraska Symposium on Motivation, 1971*. Lincoln: University of Nebraska Press, 1972.

Greenfield, P. M. Informativeness, presupposition, and semantic choice in single-word utterances. In E. Ochs & B. B. Schieffelin (Eds.), *Developmental pragmatics*. New York: Academic Press, 1979.

Harkness, S., & Super, C. M. The cultural construction of child development: A framework for the socialization of affect. *Ethos*, 1983, *11*, 221–231.

Hutchins, E. *Culture and inference: A Trobriand case study*. Cambridge: Harvard University Press, 1980.

Izard, C. E. On the development of emotions and emotion-cognition relationships in infancy. In M. Lewis & L. A. Rosenblum (Eds.), *The development of affect*. New York: Plenum Press, 1978.

Kraus, R. Über grafischen Ausdruck. *Zeitschrift für Angeweit Psychologie*, Supplement, 1930, *48*, 1–141.

Lakoff, G., & Johnson, M. *Metaphors we live by*. Chicago: University of Chicago Press, 1980.

Lewis, M., & Rosenblum, L. *The development of affect*. New York: Plenum Press, 1978.

Lundholm, H. The affective tone of lines. *Psychological Review*, 1921, *28*, 43–60.

Lutz, C. The domain of emotion words on Ifaluk. *American Ethnologist*, 1982, *9*, 113–128.

Munroe, R. H., & Munroe, R. L. Household density and infant care in an East African society. *Journal of Social Psychology*, 1971, *83*, 3–13.

Quinn, N. "Commitment" in American marriage: A cultural analysis. *American Ethnologist*, 1982, *9*, 775–798.

Schank, R. C., & Abelson, R. P. *Scripts, plans, goals, and understanding: An inquiry into human knowledge structures*. Hillsdale, N.J.: Erlbaum, 1977.

Scheerer, M., & Lyons, J. Line drawings and matching responses to words. *Journal of Personality*, 1957, *25*, 251–273.

Schieffelin, B. B. Getting it together: An ethnographic approach to the study of the development of communicative competence. In E. Ochs & B. B. Schieffelin (Eds.), *Developmental pragmatics*. New York: Academic Press, 1979.

Super, C. M., & Harkness, S. The infant's niche in rural Kenya and metropolitan America. In L. L. Adler (Ed.), *Cross-cultural research at issue*. New York: Academic Press, 1981.

Werner, H., & Kaplan, B. *Symbol Formation*. New York: Wiley, 1963.

Whiting, B. B. Transcultural code for social interaction. Unpublished manuscript, 1968.

Whiting, B. B. Culture and social behavior: A model for the development of social behavior. *Ethos*, 1980, *8*, 2.

3

Cultural Patterns and Individual Differences in the Child's Emotional Meaning System

CATHERINE LUTZ

To observe the variety of ways in which children around the world learn to be human is to observe, among other things, the socialization of emotion. This variety, however, has not been explored by those interested in affect. Virtually all of the existing studies of emotional development have been conducted in American settings. Although these studies of the development of emotional repertoires in American children have found fascinating and important types of subcultural variation (e.g., Miller, 1982), the range of variation is nonetheless quite narrow when compared with that found outside our own society. An anthropological shibboleth has it that the world's cultures present a "natural laboratory" in which the parameters of child development have been varied and the human psychosocial possibilities have been explored. This is no less the case in the area of emotional development than it is in the area of what is called social development. In this chapter, I would like to demonstrate not only that emotional development is a central aspect of social development, but that it is also importantly involved in the development in the child of a culturally specific world view.

CATHERINE LUTZ • Department of Anthropology, State University of New York at Binghamton, Binghamton, New York 13901.

CULTURE: SOME DEFINITIONS

A definition of culture is a prerequisite for any attempt to outline the relationship between culture and emotional development. Although there are almost as many conceptualizations of "culture" as there have been anthropologists, two particular views have been especially dominant.

In the first, culture is viewed as behavioral patterns; in its most successful and sophisticated version, this paradigm views the acquisition of culture in children as a process of adaptation by the child to the behavioral demands of particular interpersonal and material/environmental settings (B. B. Whiting, 1980; J. W. M. Whiting, 1973). The questions about emotional development in the cultural context that are posed by this view of culture are many; one direction for research using this paradigm is to explore the ways in which different cultural contexts require the use of particular emotional behaviors more than others. Where, for example, the exchange of children through adoption is both valued and prevalent (as it is in many societies in Oceania), a person may make his or her way through childhood and adulthood with two sets of parents. The emotional tenor of the parent–child relationship in this kind of setting is different from that in settings where children reside with their biological parents. In addition, that tenor is different in ways that are not predictable from observations of the emotional behavior of adopted children in the United States, where adoption almost always places the child in a nuclear household and severs her or his ties with any living biological parents. Thus, with this view of culture, emotional development may be examined as the process of encountering a diverse set of others who elicit particular kinds of emotional behavior. Rearing by multiple caretakers, early and extensive experience with the care of infant siblings, and interaction that is predominantly with peers rather than with adults—all of these behavioral environments have been shown to have important effects on the activities of children and should be examined for their probable impact on the emotional profiles of the children who occupy them.

Culture has also been viewed as knowledge or, more broadly, as a system of meaning. This view need not entail the reduction of the concept of culture to that of "rules"; rather, culture is here defined phenomenologically, as the lived and felt experience of the culture bearer. From this perspective, the acquisition of culture is the acquisition of a way of interpreting the world. To develop emotionally in a particular culture, then, is to develop a way of making emotional sense of everyday situations that is coherent and intelligible to others in that society. To return to the example used earlier, adoption would be viewed as an institution that means a large, complex, and relatively coherent number of things to members of the culture in which it occurs. Immersed in the cultural world in which adoption occurs, the child learns what it means to be adopted and what it means to give a child to another in the community. Although children can be said to create meaning for what they observe, this creativity occurs in the context and with the substantial aid of the individuals and the symbolic resources around them. The emotional meanings that adults ascribe to every situation are communicated to the child and form the basis for the cultural construction of emotional response.

Although these two perspectives on the nature of culture have often been taken to be antagonistic and mutually exclusive, it should be obvious that each directs our attention to important aspects of socialization contexts. An alternative perspective that makes use of both definitions of culture would examine the development in the child of cultural knowledge systems as that knowledge is provided, provoked, or elicited by particular interpersonal environments. In other words, the development of both cultural regularities and intracultural variation in emotional and other meaning systems would be examined and explained by reference to the variety of material and interpersonal conditions, or "niches" (see Harkness and Super, 1983, for an analysis of the relevance of the notion of *niche* to an understanding of child development), that are occupied by children in particular societies. Referring as it does to both the behavioral environment of the child and the construction of meaning or knowledge within and via the particular settings that the child frequents, this approach may be said to focus on the "ecology of meaning." In the body of this chapter, I present data on the ecology of emotional meaning among the children of Ifaluk atoll in the Pacific. These data will hopefully demonstrate the utility of such an approach for understanding both the emotional lives of children and the role of culture in constructing the emotional understandings that children develop.

METHODOLOGY IN THE CROSS-CULTURAL STUDY OF EMOTIONAL DEVELOPMENT

An anthropological approach to the study of emotional development is just beginning to be explicitly formulated. In the present study, traditional anthropological methods were used; these involved language learning, participant observation, and extensive interviewing of both the open-ended and the more structured type. In particular, I noted the daily use of emotion words in conversation among both adults and children, as well as the handling of emotional interaction. Adults and children were interviewed about their understanding of the meaning of the many words in their language that refer to emotion; they were also queried about their experience with emotion and emotional relationships. What emerges is a picture of the way in which Ifaluk adults and children conceptualize emotion and of the ways in which that knowledge is put to use in understanding the events of their everyday lives.

It may be objected that a methodology of this sort discovers only the "surface" of emotion, that how people "really feel" goes undiscovered by an approach that focuses on interpersonal communication (including that which occurs between the ethnographer and the informant, as well as that which occurs more generally in the community). Two responses can be made to such an objection. First, it should be noted that the complexity of the relationship between the observer and the observed is a problem that has increasingly begun to absorb anthropologists (e.g., Devereux, 1967; Dumont, 1978; Geertz, 1976). Although there has always been strong resistence within anthropology to the positivist notion of "immaculate perception" (Kaplan, 1964) in the observer, there is increased support for replacing the concept of observer bias or observer error with the more dynamic notion of interpretation; that is, participant observation is conceptualized as a process of interpersonal construction, in which the anthropologist (as well as the observed) moves back and forth between his or her own emerging view of the nature of the object and the usually quite different view held and communicated by the object. Thus, the problem of what an individual of a different cultural background actually feels would be seen not as a question of identifying a fixed (or, rather, a reified) emotion state within the individual, but as a process of successive accommodations between the views of the observer and those of the observed.

Although this first proviso does not make the question of "what they really feel" irrelevant, it does suggest that the term *really* in that phrase might be replaced with a more epistemologically appropriate one. The second proviso is one that suggests that the primacy of the question is necessitated not by the nature of emotion so much as it is by the nature of the cultural meaning system shared by Euroamerican investigators of emotion. The "theory of the subject" (Cole & Means, 1980) held by psychologists as well as by anthropologists is often an implicit one. The bulk of that theory is quite difficult to bring to the level of awareness because it constitutes what we see with, rather than what we see (Geertz, 1976). Cross-cultural comparison is the primary means by which access to the theory of the subject is accomplished; culture shock primarily consists of the realization that what we have taken as unquestioned reality is, in fact, a culturally provided apparatus for constructing reality. As an examination of the theories developed about emotion in other cultures reveals, the Euro-American concern with internal and individual definitions is by no means the only or necessarily the most parsimonious way to conceptualize emotion.[1]

This overview of an approach to the problem of anthropological method seems particularly necessary when discussing the issue of emotional development, where epistemological problems are already rife and where the assumption has often been made that emotion is an aspect of experience that is most private, least social, and therefore least amenable to the kind of approach that has been taken here.

THE CHILD'S EMOTIONAL ENVIRONMENT ON IFALUK ATOLL: SOME CULTURAL VALUES

When the Ifaluk infant lets out its first wail, those sounds reverberate in a special birth environment whose characteristics dramatically illustrate the more general nature of the setting and the values into which she will be incorporated. Present in the birthing hut with her and her mother are a multitude of kin and neighbors of the mother and the father; as many as 30 people may be present in the hut and its immediate environs waiting for news of the state of the mother and the child and for the opportunity to assist in some way in the care of the pair. The infant soon returns to her parents' household, in which reside an average of 13 people, including most probably her mother's parents and one or more of her mother's sisters and their families. Here, as later, the new Ifaluk person finds that "life is with people" and, conversely, that to be alone is not to find a valued privacy but to be outside the community. The emotions most frequently associated by adults and children with being alone are not calm or relaxation, but fear and loneliness.[2]

In the birth hut, it is also most likely that a woman is present who has asked to adopt, and has been promised, the child, and the transfer to her household will occur three to four years later. There the child will

---

[1]Although there is not space here to describe the extent and the nature of the basic assumptions that are built into most psychosocial theorizing about emotion, I have begun to do so elsewhere (Lutz, 1985a).
[2]See Lutz (1983) for a discussion of the role of the emotion of fear in the development of children on Ifaluk.

be treated quite solicitously and will live in the company of many children, children who are not necessarily immediately related either to the mother or to each other. The child may return for brief, sometimes daily visits to the household of the biological parents and finds herself with two sets of resources (including, particularly, food resources) to call on as well as two sets of adults to whom she is accountable.[3] The value placed on sharing any valued item, whether it be food, labor, or children, is communicated early and often to the child. The epithets "Bad-hearted one!" and "Stingy!" are frequently directed by adults toward children who, for example, fail to respond to a request by another child for a piece of the banana they hold. People frequently say that they feel shame or embarrassment if they are seen not sharing in some abundance, and that they feel good when they are able to share something, including their children, with another.

Gentleness in relations with others is another fundamental value on the island. A final example from the birth hut will demonstrate the value's articulation in the child's environment and its relationship to her emotional development. Physical violence, harsh words, and even unnecessarily sharp movements are all much abhorred, and people do, in fact, take much care to avoid being labeled "hot-tempered." At one birth that I attended, the first words that greeted the infant's emergence and its initial cry were "It's pissed off!" This labeling of the infant's affective state is, of course, not unique to Ifaluk (Emde, 1982, and Greif, Alvarez, & Ulman, 1981, have demonstrated the ubiquity with which affect labeling occurs in American parent–child interactions), but the meanings of the affect labels that are used are somewhat special. The emphasis on avoiding peevish anger (as opposed to the legitimate anger that the Ifaluk believe *should* accompany the violation of cultural norms) pervades the everyday experience of young children.

This necessarily brief treatment of the major value orientations and the child-rearing settings on Ifaluk suggests the extent to which emotions are involved in the maintenance of those values, and in the success of the institutions that constitute the child's social environment. Conversely, the emotional meaning system of the Ifaluk is communicated to children in such situations as adoption and other everyday settings.

---

[3]The adopting woman is frequently the infant's father's sister or mother. My 1978 census of the island revealed that 90% of all living children had been promised in adoption. (The remaining 10% most generally consisted of children who were, or who were expected to be, their biological mother's last child; it is considered inappropriate to ask to adopt such children.) Only slightly more than 40% of children over the age of 4 had, in fact, moved to the households of their adoptive parents, however. Child resistance, conflicts between the adults involved, or loss of interest on the part of the adoptive parents had resulted in the attrition that the above figures reflect.

THE ACQUISITION OF EMOTIONAL WORD MEANING: THE EXAMPLE OF *NGUCH*

Adult Uses of the Concept

The emotion vocabulary that the Ifaluk have created is relatively extensive. Children must and do learn this vocabulary in the interest of communicating with others on matters of emotional importance. One of the terms in that vocabulary that is heard very frequently in the course of an average day is *nguch*. This term may be translated as "sick and tired, bored." Although relatively adequate American English glosses can be found for many Ifaluk emotion words, it should be noted that in some cases (such as that of the term *nguch*), significant distortion of the meaning of the concept underlying the particular term would occur were one English emotion term to be used as the only translation. To translate *nguch* simply as boredom would be to cut off the sense of "being fed up," which the term also connotes. I myself found the concept of *nguch* to be a very useful one for describing a set of emotional conditions that is expressed with a relative amount of difficulty in English.

Several examples that were recorded in my field notes will serve to give the flavor of the meaning of the word.

> M. told me today that she is going to quit smoking on every day but Sunday. She has a cough and says she is afraid she will get sick from the tobacco. She says that she is also *nguch* of all the people who are always asking her for cigarettes—I think she is trying to get herself out of an emotionally wearying situation by quitting.

> Making food today with L. After we had been at it for some time and the sun had begun to set, she said she was *nguch*. She also said she was in a hurry to get home [she was making food at the house of a relative]. Then she said, "If I were a child, I'd cry."

> Some women walked past the spot where K. and I were sitting, obviously on their way to the taro gardens to work. They were singing love songs as they walked, and K. noted spontaneously that they "are doing that so that their *nguch* will leave them."

> T. said that her sister, who has just had a baby, is *nguch* because she has to stay in the house all day. [By custom, women are restricted to their household areas for 2–3 months after the birth of a child.]

A number of adults were asked to define the emotion words in their vocabulary, including *nguch*. The following sample of those collected definitions will further illustrate the meaning of the concept:

1. "We're *nguch* if every day someone comes to ask for things or if we do the same work every day, or if we have nothing to do . . . or I'm *nguch* on someone because I'm *nguch* of their talk."

2. "If someone asks us to go do something, we say 'I won't because I'm *nguch*.' It's like lazy. If you're sick, you can be *nguch*."
3. "You don't want people to talk to you, don't want to do errands. . . . It's good to say, 'No, because I'm *nguch*.' If you're working and *nguch*, you lie down and sleep. We walk around or weave. We're *nguch* of just making food. If we're a bit sick, we feel *nguch*."

Children's Use of the Concept

For children, the acquisition of a sense of the meaning of this term is a part of the process of emotional enculturation. To understand and to be able to appropriately use the term *nguch* is to become more Ifaluk in one's approach to the world. It would be erroneous to assume, however, that the meaning of this or any other word is anything but *contextual*. That is, the meaning of an emotion word for any particular child arises out of the sum of the contexts in which she or he has heard the word used. The meaning of an emotion word is not inscribed in stone (or a dictionary); rather, the meaning of the word is found in the use of emotion words to serve the purposes of the speaker. It would also be erroneous to assume that the meaning of emotion words is uniform across individuals. What the data to be described below, in fact, demonstrate is that the developmental niches (see above; see Harkness and Super, 1983) in which particular children are found play a very important role in determining how particular emotion words are construed by those children.

Some Shared Patterns

Preliminary interviews were conducted with 24 children between the ages of 8 and 13. The children were asked to say if and to describe when they had experienced five of the most basic and commonly expressed emotions, one of which was *nguch*. Specifically, they were asked questions of the form, "Are there ever times when you are *nguch*? If so, when?". They were also asked to say what they do when they experience such a state or situation. The children very rarely denied experiencing either *nguch* or any of the other emotions covered in the interview; this is consistent with the more general feeling among Ifaluk adults that it is perfectly sensible and unsanctionable for people to talk about their emotions. The interviews were conducted with all of the children of two contiguous villages, one of which was my own "home" village. All of the children had had at least some occasion to meet and speak with me prior to the interview, and many of them were quite familiar and at ease with me. The interviews were held in my home; in most cases, the children were alone with me during the interview.

The following is a sample of the responses of the children to the two questions, marked (a) and (b), asked in relation to *nguch*. It will be noticed that some children responded to the first question ("Are there times when you are *nguch*?") not only with a description of the situation involved, but also with the behavior that followed on their part. In those cases question (b) was deleted.

1. (a) "If I'm *nguch* because there are no companions with me, I'll call them to come play with me and I'll be happy" (an 8-year-old girl).

2. (a) "When we're at school, I'm *nguch*. I don't want to go. I'm *nguch* of walking in the bush. My feet hurt from the coral. But I can't lie down. I won't make food when I'm *nguch*. I sit down. I don't do things because I'm *nguch*" (a 9-year-old girl).

3. (a) "If someone tells me to go get water, I'm *nguch*. If I'm sick, I'm *nguch* of just lying down. If it's just me playing around and I have no companions, I'm *nguch*. (b) If I have no companions, I'll play ball. I'll play around. I'll climb for apples" (a 10-year-old boy).

4. (a) "Sometimes I'm *nguch*. Sometimes I'm not. If someone sends me on an errand, I'm not *nguch*. If they send me on lots of errands, I'll be a bit *nguch*. (b) I'm angry at the people who keep sending me on errands" (an 11-year-old girl).

5. (a) "I'm *nguch* of staying in the house . . . if I just sit in the house everyday. I'll walk around, play around with people, kids, go with people who are working. Another thing I do if I'm *nguch* is like if there's a wind, I'll sit around, and it's good because I'm cool" (a 13-year-old boy).

6. (a) "I'm *nguch* when the sun shines and I'm hot. If someone teases me, I'm *nguch* about it. If I just sit around, I'm *nguch*. (b) I'll play around with kids. I'll climb a coconut for a drink. I'll make some food for myself" (a 13-year-old-boy).

The situations that the children mentioned most frequently in talking about the times that they experience *nguch* include the following:

1. The performance of chores. Most frequently, children between the ages of 8 and 13 have been assigned whatever chores they do. Although children often volunteer to help at a task, self-starting at a chore is discouraged. The kinds of chores that children are assigned include many "go-fer" types of tasks, such as fetching water, collecting fallen coconuts, or going to make a request for tobacco or information from another household. As has already been mentioned, girls work earlier and more heavily (i.e., for longer periods and at more physically demanding tasks) than boys. There is a very strong work ethic, however,

which is communicated to children of both sexes by the example of adults and their judgments of each other. Someone who is a "constant worker" (a character trait term identifies such individuals) is much admired and is particularly sought after as a marriage partner. Thus, children's attitudes toward work are affected by the wider cultural valuation placed on such activity.

2. Being alone. Children frequently mentioned being alone as a source of *nguch*. To be alone is to be without playmates or adult company, rather than, as mentioned above, to have found some "private moments." Observations indicate that the children, in fact, rarely play alone, in part because virtually every child on the island lives in a home that contains children near his or her age; the institutions of the extended family and of adoption help to ensure that this will be so.

3. Being ill. To be sick is to be inactive as well as without playmates. Many children spoke of "just lying around" when sick as the factor causing *nguch*.

4. Heat. Ifaluk is located just a few degrees of latitude from the equator. Although there is frequently a good breeze blowing in off the water, the midday sun is extremely strong. In addition, the Ifaluk do not have a tradition of cutting back on or ceasing their activities during the hottest part of the day. It should be noted that the heat that the children associated with feelings of *nguch* could be intensified either by focusing on the heat or by vigorous physical activity such as play.

5. School. Although the children frequently spoke about school as a situation that they associated with happiness, many also mentioned that they were sometimes *nguch* in the classroom. From the children's perspective, two aspects of the school experience stand out from the rest of their everyday settings. In the first instance, they encounter a set of material objects (i.e., books and art supplies) that they are encouraged to manipulate; elsewhere, toys are virtually absent and they have yet to acquire the personal possessions that they will have as adults (e.g., knives and tobacco). The second contrast is a cultural one; as all of the books that are used at the school are in English, the children spend much time focusing on materials that are minimally meaningful. In addition, until very recently, many of their teachers have been Peace Corps volunteers from America whose culturally specific behavior, assumptions, and expectations may often have been too discrepant to be consistently attention-holding.

6. Having no work to do. Finally, the children frequently mentioned that they were *nguch* when they had no work to do. Implied here is the desire to work (rather than to play) and the failure of some adult to allow them to work at communal or individual tasks. Although children's labor is relatively substantial and important on Ifaluk, there

are often more hands available for a task than are needed for its completion. At least partially for this reason, children are not expected to learn, nor are they taught, many of the more complex procedures and knowledge necessary for such things as gardening, food preparation, and rope making. It has been noted elsewhere (Whiting, 1974) that children are expected to work at an earlier age in those societies where the women's work loads are heavier. On Ifaluk, the relative lightness of the work loads of both men and women is reflected in the emotional lives of their children; older children are eager to work and to demonstrate adult skills and status, but they are not encouraged as much as they would like to join in the tasks in which adults are engaged.

The above six situations constitute what the concept of *nguch* represents for children as a whole. What do these understandings tell us about the nature of emotional socialization on Ifaluk? They tell us what should be obvious but what has, in fact, been ignored in previous discussions of the socialization of emotion: they tell us about the child's emotional landscape, about the meanings that the everyday world has for the child, and they tell us that that landscape has been formed within special ecological and cultural boundaries. Although the above set of meanings is understandable to us as people who share with the Ifaluk the set of human potentials (including the ability to communicate subjective experience), to understand the child's emotional world requires, in this case, that we decenter both psychologically and culturally.

Individual Variation by Age, Gender, and Adoptive Status

With this sense of the meaning of the concept for children as a group, it is now possible to approach the issue, raised at the beginning of this paper, of subcultural variation in emotional meaning. The notion of the ecology of emotional meaning is used here to direct attention to the fact that the origins of variability (and of emotional meaning itself) may be found within particular niches occupied differentially by particular children. The three variables of age, gender, and adoption status can be used as proxies for differences in niche occupation and, hence, in experience with the situations and the individuals involved in emotional socialization.

A second set of interviews was conducted with this aim in mind. The six most common situations that the children mentioned in the first interview were depicted, in both word and picture form, on small cards. A larger sample of children ($N = 42$) was presented with the cards; the children were asked to look through them carefully and to "choose the thing that makes you the most *nguch*." These instructions were repeated until all of the cards had been chosen.

TABLE 1. Sample Characteristics: Ifaluk Children by Gender, Age, and Adoptive Status

Gender	Age	Adopted	Not adopted	Total
Female	8–10 years	2	6	8
	11–13 years	5	4	9
	Total	7	10	17
Male	8–10 years	4	4	8
	11–13 years	7	10	17
	Total	11	14	25
	Totals	18	24	42

The children who completed the ranking of situations producing *nguch* constituted virtually the entire population of the atoll between the ages of 8 and 13, inclusive. Table 1 shows the distribution of the sample among the categories that are of concern here, which are age, gender, and adoptive status. Each of these variables will now be examined in turn as it affected the children's ranking of the six situations listed above.

Only one strong trend with age can be discerned in the rankings that the children produced (see Table 2). The younger the child, the more likely it was that having no work was seen as an especially *nguch*-inducing situation. The change in emotional attitude toward work is notable; as described above, children begin to be motivated to perform their adult roles, which include particularly work roles, at an earlier age than that at which adults encourage them to do so. Young children's situational position (of more often wanting to work and not being allowed to) contrasts with that of 12- and 13-year-olds, who are actively working in many cases; this is directly reflected in the meanings that they most strongly associated with the negative emotion of *nguch*. For the older children, having no work to do may sometimes represent a respite from

TABLE 2. Multiple Regression Analysis of the Significance of Age, Gender, and Adoptive Status for Children's Ranking of Situations Associated with the Emotion of *Nguch* ("Sick and Tired, Bored"): T-Statistics and Significance Levels

	Work	Being alone	Being ill	Heat	School	No work
Age (8 years)	0.57	−0.25	−0.92	−0.23	0.15	1.42^a
Gender (female)	−0.16	−0.18	−0.11	$−1.55^a$	2.04^b	−0.39
Adoption (adopted)	$−2.36^b$	0.12	−1.13	1.30^a	0.33	1.82^b

$^a p < .10$ (one-tailed).
$^b p < .05$ (one-tailed).

the *nguch* that work itself can produce; for the younger children, having no work is seen as part of the sometimes monotonous norm.

Two of the six situations show significantly different rankings by boys and girls: heat and school. Boys ranked heat as much more *nguch*-inducing, whereas for the girls school was much more strongly associated with *nguch*. Two dramatically different aspects of the lives of girls and boys on Ifaluk explain the differential meaning of *nguch* for them. In the first instance, girls have only very recently (since approximately 1955) begun to receive formal schooling. Boys and young men, on the other hand, were sent to schools during the interwar period by the Japanese, who controlled Ifaluk and the other islands of Micronesia at that time. The association between males and schools continues to this day and, with it, the belief that girls are less capable at "school things." Girls are encouraged to drop out of school, particularly as they get older, and they are more often ridiculed at school than are boys for being "stupid." The emotional meaning of school for girls is understandable in this light.

The stronger aversion that boys have to heat also makes sense in terms of the social position in which they find themselves in contrast to girls. As noted above, boys begin their adult work activities at a much later age than do girls, so that even the oldest boys in the sample were spending much of their day in free play. They most often played on the deserted ocean side of the island (as opposed to the village areas by the lagoon) and were out in the open sun a great deal. The girls, on the other hand, were often engaged in tasks (in which their mothers were also engaged) while seated and in the shade (for example, weaving and peeling taro). In addition, when they did play, they were strongly discouraged from straying far from the household area; when not working, therefore, they were frequently found collecting leaves for their grass skirts in the wooded (and thus shaded) areas immediately behind their houses. Their activities were thus less likely than the boys' to cause them to suffer from the heat.

Adoption is the third and final variable to be considered here. The adopted child occupies a very special social and psychological niche. Although differences in the treatment of adopted versus nonadopted children are not overt and/or dramatic, parents undoubtedly distinguish in some subtle ways between their adoptive and nonadoptive children. The structural position that the adopted child occupies give him or her some power that the nonadopted child does not have. Foremost here is the fact that the child may, if he or she wishes, leave the adoptive household and not return. Although this rarely happens once the child has spent some months or years with the adoptive parents, the latter know that they may lose the child if they alienate him or her. On the

other hand, there is much pressure on parents (both adoptive and biological) to provide explicit moral guidance and direction to the child and
to teach the child good work habits and skills. These counterpressures
on adoptive parents (the fear of alienating the child versus the fear of
failing to raise the child properly) do not, however, appear to universally
balance out so that the treatment of adoptive children is indistinguish-
able from that of nonadopted children. More frequent than the complaint
that adoptive parents are being overly strict or harsh with their children
is the complaint that they are failing to teach the child proper behavior
and work skills.

These psychosocial forces may be reflected in the situations that
the adopted children more strongly associated with feelings of *nguch*.
These included heat and having no work to perform. Conversely (and
consistent with the latter ranking), the adopted children ranked being
sent on chores as less of a *nguch*-inducing situation than did the nonadopted children. This reaction strongly suggests either that the adopted
children were being assigned fewer chores (and therefore experienced
more frustration over too little—rather than too much—work) and/or
that they were being assigned chores in a much more gracious or gentle
way. Extremely polite talk is in fact frequently used as an explicit technique for endearing oneself to another and for preventing negative emotions (such as fear or anger) in others. It may be that adopted children
are also less stringently pressured to comply with a request that they
perform an errand, as was observed to be the case with boys (unusually
polite requests and greater tolerance of noncompliance mark the behavior of parents toward boys). Noncompliance by older children and by
girls is treated more harshly; this analysis suggests that such might also
be the case with biological children.

Convergent evidence for this hypothesis is found in the fact that
the adopted children also more frequently associated heat with *nguch*.
The adopted children might find that their lack of work assignments
places them in the same position as the boys whose lack of work responsibilities puts them to active play more often. In addition, both the boys
and the adopted children might find that their idle hands leave them
more time to focus on the heat of the sun.

In sum, the ranking data just described provide evidence that the
differential allocation of children of varying ages, genders, and adoptive
statuses to settings within Ifaluk society results in differences in individual emotional-meaning systems. It is important to note, however,
that no claims can or should be made that these meaning systems are
permanently acquired ones, that is, that they persist into adulthood.
Differences in emotional meaning systems, however, can be surmised
to be important sources of differences in the behavioral profiles of children.

CONCLUSION

Culture, whether defined as knowledge and meaning or as repertoires of behavior, is fundamentally involved in emotional development. This chapter has briefly reviewed some of the issues involved in an anthropological approach to emotion and its socialization. In particular, it has been emphasized that cultural values and cultural meaning systems are part and parcel of people's emotional lives. The example of the emotional meaning system of the Ifaluk people of Micronesia has been used to illustrate this approach, and data have been presented that demonstrate not only that emotional socialization involves the acquisition of an emotional vocabulary and repertoire, but that that process of socialization also entails ecological diversity within the cultural setting— a diversity that results in the differential distribution of children across settings and thus in the creation by those children of varieties of emotional meaning structures. In this conclusion, I would like to briefly expand on these two aspects of emotional development in cultural context, including the notions of "acquisition" and "creation" of emotional meaning.

The statement that children "acquire" emotional meaning requires elaboration. What is it exactly that is acquired? In the first instance, the child learns a vocabulary for speaking about emotions and emotional events. In the process of learning to speak a language, children (and the ethnographer) learn a set of concepts for emotions. The term *nguch* has provided an example of such a concept; it was left untranslated through most of this chapter to dramatize the learning process through which the child goes. Although we know what situations and feelings the concepts of *bored* and *sick and tired* are associated with, those are *associations that we have learned*. It is also important to point out that it is not simply a vocabulary, in the dictionary sense, that is acquired. Rather, emotion concepts are embedded in a wider ethnopsychology, or indigenous knowledge system that describes and explains variation in consciousness, in the behavior of others, and in social relationships. It has not been possible within the confines of this chapter to outline this wider knowledge system that Ifaluk children acquire simultaneously with their language learning (see Lutz, 1985b). This knowledge system, however, informs the meaning of emotion concepts so that children, in learning emotion words, learn much more than the labels for internal feeling states or even the labels for situations. They acquire the much broader cultural knowledge system and the set of cultural values that are part and parcel of emotion concepts and their implications.

The second aspect of emotional socialization involves a more active role for the child. Here, children are seen as themselves the source of culture, as responding creatively to the settings in which they find themselves, and as making sense of those settings emotionally. This approach not only provides a framework for understanding how emotional meanings arise in cultures; it also presents a way of explaining individual differences in emotional meaning and emotional repertoires within cultures. B. Whiting's work (1980; also Whiting & Whiting, 1975) on socialization and culture has revealed the fundamental way in which children's experience in diverse settings elicits diverse kinds of behavior. The set of possible settings is culturally constructed and culturally specific, and exposure to any particular one of those settings is controlled by the more powerful others in children's lives. As Whiting pointed out, parents—in their roles as the directors of children—allocate children to settings, and they make their decisions about where to place children on the basis of culturally informed principles such as age, gender, or adoption status. The emotional profiles of individual children thus reflect their special experiences in the settings in which they find themselves.

REFERENCES

Cole, M., & Means, B. *Comparative studies of how people think: An introduction.* Cambridge: Harvard University Press, 1980.
Devereux, G. *From anxiety to method in the behavioral sciences.* The Hague: Mouton, 1967.
Dumont, J. P. *The headman and I: Ambiguity and ambivalence in the fieldworking experience.* Austin: University of Texas Press, 1978.
Emde, R. Maternal perceptions of infant emotions from birth through 18 months. *Infant Behavior and Development,* 1982, *5,* 313–322.
Geertz, C. "From the native's point of view": On the nature of anthropological understanding. In K. Basso & H. Selby (Eds.), *Meaning in anthropology.* Albuquerque: University of New Mexico Press, 1976.
Greif, E. B., Alvarez, M., & Ulman, K. *Recognizing emotions in other people: Sex differences in socialization.* Paper presented at the meeting of the Society for Research in Child Development, Boston, 1981.
Harkness, S., & Super, C. The cultural construction of child development: A framework for the socialization of affect. *Ethos,* 1983, *11,* 221–231.
Kaplan, A. *The conduct of inquiry.* Scranton, Pa.: Chandler Publishing, 1964.
Lutz, C. Parental goals, ethnopsychology, and the development of emotional meaning. *Ethos,* 1983, *11,* 246–262.
Lutz, C. Depression and the translation of emotional worlds. In A. Kleinman & B. Good (Eds.), *Culture and depression.* Berkeley: University of California Press, 1985. (a)
Lutz, C. Ethnopsychology compared to what? Explaining behavior and consciousness among the Ifaluk. In G. White & J. Kirkpatrick (Eds.), *Person, self, and experience: Exploring Pacific ethnopsychologies.* Berkeley: University of California Press, 1985. (b)
Miller, P. Teasing: A case study in language socialization and verbal play. *Quarterly Newsletter of the Laboratory of Comparative Human Cognition,* 1982, *4,* 29–32.
Whiting, B. B. Folk wisdom and child rearing. *Merrill-Palmer Quarterly of Behavior and Development,* 1974, *20,* 9–19.

Whiting, B. B. Culture and social behavior: A model for the development of social behavior. *Ethos*, 1980, *8*, 95–116.

Whiting, B. B., & Whiting, J. W. M. *Children of six cultures: A psycho-cultural analysis.* Cambridge: Harvard University Press, 1975.

Whiting, J. W. M. *A model for psycho-cultural research.* Distinguished lecture address delivered at the annual meeting of the American Anthropological Association, New Orleans, 1973.

4

Contexts for Experience with Emotion, with Special Attention to Television

AIMÉE DORR

There are many events in everyday life that potentially involve emotion. Most of them represent opportunities for affect socialization. Usually, we think of these events as the face-to-face interactions in which children participate as principal actors. But a quick examination of how children actually spend their days readily reveals several other contexts in which they experience emotions themselves or see others' emotions. I begin this chapter by presenting a typology for categorizing these contexts. After considering the utility of this approach, I turn to an extended discussion of one special context in which children experience their own and others' emotions. It is television viewing, the pastime par excellence of American children, an activity that commands more of their time than attending school, interacting with parents, and playing with friends. To end the chapter, I present several propositions about how and when television operates in affect socialization, particularly in contrast to other affect socialization contexts that children encounter in their everyday lives.

It is easy to infer from the description of this chapter that I believe that affect socialization occurs. Several lines of evidence support this belief, but they do not need to be argued here. Others before me have

AIMÉE DORR • Graduate School of Education, University of California, Los Angeles, California 90024. The writing of this chapter was partially supported by Grant MH37611 from the National Institute of Mental Health.

made these arguments more persuasively than I, and others will after me. But before I leave the topic altogether, I want to affirm my belief in a biological base for some components of emotion. Ethologists are certainly right that our evolutionary history has endowed infants with immediate specific responses to certain eliciting stimuli (see Chance, 1980, and Hess, 1970, for examples). Perhaps, it is even true that certain forms of emotional expression are part of the human condition (see Ekman, 1973, for example). But even granting all this, I will take it as given that children in each culture learn much about how and when to express emotions, how to conceptualize and label emotions, and what emotions to feel in what situations (see Birdwhistell, 1970; Lazarus, Kanner, & Folkman, 1980; Leventhal, 1980; Mandler, 1980; and Schacter, 1964, for examples). Exactly how they learn all this has not begun to be explored. In the absence of counterevidence, I assume that all traditional socialization processes apply. These include direct explication by others, reinforcements and punishments administered by others, observation of others, self-reinforcement, and children's use of their various and sundry experiences with emotion to generate meaning, principles, conceptual systems, and/or rules. The emotions about which learning can occur will be conceived of here broadly rather than narrowly. What have been proposed as primary emotions (e.g., Izard, 1977) are certainly included, but I will add to them any and all of the more unusual, uncommon, or complex emotions. Rage, despair, ecstasy, chagrin, and foreboding stand along with interest, joy, and anger. These several beliefs about what constitutes emotions, what is learned about emotions, and how it is learned will remain implicit in most of the chapter while I focus instead on the several contexts in which such learning can occur.

A TYPOLOGY FOR CATEGORIZING CONTEXTS

To understand affect socialization fully, we must understand what is learned, the processes by which it is learned, and the contexts in which it is learned. Each area of knowledge can be tackled on its own, but ultimately, a comprehensive view of affect socialization will weld all three areas together. Indeed, even in the early stages of studying one area of affect socialization, considering a second area is likely to help refine one's study of the first. Examining the processes by which learning could reasonably occur can help sort out what could actually be learned. Whether facial expressions of emotion are posited to be learned phenomena ought partially to depend on whether we can identify reasonable processes by which they could be learned. Or identifying socialization processes will help us sort out which facial expressions could be learned.

TABLE 1. Examples of Potential Affect-Socialization Contexts Classified by Type

I. Participant in a live, ongoing experience with emotion
   Winning an important race that one's best friend also ran in
   Discussing feelings about interacting with handicapped peers
   Failing a test one studied hard for

II. Observer of a live, ongoing experience with emotion
   Hearing the new boy in day care be told that big boys don't cry
   Watching one's parents bitterly arguing and then making up
   Seeing classmates laugh uproariously at another's antics

III. Observer of a framed, ongoing experience with emotion
   Watching Arnold of "Diff'rent Strokes" cope with his very serious illness
   Hearing Madame Butterfly's undying love for her American husband and child
   Watching or reading about stoical, resourceful, sarcastic, affectionate Princess Leia

IV. Conceiver or recaller of an experience with emotion
   Figuring out why Mom shrieked and Dad only smiled when they won the Irish Sweepstakes
   Anticipating the encomiums one will receive for cooking breakfast for the family
   Recalling the killer shark attacks in *Jaws* just as one steps into the water in Hawaii

Similarly, examining contexts in which affect socialization is thought to occur can help us further to identify what is and is not socialized and how socialization occurs. It can also remind us of many potentially influential affect socialization contexts that we could use to children's benefit.

I am proposing a categorization system composed of four types of contexts, each recognized as likely to involve the child's emotional reactions or to expose him or her to the emotional reactions of others. It is in these situations, either through socialization activities directed to the child or through the child's own sense-making activity or both, that affect socialization can occur. The four types of contexts and several examples of everyday events that fit into each are presented in Table 1. For simplicity in referring to them, I will formalize the four types somewhat more than they deserve and label them Types I, II, III, and IV.

Type I: Participant in Live, Ongoing Experience

The first type of context is that in which a child is a participant in a live, ongoing experience with emotion. Most often, we think of this as involving an emotionally evocative situation for the child and an emotional response by the child, both occurring in interaction with others who are important to the child. These are the face-to-face interactions in which children participate as principal actors to which I referred at the beginning of this chapter. They are the situations that most theorists focus on, the circumstances in which a child can learn the norms for expressing anger and love, the meaning of the term *share*, and the utility of compassion for a sorrowful peer.

But Type I includes more than these face-to-face interactions. It includes children affectively engaged in solitary activities: a child experiencing the frustration of being unable to saw and hammer well enough to make the soap-box-derby car she envisioned or a child experiencing the frustration of pouring milk onto the floor as well as into his glass. It can include the consequences that each child experiences from his or her response to the frustration, whether the response is getting help, cleaning up, emptying the milk carton onto the floor, or smashing the car body with a hammer. Type I also includes other people's intentionally teaching or explaining about emotions to the child, with or without the concomitant arousal of emotions in the child: a child-care worker teaching a preschooler to growl like a lion rather than to bite when she is angry, or a father answering a child's question about why the father doesn't cry when he's unhappy, or a mother explaining why older sisters enjoy scary movies but the child doesn't.

The distinguishing features of Type I situations are several. First, they involve interactions with and/or about emotion that are occurring in real time. Second, the child is a principal actor in them, someone expected to feel an emotion, to express an emotion, to experience the consequences of expressing or not expressing an emotion or of how it is expressed, or to discuss an emotional concept or principle with another who is sensitive to the child's interests. Third, in normal environments the child's behavior in the situation is responded to contingently most of the time. Fourth, the situations are likely to be at least somewhat involving to the child, either because the situation itself is an emotionally evocative one or because the discussion topic is emotionally important to the child.

Clearly, Type I situations permit all kinds of learning about affect to occur. They are most likely, however, to socialize in areas close to what the child already understands and does. The concepts explained, the norms espoused, and the responses to affective expressions are usually adjusted to account for the developmental, social, and cultural characteristics of the child. More divergent experiences are more likely to come in Type II and III situations than in Types I and IV. Type I situations are also more likely to socialize the more common emotions in the more common situations. The infrequent emotional experiences in life—the death of a loved one, marriage, great tragedy, and supreme accomplishment—are more likely to be experienced in Type III and IV situations than in Types I and II. The socialization processes in Type I situations are those of the child's own sense making and of direct experience, explication, and reinforcement. They are also those of vicarious experience when the child is interacting with others who can serve as models for the child as well as direct influences on him or her.

Type II: Observer of Live, Ongoing Experience

The second type of context has much in common with Type I. Again it involves live, ongoing experiences with emotion, interactions with and/or about emotion that are occurring in real time and that involve real, physically present people. These people—but not the child—are the principal actors in the situations; they, and not the child, are feeling and expressing emotions, are responded to contingently, and are personally involved in the interactions. The child is an observer of, not a participant in, these situations. But—and this is important—in this type of context, the child has the option from moment to moment of becoming a participant (and thus of shifting to a Type I context). He or she can intervene in the parents' fight, join them as they hug, or comfort the lost child. He or she can join in the classmate's antics or tell a peer that little boys can cry.

As is true of Type I situations, Type II situations are likely to involve the more common emotions and situations, although they may range well beyond those immediately within the child's developmental, social, and cultural sphere. Here are the opportunities to see how older children, adolescents, and adults express anger and affection; how members of other ethnic groups feel about their own wrongdoing or failure; and how other families react to extraordinarily good news. But these are not the situations in which a child is likely to see the more infrequent emotional experiences of life. Nor are they situations in which direct socialization processes occur, unless the child chooses to become a participant in the situation. Type II situations are those in which the paramount socialization processes are observing others' behaviors, expressions, reactions, statements, and consequences and making sense of them all. They provide opportunities for attending, interpreting, categorizing, and learning, usually with less potential interference from emotional arousal. They also present the possibility of learning only a little because the situations are not immediately relevant to the child or cognitively accessible to him or her.

Type III: Observer of Framed Experience

The third type of context is notably different from Types I and II, although it represents situations that are very common in American children's lives. It includes all those situations in which children observe emotional experiences presented within "frames" that preclude becoming participants in the situation, even though the experiences are physically present in some form. It includes television programming, radio programming, books, plays, comics, operas, movies, and storytelling. As in Type II situations, children may remain emotionally uninvolved observers of these situations and may learn from them in this way, but they often respond emotionally to the humor, excitement, danger, pathos, or sorrow in the framed experience.

The range of contexts included in Type III is potentially very large. The constructed and/or staged nature of these contexts allows one to explore common and uncommon emotions and emotional experiences. Some Type III contexts can capture real but uncommon experiences and recreate them for many who could never participate in real life. Opportunities abound to use words, drawings, editing techniques, and animation to convey content that never occurs in the real world. Depictions can be constructed so as to remove irrelevancies and distractions, to heighten expressiveness, to manipulate arousal, and to direct attention to a few important elements. The actors, the eliciting events, and the emotional reactions can each vary from extremely realistic to extremely unrealistic in terms of both their style of representation and their interpreted meaning.

These characteristics of Type III situations make it difficult to say what meaning the situations will have for children. When the material being presented is true and the presentational style is realistic (for example, in the news reports of the My Lai massacre), the situation is still presented in a frame that could isolate the child from it in potentially significant ways. On the other hand, even an allegory in a very unrealistic presentational style (for example, the animated television version of *The Lion, the Witch, and the Wardrobe*) can be properly interpreted by some children as depicting religious conversion and can be responded to accordingly.

These interpretive problems in Type III contexts are compounded by the fact that the range of emotions possible for human beings, the range of ways in which they are displayed, and the range of situations evoking them are enormously large if one includes all possibilities rather than simply those that are common singly and in combination. For example, most human beings find the murder of another human being abhorrent, but a few people kill for pleasure and a few more kill for business. What, then, should one consider an authentic emotional response to killing? The feelings of the Manson family members as described in *Helter Skelter*? The reactions of the soldiers in *All Quiet on the Western Front*? The emotions of Lord or Lady Macbeth? With any appreciation of the great diversity in human emotional systems, one can view as a potential socializer almost any Type III emotional experience presented in a reasonably realistic style. Moreover, given the human ability to attribute meaning to any content, even that presented in less realistic and unrealistic styles, that communicated as allegory or metaphor, and that contained in frames saying "opera," "situation comedy," or "detective novel," it is clear that virtually any framed experience could be a socializing one.

The urge is great to characterize Type III situations neatly as potentially contributing X, Y, and Z to affect socialization, but the preceding discussion makes it clear that one must refrain from too simple an approach. The great variety of content and presentational form represented in Type III situations and the substantial interpretive opportunities that they present to children mean that highly qualified statements are the order of the day. This is not the place to pursue them; it should be apparent what they would be like. What is important to add here to complete the discussion of Type III situations is that, unlike Type I and II situations, they are more likely to provide children with access to the uncommon emotional experiences and to do so in impactful ways. Also, whatever affect socialization occurs in Type III situations will occur through observational learning and sense-making activities of the child, the processes most common in Type II situations as well.

Type IV: Conceiver of Experience

The fourth and last type of context is that in which a child conceives of or recalls an experience with emotion. For some theorists, this is not socialization at all because the term *socialization* implies others' imposition on the child of the understandings, beliefs, behaviors, and norms of his or her society (for illustration, peruse the chapters in Goslin, 1969, especially by Campbell [1969] and by McCandless [1969], and the chapters in Part IV of Mussen, 1970). For me, however, the child's cognitive work is as much a part of the socialization process as is the work of the people, the institutions, and the media in the child's environment. All are needed for socialization to occur.

In Type IV contexts, the child draws on all that he or she has experienced directly (Type I) or experienced vicariously (Types II and III) and uses all his or her own cognitive and creative abilities to construct experiences with emotion. These include reliving previous experiences just as they occurred or with specific alterations, anticipating future experiences, and simply imagining unlikely or impossible experiences. These are the times when children imagine the thrill of soaring like Icarus or Superman, feel anxious as they anticipate their parents' finding that the bed is wet, and relive the doctor's visit, making themselves this time outwardly brave instead of fearful. Children may engage in these experiences entirely through internal representations, through such expressive acts as speech, drawing, singing, and dance, or through dramatic play. As in Type I situations, the child is more a participant than an observer, although in Type IV situations, the child participates by his or her cognitive creation of a situation rather than by serving as a principal actor in a situation jointly determined by the child and others.

The emotions and the experiences in Type IV situations may not be very common in a child's life nor very well adapted to the child's developmental, social, or cultural characteristics, yet they must be enough within the child's cognitive grasp so that he or she can construct and reconstruct them. They must be interesting or important enough so that the child is willing to invest the energy needed to bring these experiences into being, giving them more in common with Type I than with Type II and III situations. Clearly, the primary socialization process here is the child's own generation of meaning, principles, conceptual systems, and rules.

REFLECTIONS ON THE PROPOSED TYPOLOGY

Now that the four types of contexts for affect socialization have been proposed, what can be said about the typology? It illustrates the plethora of emotional events that children may experience. It suggests a simple, reasonably compelling system for categorizing these events, a system that conforms to commonsense thinking about the kinds of experiences that children have with emotion. It implies a wide range of socialization processes and a broad view of what is socialized. What it does not do is provide a clean list of potent variables that differentiate affect socialization experiences. Instead, it takes commonly recognized types of situations and examines their characteristics. Some variables arise from this examination as dimensions along which affect socialization contexts can vary. They are presented in Table 2, along with a rough indication of where each type of context falls on each dimension.

Seven dimensions have been used to characterize the proposed four types of affect socialization contexts. The dimensions represent aspects of the child's role in the situation, the extent to which the child and the situation can impact on each other contingently, the extent to which the situation is geared to the child himself or herself, and the naturalness and completeness of the ways in which the event is communicated. Most of the dimensions are assumed to be continuous, with situations varying all along them. For ease of presentation in the table,

TABLE 2. Variations of Four Types of Contexts along Seven Dimensions

	I	II	III	IV
Child's role in situation	Participant	Observer	Observer	Cognizer/creator
Physical presence of events	Tangible	Tangible	Tangible	Intangible
Child's opportunity to influence event	High	Moderate	None to low	High
Immediate responsivity to child	High	None to low	None	None
Current relevance to child	High	Low to high	Low to high	Moderate to high
Number of communication codes available for use	Moderate to high	Moderate to high	Low to high	Low to moderate
"Constructedness" of event	None to moderate	None to moderate	High	High

however, I have represented this variation as "None," "Low," "Moderate," and "High," or as ranging between two points so specified. Two dimensions were not handled in this way. For the child's role, three distinct roles were specified. These could, however, be roughly interpreted as three points on a continuum, as the role of observer includes that of cognizer/creator to some extent, and the role of participant includes those of observer and cognizer/creator. For physical presence, only the states of tangible and intangible were used, although the dimension could probably be reformulated to represent the number of senses and communication modes (e.g., time and space) that can be utilized in a type of context (see Short, Williams, & Christie, 1976, for such a formulation).

Analysis of the entries in Table 2 suggests several things about the adequacy of the proposed typology. On the positive side is the fact that the four types of contexts do indeed have different profiles of characteristics. None is a replica or a subset of another. Moreover, at least some of the ways in which the four types differ among themselves are considered important by laypeople and researchers alike. On the negative side is the fact that, for several of the dimensions, one or more of the types of contexts include situations that vary considerably in where they fall on the dimension. For instance, Type I contexts vary from moderate to high in the number of communication codes used and from none to moderate in their constructedness. These variations are largely accounted for by the fact that I included in Type I contexts both those involving ongoing, emotionally toned face-to-face interactions of the child with objects and people and those involving a more abstract discussion or explication related to emotion (although these still involve interaction between the child and other people). Perhaps these two kinds of participatory, live, ongoing experiences with emotion should be separated into two types, so that Type I contexts do not vary so much in their placement on several dimensions. Similar analyses would suggest breaking each of the other three types of contexts into several more types. The number of such further divisions would probably be the smallest for Type IV and the largest for Type III contexts.

Adopting this strategy would have two rather undesirable consequences. First, it would lead to identifying the types of contexts on the basis of both the socialization techniques used and the socialization content. I chose, although not completely successfully, to eschew this approach, and I continue to believe that this is the most promising option now. Second, it would proliferate the types of contexts well beyond anything that would make sense or be useful to researchers. For those imbued as I am with an appreciation of combinatorial analysis and other formal operations, the dimensional approach strikes a resonant chord. The end result is, however, antithetical to the functioning of most human beings, even most scientists, most of the time. The number of types suggested would be too large, whereas the number of dimensions and the amount of variation accepted along them would be too small. To categorize the full range of affect socialization contexts into groups that are recognizable to and usable by researchers and practitioners alike, we seem to need a messier reality, one that is not bound by the canons of formal operational thought. The typology, dimensions, and levels of variation proposed here are an attempt to represent such a reality.

But to describe a typology for characterizing the contexts in which emotions are encountered and the dimensions that it suggests is not to imply that the proper theoretical base for such a description is already established. It is not. The present discussion suggests that the proposed typology is inadequate and/or incomplete, but it is hard to do much better right now. Some aspects of current theory and practice suggest one kind of system, others suggest other systems, and still others simply do not address this concern at all. A few of the most prominent examples of the uncertainties in which we find ourselves should suffice.

Our research practices, for example, often make implicit statements about a typology and the critical variables underlying it. Consider the use of photographs or videotapes to present emotions to be recognized (e.g., Deutsch, 1974; Walden & Field, 1982). Because the researchers usually wish to understand the recognition of emotions in ordinary face-to-face encounters (not in photographs or videotapes), they must assume that a mediated presentation provides the same (or sufficiently similar) cues as would a face-to-face one. Or consider the use of oral synopses of events to study children's attributions about emotions (e.g., Mood, Johnson, & Shantz, 1978; Weiner & Graham, 1984). The research interest here is not in children's attributions of storybook characters' emotions but in attribution processes in everyday life. It is easy for one to infer that researchers employing these stimuli believe that live (Types I and II) and mediated (Type III) contexts do not differ in ways importantly related to the recognition or attribution of emotions—and maybe they don't.

Other work can also be used to argue that the affect socialization processes underlying mediated (Type III) versus unmediated (Types I and II) and observed (Types II and III) versus participatory (Type I) contexts are not appreciably different. The substantial body of work on observational learning and vicarious reinforcement asserts, and largely demonstrates, that principles that hold in participatory, unmediated circumstances also hold in observational circumstances, both mediated and unmediated (e.g., Bandura, 1977a; Rosenthal & Zimmerman, 1978; Rushton, 1979, 1982). People can learn how to express anger or love by watching peers, parents, or television; by reading; by listening; or by trying it out themselves. A prior history of frightening interactions with dentists can be counteracted by repeated exposure to videotapes of engaging dentists in pleasurable interactions with patients. Another body of work demonstrates that even infants generally equate mediated representations, such as those in drawings, slides, photographs, and videotapes, with the real thing (Cohen, DeLoache, & Pearl, 1977; Daehler, Perlmutter, & Myers, 1976; DeLoache, Strauss, & Maynard, 1979; Dirks & Gibson, 1977; Field, 1976). Even much television research may be interpreted as supporting the assertion that an experience mediated through television operates similarly to an unmediated one (e.g., Comstock, Chaffee, Katzman, McCombs, & Roberts, 1978; Pearl, Bouthilet, & Lazar, 1982; Surgeon General's Scientific Advisory Committee, 1972).

But the opposite assertion—that there are meaningful differences between different types of contexts—can also be argued. Even those most closely associated with observational learning theory and behaviorism provide some of the ammunition. A close look at any of their clinical practice and more recent research indicates that at least the following dimensions are seen as important: cognitively constructed versus physically present (Type IV vs. Types I, II, and III), mediated versus-unmediated (Type III vs. Types I and II), and observational versus participatory (Types II and III vs. Types I and IV) (e.g., Bandura, 1969, 1977b, 1978, 1982; Wolpe, 1974).

I have just reviewed bits of theory, research, and practice that suggest that it is legitimate to differentiate among the four types of contexts as I have proposed—at least under some circumstances. But they also suggest that perhaps some other types of contexts should be proposed and that, under other, as yet not well-specified, circumstances, the proposed differentiations may be irrelevant. Given this situation, it is probably best to assume that the typology proposed here, or something similar, is worth keeping until other evidence indicates that it does not function for specific identifiable aspects of affect socialization. Should such evidence arise, we could then develop a more differentiated theory of how specific areas of affective knowledge and behavior are socialized. For now, there is sufficient evidence to suggest that it is worthwhile to differentiate the contexts from each other, at least some of the time. And that, of course, is exactly what someone particularly interested, as I am, in one type of context wants to establish.

FRAMED EXPERIENCES WITH EMOTION

Having presented a typology for characterizing the contexts in which children experience emotion and having suggested that its utility and validity be explored further, let me try this for Type III situations, those in which a child observes ongoing but "framed" experiences with emotions. Here, the child is an audience member, a consumer, with no possibility of becoming a real participant. The other chapters in this book, I know, focus on other types of situations, especially those involving face-to-face interactions in which the child participates, as defined by Type I. What I intend to do here, then, is to present a small counterpoint to this emphasis and ultimately to propose how framed contexts may and may not differ from other types of contexts in their contributions to affect socialization.

Framed experiences abound in modern American society. They began long ago, when someone first told stories around a campfire or painted ritualistic animals in caves. Such experiences have increased in number and have diversified in kind throughout history. Today, much of our time is given to framed experiences, and at least some portion of these experiences is personally or socially significant. For children, and indeed for adults, many of these framed experiences, especially those involving emotions, are regarded as entertainment. They are thought of as leisure-time activities that nonetheless can co-occur with eating meals, playing, conversing, socializing with others, and laboring in the workplace or at home.

The relevance of framed experiences to affect socialization derives from a complex set of interrelated circumstances that together produce an environment in which children can consume many framed experiences involving human emotions. What are these circumstances? One is that framed experiences abound in the United States and are widely available to children. Moreover, the means of production and distribution are largely owned by private companies whose predominant goal is making money. Also, profits tend to increase when emphasis is placed on the entertainment—rather than on the information—potential of framed experiences, and entertainment is most easily delivered in stories that, by their nature, tend to involve the emotions of both characters and viewers (cf. Cantor, 1980). These stories about people or anthropomorphized animals are variously known as tragedies, comedies, human interest stories, opéra bouffe, adventures, mysteries, and science fiction. Their focus is not usually on emotions, but inherently they involve emotions, positive and negative, common and uncommon. Framed experiences need not involve emotions, and, of course, some of the time they do not. But what is relevant to this chapter is that children prefer and most often use entertaining content and that entertainment comes primarily from telling interesting stories that turn out to involve human emotions.

Among all the Type III experiences that children encounter, most research attention today is given to viewing television. The rationality of such an emphasis is often questioned by those who grew up without television, those with a strong liberal-arts education, those with personal interests in high culture and not popular culture, and those aware of intellectuals' responses to such earlier framed experiences as opera, novels, radio, and comics. These doubts are not without some merit. Television is only one of many framed experiences available to American children today. Television is only the most recent of a long line of means of conveying popular and high culture. Television's popularity is likely to be supplanted by an even more sophisticated technology of the future. And finally, television probably does operate in ways similar to those of the other purveyors of framed experiences.

Nonetheless, there are several reasons that anyone interested in affect socialization and willing to consider Type III contexts at all probably ought to pay particular attention to television viewing. It begins earlier in a child's life than does the use of any other form of framed experience (Comstock et al., 1978; Lyle & Hoffman, 1972a, b; Schramm, Lyle, & Parker, 1961). Some children may have concurrent experience with picture books, but many do not. The amount of time devoted to television viewing is far greater than that given to any other form of framed experience except during adolescence, when some may devote more time to music listening (Lyle & Hoffman, 1972a; Schramm et al., 1961).

Except for film, no other purveyor of Type III experiences with emotion presents content that is as easily decoded (Salomon, 1979; Short et al., 1976). Television utilizes the primary modes of face-to-face communication in everyday life. Behaviors, expressions, postures, positions in space, speech, paralinguistic features, and changes over time are all modes of communication that are more easily decoded than the modes and codes used in print, dance, music, opera, and other framed experiences. Moreover, the multiplicity and the redundancy of communicative features that can be, and ordinarily are, used in television programming are greater than those used in any other purveyor except film. The communicative features available for use in television programming are more like those of everyday life than are those for most other Type III contexts (Short et al., 1976). Yet, unlike everyday life, television programming can emphasize and delimit experience by camera angles, picture composition, editing, well-chosen words, music, the juxtaposition of scenes, voice-overs, and the like. The amount of metal to dross, so to speak, is much higher in television programming than in everyday life.

Finally, suggesting that television should be disregarded because it is only a descendent of radio and comics may be likened to suggesting that life today, with the automobile, the airplane, and mass transit, can be fully understood by drawing on our knowledge of life with the horse and buggy, the sailing ship, and feet. The past is, of course, prologue to the present, but it is only prologue. If we are interested in the ways in which affect socialization occurs for the present generation of children, we should understand both the present as it is and the past as it contributes to the present. Now that I have made a brief apologia for my focus, let me turn to a more extended discussion of television as a context for affect socialization.

TELEVISION EXPERIENCES WITH EMOTION

Television presents numerous opportunities for learning about emotions. The average child or adolescent views 2–5 hours a day, almost all devoted to entertainment programming. It is a *sine qua non* of such programming that it cannot be dull, it cannot leave one unaffected emotionally. One must laugh or be frightened or feel relief or cry. One feels these emotions because one sees other people or anthropomorphized animals making jokes, playing tricks, taking pratfalls, being endangered, feeling angry, being frightened, succeeding, failing, being hurt, being aggressed against, and so on. One sees virtually the whole range of human experience except for the truly mundane, unaffecting trivia that consumes hours of daily life. Even if viewers are not as emotionally responsive to television context as I have implied, given the nature of entertainment programming they cannot fail to be exposed to much "information" about emotions.

Television viewing is an experience in which emotional situations are crowded together with an intensity and at a rate not frequently experienced in real life. The characters who participate in the situations are usually well known to the viewer. Many other viewers share the experiences and reactions. Yet, for all their frequency and potential intensity, these emotional situations are clearly removed from one's own environment and are confined in the set. They require no overt reaction, and they permit none that has any impact on the unfolding events or the characters. Nor can there be any real consequences for any of the viewers' concurrent behaviors. Television experiences with emotion are almost entirely safe. But watching them provides pleasure that keeps viewers coming back for more.

Such television programming can relate to affective development in at least four ways. First, children can learn from experiencing many emotions during television viewing. Most programmers intend to provoke emotions, and research shows that they generally succeed. Second, children can experience pleasure associated with entertainment, perhaps because of the many other emotions that they and the television characters experience. Third, children can acquire much cognitive knowledge about emotion, including likely situations, labels, and display rules for emotions. The reason is that most programming portrays people and anthropomorphized animals experiencing and expressing emotions in situations in which emotions would ordinarily occur. Fourth, and finally, because of the nature of the programming, children have many opportunities to practice interpreting and/or inferring emotions from the behavioral, verbal, nonverbal, paralinguistic, contextual, and historical cues provided in the programming.

Experiencing Emotions

The television programs that children watch are expected, as I have said, to evoke emotions. They succeed. Whether measured physiologically, by self or other report, or through observation, and whether assessed as arousal or specific emotions or affective tone, emotions have been shown to be aroused in children viewing content on television, film, videotape, and slides. Not all emotions, all content variations, or all types of children singly or in all possible combinations have been assessed, but more than enough work has been done to affirm the general phenomenon for preschoolers, children, adolescents, and adults. Several studies have shown that fear or anxious anticipation can be aroused (Cantor & Reilly, 1982; Cline, Croft, & Courrier, 1973; Dysinger & Ruckmick, 1933; Eyre-Brook, 1972; Feilitzen & Linne, 1969; Filipson, Schyller, & Hoijer, 1974; Garry, 1970; Himmelweit, Oppenheim, & Vince, 1958; Linne, 1971; Lyle & Hoffman, 1972a; Schramm et al., 1961; Zillmann, 1980; Zillmann & Bryant, 1975; Zillmann, Hay, & Bryant, 1975). Other negative emotions, such as disgust, hatred, and anger, have also been reported as responses to television programs, usually by older children and adolescents (Eyre-Brook, 1972; Filipson et al., 1974; Garry, 1970). Among the positive emotions, interest, pleasure, and humor are the most frequently assessed. All have been shown to be regular responses of preschoolers, children, and adolescents (Ekman, Liebert, Friesen, Harrison, Zlatchin, Malmstrom, & Baron, 1972; Laosa, 1976; Lesser, 1974; McGhee, 1980; Sproull, 1973; Zillmann, 1982; Zillmann, Bryant, & Sapolsky, 1979). Loving and romantic emotions can also be aroused by television programming, more reliably among older children and adolescents than among younger children (Dysinger & Ruckmick, 1933). Thus, it is clear that children experience a wide range of emotions, common and less common, while viewing television programming. How frequently various emotions are experienced during viewing and how this rate compares to experiences during the rest of day-to-day life have not been established, although most assume that the rate of at least mild emotional experiences per unit time is higher during television viewing than during daily face-to-face interaction.

Because television programs have been shown to produce changes in arousal level and experienced emotion, something must be conveyed by the programs to produce these responses. Several possibilities present themselves: the story line and the actions themselves, the emotional displays of the characters, a narration or an audience's emotional responses carried on the soundtrack, the music, the pace at which content is presented, and other production techniques. One or another study has presented evidence that each of these can function to produce emotional responses in child viewers (see Dorr, Doubleday, & Kovaric, 1983, for a review), but none really explains how they work individually or in concert for which content and which viewers. That is not important for this argument. What is important to note is that emotions are aroused, that one or more program elements create the arousal, and that, when emotion is experienced, the program has been or is depicting specific characters, settings, actions, and events. This means that these television experiences with emotion are opportunities for the conditioning or habituating or desensitizing of emotional responses to particular stimuli, which is clearly affect socialization.

Numerous possibilities for real-life conditioning, habituation, and desensitization through television viewing are suggested by research demonstrating that these phenomena can occur (see Bandura, 1977b; Berger, 1962; Rushton, 1979, 1982; and Zillmann, 1982; for reviews). The firstborn child who has not yet gone to any school may develop positive emotional responses to school if he or she has watched a lot of "Sesame Street" (Bogatz & Ball, 1971). The child afraid of large dogs may become less frightened after repeated viewing of a series like "Lassie" (Bandura, Grusec, & Menlove, 1967). The youth who consumes large doses of televised aggression and violence may become less upset when peers fight (Drabman & Thomas, 1974). The child who watches programming in which frightening sound effects and fright reactions of characters are paired with the catacombs, something the child has never seen before, may subsequently find the real catacombs and other similar places frightening (Venn & Short, 1973). One does not want to go too far here. In the absence of the critical data, there are no claims being made that television could reliably produce these effects or that its messages are so consistent that they would be able to produce such effects. Rather, the intent is to describe possibilities, to cite supportive evidence, and to provoke further consideration of such contributions to a child's affective development, particularly for the less common emotions, forms of emotional expression, situations eliciting emotions, and emotion–situation combinations.

Pleasure and Emotional Experience

In addition to momentary changes in emotions as a program unfolds, one must assume from the hours that youth give to television that the entire viewing experience is pleasurable. Self-reported motivations for viewing, or the gratifications obtained from it, certainly include such positively toned feelings as relaxation and enjoyment (for recent reviews, see Comstock *et al.*, 1978; Murray & Kippax, 1979), and children usually report that they would be very reluctant to give television up (Comstock *et al.*, 1978). Further evidence of the pleasure associated with television viewing can be inferred from the fact that the major forms of parental control on television viewing are using withdrawal of viewing privileges as a punishment for bad behavior and using the opportunity to view television as an incentive for finishing homework or household chores (Comstock *et al.*, 1978; Dorr, 1981; McLeod, Fitzpatrick, Glynn, & Fallis, 1982).

Where does the pleasure associated with television come from? The possible sources are several. Television stories are interesting and interestingly presented. Television viewing is an easy, often soothing, relaxing way of spending time. It often allows one to avoid more onerous tasks and interpersonal interchanges. Emotional arousal, especially in a completely safe situation, is a pleasant experience. Thus, for several reasons, children derive pleasure from, or associate it with, viewing others' experiences with emotion and experiencing emotion themselves. American children spend hours each day obtaining pleasure from this activity centered on emotional experience. No one knows if this activity is part of affect socialization in the United States. We should find out, for the association of pleasure and emotional experience provided by television stands in marked contrast to many of a child's experiences and to the experiences of all but the most recent generations of children.

Cognitive Learning about Emotion

Television programming provides many opportunities to learn about emotions. Some programming teaches affective labels for behavioral displays and/or physiological experiences. Most programming teaches about relationships between situations and the emotions that are felt and/or displayed in them and about how felt emotions can be displayed to others in meaningful ways. Television provides some kind of a rough map of the American emotional landscape. It does so for everyday emotions, expressions, and situations, but significantly, it also does so for the less common emotional experiences of everyday life. The technology's ability to highlight and emphasize content, the storytelling mode that it uses, and the many hours that children watch each week mean that television has an almost unparalleled opportunity to influence cognitive learning about emotions.

Some television programs have established an explicit goal of teaching about emotions, but their success has generally not been evaluated. "Mister Rogers' Neighborhood" and "Sesame Street" intend to teach children to recognize their own and others' emotions, to label them properly, to accept them, and to work through them. "Mister Rogers' Neighborhood" gives much more program time to these matters, but only "Sesame Street's" affective segments have been formally evaluated. Heavier viewers were found to associate emotions and evocative situations better (Bogatz & Ball, 1971), but the effect was relatively weak, perhaps because small amounts of program time were given to the topic. At the elementary level, the mental health series "Inside/Out" (1973) explores situations evoking such emotions as sadness, jealousy, and regret and reportedly provokes much subsequent classroom discussion. Even some primetime entertainment programming teaches quite explicitly about emotions. More than one episode of "Mork and Mindy" dealt with human—as opposed to Orkian—emotions. Mork displayed them behaviorally; he and/or Mindy labeled them and discussed what evoked them, who else feels them, and what to do with them. Family comedy and drama such as "Eight Is Enough," "One Day at a Time," and "Diff'rent Strokes" and some medical, law, and police series also sporadically deal with emotions in a reasonably forthright, instructive manner. Other genres—except perhaps soap operas—rarely do.

Nearly all programming teaches explicitly or implicitly about display rules or about the emotions that are likely in different situations. What is taught depends more often on the viewer's cognition than on what television portrays. If Cagney or Lacey is fearless in a situation that would turn most knees to jelly, one may decide that it is a situation in which to hide one's fear or, alternatively, a situation in which some people are unafraid. Of course, one may just dismiss the whole episode as entertainment irrelevant to real life. But one does not always do this, and so television programming of all kinds can teach about the relationships between situations and emotions by virtue of the emotions that people display and those that they fail to display in particular situations. Research suggests—where any learning at all occurs—an adult would learn more about display rules than about situation–emotion relationships per se, whereas a younger child would learn more about relationships than about display rules (DePaulo, Jordan, Irvine, & Laser, 1982; Flapan, 1968; Frijda, 1969; Gnepp, 1983; Harris, Olthof, & Terwogt, 1981; Saarni, 1979, 1980, 1982). The reason is that, in ascribing emotions to others, young children are more likely to focus on what "emotions" are displayed, whereas adults are more likely to rely on their knowledge of what people "usually feel" in a given situation, regardless of what they display.

Programming can also teach about the variety of ways in which a particular emotion may be expressed, ways that are all likely to be interpreted by other members of the culture as expressive of that emotion. The sheer quantity of programming that intends to convey the emotional experiences of characters and the program creators' ever present striving for originality virtually guarantee that children will see many different expressions of the same emotion. It may be, as some have argued, that there is a close correspondence between facial expression and the emotion attributed to the expressor (Ekman & Friesen, 1975); however, the means of conveying emotions are greater and more varied than a singular focus on facial expression implies. Posture and gesture, speed and smoothness of movement, clothing, adornments, and symbols can all convey emotion (Harrison, 1974). Television programming seems quite able to provide children with many different examples of how to express anger, dismay, fear, chagrin, happiness, and humor, and, for each emotion, these are examples of optional variations in expressive style rather than examples of different display rules.

Interpreting Depicted Emotions

In addition to teaching labels for emotions and norms for experiencing and expressing them, television programming provides countless opportunities for viewers to interpret emotions. In virtually all situations, except some research asking people to label emotions based simply on a photograph of a face or a written or oral description of a momentary situation, the proper interpretation of emotions can require complex mental activity. One must first assess a person's statements and other emotional expressions; the present situation and the relevant preceding events; and the person's goals, intentions, and personality. Attributing an emotional experience to that person ordinarily then requires some complex combining of all these assessments. The correct attribution is not always easily made, even if human beings do it as a matter of course. The process draws on much of the cognitive knowledge described in the preceding section, but it goes further by using that knowledge in a cognitively complex assessment and judgment process.

Ordinarily, television programming is replete with cues that can be used to attribute emotions to characters. Children and adolescents may use, singly or in combination at any given moment or assessed over time, any of several types of cues: facial expressions, other non-verbal behaviors, spoken descriptions, paralinguistic features, the actions and reactions of other characters, the present situation, the preceding events, the character's goals and personality, and such production features as music and slow motion. Program creators ordinarily use several of these types of cues to convey each emotion, thereby increasing the likelihood that children will correctly interpret the characters' emotions. Indeed, there is some evidence that better or more mature performance is obtained when the stimulus materials are richer in the number and range of the cues provided; for example, videotaped performances yield better judgments than do orally presented stories (Chandler, Greenspan, & Barenboim, 1973; Shultz & Butkowsky, 1977). As children use some of the several available cues to interpret characters' emotions, it is likely that they will also come to associate other available cues with that emotion as well. Thus, in the process of interpreting characters' emotions, children may learn more about what cues can be used, as well as becoming more adept at carrying out a complex attributional process using the cues that they already know.

Proper recognition of emotions is often important to the proper understanding of program content. Although it is not a wise assumption to make about some viewing by preschoolers and young children, it is generally safe to assume that children usually strive to understand the television programs that they view. Television, then, provides children with numerous opportunities to practice interpreting the depicted emotions and motivates children to engage in such practice and to improve their performance. It seems important to develop our understanding of television's relationship to children's abilities to interpret expressions of emotions. For some, such understanding will elucidate television's role in affect socialization, whereas for others, who use television or televisionlike materials as though they were no different from other types of materials or real-life experiences, it will show when these practices are appropriate and when they are not.

Summary

These several observations suggest that television may have some role to play in affective life. It may help to cultivate healthy affective responses when it shows constructive ways of handling anger or overt expressions of pleasure in caring for others. It may also contribute to less healthy affective responses in ways too frequently lamented to be worth describing here. It may contribute to the development of emotional lability or, alternatively, of reduced emotional responsivity. It may help people to become more adept at recognizing emotions and more knowledgeable about the display rules for emotions. Thus, in several ways, the "safe" mediated experiences with emotions that television provides during much of each day may play some role in the affective socialization of today's youth.

OBJECTIONS TO TELEVISION AS A SOCIALIZER

Having said all this about television's place in children's emotional lives, about its plethora of stories involving characters in evocative situations and emotional displays, about its evocation of pleasant and unpleasant emotions in viewers, and about its ultimate provision of pleasure to child viewers, let me hasten to say that I recognize the usual arguments against television's having a significant role in children's affective development.

The most common arguments against television's being an agent in affect socialization can be reduced to three major points. One is that most of what television presents is fantasy, recognized as such by children and therefore discounted by them. Another is that television's content, whether fantasy or not, is irrelevant to children's lives. How superheroes, police officers, private detectives, rabbits, and birds feel about danger and pain has no relevance to children. The feelings, emotional displays, and conceptual schemes of the characters in situation comedies are so exaggerated for humorous effect as to be irrelevant to children. And the emotional experiences of dramatic characters are so idealized as to be, once again, irrelevant to children functioning in normal families with their less-than-ideal systems. The third common argument is that television is noninteractive. Its actions are not addressed to any particular child and are not contingent on or responsive to what he or she does. The child cannot in any way act on the emotional experiences in the program or respond to the affect aroused. How legitimate are these arguments against television, or, indeed, any other Type III context, having a role in affect socialization?

Television Content as Fantasy

It is indubitably true that most of what children watch on television is fantasy material, in the sense that it has been scripted and acted or animated. It takes children a while to learn this, however (Dorr, 1983;

Fernie, 1981; Hawkins, 1977). By the age of 4 or 5, most children understand that animated programs and those employing puppets are made up, and they recognize that the news is real. From an adult's perspective, they are still likely to be confused about situation comedy, action adventure, family drama, and crime. All but crime programs are likely to be viewed frequently by children at this age, but they are not sure how real or pretend they are. By about the age of 8, most children know that most of the programs that they watch are scripted and acted, but "serious" programs can still present interpretive problems. Many believe that serious topics—diseases, legal cases, murders, medical procedures, and police activities—cannot be falsified. Although children may know that these programs are scripted and acted, they tend to believe that they are nonetheless faithful to reality. By the end of elementary school, most children recognize that even content such as this need not be realistic.

So, for a significant period of time, children watch at least some programming that they believe is real or factual. During this time, for this programming, this argument against television is not pertinent. But even very young children understand that some programming is fantasy, and as they develop, they understand that more of it is fantasy. Does this fact support the first argument against television as an agent in affect socialization? Not really. Crucial to this argument is the assumption that program content is discounted once children realize that it is scripted and acted. This simply is not what happens.

The earlier description of children's emotional reactions to programming suggests that, while viewing, they can, and often do, temporarily ignore whatever they know about programming being created and take the content seriously enough to respond emotionally to it. After viewing, those children and adolescents who understand that the programming was created will tell you so. It does not follow that they will therefore discount all its content. On the contrary, they can and will examine the content and select from it, using several rather complex decision-making criteria, what they will treat as important (Dorr, 1983). Younger children are likely to select examples of "what is" as important, whereas older children and adolescents also select "what could be," the ideal of what is possible not just the reality of what is.

Finally, when older children have been asked why they choose to view different entertainment programs, they report that some are viewed explicitly to give them ideas about how to get along with others, how to display their feelings, and the like (Kovaric, Dorr, & Nicol, 1983). The programs so chosen are ones that all children of this age understand are created for entertainment purposes. Still, their content is considered informative. Thus, several lines of evidence suggest that the first argument against television as an agent in affect socialization is not entirely correct. The argument and the evidence pertaining to it point, however, to some ways in which television and other Type III contexts may operate differently from other types of contexts. I will come back to these differences at the end of the chapter.

Television Content as Irrelevant

The second argument against television as an agent in affect socialization centers not on the fact that programming is created rather than real, but on the presumption that what is created is far too removed from a child's everyday life to be relevant. Rebutting this argument is rather problematic because certain crucial data are not available. No one has done a content analysis to determine how much frequently viewed programming presents emotional behaviors and situations that would be immediately relevant to children's lives. Personally, I believe that more series do so than one would at first imagine. Consider, for example, the content of "The Brady Bunch," "The Partridge Family," "Eight Is Enough," "One Day at a Time," "Fame," "All in the Family," and "Little House on the Prairie." All present realistic children and adolescents in realistic, emotion-related circumstances. Even when programs present emotional content that is not immediately relevant to children's lives, it may well be that such content is stored as images and ideas that will be referred to when the children become adolescents or adults, when they encounter the more uncommon emotional experiences of life, or when they need the more uncommon forms of emotional display. Thus, even apparently irrelevant content has potential significance in a broad view of affect socialization.

Much television programming involves fantastic characters, fantastic settings and events, overblown humor or drama, unusual emotional displays and experiences, and idealized people and relationships, each of which seems at first glance to make the content irrelevant to children's lives. The discussions in the preceding section and in the general description of Type III contexts make it clear, however, that one cannot safely assume that children and adolescents completely reject such content. I have tested children who found Pebbles Flintstone to be a good model of how to relate to one's father and who understood that colored, musical, moving dots illustrated a good moral about the pain of social ostracism. In both cases, and in many others, I agreed with the children's judgment of the relevance of apparent irrelevancies. As already discussed, research clearly suggests that children do not use single or simple criteria for evaluating individual bits of content. This suggestion leaves open the possibility that they may selectively use even fantastic, overblown, or idealistic content to develop their own cognitive and enacted emotional systems. It is perhaps especially important to highlight older children's possible use of idealized portrayals of people and their emotions to establish scripts for what could be, as well as for what is.

Television Content as Noncontingent

The third argument against television as an agent in affect socialization rests on undeniable differences in the experiences possible in Type III versus Type I and II contexts and then on some assumptions about the significance of these differences (see Leifer, 1975, for a discussion of differences between television and the family in socialization techniques and their significance). Without a doubt, television programming cannot react directly to a child. It cannot gear its presentation to the momentary interests of a particular child, and it cannot react to the child's behaviors. This does not mean that, on the average, programming cannot be interesting to and directed toward children. It can most assuredly be child-oriented. In many cases, programming can even deliver clearer, more emphatic, and more riveting messages than those delivered in other types of contexts. These several facts suggest that television's inability to interact contingently with children only circumscribes rather then precludes its potential for affect socialization. Television should have limited effectiveness as a socializer of the child's emotional behavior, because such behavior is surely shaped by contingent responses unavailable from television. It could, however, be more effective as a socializer of the child's cognitions about emotion.

CONCLUDING PROPOSITIONS

These several responses to the most common arguments against television and other Type III contexts having any role in affect socialization, the earlier review of research about television and emotion, and the initial description of a possible typology for affect socialization contexts together suggest several propositions about the ways in which television, as compared to Type I, II, and IV contexts, may operate in affect socialization. By extension, the propositions also apply to comparisons involving other Type III contexts. However, I will state them in terms of television contrasted to other contexts labeled simply as Types I, II, and IV, because that is how most of the discussion has been couched. The propositions will be divided into those addressing cognitive learning about emotion and those addressing emotional responding. I will state them baldly. The supporting argumentation has already been presented and need not be repeated here.

Propositions about Cognitive Learning about Emotion

1. Like Type I, II, and IV contexts, television is accepted as providing a rough cognitive map of emotional life in America.
2. Cognitive learning from television is more readily changed by conflicting Type I and II experiences than learning from Type I and II contexts is changed by conflicting television experiences.
3. Television, as compared to Type I and II contexts, is more likely (a) to affect initial learning about uncommon emotions, situations, emotional displays, and emotion–situation combinations and (b) to reinforce initial learning in other contexts about common emotions, situations, displays, and combinations.
4. The cognitive socialization effects of television are likely to have greater variability than are those of Type I and II contexts.
5. For older children and adolescents, television can be used to develop an ideal cognitive map against which Type I and II contexts are measured.

Propositions about Emotional Responding

6. Like Type I and II contexts, television programming can evoke, condition, habituate, and desensitive emotional responses.
7. When television's messages are generally consistent, they may condition, habituate, and desensitize more effectively than Type I and II contexts.
8. Where the conditioning, habituating, and desensitizing messages of television diverge from those of Type I and II contexts, those of television are more easily amended or rejected than vice versa.
9. Unlike Type I and II contexts, television can cultivate a "cheap thrills" orientation to emotional life.
10. Unlike Type I and II contexts, and more like Type IV contexts, television programming can be a strong stimulus for sorting out the culturally determined legitimacy of certain emotional responses to certain elicitors (for example, fear of ghosts or witches).
11. Television's influence on emotional responding and behavior is likely to be less than its influence on cognitive learning about emotions.

It is clear from all that has been said that thought about the contexts for affect socialization is not without merit and that the existing body of knowledge gives us plenty to argue about and little to settle on. At the very least, however, the research to date suggests that face-to-face interaction is unlikely to be the sole context in which affect socialization occurs. In particular, the less common emotions, the less common emotional experiences, the less common emotion–experience combinations, and those emotions and experiences less directly related to the child's current developmental, social, and cultural status are likely to be socialized in contexts other than those of face-to-face interaction directly involving the child. My own interest is in mapping out the roles that the most common Type III context, television programming, plays in affect socialization and in contrasting these roles to those of the family during childhood and adolescence. In other words, I am interested in contrasting a Type III context with Type I and II contexts. But whatever one's particular interest, work in affect socialization is likely to advance somewhat better if we remain sensitive to the ways in which varieties of human experience with emotion may be substituted for each other and to the ways in which they must be regarded as unique contexts for affective development.

ACKNOWLEDGMENTS

I am grateful to Catherine Doubleday, Peter Kovaric, and Carolyn Saarni for helpful comments on an earlier version of this chapter.

REFERENCES

Bandura, A. Social learning theory of identificatory processes. In D. A. Goslin (Ed.), *Handbook of socialization theory and research.* Chicago: Rand McNally, 1969.

Bandura, A. Self-efficacy: Toward a unifying theory of behavioral change. *Psychological Review,* 1977, *84,* 191–215. (a)

Bandura, A. *Social learning theory.* Englewood Cliffs, N.J.: Prentice-Hall, 1977. (b)

Bandura, A. The self system in reciprocal determinism. *American Psychologist,* 1978, *33,* 344–358.

Bandura, A. Self-efficacy mechanism in human agency. *American Psychologist,* 1982, *37,* 122–147.

Bandura, A., Grusec, J. E., & Menlove, F. L. Vicarious extinction of avoidance behavior. *Journal of Personality and Social Psychology,* 1967, *5,* 16–23.

Berger, S. M. Conditioning through vicarious instigation. *Psychological Review,* 1962, *69,* 450–456.

Birdwhistell, R. L. *Kinesics in context.* Philadelphia: University of Pennsylvania Press, 1970.

Bogatz, G. A., & Ball, S. *The second year of Sesame Street: A continuing evaluation.* Princeton, N.J.: Educational Testing Service, 1971.

Campbell, E. Q. Adolescent socialization. In D. A. Goslin (Ed.), *Handbook of socialization theory and research.* Chicago: Rand McNally, 1969.

Cantor, J., & Reilly, S. Adolescents' fright reactions to television and films. *Journal of Communication,* 1982, *32*(1), 87–99.

Cantor, M. G. *Prime-time television: Content and control.* Beverly Hills, Calif.: Sage, 1980.

Chance, M. R. A. An ethological assessment of emotion. In R. Plutchik & H. Kellerman (Eds.), *Emotion: Theory, research and experience* (Vol. 1). New York: Academic Press, 1980.

Chandler, M., Greenspan, S., & Barenboim, D. Judgments of intentionality in response to videotaped and verbally presented moral dilemmas: The medium is the message. *Child Development,* 1973, *44,* 315–320.

Cline, V. B., Croft, R. G., & Courrier, S. Desensitization of children to television violence. *Journal of Personality and Social Psychology,* 1973, *27,* 360–365.

Cohen, L. B., DeLoache, J. S., & Pearl, R. A. An examination of interference effects in infants' memory for faces. *Child Development,* 1977, *48,* 88–96.

Comstock, G., Chaffee, S., Katzman, N., McCombs, M., & Roberts, D. *Television and human behavior.* New York: Columbia University Press, 1978.

Daehler, M. W., Perlmutter, M., & Myers, N. A. Equivalence of pictures and objects for very young children. *Child Development,* 1976, *47,* 96–102.

DeLoache, J. S., Strauss, M. S., & Maynard, J. Picture perception in infancy. *Infant Behavior and Development,* 1979, *2,* 77–89.

DePaulo, B. M., Jordan, A., Irvine, A., & Laser, P. S. Age changes in detection of deception. *Child Development,* 1982, *53,* 701–709.

Deutsch, F. Female preschoolers' perceptions of affective responses and interpersonal behavior in videotaped episodes. *Developmental Psychology,* 1974, *10,* 733–740.

Dirks, J., & Gibson, E. Infants' perception of similarity between live people and photographs. *Child Development,* 1977, *48,* 124–130.

Dorr, A. Interpersonal factors mediating viewing and effects. In G. V. Coelho (Ed.), *Television as a teacher: A research monograph.* Rockville, Md.: National Institute of Mental Health, 1981.

Dorr, A. No shortcuts to judging reality. In J. Bryant & D. R. Anderson (Eds.), *Children's understanding of television: Research on attention and comprehension.* New York: Academic Press, 1983.

Dorr, A., Doubleday, C., & Kovaric, P. Emotions depicted on and stimulated by television programs. In M. Meyer (Ed.), *Children and the formal features of television.* New York: Saur, 1983.

Drabman, R. S., & Thomas, M. H. Does media violence increase children's toleration of real-life aggression? *Developmental Psychology,* 1974, *10,* 418–421.

Dysinger, W. S., & Ruckmick, C. A. *The emotional responses of children to the motion picture situation.* New York: Macmillan, 1933.

Ekman, P. (Ed.). *Darwin and facial expression: A century of research in review.* New York: Academic Press, 1973.

Ekman, P., & Friesen, W. *Unmasking the face.* Englewood Cliffs, N.J.: Prentice-Hall, 1975.

Ekman, P., Liebert, R. M., Friesen, W. V., Harrison, R., Zlatchin, C., Malmstrom, E. J., & Baron, R. A. Facial expressions of emotion while watching televised violence as predictors of subsequent aggression. In G. A. Comstock, E. A. Rubinstein, & J. P. Murray (Eds.), *Television and social behavior. Vol. 5: Television's effects: Further explorations.* Washington, D.C.: U.S. Government Printing Office, 1972.

Eyre-Brook, C. (Ed.). *Young people and television: An international study of juries, producers and their young audiences based on the prize-winning programmes of Prix Jeunesse 1970: Man in metropolis and baff.* Munich: Internationales Zentralinstitut für das Jugend-und Bildungsfernsehen, 1972.

Feilitzen, C., von, & Linné, O. *Living habits and broadcast media behavior of 3–6 year olds.* Sveriges Radio, Audience and Programme Research Department, February 1969.

Fernie, D. E. Ordinary and extraordinary people: Children's understanding of television and real life models. In H. Kelly & H. Gardner (Eds.), *Viewing children through television.* San Francisco: Jossey-Bass, 1981.

Field, J. Relation of young infants' reaching behavior to stimulus distance solidity. *Developmental Psychology,* 1976, *12,* 444–448.

Filipson, E., Schyller, I., & Hoijer, B. *Pretesting of the programme "Why Must We Die?"* Swedish Broadcasting Corporation, Audience and Programme Research Department, July 1974.

Flapan, D. *Children's understanding of social interaction.* New York: Teacher College Press, 1968.

Frijda, N. H. Recognition of emotion. In L. Berkowitz (Ed.), *Advances in experimental social psychology* (Vol. 4). New York: Academic Press, 1969.

Garry, R. (Ed.). *Findings and cognition on the television perceptions of children and young people based on the prize-winning program of Prix Jeunesse 1968: The Scarecrow.* Munich: Internationales Zentralinstitut für das Jugend- und Bildungsfernsehen, November 1970.

Gnepp, J. Children's social sensitivity: Inferring emotions from conflicting cues. *Developmental Psychology,* 1983, *19,* 805–814.

Goslin, D. A. (Ed.). *Handbook of socialization theory and research.* Chicago: Rand McNally, 1969.

Harris, P. L., Olthof, T., & Terwogt, M. M. Children's knowledge of emotion. *Journal of Child Psychology and Psychiatry,* 1981, *22,* 247–261.

Harrison, R. *Beyond words: An introduction to nonverbal communication.* Englewood Cliffs, N.J.: Prentice-Hall, 1974.

Hawkins, R. P. The dimensional structure of children's perceptions of television reality. *Communication Research,* 1977, *4,* 299–320.

Hess, E. H. Ethology and developmental psychology. In P. H. Mussen (Ed.), *Carmichael's manual of child psychology* (Vol. 1). New York: Wiley, 1970.

Himmelweit, H. T., Oppenheim, A. N., & Vince, P. *Television and the child.* London: Oxford University Press, 1958.

Inside/out: A guide for teachers. Bloomington, Ind.: National Instructional Television Center (NITVC), 1973. (ERIC Document Reproduction Service No. ED 084 864)

Izard, C. *Human emotions.* New York: Plenum Press, 1977.

Kovaric, P., Dorr, A., & Nichol, J. *What's gratifying about different types of television programs.* Unpublished manuscript, University of Southern California, January 1983.

Laosa, L. M. Viewing bilingual multicultural educational television: An empirical analysis of children's behaviors during television viewing. *Journal of Educational Psychology,* 1976, *68,* 133–142.

Lazarus, R. S., Kanner, A D., & Folkman, S. Emotions: A cognitive-phenomenological analysis. In R. Plutchik & H. Kellerman (Eds.), *Emotion: Theory, research and experience* (Vol. 1). New York: Academic Press, 1980.

Leifer, A. D. Research on the socialization influence of television in the United States. *Fernsehen und Bildung,* 1975, *9,* 111–142.

Lesser, G. S. *Children and television: Lessons from Sesame Street.* New York: Random House, 1974.

Leventhal, H. Toward a comprehensive theory of emotion. In L. Berkowitz (Ed.), *Advances in experimental social psychology* (Vol. 13). New York: Academic Press, 1980.

Linné, O. *Reactions of children to violence on TV.* Sveriges Radio, Audience and Programme Research Department, July 1971.

Lyle, J., & Hoffman, H. R. Children's use of television and other media. In E. A. Rubinstein, G. A. Comstock, & J. P. Murray (Eds.), *Television and social behavior. Vol. 4: Television in day-to-day life: Patterns of use.* Washington, D.C.: U.S. Government Printing Office, 1972. (a)

Lyle, J., & Hoffman, H. R. Explorations in patterns of television viewing by preschool-age children. In E. A. Rubinstein, G. A. Comstock, & J. P. Murray (Eds.), *Television and social behavior. Vol. 4: Television in day-to-day life: Patterns of use.* Washington, D.C.: U.S. Government Printing Office, 1972. (b)

Mandler, G. *Mind and emotion.* New York: Wiley, 1980.

McCandless, B. R. Childhood socialization. In D. A. Goslin (Ed.), *Handbook of socialization theory and research.* Chicago: Rand McNally, 1969.

McGhee, P. E. Toward the integration of entertainment and educational functions of television: The role of humor. In P. H. Tannenbaum (Ed.), *The entertainment functions of television.* Hillsdale, N.J.: Erlbaum, 1980.

McLeod, J. M., Fitzpatrick, M. A., Glynn, C. J., & Fallis, S. F. Television and social relations: Family influences and consequences for interpersonal behavior. In D. Pearl, L. Bouthilet, & J. Lazar (Eds.), *Television and behavior: Ten years of scientific progress and implications for the eighties* (Vol. 2). Rockville, Md.: National Institute of Mental Health, 1982.

Mood, D. W., Johnson, J. E., & Shantz, C. U. Social comprehension and affect-matching in young children. *Merrill-Palmer Quarterly,* 1978, 24, 63–66.

Murray, J. P., & Kippax, S. From the early window to the late night show: International trends in the study of television's impact on children and adults. In L. Berkowitz (Ed.), *Advances in experimental social psychology* (Vol. 12). New York: Academic Press, 1979.

Mussen, P. H. (Ed.) *Carmichael's manual of child psychology* (Vol. 2). New York: Wiley, 1970.

Pearl, D., Bouthilet, L., & Lazar, J. (Eds.). *Television and behavior: Ten years of scientific progress and implications for the eighties* (Vols. 1 and 2). Rockville, Md.: National Institute of Mental Health, 1982.

Rosenthal, T. L., & Zimmerman, B. J. *Social learning and cognition.* New York: Academic Press, 1978.

Rushton, J. P. Effects of prosocial television and film material on the behavior of viewers. In L. Berkowitz (Ed.), *Advances in experimental social psychology* (Vol. 12). New York: Academic Press, 1979.

Rushton, J. P. Television and prosocial behavior. In. D. Pearl, L. Bouthilet, & J. Lazar (Eds.), *Television and behavior: Ten years of scientific progress and implications for the eighties* (Vol. 2). Rockville, Md.: National Institute of Mental Health, 1982.

Saarni, C. Children's understanding of display rules for expressive behavior. *Developmental Psychology,* 1979, 15, 424–429.

Saarni, C. *Observing children's use of display rules: Age and sex differences.* Paper presented at the meeting of the American Psychological Association, Montreal, September 1980.

Saarni, C. Social and affective functions of nonverbal behavior: Developmental concerns. In R. Feldman (Ed.), *Development of nonverbal behavior.* New York: Springer Verlag, 1982.

Salomon, G. *Interaction of media, cognition, and learning.* San Francisco: Jossey-Bass, 1979.

Schachter, S. The interaction of cognitive and physiological determinants of emotional state. In L. Berkowitz (Ed.), *Advances in experimental social psychology* (Vol. 1). New York: Academic Press, 1964.

Schramm, W., Lyle, J., & Parker, E. B. *Television in the lives of our children.* Stanford, Calif.: Stanford University Press, 1961.

Short, J., Williams, E., & Christie, B. *The social psychology of telecommunications.* New York: Wiley, 1976.

Shultz, T. R., & Butkowsky, I. Young children's use of the scheme for multiple sufficient causes in the attribution of real and hypothetical behavior. *Child Development,* 1977, *48,* 464–469.

Sproull, N. Visual attention, modeling behaviors, and other verbal and nonverbal metacommunication of prekindergarten children viewing *Sesame Street. American Educational Research Journal,* 1973, *10,* 101–114.

Surgeon General's Scientific Advisory Committee. *Television and growing up: The impact of televised violence.* Washington, D.C.: U.S. Government Printing Office, 1972.

Venn, J. R., & Short, J. G. Vicarious classical conditioning of emotional responses in nursery school children. *Journal of Personality and Social Psychology,* 1973, *28,* 249–255.

Walden, T. A., & Field, T. M. Discrimination of facial expressions by preschool children. *Child Development,* 1982, *53,* 1312–1320.

Weiner, B., & Graham, S. An attributional approach to emotional development. In C. Izard, J. Kagan, & R. Zajonc (Eds.), *Emotions, cognition, and behavior.* Cambridge: Harvard University Press, 1984.

Wolpe, J. *The practice of behavioral therapy.* New York: Pergamon, 1974.

Zillmann, D. Anatomy of suspense. In P. H. Tannenbaum (Ed.), *The entertainment functions of television.* Hillsdale, N.J.: Erlbaum, 1980.

Zillmann, D. Television viewing and arousal. In D. Pearl, L. Bouthilet, & J. Lazar. (Eds.), *Television and behavior: Ten years of scientific progress and implications for the eighties* (Vol. 2). Rockville, Md.: National Institute of Mental Health, 1982.

Zillmann, D., & Bryant, J. Viewer's moral sanction of retribution in the appreciation of dramatic presentations. *Journal of Experimental Social Psychology,* 1975, *11,* 572–582.

Zillmann, D., Hay, T. A., & Bryant, J. The effect of suspense and its resolution on the appreciation of dramatic presentations. *Journal of Research in Personality,* 1975, *9,* 307–323.

Zillmann, D., Bryant, J., & Sapolsky, B. S. The enjoyment of watching sport contests. In J. H. Goldstein (Ed.), *Sports, games, and play: Social and psychological viewpoints.* Hillsdale, N.J.: Erlbaum, 1979.

II

Processes of Socialization

5

Signals, Symbols, and Socialization
The Modification of Emotional Expression in Human Development

CAROL ZANDER MALATESTA AND
JEANNETTE M. HAVILAND

> Very few adult males cry in public. Almost no adults have tantrums. Few
> adults publicly hang their head in shame. Only rarely do adults shout with
> joy in public. Very few publicly show intense excitment, sexual or otherwise.
> It is uncommon to express contempt by raising the upper lip and pulling the
> face back. Very few male adults publicly express extreme fear by a shriek.
> (Tomkins, 1962, p. 305)

As Tomkins (1962) observed, the human adult, and especially the male
of the species, rarely displays intense emotional feelings publicly. When
we think about the intense volatility of young children's feelings and
displays and compare it with adult behavior we are naturally struck by
the contrast. The motivations to control affective display are powerful
and varied. In adults, Tomkins (1962) suggested, the facial display of
affect is brought under strict social control in order to prevent affect
contagion and escalation and in order to prohibit others from achieving
control through knowledge of one's otherwise private feelings. According to the work of Saarni (1979, 1981, 1982), the motivations of children

CAROL ZANDER MALATESTA • Graduate Faculty, New School for Social Research, New
York, New York 10003.   JEANNETTE M. HAVILAND • Department of Psychology, Rutgers University, New Brunswick, New Jersey 08903.

are equally commanding and involve defense of self-esteem, avoidance of punishment and disapproval for revealing unregulated negative expressive behavior, concern over hurting other people's feelings, and gaining advantage in interpersonal situations. Gradually, of course, children acquire the skills that are necessary for the regulation of emotion, and they adopt culturally specific conventions of expression. What is not so readily understood, however, is *how* children learn to regulate their expressive behavior and their underlying feelings. In this chapter, we take on the task of framing a working model of affect socialization in an attempt to answer this question. We start with certain premises about the nature of emotion as a motivational system and about the nature of emotional expression.

THE NATURE OF AFFECT

Current research on infant emotion has progressed far enough so that dispute over basic concepts has arisen as we attempt to form new theories of affect development and expression. To refamiliarize the reader with the issues that are especially germane to the concepts treated in this chapter, we describe a friendly debate that took place not long ago over lunch at a conference on infancy studies, one that recapitulated some of the more important developmental issues and controversies.

The central problem under discussion could be described as "How do you tell an infant emotion from any other infant reflex, and why accord it special status?" The conversation was originally launched with the outlining of a plan of research involving the elicitation of emotional behavior in neonates; the proposed behavior was the gustofacial response of disgust. One person balked at the description of this as *emotional* behavior, preferring to view it, as well as the smiles and frowns of young infants, as simple motor acts devoid of affective "meaning." These expressions, he thought, were more like behaviors such as the tonic neck reflex, the Moro, and the stepping reflex. Even though such early behaviors might have a passing resemblance to later developments as in the resemblance of stepping to walking, the speaker felt very strongly that they should not be confused with *voluntary* actions occurring later in infancy and childhood; that is, they were not to be considered phenotypic variants of the same underlying system. Thus, the disgust configuration accompanying the repulsion of a bitter substance was to be regarded as nothing more than a primitive stepping reflex of the face, a spurious, accidental behavior rather than true affect. The implication, of course, was that only conscious emotion qualifies as genuine emotion.

Emotion must be apprehended by the person doing the emoting and must be *processed* in some way.

Debate ensued, for not everyone was content with this cognitive definition of affect. Although none denied that there were cognitive embellishments developmentally, it seemed, at least to some, to be an unnecessary constraint for affect to be defined by cognitive criteria. This approach also seemed to be at violent odds with evolutionary theory because such an assumption automatically excludes all nonsymbolic animals from the experience of emotion, an unlikely state of affairs.

Eventually, it was suggested that emotion, even at a primitive level, involves a motivational state in addition to the motor act, a definition serving to distinguish it from other reflexes. This distinction has been favored in almost all classical theories of emotion. The importance of emotion in providing the "motion" or direction for behavior has been eloquently discussed by Tomkins (1962) and Izard (1971, 1977), and we therefore do not recapitulate that argument here. The motoric behaviors that accompany the emotion/motivational state are usually intrinsic to the emotion expression. The affective behavior *serves* the function of the motivation, opening the sensory system in interest, closing it in disgust, and so forth. These behavioral properties of the emotional response are so characteristic that they may be counted on as reliable signals of the affective state until the organism has acquired the ability to use these signals in impression management. (At that point, they retain signal value but lose their effectiveness as direct links to the automatic affective response [Leventhal, 1980; Tomkins, 1962].) It is no accident that parents attend to the affective expressions of their infants and use these as cues to care for the infant. Although some psychologists are reluctant to believe that there is an isomorphism between an infant's affective state and its affective expression, the argument is almost irrelevant when considered pragmatically, as the caregiver will respond as if the expression were indeed isomorphic with the state.

All of this is by way of indicating that perhaps one of the more important properties of infant affect is its salience to the caregiver as a signal of emotion. Now, more interestingly, because these are *social* signals (i.e., interactive in nature), and because they are not viewed as content-devoid reflexes, at least by caregivers, but as communications, they are subject to interpretation and, like the objects of Heisenberg's uncertainty principle, well on their way to being transformed.

It is to the process of transformation that we now turn. In using the term *transformation*, we are assuming two things, namely, that (a) affects are innately modifiable, and (b) that something about the *affect itself*, and not just the meaning assigned to it by others, is changed.

First, let us consider the substrate on which such transformations must operate.

Affects as Displays

The transformations that are mentioned above must operate on observable behavior, behavior that takes the form of emotional "expressions." We view the very first expressions as raw emotion signals, homologues of the primate displays of the ethological literature. In the course of development, it is these originally hard-wired displays that are transformed into the variable forms used in social communication. Such an assumption implies that affect expressions cannot be randomly cross-wired across individuals. Under conditions of normal development, one does not signal anger when happy. The responses of bellowing, stamping the feet, and gritting the teeth are incompatible with those of joy. If one learns, by some chance, to signal anger and to be angry when most people are joyful, that is a different matter entirely, and would have a multitude of consequences that go beyond the signal itself.

Types of Displays

In order to deal with the socialization of emotion display, it is necessary to consider the types of expressions that can be modified and the various kinds of linkages between expression and state. Displays may represent spontaneous responses to emotion-eliciting cues or they may occur as voluntary behaviors used in the service of impression management. In the latter case, they function as a kind of stimulus more than a response to stimulation. In order to make this distinction a bit clearer, it is helpful to refer to Zivin's (1982) taxonomy of nonverbal signals.

Zivin distinguishes between the classic displays of the ethological literature (i.e., expression linked directly to biogenetically prewired programs), on the one hand, and those signals acquired through learning that serve a wide variety of purposes in social commerce, on the other. Classical displays are said to index immediate internal emotional and motivational states, although anecdotal evidence (Darwin, as cited by Ekman, 1973), as well as more recent empirical evidence (Steklis & Raleigh, 1979), indicates that, even among nonhominid primates, experience can play a role in the *adaptation* of displays for social purposes.

Biologically based and conventionalized signals are rendered as "hard" and "soft" signals in Zivin's systems, and several forms of these two types of signals are distinguished. The heuristic value of Zivin's taxonomy lies in emphasizing the variable linkage between emotional state and overt expression and in its specification of the likely mechanisms involved in transforming the original hard, biologically based propensities to fit the need for variable social communication. In brief outline the taxonomy is as follows:

1. *Hard signals.* These signals have deep roots in biological organization, and there is a reliable link between the appearance of a signal and the presence of the internal state that it is thought to index. There are two types of hard signals, fixed and firm.

a. *Fixed signals* are the classically conceived, genetically prewired displays. An example might be the pure anger expression of an enraged animal.

b. *Firm signals* are those that seem universal but are not necessarily linked directly to internal emotional states. They may, for example, index processing states that incidentally co-occur with other states such as emotions. Through classical conditioning, the behavior can come to be elicited by the previously co-occurring emotion and can reliably function as an index of it.

2. *Soft signals.* These are signals that arise in the course of social learning and that may or may not be involved in the conditioning of behavior to state. There are three types of soft signals:

a. *Forced signals* are those that are modifications of fixed signals. They involve a conscious modification of fixed patterns according to display rules. Display rules operate in impression management and can include *intensification* or exaggeration of affect, *minimization* or reduction, *neutralization,* and *dissimulation* or substitution of innate expressions (Ekman & Friesen, 1975).

b. *Flexible signals* are those learned through imitation and instrumental conditioning, and they include such behaviors as learning to pout when frustrated, the way a sibling does.

c. *Fluid signals* provide no reliable knowledge of state, although states are sometimes inferred by others. Included in this subclass are most paralinguistic behaviors and idiosyncratic nonverbal mannerisms.

The foregoing taxonomy encompasses the full range of hard-wired, biologically based signals and conventionalized social expressions. As Zivin indicated, this taxonomy lends itself to developmental predictions, predictions that rest on the implicit assumptions of ontogenetic plasticity and developmental change. Predictions about development might include assuming that the preponderance of hard signals will give way in early childhood to soft signals. In fact, Zivin suggests that the soft signals do not appear until late infancy or early preschool and may first occur during the time of overall conversational mastery. Hard signals readily lend themselves to phenotypic differentation. The affect system not only *enables* most kinds of learning to take place by supplying motivation but is itself transformable, thus permitting the kind of learning that goes into the development of individual personality and cultural diversity in emotion expression. With this discussion as background, let us turn to a more detailed examination of the way in which affect may be transformed.

AFFECT TRANSFORMATION

Both Freud (1938) and Tomkins (1962, 1963), as well as most psychodynamic psychologists and most practitioners of psychosomatic medicine, have viewed emotion as a somewhat closed energic system with some need of expression. Although emotions themselves may be transformed (indeed, plasticity is their hallmark), the energy of emotion is conserved rather than lost to the organism. In Freud's system, repressed emotion finds expression in psychosomatic or symbolic form. In Tomkins's system, emotion that is blocked—either in awareness or somatically, say, in a dampened facial response—may find heightened expression in the voice or may be experienced as tension in a particular site in the body. Tomkins also suggested that emotion may be delayed or put on hold, as in the automatic gating out of the fear response during the negotiation of maneuvers associated with avoiding an automobile accident; the original response is momentarily blocked but may be experienced in full force seconds or minutes later. The ability to postpone emotion may be an especially well-learned mode of functioning for certain individuals, or for a whole class of individuals within a particular culture. The "nonemotional" nature of men in Western culture is revealed as a hoax to anyone who has ever listened to the screams, hoots, and wails that attend football games and other sports, or to the loud boisterous laughter that accompanies poker games. The generally muted affect of males has its own ritualized outlets. The point is that emotion typically finds some form of expression, even if it is in a miniature form or is permitted only periodic outlet.

The feeling component of emotion may also undergo modification developmentally, although some form of emotional feeling is likely to be preserved. A profound obliteration of feeling is even less likely than the wholesale reduction of display, except in extreme pathological conditions, for two reasons. First, the covert nature of feeling makes it a less readily accessible target of socialization. Second, the basic nature of emotion tends to work against its obliteration. According to Tomkins (1962), there are four basic human functional blueprints or goals related to feelings that regulate the conduct of human lives: the minimization of negative affect, the maximization of positive affect, the goal of achieving all other goals, and the goal of the minimization of affect inhibition. The latter, roughly translated, means that humans like to feel, and that for the most part, they like to feel intensely, no matter what the culture says about modulating overt expression. Saul Bellow put it somewhat more vividly in *Mr. Sammler's Planet* (1969):

> When people had found a name for themselves, human, they spent a lot of time acting human, laughing and crying and getting others to laugh and cry, seeking occasions, provoking, taking such relish in wringing their hands, in drawing tears from their glands, and swimming and boating in that cloudy, contaminated, confusing, surging medium of human feelings, taking the passion-waters, exclaiming over their fate. (p. 234)

Feeling good or bad is better than feeling numb.

Finally, although this point is less obvious, changes within the emotion system may occur at the physiological level as well. The clearest cases are those involving the somatization of blocked affect in muscular tension and cardiovascular pathology. Frequently, there are also changes in the neuroendocrine system caused by stress and other forms of emotional disturbance (Selye, 1956).

In summary, emotion finds expression in physiology, feeling states, and motor behavior. In the course of development, any or all of these aspects may undergo transformation to varying degrees. In unsocialized human beings, such as infants, affect expression is a whole body experience, presumably involving all aspects. Later, under the impact of environmental contingencies, as well as of self-directed modulation and the development of symbolic function, favored modes of expression develop. Socialization may be directed at training in one or all of these channels. Let us now take a closer look at the workings of each system and at some of the social mechanisms operating to bring about developmental change. Finally, we present a developmental model suggesting that socialization begins with attempts to change display properties and, ultimately, feeling states.

ASPECTS OF AFFECT SOCIALIZATION

The Socialization of Physiological Reactions

Much of the history of the psychology of emotion has been concerned with its physiological manifestation. Does emotion consist of discriminable patterns of physiological arousal? Does the central or peripheral nervous system play a more important part? Is emotion simply the perception of autonomic arousal? In the more recent literature concerning infants and children, physiological factors have been important indices of emotional arousal, as in studies of fear, wariness, interest, and pleasure (e.g., Lewis, Brooks, & Haviland, 1978). The more complex questions, such as those involving individual developments in the socialization of physiological mechanisms, have been largely ignored, and yet, there is growing evidence that physiological responses are susceptible to change in the context of certain learning situations.

It has been known for quite some time that there are distinct individual differences in patterns of the autonomic and glandular responses to cognitive and affective stimuli. John and Beatrice Lacey (Lacey, 1950; Lacey & Lacey, 1958, 1962) were among the first to call attention to and to document not only the fact that automatic responsiveness is highly individualized, but that patterns of responsivity show transsituational specificity. Idiosyncratic patterns of autonomic nervous system arousal have been observed in infants as well (Kagan, 1982; Lewis et al., 1978).

Neuroendocrine responses to emotional situations can also vary considerably from individual to individual. Tennes (1982) reported differential patterns of behavioral distress and cortisol production in infants' response to maternal departure; the fact that individual levels of excreted cortisol were significantly correlated across control and experimental conditions suggested that individual differences in the chronic level of adrenocortical activity may be greater than variability in the response to experimental stress, a possibility confirmed by a subsequent longitudinal follow-up into the third year of life. There were high correlations between the mean levels of cortisol excreted for 8 hours 2 years apart in the same subjects. Another interesting finding of this study was that when children's behavioral responses to maternal departure and reunion were classified in terms of types of attachment, the levels of cortisol response predicted the classifications. The pattern of high intraindividual stability in adrenocortical response over time in concert with the finding of a relationship between affective responses to separation and levels of cortisol suggested two alternative explanations for the relationship: (a) the stability of the adrenocortical response is conceivably a function of a physiologically determined predisposition that also impacts on attachment and (b) alternatively, early experiences that the infant has with the mother may serve both to shape the attachment and to condition the pattern of adrenocortical response. Studies from the laboratories of Stern and Shields (discussed below) suggest that idiosyncratic patterns of physiological responsivity are, at least in part, mediated by experiences within the family and possibly in the broader culture.

It is not unusual for people to be consciously aware of their automatic responses during a state of emotional arousal. Sweating palms, accelerated heart rate, gastrointestinal upset, and flushed face are just a few of the symptoms that people perceive in states of arousal and agitation. Research has demonstrated that adults are able not only to articulate the various physiological responses that they experience, but also to report their *primary* physiological response (Stern & Higgins, 1969). In addition, Stern and colleagues (Stern, 1973; Stern & Kaplan, 1967; Stern & Lewis, 1968) have found that, at least in some modalities, subjects' reports of their primary bodily response coincide with an ability to control the response; people who typically respond with palmar sweating under conditions of real-life stress have demonstrated the ability to control their skin-conductance responses. The ability to modulate autonomic nervous system responses in certain modalities suggests two possibilities, that there is either a greater relative magnitude of response in the physiological system in question or a greater sensitivity to activity in that system. The sensitivity itself may, in turn, be related to a lower system-specific feedback threshold and/or to cognitive factors that enhance awareness of the activity in the particular organ system. Although there is considerable evidence that awareness is associated with magnitude of reactivity (Stern, 1973; Stern & Lewis, 1968; Wack, 1972), it is also certainly possible that sensitivity to a particular response may be developed or sharpened through the training of awareness. Such training may consist of parents' drawing attention to a particular concomitant of stress or anger or, as Shields and Stern (1979) suggested, of the salience of a recent event on which the individual focuses (for example, being conscious of heart rate changes after a friend has had a heart attack).

Socialization factors would seem to be implicated in a study of college students' and their parents' perception of autonomic responses to stress situations. Stern and Higgins (1969) found that the probability was greater that students would report a particular somatic response if either parent reported that response than if neither parent reported the symptom. However, it was not clear whether this pattern of results should be attributed to similar genetic background or to socialization influences within the family. Another study by Shields and Stern (1979) more clearly demonstrates the contribution of socialization. Children between the ages of 7 and 10 were presented with a scenario that most would agree creates considerable anxiety: having to report to the principal for an accidentally broken school window. These children not only were interviewed about their own physiological responses but were also asked to guess what their parents might experience on an equivalently stressful occasion for them. The authors found that fathers' agreement with either son or daughter did not exceed the agreement found between fathers and randomly paired children; in contrast, both mother–son and mother–daughter agreement was significantly greater than agreement between mothers and unrelated children. This pattern of finding would seem to discount genetics as the sole contributor to similar patterns between parents and children.

The Socialization of Phenomenology

To judge from semantic differential studies (Block, 1957; Marsella, Murray, & Golden, in press), the phenomenology of what we have come to regard as the basic, fundamental human emotions can vary in shades of experience, in accord with particular patterns of socialization, for example, by culture and gender. Block (1957) studied the semantic differential responses of college students to a set of 15 emotion words. He found that although the responses of males and females showed substantial overlap in phenomenology for descriptions of 14 of the affect terms, there was a considerable difference in the rendering of *grief*. For women, *grief* was described as relatively low, green, weak, smooth, and rounded, whereas for men, *grief* was described as relatively high, red, strong, rough, and angular. This study also examined the isomorphism of the relationships *among* 15 emotion variables by comparing correlation matrices for males and females; Block found that the emotions interrelated in the two sexes with full equivalence, a finding suggesting that the sex differences in expressed emotionality (with women being the more overt and accurate encoders of affect; see Buck, 1981, and Hall, 1978) are probably not due to differences at the level of experience, except, apparently, for grief.

Cross-cultural differences have also been reported. In Block's 1957 study, the responses of Americans and Norwegians were compared. Although the emotions stood in roughly the same relation to one another in the two cultures, specific correlations between Norwegian and American responses for individual emotions showed some variation, with the correlation between the groups for the phenomenology of nostalgia, grief, and anticipation being the lowest, and of pride and love the highest. In examining the semantic differential responses of groups of Caucasian-Americans, Japanese-Americans, and Chinese-Americans for the emotion of shame, Marsella *et al.* (in press) detected a number of apparent differences in the phenomenology of this emotion. The Caucasian-Americans rated shame as significantly more low, weak, and dull than the two Oriental groups, a finding suggesting that shame is less clearly identifiable or understood by the Caucasian group. The authors speculated that the reason is that shame may be used as a technique of social control more often in Oriental societies; Oriental children would consequently have a greater incentive to learn to read the organismic and situational cues for shame. Another finding was that all three groups rated shame as a "serious" experience, but the Caucasian-Americans and the Chinese-Americans rated it as significantly more serious than did the Japanese-Americans. Another study by Marsella and colleagues (Marsella, Kinzie, & Gordon, 1973) demonstrated that depression is manifested differently among various ethnic groups. There is some evidence that such a result is attributable to differences in how various ethnic groups verbalize mood states. Chinese-Americans are reluctant to say that they are depressed and instead report that they are fatigued, tired, nervous, and suffering from numerous somatic complaints.

How are such phenomenologically different feelings acquired? As Hochschild (1979) has suggested, people try to modulate feeling states as well as overt expressions. They know what they *should* feel in order to be socially appropriate. "Conventions of feeling become surprising only when we imagine, by contrast, what totally unpatterned, unpredictable emotive life might actually be like at parties, funerals, weddings, and in the family or work life of normal adults" (p. 552). Conscious of normative standards, people *work* at getting their emotions to conform to what is expected, as captured by such expressions as trying to get oneself "psyched up" for something , or conversely "calmed down."

Conventions about feelings can be subsumed under the term *feeling rules*. These rules delineate the "zone within which one has permission" to feel such-and-such a way. "Such zoning ordinances describe a metaphoric floor and ceiling" (Hochschild, 1979, p. 552). Feeling rules differ not only across different cultures, but within cultures as well, according to differences such as gender and social class. It is possible that the phenomenological difference in the experience of grief for men and women is related to the assumption that their natures are basically different, especially with respect to the elicitation and experience of affects related to sadness. Parents apparently socialize their children's feelings according to social class as well as gender (Hochschild, 1979). Middle-class parents tend to exert control over behavior via appeals to feelings, and the control is more concerned with feelings; the child of a middle-class family may be reprimanded for feeling the wrong way ("You should be ashamed of yourself for taking that child's toy"; "You should be grateful that your grandmother gave you that set of knit socks instead of the new Atari cartridge you wanted"). In contrast, the working-class parent tends to control via appeals to behavior, and the control is more directed toward behavior and its consequence.

The Socialization of Display Behavior

The socialization of display consists of both deliberate and unconscious efforts of parents to encourage children to regulate their expressive behavior in accord with culturally defined norms. Although facial and vocal affect, physiological reactivity, and phenomenology can all be altered, it is likely that socialization efforts are differentially focused depending on the age of the child. For example, facial and vocal affect are the most directly visible forms of emotion in infants, and therefore, these become the most immediate targets of deliberate parental socialization. It is obvious that parents will want to curb the rageful responses of toddlers in the throes of the "terrible twos," that they will want to encourage smiling from young infants in response to relatives, and so on. It is not so immediately obvious how these goals are accomplished. Is its verbally, nonverbally, or through some combination of the two? Or must modulated affect display simply attend maturational changes in the nervous system, with relative independence of parental efforts. Because it is our thesis that socialization efforts are first directed at display, developmentally, we discuss the socialization of expressive behavior further in the following section.

To summarize thus far, we have seen that emotion socialization may include display behavior, phenomenology, and physiological responses as targets, and that these systems are, to a greater or lesser extent, modifiable in form. The details of modification, specification of principles, and a working developmental model are presented below.

MECHANISMS OF EMOTION SOCIALIZATION AND A DEVELOPMENTAL MODEL

Overview

Earlier, we asserted that affects start out developmentally as hard-wired displays linked to state. These are the *hard* signals of the taxonomy of Zivin (1982). We would like to propose that *flexible* signals evolve originally within dyadic interchange between mother and infant. We also suggest that this same occasion supports the development of forced and fluid signals, although we presume that, for the young infant, these processes are preconscious. (Though the processes may not be conscious in a self-reflective way, we would argue along with Buck, 1981, Leventhal, 1979, Panksepp, 1982, and Izard, 1983 that affects and affect modifications are probably felt or sensed in some primitive, subjective way in even the very young, preverbal infant; the "sensorimotor" stage of development described by Piaget surely includes a sensoriaffective mode of experience with the world.) In the course of development, state and expression may become partially uncoupled, with subsequent flexibility in the use of the original displays. Further transformations of both expressions and feelings proceed apace with further maturation and experience with the social world. Several processes are involved: (a) modification of hard display; (b) addition of firm display; (c) addition of soft display (all of the foregoing in response to an appropriate stimulus); and (d) management of signal to *produce an effect*, rather than *as a response*. What we are saying is that signals may function originally only as responses, but that eventually they may be employed as stimili during interactive processes. In this stimulus form, they may or may not be initially congruent with the response state of the signal sender. The developmental course is elaborated below.

Infancy

We begin with infancy because much recent cross-cultural research on mother–infant interaction demonstrates that enculturation for social and emotional behavior beings in the cradle or its equivalent (Field, Sostek, Vietze, & Leiderman, 1981). Super and Harkness (1982), for example, have noted that the parents' expressive interaction with their infants reflects the larger cultural values concerning emotional states and expressions. This fact is readily observed in face-to-face play, an important medium for the mother's enactment of formalized (and usually exaggerated) versions of social decorum concerning emotion displays and patterns of gazing in social interaction. The form of etiquette varies considerably across cultures and tends to reflect the culture's stance toward emotions: how it construes emotion, interprets its signals, and deals with issues of control. Perhaps one of the best examples of the relations among parental beliefs, cultural ideals, and parental practices in working to promote the adoption of local cultural ideals is seen in a study of mother–infant interactions among the Gusii of Africa (Dixon, Tronick, Keeler, & Brazelton, 1981).

The Gusii are a community of Bantu-speaking people living in southwestern Kenya. Interactions among adults are pervaded by tacit rules proscribing the display of intense emotion, rules, that is, for the minimization of affect. The buildup of either positive or negative feeling between interactants is prevented by the practice of constant gaze aversion and use of a bland countenance. Immediate parallels are to be found in the pattern of mother–infant contact, where face-to-face play is rare, eye contact is avoided, and interaction is characterized by affective restraint. When the investigators asked mothers to engage in face-to-face play with their infants, their behavior appeared awkward, for the infant is rarely held in an enface position in this culture. Gusii mothers believe that the infant is incapable of communicative intent aside from the signaling of hunger or distress, and that affective intensity is dangerous and to be avoided. In concert with these beliefs, mothers avoid lengthy bouts of play with their infants that might overly excite them, they do not use the exaggerated baby talk seen among American mothers, and their facial expressions are bland, rather than animated. This behavior appears to put a damper on infant affectivity. When an infant does become excited, the mother exercises a variety of immediate strategies to terminate this excitement. She averts her gaze or blinks frequently to break contact with the infant, and she may use physical restraint, such as holding a down a child's arms, if its movements become large or excited. Thus, the cultural norms that preclude intense social interaction among adults are introduced as a matter of course in the earliest interpersonal encounters that the infant experiences.

Yet another example of the relationship between parental beliefs and practices concerning emotion comes to us from our own culture. In a recently completed study from our own lab (Malatesta & Haviland, 1982), we looked at the characteristic facial play between American mothers and their young 3- to 6-month-olds. The findings appear to reflect the local cultural ideals of middle-class American mothers.

Drawing from a variety of sources (Dixon, et al., 1981; Kagan, 1979; Lutz, 1982; Tomkins, 1962, 1963), including personal observation, we present the following as constituting some of the implicit beliefs about emotion in this culture. First of all, American mothers believe that infants are helpless and dependent and that they require help in developing autonomy. Middle-class American mothers regard spontaneity, rather than control and obedience, as a favorable trait to be encouraged. Attitudes toward emotion include beliefs that emotions are powerful forces; that they should be expressed in at least some form, rather than suppressed; and that free access to affect is adaptive, whereas repression leads to negative consequences. However, this "enlightened" attitude toward emotional expression includes some ambivalence about negative affect. Today's mothers, having themselves been reared in a post-Freudian climate imbued with notions of infant vulnerability and susceptibility to pathology from distress and anxiety, feel called on to defend their helpless infants against the experience of negative emotion. Mothers also hold beliefs about the differential vulnerability to distress of male and female infants and the need for girls to be more conversant with a wider range of emotional feelings than boys. In analyzing our results, we found that all of the foregoing values and beliefs were manifest in face-to-face play behavior, and we were, moreover, able to identify some of the behavioral mechanisms that mediate the socialization of emotion during this early stage of development.

Here, we briefly summarize some of the findings that illustrate how cultural values, translated through maternal behaviors, act to socialize the expression of emotion in infants. In the study, we videotaped play and reunion sessions; we then subjected the tapes to the Max (Izard, 1979) facial-affect coding system, thus generating a body of sequential data on second-to-second changes in maternal and infant expressions.

First of all, we found that infants display a wide range of categorical emotional expressions and signals as early as 3 months of age, including interest, enjoyment, surprise, sadness/distress, anger, knit brow, discomfort/pain, and brow flash. Infants also showed a high rate of change in their facial expressions. The 3-month-olds were found to change their expression once every 7 seconds; the 6-month-olds, once every 9 seconds. These two foregoing findings, that young infants have such a wide repertoire of expressions, in combination with the finding of high lability, suggested to us that caregivers have a tremendous opportunity to respond to infant affect and conceivably to shape it via instrumental conditioning, a point to which we will return momentarily.

The mothers showed a density of expression change that was similar to the rate found in the infants; they displayed an average of eight emotional expressions per minute during play. However, the mothers did not duplicate their babies' wide range of expressions. Instead, the maternal facial expressions were found to be basically restricted to the emotions of interest, enjoyment, and surprise, and to a positive brow-flash signal. Maternal modeling, therefore, is primarily of the positive emotions and signals, a finding supporting the implicit premium on positive affect. The mothers were found to make contingent facial-change responses to at least 25% of the infant facial-expression changes, and most of these were given when the baby was visually engaged with the mother. The lag between maternal expression change and infant expression change was found to be less than half a second; thus, maternal responses fall within the most optimal range for "instrumental conditioning." Because the contingency patterns differed subtly according to the age and the sex of the child, we presume that differential learning could have been taking place.

Of special interest was the interplay between infant expressions and maternal contingent responses. Although infant males and females displayed the same type and rate of facial expression change, with the one exception that infant females displayed more interest expressions, the mothers responded differentially to the two sexes. The mothers showed a significant increase, over infant age, in contingent responding (especially contingent smiling) to the smiles of infant males and a decrease for females. We speculate that this difference may reflect the great investment that mothers may have in reinforcing the positive affect of male infants, as male babies seem to have a greater predisposition to irritability (Haviland & Malatesta, 1981). Another sex-differentiated maternal behavior was found within the patterns of contingent responding. The mothers were found to give similar or matching responses more to male than to female expressions, and they followed more female, as opposed to male, expressions with dissimilar responses. Matching responses, or imitations, appear to sustain infant attention, especially among infants with vulnerability to irritation (Field, 1977) and prevent overarousal; the arousal-shielding functions of matching may partially account for the sex difference, if we assume that mothers are sensitive to their infants' level of stimulus tolerance. This differential pattern of maternal respond- ing also means that females are exposed to a wider range of emotional expressions. If female infants continue to be exposed to a wider range of expressions than male infants as they progress developmentally, then we have at least a partial explanation of why, at all ages, girls are better at decoding emotional expression than boys (Hall, 1978).

In summary, then, we find that mothers in face-to-face play with their infants behave in ways that might be predicted, *a priori*, on the basis of our knowledge of prevailing socioemotional cultural ideals. Con- gruent with this culture's emphasis on spontaneity and overtness with respect to the more sanguine, social emotions, and congruent with its notions about females as the more "emotionally sensitive" sex, mothers display and reinforce positive affect in both sexes and display a wider range of contingent emotional expressivity with females; mothers encourage the initially more irritable and labile male to become "stoical" by reinforcing positive affect expressions when they occur and by min- imizing the occasions for overstimulation that would propel the child into a state of distress.

Implicit in these findings is the assumption of certain learning mechanisms that promote the adoption of conventionalized forms of expression, that is, (a) observational learning of modeled expressions and imitation and (b) instrumental learning. Given that these abilities have already been established in young infants in a number of simple learning paradigms, we need only demonstrate their existence in this domain of behavior.

1. *Imitation of modeled expressions.* Mothers display an average of 8.05 emotion-signal changes per minute. At that rate, assuming that a mother spends about 3 hours a day in face-to-face interaction with her infant, with the infant attending to her face one quarter of the time (Hittelman & Dickes, 1979), the average infant is exposed to 362 exem- plars of emotion signals per day, or about 32,580 during the third to the sixth month, a period of time identified as the peak period in face-to- face play (Field, 1979). We assume that this is not a trivial learning opportunity for the infant, and that it is a crucial early component of emotion socialization. Although there is some controversy about the ability of young infants to imitate modeled expressions, our own recent

review of the literature (Malatesta & Izard, 1983) indicates that there is more support for the case than against it. Moreover, in our own study we found that older infants are more like their mothers, in their facial expressive behavior, than are younger infants. More direct evidence could be obtained with longitudinal data, a project that is now under way in our own laboratory. Collectively, the literature indicates that young infants are capable of matching elements or whole facial expressions of models with similar expressions of their own. Although we hesitate to infer intentionality in these matching responses, the capacity to mimic another would seem to be a vital developmental process contributing to emotions ontogenesis.

2. *Instrumental learning.* Mothers have the option to respond or not respond to infant expressions, and these behaviors can be regarded as constituting reinforcement or extinction training. The type of response that a mother makes (i.e., the class or classes of infant expression to which she responds or does not respond) and the type of the emotional *content* of her response may be additional important aspects of affect socialization; research on this subject has only just begun (e.g., Cohn, 1981). We do know that maternal responses are typically contingent and immediate and that the lag between infant and maternal expression changes is in the most optimal range for instrumental learning.

How might the foregoing mechanisms begin to impact on infant affect? At the display level, facial expressions may undergo a variety of changes, most notably in *frequency, range, discreteness,* and *pattern.* The preceding study, as well as work by Demos (1982a, b) with older infants, speaks to these changes. In our own study, we found that there was a significant decline in the frequency of facial expression changes from 3 to 6 months, from a rate of one change every 7 seconds at 3 months to one every 9 seconds at 6 months. We also found that there was proportionately more reduction in expressions of negative affect than in those of positive affect from 3 to 6 months. Thus, there was a reduction in both the *frequency* and the *range* with age. Beyond a certain point, however, we would expect expressions to start becoming less discrete in terms of their "purity," as affect blends characterize more mature individuals (Ekman & Friesen, 1975). In fact, in Demos's naturalistic study of the expressive behaviors of 7- to 24-month-old children (1982a, b), she noted that blends were relatively rare at the youngest ages and become increasingly likely with age. Interestingly, Demos found that when blends did occur, they were most commonly blends involving the smile: a surprise smile, an excited smile, a smile with lowered, angry brows. The preference for smile blends may reflect this culture's emphasis on maintaining sociability with others and the ease with which smiling may be used to mask all kinds of other unacceptable emotions. It is certainly consistent with mothers' preference for smiling (the most frequent of all facial displays—Malatesta & Haviland, 1982) and the presumed effects of maternal modeling on infant affect change.

As far as changes in *pattern* go, we suspect that patterns become more idiosyncratic with age, depending on social learning and the kinds of patterns of affective expression to which the child is exposed. In the study described above, we found that the members of each mother–infant pair shared commonalities in how they used their facial muscles, both in their discrete facial movements, and in their preference for certain categorical expressions; moreover, the strength of the correlations between the mothers and the infants for types of facial movement increased with the infant's age. The older the infant, the more similar were its facial expressions to those of its mother. In a similar vein, Demos (1982a, b) found evidence of what she called "emblems" during the second half of the first year, and these appear to be imitations of adult expressions, such as the raised brow to signal a question; these data would seem to support our own observations of soft signal mastery in the first year of life.

What kind of changes in phenomenology might accompany the changes in display that we have just described? At the phenomenological level, we can only speculate. However, if we assume a more-or-less one-to-one link between state and display in infancy, as proposed by Zivin (1982) and Demos (1982a), we must presume a changing affect phenomenology as well. The changes in facial display described above suggest that the infant may be experiencing a more stabilized affective world from the third to the sixth month, in that the rate of facial expression change is diminishing. In her study of older infants, Demos found no evidence of attempts to deintensify or minimize (distress) affect in her youngest (7 to 12-month-old) subjects, although examples of what appeared to be exaggerations or amplifications of affects were seen for older children. Only later was there evidence of one child's attempt to control distress by sucking in the lips and producing a lip funnel.

The theory that we are working on says that the voluntary, intentional modification of affective expression—as in the modes of intensification, minimization, neutralization, and dissimulation—become possible only around the time of the fifth stage of sensorimotor development (around 10–12 months of age), at the same time as the emergence of other intentional behavior (Bates, Camainoni, & Volterra, 1975; Bruner, 1975, Harding & Golinkoff, 1979). We also suspect that such a capacity is dependent on two other prior changes in the affect system: (a) stabilization and clarification of emotional state and (b) some rudimentary symbolization of affect. As noted earlier, early infant affect is extremely labile. Expressions change quickly, and one often sees gen- uinely "mixed emotions" in which one emotion seems to be competing with another, as in the rapid alternation between tears and smiles in the young infant whose mother is trying to divert it with games. We speculate that contingent responding, as described earlier, contributes to the stabilization of infant affect and perhaps even to the consolidation of particular patterns of affective expression. It may be that the infant develops a clearer sense of his or her own change of state and a grasp of the differences among categorical feeling changes by the very timing and patterning of the mother's contingent responding and mirroring of state. Here, we are suggesting not that the mother *brings about* differ- entiation of the infant's emotions (discrete emotions appear already to exist), but that it is through her contingent behaviors that she contributes to the infant's general affect awareness, its eventual awareness of the differences among feeling states, and its ability to use affective states differentially and instrumentally.

In our own study, we found that the mothers appeared to be encouraging the dampening of affective expressions with increasing infant age. The mothers of 6-month-olds were found to use significantly fewer brow flashes than were the mothers of 3-month-olds. The brow flash has been described as a signal of acknowledgment and agreement (Eibl- Eibesfeldt, 1979; Ekman, 1979). Thus, mothers of older infants show reduced nonverbal acknowledgment of infant affect. In addition, these mothers do not compensate for a reduction in nonverbal response with an increase in verbal response. On the contrary, the verbal records are consistent with the nonverbal records. Transcriptions of maternal speech to infants in face-to-face play indicate that mothers make fewer com- ments about their infant's affect with age and also make fewer statements that encourage affective displays. These apparent "affect-reduction strat- egies" employed by mothers are consistent with the cultural ideals dic- tating suppression of the overt display of affect with age (Tomkins, 1962, 1963). However, in accord with the psychodynamic model of emotion mentioned earlier (Freud, 1938; Tomkins, 1962, 1963), we would expect that actual attenuation of overtly displayed affect (affect minimization), of necessity, awaits other maturational changes. Because displays and states appear to be directly linked, at least in early infancy, modification of both displays and state may attend the capacity to symbolize the sensate and/or display properties of affect. The following suggests a way in which overt displays may become internalized.

First of all, the high rate of maternal expression-modeling provides the infant with abundant exemplars for the formation of elemental sche- mas of categorical expression, especially during the peak period of face-to-face play, that is, during the third to the sixth month. Second, as we have proposed, the mother's contingent responding to infant expressions accentuates the infant's awareness of his or her own state changes and thus assumedly aids in the ability to discriminate among various emotions. Particular types of contingent responding provide yet another means of promoting the development of a shift to "representational" emotion: affect imitations and affect–affect sequences. In the first type, imitations, "mirrored" expressions permit simultaneity in the "viewing" and the "feeling" of affect and thus the development of an association between images and feelings. The second type, wherein a particular infant expression is regularly followed by a dissimilar but predictable response, as when the infant's smile is regularly followed by maternal mock surprise, permits the development of expectations about affect sequences. In both cases, images of affect, formed by viewing modeled expressions and developed from kinesthetic feedback from the infant's own face, eventually stand in for, or represent, overt emotional expression. Once perceptual differentiation has occurred, assisted by the above processes, and once overt expressions (those of both the mother and the infant) have been internalized in the form of rudimentary representational images, greater modulation of affect becomes possible, and the child is well on his or her way to the ability to develop and use forced, or conventionalized, signals intentionally.

Socialization of Affect in Older Infants and Children

As the infant matures, the mother and child show changes in interactive behavior that are germane to an understanding of the socialization of affect beyond the first few months of life. Starting when infants are about 3 months old, mothers begin to show a decline in the frequency with which they use facial expressions, reaching a low point at 36 months, according to an observational study by Ling and Ling (1974). Although infants also show a decrement in facial expressions over time, the decline for mothers appears to be sharper than for infants, a finding suggesting that the mothers are taking the lead. Demos (1982b) coded the tonal quality of maternal utterances to their 9- to 21-month-old infants, as well as the verbal content. She found that maternal evaluation and affective comments to 9- and 15-month-olds were mainly of positive statements and tones; by 21 months, however, there was a considerable shift to the increasing inclusion of irritated, perfunctory, and didactic tones. Malatesta (1980) found that mothers' contingent responses to 3- and 6-month-old infant expressions shifted from mainly contingent responding to positive affect, to greater attention to negative affect with infant age, a trend that appears to be consistent with the data obtained by Demos.

It is perhaps the case that mothers focus more on positive affect expressions in early infancy in an attempt to expand the frequency of positive affect, and then, with the greater stabilization of positive affect that occurs between 3 and 6 months, they switch to a different strategy to deal with the residual negative affect.

Infants, for their part, also show changes, some of which probably reflect maturation of the nervous system, others of which reflect the impact of early socialization. Kaye and Fogel (1980), looking at the temporal structure of face-to-face communication between mothers and their 1½- to 6½-month-olds, found that, in the first months, infant expression changes appeared to be mainly under the control of maternal elicitation; at 3 months, there was more frequent reciprocal behavior; and at 6½ months, there emerged infant-initiated greetings, demonstrating greater autonomy in the infant's social interchange with age. Interestingly, the mean proportion of time during which infants were oriented toward their mothers' faces declined with age, as did the state of *attention* to the mother's face. However, although there was a steep decline in these behaviors, with the older infant spending more time looking at things besides the mother's face, this time was deleted from the time it had spent watching the mother's *resting* face; it continued to spend just as much time watching the more expressive behavior. Thus, infants continue to regard the more informationally meaningful aspects of their mothers' faces. In fact, infant attention to maternal affective reactions may become more highly motivated with age. Malatesta (1980), for example, observed that 6-month-old infants were less likely to close their eyes when crying than were 3-month-olds and, instead, typically regarded their mothers through partially opened eyes during the majority of the time that they cried, as though checking their mother's reactions. Stenberg (1982) also noted this tendency. Social referencing, a term used to describe the child' s use of its mother's facial, vocal, and gestural cues during situations of uncertainty (Campos & Stenberg, 1981), is another example of how infants continue, through the second half of the first year and beyond, to use the affective expressions of others as guideposts to behavior. Such continued observance of the emotional behaviors of others permits further opportunities to learn about the display characteristics of people whose expressions transmit the larger culture's values concerning the overt display of affect; it also provides further opportunities for the social world to impact on the child's development of affect modulation. This kind of social comparison of affect probably continues throughout life. However, it is likely that, in addition to the nonverbal learning that takes place all through life, an added component of emotion socialization enters as the child gradually masters an understanding of the symbols of language. Although the phenomenological experience of children is difficult to ascertain, we know that preschoolers have an understanding of and a vocabulary for emotional states that describes both themselves and others (Bretherton, McNew, & Beeghly-Smith, 1981). This vocabulary is use to describe internal states and to attribute intention. Although it is not clear how broad or how well-differentiated this phenomenon is, studies of slightly older children indicate that they have a relatively accurate understanding of basic emotional states and can label emotional expressions quite accurately, although there continues to be general improvement up to adolescence (Charles-worth & Kreutzer, 1973; Izard, 1971).

Although Izard (1971) and others have suggested that further affect modulation becomes possible with the development of semiotic functions such as memory and language, there has yet to be a study of the way in which the developmental course of language may or may not coincide with the ability of children to further displace overt display with internal representations. Let us examine the ways in which the growth of linguistic function, as well as more general symbolic function, may assist in the further desomatization of affect as a developmental feature in the socialization of affect.

Language and Emotion in Older Children and Adults

Lutz (1982) and others (Geertz, 1959; Levy, 1980) have suggested that the emotion words of a culture exert a powerful influence on the actual experience of emotion. Here, we would like to examine that thesis in more detail.

Although the range and quality of emotional experience is potentially the same for all human beings (Geertz, 1959), the anthropological literature demonstrates that this potential range becomes altered in various ways, so that certain qualitative aspects are attenuated, emphasized, or embroidered upon. Indeed, once the child has learned his or her culture's nomenclature for the various constituents of emotion and the various shades of meaning, these terms become the tools that enable further socialization of emotion. Although we presume that parents and others continue to exert influence on the display aspects of their children's emotion through the use of nonverbal commentary (as in signaling disapproval of a behavior by a raised brow), as the child develops language verbal forms of communication begin to play an increasingly important part in altering behavior and structuring emotional experience.

Let us examine some of the ways in which language helps to socialize emotion in children. First of all, as Izard (1980) has demonstrated, cultures vary in the number of words they have to describe particular emotions. The culture thus imposes constraints on how parents may use language to promote social goals. The sheer number of emotion words that pertain to an emotion is a good index of how important that emotion is in the culture (Levy, 1980), be it highly celebrated or regarded as dangerous and in need of tight social control. An emotion with a large array of terms to describe it is said to be *hypercognized*, whereas an emotion with relatively few terms to index it is said to be *hypocognized* (Levy, 1980). When there are varied ways of referring to a particular experience in an explicit fashion, as when the emotion is hypercognized, the emotion itself is brought into the social domain, where it can become a focus of community regulation. An experience that is variously and endlessly described can be "chewed" to death so that it loses its potency. Such a treatment of an emotion would constitute a type of emotion "desensitization," with consequent affect reduction.

On the other hand, an emotion that is hypocognized is less distinct and less available to reflective consciousness. However, unless the usual eliciting conditions are entirely eliminated from the environment, the fundamental emotions are still capable of being activated. In the case of cultures where responsibility of behavior is considered largely external to the individual, there may be few words for *guilt* and few experiences of it. However, for other emotions, where eliciting conditions still prevail (situations capable of recruiting disgust, for example) the emotion itself is activated, though it may or may not cross the limen of reflective self-awareness; it is less available for further processing because it does not receive the focus of social attention achieved by more hypercognized emotions and remains primarily at a sensate, organismic level of awareness.

Second, language is used to sharpen awareness by drawing attention to some ongoing or *remote process*. Parents use an emotional vocabulary in interacting with their children even in the early months of life, and they regularly comment on their children's emotional displays. Many of the comments are directive. In our study of American mothers and their infants, we distinguished three types of maternal affect commentary: the first type consisted of "affect encouragement" (e.g., "Smile for Mommy"); the second type was "discouragement" (e.g., "Don't be sad"; "Stop crying"); and the third type was a nondirective "Rogerian" sort that consisted of an emotional reflective listening (e.g., "You're feeling unhappy, aren't you?"). Although we have no data yet on older children that allows us to judge developmental trends, we suspect that the bulk of affective commentary by parents focuses on immediate state in infants and young children and gradually expands to include comments on remote emotional events, anticipated or past, in concert with the child's maturing cognitive capacities. Both kinds, however, serve to bring emotion into the domain of consciousness. At the same time, the child learns valuable things about when, where, and in what form the emotion that has been evoked verbally should or should not be expressed, thus linking internal state (as it is currently apprehended or in its evoked form as a past or future experience) with its socially acceptable form of expression and the appropriate eliciting conditions. Eventually, this verbal commentary, as in the case of its nonverbal counterpart, further promotes the transformation of display, physiological response, and phenomenology in accord with local cultural ideals.

Third, language permits the further development of idiosyncratic or familial associations between state and phenomenology to occur as a function of particular patterns of training. As Lewis and Michalson have (1982) pointed out, parental interpretative labeling of emotional behaviors and reported states has various outcomes. An emotion that is inappropriately labeled by the parent can set the stage for mixed feelings and substitution of experience; emotions that are ignored are exposed to a kind of extinction training; parents may also promote undue inhibition of emotions through extreme responses to their display.

Finally, language facilitates the eventual development of schematic emotional memory and probably also contributes to the development of an abstract conceptual system related to emotion (Leventhal, 1979). Schematic, emotional memory, as conceived of by Leventhal (1979), is portrayed as a relatively concrete, iconic affair whose key perceptual features are the emotion-eliciting situations; a representation of the primary, expressive motor reactions accompanying these episodes, an associated set of automatic reactions; a code of the subjective emotional feeling itself; and various overt, instrumental coping responses. We would add to this list an assortment of related lexical labels that serve to facilitate the retrieval of the emotional memories. Emotional schemata are said to play a crucial role in creating or structuring emotional experience in that they act as selective devices permitting rapid reactions to affectively significant situations, in directing attention to the perceptual field, in elaborating a trace of a current situation, and in amplifying or strengthening inputs to give them a place in focal awareness. They also permit the blending of experiences and the development of subtler feeling states by permitting the attachment of existent emotion to new situations and the alteration of emotion by generating new combinations of stimulus traces and motor patterns of expressive behaviors along with autonomic and instrumental responses. Thus, emotional schemas are said to support the development of higher order emotional responses, such as the capacity for feelings of empathy, intimacy, and pride.

The abstract conceptual system (Leventhal, 1979) contains abstractions from more concrete or episodic experience; it is a repository of memories and operations *about* feelings. It is also likely to be associated with global lexical terms such as *sadness, happiness,* and *anger.* The abstract conceptual processing system is especially useful for controlling feelings, doing so by accessing emotional feelings of the more specific, concrete, prototypical type, and by volitional regulation of expressive behavior. Eventually, this system permits one to summon up a "happy" or "angry" attitude or feeling, and thus engage in what Hochschild (1979) refers to as "deep acting." Deep acting calls for re-creating authentic feeling (versus merely adopting a display or mask) in the absence of a natural eliciting condition, to voluntarily *feel* the emotion that is socially required.

SUMMARY AND CONCLUSION

Emotion starts out developmentally as complex reflexlike behavior consisting of state-linked display behavior. This behavior is subsequently altered through parental nonverbal contingencies, neuromuscular maturation, and self-regulating properties of the affect system, leading to the development of two kinds of soft signals, the fluid and the flexible. Voluntary control of display behavior begins to develop through the imitation of the modeled expressive behavior of caregivers and the maturation of the pyramidal motor system, leading to the eventual attainment of forced signal mastery with the capacity to intensify, minimize, neutralize, and dissimilate expressions of emotion. Linguistic labels for the emotions, gradually acquired over time and variously linked with current and remote emotional experience, lead to further clarification of emotional experience and greater voluntary control over affective experience and behavior. Language also assists the development of emotional schematic memory, as well as of an abstract conceptual structure, systems that permit the merger of display and feeling as required by social contingencies. Thus, human development consists of uncoupling preadapted display/state/experience emotional coherences early in life, to eventually form new display/state/experience coherences to suit culturally specific requirements; if the hallmark of intelligent behavior is adaptability, the emotion system would appear to be fairly intelligent.

REFERENCES

Bates, E., Camainoni, L., & Volterra, V. The acquisition of performatives prior to speech. *Merrill-Palmer Quarterly,* 1975, *21,* 205–226.

Bellow, S. *Mr. Sammler's planet.* New York: Viking Press, 1969.

Block, J. Studies in the phenomenology of emotions. *Journal of Abnormal and Social Psychology,* 1957, *54,* 358–363.

Bretherton, I., McNew, S., & Beeghly-Smith, M. Early person knowledge as expressed in gestural and verbal communication: When do infants acquire a "Theory of Mind?" In M. E. Lamb & L. R. Sherrod (Eds.), *Infant social cognition*. Hillsdale, N.J.: Erlbaum, 1981.

Bruner, J. S. The ontogenesis of speech acts. *Journal of Child Language*, 1975, 2, 1–19.

Buck, R. The evolution and development of emotion expression and communication. In S. S. Brehm, S. M. Kassin, & F. X. Gibbons (Eds.), *Developmental social psychology*. New York: Oxford University Press, 1981.

Campos, J. J., & Stenberg, C. R. Perception, appraisal and emotion: The onset of social referencing. In M. E. Lamb & L. R. Sherrod (Eds.), *Infant social cognition*. Hillsdale, N.J.: Erlbaum, 1981.

Charlesworth, W. R., & Kreutzer, M. A. Facial expressions of infants and children. In P. Ekman (Eds.), *Darwin and facial expressions*. New York: Academic Press, 1973.

Cohn, J. F. *Three-month-old infants' reaction to simulated maternal depression*. Paper presented at the meeting of the Society for Research in Child Development, Boston, Mass., April 1981.

Demos, V. Facial expressions of infants and toddlers: A descriptive analysis. In T. Field & A. Fogel (Eds.), *Emotion and early interaction*. Hillsdale, N.J.: Erlbaum, 1982. (a)

Demos, V. The role of affect in early childhood: An exploratory study. In E. Z. Tronick (Ed.), *Social interchange in infancy*. Baltimore: University Park Press, 1982. (b)

Dixon, S., Tronick, E., Keeler, C., & Brazelton, T. B. Mother-infant interaction among the Gusii of Kenya. In T. M. Field, A. M. Sostek, P. Vietze, & P. H. Leiderman (Eds.), *Culture and early interaction*. Hillsdale, N.J.: Erlbaum, 1981.

Eibl-Eibesfeldt, I. Human ethology: Concepts and implications for the sciences of man. *Behavioral and Brain Sciences*, 1979, 2, 1–57.

Ekman, P. Epilogue. In P. Ekman (Ed.), *Darwin and facial expression*. New York: Academic Press, 1973.

Ekman, P. About brows: Emotional and conversational signals. In M. von Cranach, K. Foppa, W. Lepenies, & D. Ploog (Eds.), *Human ethology*. Cambridge: Cambridge University Press, 1979.

Ekman, P., & Friesen, W. V. *Unmasking the face*. Englewood Cliffs, N.J.: Prentice-Hall, 1975.

Field, T. Maternal stimulation during infant feeding. *Developmental Psychology*, 1977, 13, 539–540.

Field, T. M. Visual and cardiac responses to animate and inanimate faces by young term and preterm infants. *Child Development*, 1979, 50, 188–194.

Field, T. M., Sostek, A. M., Vietze, P., & Leiderman, P. H. (Eds.), *Culture and early interactions*. Hillsdale, N.J.: Erlbaum, 1981.

Freud, S. *The basic writings of Sigmund Freud*. A. A. Brill, trans. New York: Random House, 1938.

Geertz, H. The vocabulary of emotion. *Psychiatry*, 1959, 22, 225–237.

Hall, J. A. Gender effects in decoding nonverbal cues. *Psychological Bulletin*, 1978, 85, 845–857.

Harding, C. G., & Golinkoff, R. M. The origins of intentional vocalizations in prelinguistic infants. *Child Development*, 1979, 50, 33–40.

Haviland, J. J., & Malatesta, C. M. A description of the development of nonverbal signals: Fallacies, facts and fantasies. In C. Mayo & N. Henley (Eds.), *Gender and nonverbal behavior*. New York: Springer, 1981.

Hittelman, J. H., & Dickes, R. Sex differences in neonatal eye contact time. *Merrill-Palmer Quarterly*, 1979, 25, 171–184.

Hochschild, A. R. Emotion work, feeling rules, and social structure. *American Journal of Sociology*, 1979, 85, 551–575.

Izard, C. *The face of emotion*. New York: Appleton-Century-Crofts, 1971.

Izard, C. E. *Human emotions*. New York: Plenum Press, 1977.

Izard, C. E. *The Maximally Discriminative Facial Movement Coding System (Max)*. Newark: University of Delaware, 1979.

Izard, C. Cross-cultural perspectives on emotion and emotion communication. *Handbook of cross-cultural psychology*. Boston: Allyn and Bacon, 1980.

Izard, C. E. Emotion-cognition relationships and human development. In C. E. Izard, J. Kagan, & R. Zajonc (Eds.), *Emotion, cognition, and behavior*. New York: Cambridge University Press, 1983.

Kagan, J. Overview: Perspectives on human infancy. In J. D. Osofsky (Ed.), *Handbook of infant development*. New York: Wiley, 1979.

Kagan, J. Heart rate and heart rate variability as signs of a temperamental dimension in infants. In C. E. Izard (Eds.), *Measuring emotions in infants and children*. Cambridge: Cambridge University Press, 1982.

Kaye, K., & Fogel, A. The temporal structure of face-to-face communication between mothers and infants. *Developmental Psychology*, 1980, 16, 454–464.

Lacey, J. I. Individual differences in somatic response patterns. *Journal of Comparative and Physiological Psychology*, 1950, 43, 338–350.

Lacey, J. I., & Lacey, B. C. Verification and extension of the principles of autonomic response stereotypy. *American Journal of Psychology*, 1958, 71, 50–73.

Lacey, J. I., & Lacey, B. C. The law of initial value in the longitudinal study of autonomic constitution: Reproducibility of autonomic responses and response patterns over a four-year interval. *Annals of the New York Academy of Sciences*, 1962, 98, 1257–1290; 1322–1326.

Leventhal, H. A perceptual-motor processing model of emotion. In P. Pliner, K. R. Blansten, & I. M. Spigel (Eds.), *Perception of emotion in self and others*. New York: Plenum Press, 1979.

Leventhal, H. Toward a comprehensive theory of emotion. In L. Berkowitz (Ed.), *Advances in experimental social psychology* (Vol. 13). New York: Academic Press, 1980.

Levy, R. I. *On the nature and functions of the emotions: An anthropological perspective*. Unpublished manuscript, 1980.

Lewis, M., & Michalson, L. The socialization of emotions. In T. Field & A. Fogel (Eds.), *Emotion and early interaction*. Hillsdale, N.J.: Erlbaum, 1982.

Lewis, M., Brooks, J., & Haviland, J. Hearts and faces: A study in the measurement of emotion. In M. Lewis & L. Rosenblum (Eds.), *The development of affect*. New York: Plenum Press, 1978.

Ling, D., & Ling, A. H. Communication development in the first three years of life. *Journal of Speech and Hearing Research*, 1974, 17, 146–159.

Lutz, C. The domain of emotion words on Ifaluk. *American Ethnologist*, 1982, 9, 113–116.

Malatesta, C. Z. *Determinants of infant affect socialization: Age, sex of infant and maternal emotional traits*. Unpublished doctoral dissertation, Rutgers University, 1980.

Malatesta, C. Z., & Haviland, J. M. Learning display rules: The socialization of emotion expression in infancy. *Child Development*, 1982, 53, 991–1003.

Malatesta, C. Z., & Izard, C. E. The ontogenesis of human social signals: From biological
    imperative to symbol utilization. In N. Fox & R. J. Davidson (Eds.), *Affective devel-
    opment: a psychobiological perspective*. Hillsdale, N.J.: Erlbaum, 1983.
Marsella, A., Kinzie, D., & Gordon, P. Ethnic variations in the expression of depression.
    In W. Lebra (Ed.), *Culture-bound syndromes, ethnophyshiatry, and alternate therapies*,
    Vol. 2 of *Mental health research in Asia and the Pacific*. Honolulu: University of Hawaii
    Press, 1973.
Marsella, A. J., Murray, M. D., & Golden, C. Ethnic variation in the phenomenology of
    emotion: I. Shame. *Journal of Cross-Cultural Research*, in press.
Panksepp, J. Toward a general psychobiological theory of emotions. *The Behavioral and
    Brain Sciences*, 1982, *5*, 407–467.
Saarni, C. Children's understanding of display rules for expressive behavior. *Developmental
    Psychology*, 1979, *15*, 424–429.
Saarni, C. *Emotional experience and regulation of expressive behavior*. A paper presented at the
    meeting of the Society for Research in Child Development, Boston, April 1981.
Saarni, C. Social and affective functions of nonverbal behavior: Developmental concerns.
    In R. Feldman (Ed.), *Development of nonverbal behavior*. New York: Springer Verlag,
    1982.
Selye, H. *The stress of life*. New York: McGraw-Hill, 1956.
Shields, S. A., & Stern, R. M. Emotion: The perception of bodily change. In P. Pliner,
    K. R. Blankstein, & I. M. Spigel (Eds.), *Perception of emotion in self and others*. New
    York: Plenum Press, 1979.
Steklis, H. D., & Raleigh, M. J. Behavioral and neurobiological aspects of primate vocal-
    ization and facial expression. In H. D. Steklis & M. J. Raleigh (Eds.), *Neurobiology
    of social communication in primates*. New York: Academic Press, 1979.
Stenberg, C. R. *The development of anger facial expressions in infancy*. Unpublished doctoral
    dissertation, University of Denver, 1982.
Stern, R. M. Voluntary control of GSR and reports of sweating. *Perceptual and motor skills*,
    1973, *36*, 1342.
Stern, R. M., & Higgins, J. D. Perceived somatic reactions to stress: Sex, age, and familial
    occurrence. *Journal of Psychosomatic Research*, 1969, *13*, 77–82.
Stern, R. M., & Lewis, N. L. Ability of actors to control their GSRs and express emotion.
    Psychophysiology, 1968, *4*, 294–299.
Super, C. M., & Harkness, S. The development of affect in infancy and early childhood.
    In D. A. Wagner & H. W. Stevenson (Eds.), *Cultural perspectives on child development*.
    San Francisco: W. H. Freeman, 1982.
Tennes, K. The role of hormones in mother-infant transactions. In R. N. Emde & R. J.
    Harmon (Eds.), *The development of attachment and affiliative systems*. New York: Plenum
    Press, 1982.
Tomkins, S. *Affect, imagery, consciousness. Vol. 1: The positive affects*. New York: Springer,
    1962.
Tomkins, S. *Affect, imagery, consciousness. Vol. 2: The negative affects*. New York: Springer,
    1963.
Wack, D. *An exploratory study of focusing*. Unpublished doctoral dissertation, Pennsylvania
    State University, 1972.
Zivin, G. Watching the sands shift: Conceptualizing development of nonverbal mastery.
    In R. Feldman (Ed.), *The development of nonverbal behavior in children*. New York:
    Springer-Verlag, 1982.

6

What Do Children Know about Emotions and When Do They Know It?

LINDA MICHALSON AND MICHAEL LEWIS

Although researchers have learned much about children's social knowledge in the last decade, little is known about children's understanding of emotions and emotional expressions. Investigations of children's knowledge of emotions and the socialization of emotional behavior have been restricted in part by a powerful theory of emotion, which was suggested by Darwin (1872) and later elaborated by Tomkins (1962, 1963) and Izard (1977). This biological view of emotion was characterized by Hochschild (1979) in the following description of emotional behavior:

> The image that comes to mind is that of a sudden, automatic reflex syndrome—Darwin's instant snarl expression; Freud's tension discharge at a given breaking point of tension overload; James' and Lange's notion of an instantaneous, unmediated visceral reaction to a perceived stimulus, the perception of which is also unmediated by social influence. (pp. 553–554)

Emotions are viewed as analogous to knee jerks or sneezes, unlearned, biologically controlled, and subject to relatively little socialization influence.

Strong forms of the biological model that do not require cognitive or socialization explanations do not even raise the question of the origins of facial expressions in explaining their production. If one believes that

LINDA MICHALSON AND MICHAEL LEWIS • Department of Pediatrics, UMDNJ-Rutgers Medical School, Institute for the Study of Child Development, New Brunswick, New Jersey 08903.

the facial expressions of a 2-year-old, for example, are controlled directly by a set of stimulus events, then one does not need to pursue questions about the role of socialization and cognition in their appearance. The limited roles of cognition and socialization in the biological model appear later in development and are not seen as part of the creation of emotional expressions themselves. In this view, an elicitor (situation) produces an emotional expression automatically. However, alternative views can be adopted about the roles of socialization and cognition as they affect the connection between an emotional elicitor and an emotional response.

MODELS OF EMOTIONAL ELICITOR–EXPRESSION RELATIONSHIP

We can construct two models to explain the connection between an emotional elicitor (a stimulus) and the resultant emotional expression (see Figure 1). In the first, the biological model, an elicitor directly produces an emotional expression. A hypothetical neurological connection is postulated to exist between the elicitor and the behavior so that the elicitor automatically evokes a particular emotional expression.

The alternative model—the cognitive/socialization model—is one in which an elicitor produces an emotional expression not directly, but only through the mediation of a cognitive connection. This cognitive connection may take several forms. It may consist of understanding the nature of the stimulus and comparing it to past events or associations, or it may be in the form of connecting the stimulus and the response with "appropriate" social rules. The latter connection may be represented in the form of an implicit question in the mind of the subject: "What is the emotion that I am supposed to feel or show?" As a consequence, an elicitor that evokes anger in one subject may evoke sadness

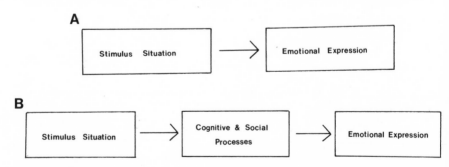

FIG 1. Contrasting models of the connection between stimulus situations and the resulting emotional expressions.

in another, as a function of individual differences in cognition or in the action dictated by the cognition. In other words, the elicitor is processed by a subject in such a way that the subject asks, at either a conscious or an unconscious level, "What is the socially appropriate expression in this particular situation?"

This cognitive/socialization view of the connection between elicitor and expression allows us to consider the possibility that emotional expressions can be the result of a mediating cognitive structure rather than the product of an event external to the subject. As we shall argue, in cases where a mediating structure and a stimulus carry the same meaning, emotional expressions are related to the stimulus event. To the extent that the stimulus and the cognitive structure have discrepant meanings, one would expect an expression to be the product as much of the mediating cognitive structure as of the external event.

CHILDREN'S KNOWLEDGE OF EMOTIONAL EXPRESSIONS AND SITUATIONS

A growing body of work on the socialization of emotion gives us good reason to believe that emotional elicitors, expressions, states, and experiences are not necessarily linked to each other in a direct way and that strong socialization forces act to alter infants' emotional behaviors as early as the age of 3 months (Brooks-Gunn & Lewis, 1982; Malatesta & Haviland, 1983). Children's knowledge of how other people feel in certain situations, the consequence of learning and socialization, has received considerable attention in the research literature. Data show that children 3–6 years old understand the "appropriate" people to interact with in different situations (Edwards & Lewis, 1979). For example, 3-year-olds choose to play with peers, to seek help from adults when hurt, and to get information from older children. Although not directly related to children's social knowledge of emotions, these data indicate that young children are capable of situational analyses and have very clear social preferences as a function of particular situations.

There is also research suggesting that young children show emphatic awareness of the emotions of others (Eisenberg, 1983). For example, a 2-year-old may comfort, hold, and pat a father who is sad (Borke, 1971). In this situation, one does not know, however, whether the child has any *understanding* of the situation that produced the emotion or whether the child is responding only to the father's *expression* of sadness. Whether knowledge of the feelings of other people is derived through empathy or other learning processes is a question not yet answered in the research literature.

Children's Knowledge of Situations

Of specific interest in the present discussion are studies showing that, at relatively young ages, children know how others feel and how these feelings are related to certain situations. It is possible that children's knowledge about situations is derived through their observations of the expressions of other people *in* particular situations. The observations may, in turn, provide information about the sitautions as well as about expressions. On the other hand, children may have some understanding of the situational requirements apart from the behavioral expressions of emotion in the situation. The studies most relevant to children's knowledge about situations and appropriate emotions are studies that eliminate behavioral clues to the emotion.

In these studies, subjects typically were told a short story that was accompanied by a picture depicting the situation (e.g., Borke, 1973; Feshbach & Roe, 1968; Gnepp, 1983). The story might be about a birthday party or a broken toy, for example. The subjects were asked, "How does the child in the story feel?" or "How would you feel?" The extent to which the picture did not contain clues to emotional expression was the extent to which the children's answers reflected their own understanding (as opposed to the experimenter's understanding) of the emotional sequelae of the situations depicted. The results of such studies indicate that, by age 4, and sometimes as young as age 3, children understand what adults would consider to be "appropriate" emotional responses in some situations (Borke, 1971, 1973; Gnepp, 1983; Mood, Johnson, & Shantz, 1974). In reviewing this literature, Shantz (1975) suggested that simple situations eliciting happy responses are reliably understood by children as young as age 4. Between 4 and 7 years, children show an increasing ability to understand situations eliciting fear, sadness, and anger.

Similar results were reported by L. Camras and J. Brusa (personal communication, 1981), who interviewed kindergarten children about their knowledge of the appropriate emotions in specific situations as well as the relative intensities of the emotions. Among the different stories told the children was the following: "My friend came home from school one day and his mother told him that the family dog just had puppies. My friend didn't even know his dog was going to have puppies." The children were asked about the presence or absence of several emotions—in this example, happiness, surprise, and disgust. They were also asked about the intensity of the emotion ("a lot" or "a little"). A preliminary analysis indicated that the kindergarteners could judge both the presence and the intensity of the emotions of other children in the various situations. They understood that more than one emotion may be elicited by a situation. In the example of the dog having puppies, the children reported that the feelings were equal amounts of happiness (mean = 1.50) and surprise (mean = 1.56) and some disgust (mean = 0.67), on a 3-point scale of intensity.

The process of identifying the emotions appropriate to particular situations is facilitated by a similarity between the subject and the child in the story. When the person in the situation is more like the subject (i.e., of similar age or sex), the subject's accuracy in identifying the emotion is increased (Shantz, 1975). Such findings suggest that empathy and the concept of self may play important roles in understanding situations and emotions (Lewis & Brooks-Gunn, 1979).

It is interesting that studies incorporating an ambiguity in the story situation through a discrepancy between situational and facial cues find that children differentially use situational and facial cues in judging the emotion of the story character (Burns & Cavey, 1957). Gnepp (1983) reported that preschoolers preferred to base inferences about emotion on facial expressions rather than on situational contexts. This preference decreased with age. Yet, in response to conflicting situational cues, the children tended to reinterpret facial cues. Too few data exist on this topic for us to look for a developmental trend, but evidence indicates that adults also rely primarily on situational cues (Tagiuri, 1969). Situational cues seem to affect adults' emotional responses more powerfully than their own facial expressions (Laird, 1974). It appears that social knowledge about situations in which emotions occur is acquired early in life.

Children's Knowledge of Expressions

In addition to this body of research on knowledge of situations, another important body of research exists about children's ability to discriminate the facial expressions of others. The evidence is conflicting about when infants are first able to discriminate gross facial configurations (Charlesworth & Kreutzer, 1973; Ekman & Oster, 1979; Oster, 1981). Many studies do not find clear evidence of infant discrimination of positive or negative expressions before the age of 5 or 6 months (Charlesworth & Kreutzer, 1973), although LaBarbera, Izard, Vietze, and Parisi (1976) found that 4-month-olds preferred to look at joy faces than to look at anger or neutral faces. Young-Browne, Rosenfeld, and Horowitz (1977) reported that infants as young as 3 months could distinguish happy from surprised faces, although they could not discriminate happy from sad faces.

More recently, Caron, Caron, and Myers (1982) introduced a series of controls in an investigation of facial discrimination in order to separate what they considered the irrelevant aspects of facial expressions from the more critical features. Their work strongly suggests that not until 7 or 8 months of age can infants discriminate facial expressions independent of such irrelevant details as "toothy smiles." A careful examination of the role of superfluous stimuli in facial discrimination studies indicates that infants do not discriminate emotional expressions much before the beginning of the second semester of life.

CHILDREN'S LEXICAL KNOWLEDGE

Few studies have looked at older children's knowledge of emotional expressions and at the same time assessed children's lexical ability. To what extent are the subject's knowledge of and ability to use emotional terms related to other emotional knowledge? If, for example, an investigator wants to examine children's understanding of particular facial expressions, she or he may use or require the subjects to use terms such as *happiness, sadness,* or *anger.* If children do not have these words in their lexicon, then the investigator's finding about what these children know about emotional expressions are limited. In any study of children's knowledge of emotional expressions, one must first assess the children's lexical knowledge.

Although investigations of children's acquisition of language are numerous, few data are available on children's acquisition of emotion labels. Researchers study the acquisition of nouns, verbs, pronouns, and more recently, personal pronouns, but the acquisition of words that label emotions is not usually examined. Some work has been done on the language of emotions, that is, how children and adults talk about their feelings (e.g., Davitz, 1969; Lewis, Wolman, & King, 1972a, b; Russell & Ridgeway, 1983; Wolman, Lewis, & King, 1971, 1972a, b); but little is known about how labels are acquired for these feelings. Amen (1941) found that by 4 years, children already use a limited number of affect terms, including *happy, sad, mad, angry,* and *scared.* Izard (1971) reported that children can discriminate emotions earlier than they can label them, and that although the ability to recognize and discriminate emotions increases with age, emotion labeling is not strongly related to chronological age. More recently, Zahn-Waxler, Radke-Yarrow, and King (1979) found that as early as the age of 2, children begin to understand and even produce verbal labels for emotional behaviors such as crying and laughter. It is surprising that so little work has been done in this area, as infants' ability to differentiate emotional expressions of the face by 8 months should provide a structural basis for lexical differentiations.

The general rules of language learning may apply to the learning of emotion labels. Theory and empirical evidence support the proposition that comprehension precedes production, at least at the one-word utterance stage. This phenomenon is based on a belief that children need to hear and understand speech before producing it. In empirical studies of children's lexical knowledge, one finds that children's comprehension is better than their production (Bloom, 1978).

To examine children's knowledge as it applies to emotion labels, we tested 35 children 2 (N = 10), 3 (N = 11), 4 (N = 9), and 5 (N = 5) years old in the following way. We first showed the children Polaroid snapshots of a 10-year-old girl (Felicia) posing six different facial expressions of emotion: happiness, sadness, anger, fear, surprise, and disgust (see Figure 2). These six expressions were chosen because they are believed to represent primary emotions that appear early in life (Izard, Huebner, Risser, McGinnes, & Dougherty, 1980). The validity of the expressions was established by subjecting them to the Max facial-coding system (Izard, 1979).

Production

To test the children's ability to produce verbal labels of emotion, for each of the six photographs we asked the children, "What kind of face is Felicia making?" The order of presentation of the six photographs was randomized across subjects. The subjects' responses were recorded verbatim on a scoring sheet. Faces that were labeled in terms of a behavior were not considered correct in the tabulation of the production data. For example, several children labeled the happy face "smiling," the sad face "crying," and the disgust face "sticking out the tongue." The only synonyms that were accepted were *mad* for the angry face and *scared* or *afraid* for the fear face.

Figure 3 presents the percentage of subjects by age who could label the facial expressions of emotion. In cases where the subjects did not finish the task, the data were not included in the percentage computations. These cases apply only to instances when the subjects would not look at the stimulus. Instances in which the subject looked at the picture but did not answer were coded as "did not know" and included in the "wrong answer" category.

The data indicate that the 2-year-olds had few verbal labels (see Figure 3). Only the "happy" and "sad" labels were used, and then only by one subject. By age 3, 27% of the children used the "happy" label, and 45% were able to use the "sad" label. In addition, some subjects used the "surprise" and "anger" labels. Over 50% of the 4-year-olds had

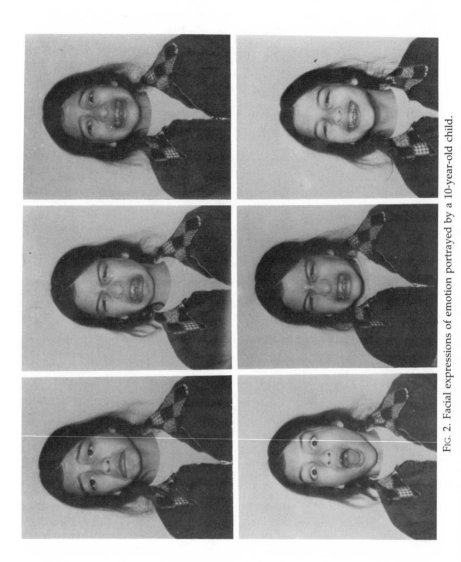

FIG. 2. Facial expressions of emotion portrayed by a 10-year-old child.

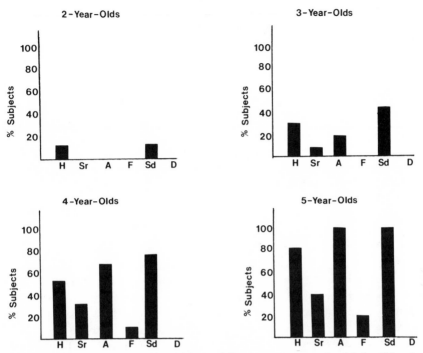

FIG. 3. Age and emotion effects in children's ability to produce emotion labels. Abbreviations: H, happy; Sr, surprise; A, anger; F, fear/afraid; Sd, sad; D, disgust.

labels for happiness, sadness, and anger. By age 5, 80% of the children had the happiness label, all had labels for sadness and anger, and relatively few had labels for surprise and fear. No subject had a label for the disgust face. The data reveal both interesting emotion and age effects.

Emotion Effects

The labels of happiness and sadness were the first labels learned. Anger was the next emotion label acquired. Of the 3-year-olds, 18% had the label, and 67% of the 4-year-olds had a label for the angry face. Surprise and fear had a much lower rate of acquisition. Even by age 5, fewer than 40% of the subjects produced these two labels. Disgust was a facial expression that even by age 5 was not labeled.

It should be noted that "happy" and "sad," the two labels acquired earliest, are considered the bipolar emotional tones of infants at birth. To discover that these are the first two emotions labeled by children reflects their importance in this early age period. The finding suggests that mothers may be using these labels to characterize their children's first emotional states, although there is evidence that mothers believe many states other than happiness and sadness occur during infancy and that they use other labels in addition to "happy" and "sad" (Lewis & Michalson, 1982).

Age Effects

The use of emotion labels was directly related to the age of the child, with an increase in verbal labeling through 5 years of age. Interestingly, no important differences between the emotion labels of 4- and 5-year-olds were detected, a finding that suggests that labels used by 5-year-olds have already been learned by age 4.

Comprehension

To test children's comprehension of emotion labels, we asked subjects to point to the face (photograph) that matched the word (emotion label) given by the experimenter. The correct face (i.e., the face that represented the label) was embedded in a set of four different faces displayed in a photograph album. Two different orders of the recognition task were given to each subject. For data analysis purposes, a correct response was scored only if the child pointed to the correct face in both orders.

As expected, the children's comprehension of emotion labels was far superior to their ability to produce labels. Figure 4 presents the data on the comprehension tasks by age and by facial expression. Several points can be made in observing these data. First, at every age, the children were better at comprehending labels than producing them. This phenomenon was most dramatic at age 2. Although very few 2-year-olds produced the verbal label, most understood at least some of the labels. Over 80% of the 2-year-olds pointed to the happy and sad faces, and over 40% pointed to the surprised and angry faces in response to the respective labels. The fear and disgust labels were the least understood. The ability to comprehend these labels did not appear before 4 years of age. The main difference between the 4- and 5-year-olds and the younger children occurred in response to the fear and disgust labels. Of the older children, 40%–80% showed recognition of the label by pointing to the correct face, compared to approximately 20% of the 2- and 3-year-olds.

These data underscore the fact that certain emotion labels are more readily learned. "Sad," "happy," and "angry" are learned first, whereas "fear" and "disgust" take longer to acquire. One emotion label showed a strong discrepancy between comprehension and production ability, and that was "surprise." Whereas relatively few children at any age

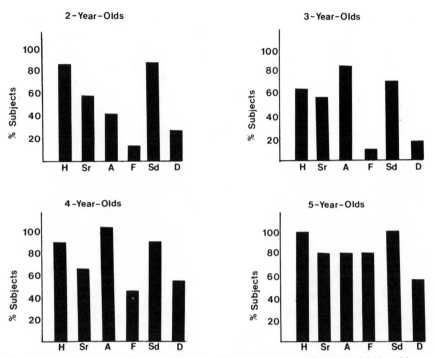

FIG. 4. Age and emotion affects in children's ability to comprehend emotion labels. Abbreviations: H, happy; Sr, surprise; A, anger; F, fear/afraid; Sd, sad; D, disgust.

labeled the surprised face, most children between 2 and 5 years of age were able to recognize it. One possible explanation is that *surprise* is a complex word to produce, with more letters than the other emotion terms.

In summary, when one looks at the emotion lexicon of children from 2 to 5 years old, one is rather impressed with what children know about the representation of facial expressions and the vocabulary that corresponds to them. With the exception of fear and disgust, 40% or more of the children comprehended emotion labels, specifically, "happiness," "surprise," "anger," and "sadness." That children as young as 2 years old matched the labels with the faces suggests that one does not need to use emotion terms themselves and instead can rely on pictorial representations of the terms to examine children's knowledge of emotional expressions and their contexts.

It is clear that, by 2 years of age, children understand emotion labels. Comprehension ability reflects the minimal level of knowledge necessary to support children's cognitive structures underlying the display of emotion in social situations. Finding that children have this basic knowledge encouraged us to explore more complex questions about their knowledge of emotional expressions. In particular, we decided to investigate whether children understand the relationship between particular elicitors (situations) and the facial expressions likely to occur in response to those situations. Such a demonstration of children's knowledge would establish the legitimacy of addressing the proposition discussed earlier, namely, that the connection between particular elicitors and particular emotional responses is predicated in part on what people know about the appropriateness of emotional expressions in particular situations.

SITUATIONAL KNOWLEDGE

To explore children's knowledge of facial expressions of emotion in their situational contexts, we gave each subject a third task, in addition to the comprehension and production tests. In this task, an experimenter told the subjects six simple stories in which a little girl (Felicia) was involved in situations likely to elicit an emotional response. The stories were illustrated by line drawings in which the faces of the characters were left blank (see Figures 5–10). Each story focused on a simple situation that might occur in the life of a child. For each of the stories, we judged *a priori* which emotion would appear. For example, happiness was judged to be the primary emotion associated with Felicia's birthday party. The stories are depicted in Figures 5–10. After each story, the experimenter asked the child to point to the face that Felicia would have made

FIG. 5. Birthday party.   FIG. 6. Mother with pink hair.

FIG. 7. Dog runs away.

FIG. 8. Awful-tasting food.

FIG. 9. Sister knocks over tower of blocks.

FIG. 10. Lost in grocery store.

in that situation. In addition to the face that represented the "correct" response (i.e., the face that we assumed to be the correct response), three other faces were randomly selected to constitute the array of faces from which the subject had to choose. Four faces were presented for each story, rather than all six, because pilot testing showed that six options were too confusing for children this young.

The data for this task are presented in Figure 11 in terms of the percentage of subjects at each age who chose the various faces associated with each story. Note that, in this figure, a fifth age point is shown: that for adult subjects. We also gave the task to 10 adult subjects to ensure that the "correct" faces, in terms of the situations chosen, had some validity in the adult world. In a sense, the adults' performance constituted a criterion measure with which the children's performances could be compared.

Consider the happy situation first (see Figures 5 and 11). Of the 2-year-olds, 70% selected the happy face to go with the situation "birthday party." Moreover, there appeared to be little age change between 2 and 5 years. Indeed, the adults picked the happy face for the happy situation.

A different pattern emerged for the surprise situation. Although 60% of the 2-year-olds understood "surprise" in the comprehension task, only 40% picked the surprise face in the situation "mother with pink hair" (see Figures 6 and 11). Few differences appeared among 2- and 3-year-olds in identifying the surprise face in this situation. The 5-year-olds, on the other hand, showed 100% correct responses, and their performance was most similar to the adults'. This age pattern reflects a strong developmental trend.

The situation "dogs run away" elicited a completely different pattern of response (see Figures 7 and 11). The adults corroborated our judgment by identifying the sad face with the story. Only 30% of the 2-year-olds associated the sad face with the story. Few differences were found among the 3-, 4-, and 5-year-olds' performances, with between 60% and 90% choosing the sad face.

The responses to the disgust situation by 5-year-olds resembled those of the adults. The children's responses in this situation showed a developmentally oriented pattern (see Figures 8 and 11). All 5-year-olds associated the disgust face with the situation, compared with 70% of the 4-year-olds, 50% of the 3-year-olds, and 10% of the 2-year-olds.

In the happy, surprise, disgust, and sad situations, the 5-year-olds' performance matched the performance of the adults. The 2-, 3-, and 4-year-olds showed some increase in "correct" responding in the surprise, sad, and disgust situations.

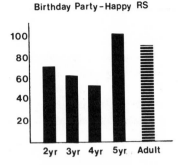

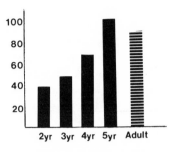

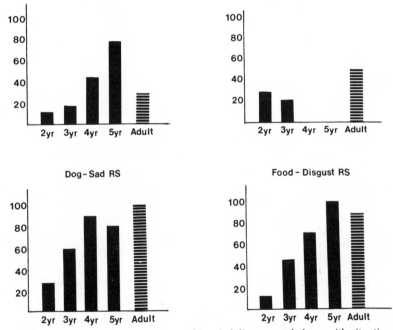

FIG. 11. Age and affect differences in subjects' ability to match faces with situations.

In the two other situations, we uncovered surprising results. The anger situation was chosen in the belief that when one's sister knocks over a tower of blocks, one will feel anger. However, only 30% of the adults thought that this situation would elicit anger (see Figures 9 and 11). Except for the 5-year-olds, similar percentages of the children also selected the angry face in this situation. Thus, although "sister knocks over tower of blocks" may not have been a good example of an anger-provoking situation, the data suggest that children at this age have an understanding of the situation similar to that of adults.

What other faces did the subjects select in the anger situation? For all subjects, whether children or adults, the competing emotional expression chosen was sadness. Indeed, over 40% of the 2-, 3-, and 4-year-olds and 40% of the adults pointed to the sad face in this situation. Thus, even though we may have misjudged the emotion associated with this situation, there is nevertheless support for the proposition that very young children match facial expressions of emotion with situations in a manner similar to that of adults. This parallel between children's and adults' performances confirms our contention that emotional knowledge is acquired early in life.

Another interesting result involved the situation that we judged would elicit fear in young children. The situation was a young child getting lost in the grocery store and not being able to find her mother (see Figures 10 and 11). In this situation, 50% of the adults, but almost none of the children, pointed to the fear face. The findings from the adult sample suggest that the situation may not have been the best exemplar of a fear-eliciting situation. Observations of differences in judgment are instructive. Whereas half the adults chose the fear face, the other half chose the sad face. Looking at the children's responses, we found that 20% of the 2-year-olds, 50% of the 3-year-olds, and 100% of the 4- and 5-year-olds also selected the sad face. Thus, even though experimenter bias may have occurred in selecting the situation, the children matched emotional expressions with social situations in a manner similar to that of most adults.

In the situation of loss, three developmental phases can be observed: the youngst children selected both sadness and fear, the 4- and 5-year-olds almost always selected sadness, and the adults selected sadness and fear. In terms of understanding this situation, then, the developmental process may be incomplete by age 5. In other situations, the 5-year-olds showed a percentage of correct responses similar to that of adults. In this situation, however, they differed from adults.

Mixed Emotions

These data provoke discussion in two areas. First is the possibility that elicitors or stimulus events can evoke more than one emotion. We have suggested elsewhere that the issue of mixed emotions has not been thoroughly examined (Lewis & Michalson, 1983). In four of our six situations, the children's and the adults' responses showed a pattern in which a single emotion was expressed; their other choices were not systematic. In the situations "sister knocks over tower of blocks" and "lost in the grocery store," the subjects chose two different emotions with almost equal frequency. Moreover, the subjects choosing one response tended to choose the other response as their second-choice emotion. Such data have two possible explanations, which are not necessarily contradictory. That two emotions were chosen (as a first or a second response) suggests that the situation elicits a mixed emotion, comprised of two emotions. Alternatively, individual differences in subjects' understanding of the response to the situation may account for the different choices. In methodologies where the experimenter asks subjects to select a predominant emotion elicited by a stimulus, whether the chance to make a second choice is given, one cannot answer the question of whether the situation elicits more than one emotion, that is, a mixed emotion. At this point, there is no way to answer the question of mixed emotions, as in the present study the subjects were not given the opportunity to report two *simultaneous* feelings.

Rules of Evocation

The second issue that these data raise pertains to the fact that different situations may elicit different intensities of a particular emotion. That is, even though we may agree on a class of situations likely to evoke one emotion, the situations may differ in terms of their power to elicit that emotion. For example, receiving a telegram and meeting a stranger in a dark alley are two situations likely to evoke fear in many people. Yet, these situations may r.Jt produce similar levels of fear either within or between individuals. One could reasonably argue that one situation—the stranger—would elicit more fear than the other.

An analysis of the evocative power of situations or stimuli leads to a discussion of the nature of the stimulus. The classification of situations according to their ability to elicit emotions is complex. Perhaps, it is best at this point solely to point out that there appears to be some agreement within a society or a social group about ordering situations and stimuli according to their likelihood of evoking particular emotions. As we mentioned, we can be sure that most people would be more afraid when encountering a stranger in a dark alley than when receiving a telegram. If one stimulus is more likely than another to elicit a uniform response, the question then is, What causes this similarity at the group level? On the one hand, one could argue that the uniformity of response to a particular evocative situation is evidence of strong biological processes that act on the species to produce similar behavior. On the other hand, one might argue equally well that the similarity of behavior within a group is proof of socialization forces that define the group, because the goal of socialization is to raise children to behave as do other members of the group.

In situations in which large individual differences exist in the associations of emotional responses with particular situations, one usually assumes that these differences constitute proof of the weak influence of biological pressures and the powerful influence of socialization. If socialization pressures are used as explanatory devices, it is necessary to postulate the existence of "idiosyncratic" socialization pressures. That is, some socialization pressures cause individuals of the group to act not similarly but "idiosyncratically." Thus, socialization theories can explain uniformity as well as differences in response to an emotion-eliciting situation.

In discussions of socialization forces that explain uniformity and/or differences in behavior, one might argue that, in cases where socialization accounts for uniformity, the information provided to the child may come from a *variety* of sources and may be influenced by the culture in general, rather than by a particular socialization agent. Furthermore, one might suspect that when socialization forces produce idiosyncratic responses, a particular socialization agent is more likely to be the responsible agent. In a certain sense, the responses linked to evocative events that possess culturewide generality can be located in aspects of that culture, and learning takes place from a variety of agents. In other situations, the variability of responses across individuals indicates that children's learning any particular response is likely to be specific to a particular socialization agent.

In our data, situations such as "birthday party," "mother with pink hair," "dog runs away," and "disgusting food" were associated by most subjects with a uniform emotional expression. Situations involving anger or fear seemed to be more ambiguous in their behavioral demands; the result was a lack of uniformity within our groups of subjects. The socialization rules governing the appropriate behavior in these situations appear to be learned at the individual level. In regard to this point, we examined the verbal and behavioral responses of mothers of 1-year-olds to their children's responses to being left alone in a room (a situation similar to the situation "lost in the grocery store"). We found that about 25% of the mothers labeled their children's distress expressions as "sad," whereas an equal number used the label "afraid." Another 25% used the label "angry." Thus, individual mothers may be using personal interpretations to give meaning to their infant's actions. Children's behavior, whatever it might be, is labeled according to this individual expectation and attribution (Lewis & Michalson, 1982, 1983).

Most socialization models of emotion address the problem of how given connections between situations and expressions are altered by individual factors. This is a reactive view of the socialization of emotion in which socialization processes have only an adverse or modifying effect on natural biological processes. In the absence of "abnormal" socialization experiences, the natural or biological connection will emerge and be maintained. In some sense, socialization "fouls up" the process.

In the model depicted in Figure 1, we suggested that socialization serves as a natural intervening process between an elicitor and an expression. In its simplest form, this view posits that some, but not necessarily all, joys are unlearned. The accumulation of excess wealth is an example of a socialized, or learned, elicitor of joy. That many children as young as age 2 understand what faces are associated with particular situations is a fact that provides a logical reason to introduce an intervening variable—socialization influences—between elicitors and expressions. If a subject knows what a response will be independent of direct experience with the elicitor of that response, then one cannot conclude that the elicitor *per se* produces that response. That is, the subject's *knowledge* of the expected response could produce the response, independent of the external stimulus.

Another possible role of socialization in emotional processes is one that links the elicitor to the emotional expression. To understand this role, one must consider emotional states as intervening processes between emotional elicitors and expressions. Under these circumstances, socialization can affect the elicitor–expression relationship by influencing the child's emotional states. For example, the mother or the socializing agent who *believes* that a child feels fear when left alone or lost is likely to interpret and respond to a crying child *as if the child feels fear*. This behavior contrasts with that of the mother who, in the same situation, believes that the crying child is sad. The intergenerational transmission of connections between emotional elicitors and particular states and expressions, through individual attribution and social responsivity mechanisms, provides the means for positing individual differences in emotional responses to particular elicitors. In other words, if a mother believes that a "fear-eliciting situation" (i.e., a situation that elicits fear in most children) is, in fact, a sad one, then the mother's interpretation is likely to influence the child's judgment of the situation as one that produces sadness. As a result, psychopathology may develop as a function of socialization differences between individuals and the group (see Lewis & Michalson, 1982).

In short, although biological theories usually acknowledge some role of socialization in affecting emotional expressions (e.g., Ekman,

1977), the effect of socialization is likely to distort the "natural connection" between elicitor and response. Our own position expands this role by suggesting that the undifferentiated emotional behavior of children is often interpreted by parents as a reflection of a particular emotion that the mother thinks is connected to the elicitor (see Pannabecker, Emde, Johnson, Stenberg, & Davis, 1980). The behaviors, verbal labeling, and responses of parents are likely to reinforce emotional connections or even to *create* connections between particular emotional states and expressions. When all members of a society subscribe to the same expectations and adopt similar socialization practices, children should develop similar state and expression connections. However, in ambiguous situations, particular socialization experiences, family dynamics, or life events may influence the connections on an individual basis.

The finding that children as young as 2 and 3 can associate facial expressions with situations is important to an investigation of the development of emotional expressions and knowledge. Recall that we used faces of emotion as response options to avoid the problem of inadequate language ability in young subjects. It was clear from our data that children's productive ability vis-à-vis emotional terms lagged behind their comprehension of these terms. Procedures that rely on linguistic responses may produce indeterminate results. Even though children's comprehension was better than their production, the comprehension task also required that the children understand verbal labels. Again, the demonstration of their ability was predicated on language skills. The presentation of faces and pictures of situations explained in simple language provided an alternative means for assessing children's knowledge of emotional expressions that required minimal language skills on the part of the subjects.

To determine whether language skills and situational knowledge are related, we compared subjects with and without comprehension lexical skills. The results showed no significant differences between the two groups. Such findings suggest that the ability to link emotional expressions to situations is a skill acquired readily and one that does not require an elaborate lexicon of emotional terms. The learning of these relationships is an important aspect of the social-affective curriculum of childhood. We believe that learning this curriculum is vital because it provides a script that enables children to *act* emotionally in particular situations and to anticipate the actions of others (see Abelson, 1976).

The demonstration that children understand these relationships as early as age 2 raises a more general issue: Can one claim that an elicitor–state–expression correspondence in emotions is a biological product if it can be demonstrated that subjects *know* what people are likely to feel in response to an elicitor? As Orne (1973) pointed out, the subjects' knowledge of the likely outcome of an experimental manipulation reduces the logical necessity of a causal link between the experimental manipulation and the subjects' response. The causality between the manipulation and the outcome is questionable. Similarly, the knowledge that people feel sad at a funeral precludes the logical necessity that the funeral itself produced sadness. This argument returns us to the model in Figure 1. Although one might prefer one of the paths, it is likely that both operate in connecting elicitors to expressions. The utilization of both paths allows one to explain both the production and the development of facial expressions. The socialized knowledge, for example, that a funeral will elicit sadness is just as likely to produce an emotional state of sadness as is any biological connection (e.g., between the crying of others and the sadness of oneself). The early acquisition of emotional knowledge suggests that emotional behavior is central to social adaptive functioning. Socialization rules create emotional knowledge both for the group as a whole and for specific individuals.

REFERENCES

Abelson, R. Script processing in attitude formation and decision making. In J. S. Carroll & J. Payne (Eds.), *Cognition and social behavior*. Hillsdale, N.J.: Erlbaum, 1976.

Amen, E. Individual differences in apperceptive reaction: A study of the responses of preschool children to pictures. *Genetic Psychology Monographs*, 1941, *23*, 319–385.

Bloom, L., & Lahey, M. *Language development and language disorders*. New York: Wiley, 1978.

Borke, H. Interpersonal perceptions of young children: Egocentrism or empathy. *Developmental Psychology*, 1971, *5*, 263–269.

Borke, H. The development of empathy in Chinese and American children between three and six years of age: A cross-cultural study. *Developmental Psychology*, 1973, *9*, 102–108.

Brooks-Gunn, J., & Lewis, M. Affective exchanges between normal and handicapped infants and their mothers. In T. Field & A. Fogel (Eds.), *Emotion and early interaction*. Hillsdale, N.J.: Erlbaum, 1982.

Burns, N., & Cavey, L. Age differences in empathic ability among children. *Canadian Journal of Psychology*, 1957, *11*, 227–230.

Caron, R. F., Caron, A. J., & Myers, R. S. Abstraction of invariant face expressions in infancy. *Child Development*, 1982, *53*, 1008–1015.

Charlesworth, W. R., & Kreutzer, M. A. Facial expressions of infants and children. In P. Ekman (Ed.), *Darwin and facial expressions: A century of research in review*. New York: Academic Press, 1973.

Darwin, C. R. *The expression of the emotions in man and animals*. London: John Murray, 1872.

Davitz, J. R. *The language of emotion*. New York: Academic Press, 1969.

Edwards, C. P., & Lewis, M. Young children's concepts of social relations: Social functions and social objects. In M. Lewis & L. A. Rosenblum (Eds.), *The child and its family*. New York: Plenum, 1979.

Eisenberg, N. (Ed.). *The development of prosocial behavior*. New York: Academic Press, 1982.

Ekman, P. Biological and cultural contributions to body and facial movement. In J. Blacking (Ed.), *Anthropology of the body*. New York: Academic Press, 1977.

Ekman, P., & Oster, H. Facial expressions of movement. *Annual Review of Psychology*, 1979, 30, 527–554.

Feshbach, N., & Roe, K. Empathy in six- and seven-year-olds. *Child Development*, 1968, 39, 133–145.

Gnepp, J. Children's social sensitivity: Inferring emotions from conflicting cues. *Developmental Psychology*, 1983, 19, 805–814.

Hochschild, A. R. Emotion work, feeling rules, and social structure. *American Journal of Sociology*, 1979, 85, 551–575.

Izard, C. E. *The face of emotion*. New York: Appleton, 1971.

Izard, C. E. *Human emotions*. New York: Plenum Press, 1977.

Izard, C. E. *The Maximally Discriminative Facial Movement Coding System (MAX)*. Newark, Del.: Instructional Resources Center, University of Delaware, 1979.

Izard, C. E., Huebner, R. R., Risser, D., McGinnes, G. C., & Dougherty, L. M. The young infant's ability to produce discrete emotion expressions. *Developmental Psychology*, 1980, 16, 132–140.

LaBarbera, J. D., Izard, C. E., Vietze, P., & Parisi, S. A. Four- and six-month-old infants' visual responses to joy, anger, and neutral expressions. *Child Development*, 1976, 47, 535–538.

Laird, J. D. Self-attribution of emotion: The effects of expressive behavior on the quality of emotional experience. *Journal of Personality and Social Psychology*, 1974, 29, 475–486.

Lewis, M., & Brooks-Gunn, J. *Social cognition and the acquisition of self*. New York: Plenum Press, 1979.

Lewis, M., & Michalson, L. The socialization of emotions. In T. Field & A. Fogel (Eds.), *Emotions and early interaction*. Hillsdale, N.J.: Erlbaum, 1982.

Lewis, M., & Michalson, L. *Children's emotions and moods: Developmental theory and measurement*. New York: Plenum Press, 1983.

Lewis, W. C., Wolman, R. N., & King, M. The development of the language of emotions: III. Type of anxiety in the experience of affect. *Journal of Genetic Psychology*, 1972, 120, 325–342. (b)

Lewis, W. C., Wolman, R. N., & King, M. The development of the language of emotions: II. Type of anxiety in the experience of affect. *Journal of Genetic Psychology*, 1972, 120, 325–342. (b)

Malatesta, C. Z., & Haviland, J. M. *Age- and sex-related changes in infant affect expressions*. Paper presented at the meeting of the Society for Research in Child Development, Boston, 1981.

Mood, D., Johnson, J., & Shantz, C. U. *Affective and cognitive components of empathy in young children*. Paper presented at the meeting of the Society for Research in Child Development, Chapel Hill, North Carolina, 1974.

Orne, M. T. Communication by the total experimental situation: Why it is important, how it is evaluated, and its significance for the ecological validity of findings. In P. Pliner, L. Krames, & T. Alloway (Eds.), *Communication and affect: Language and thought*. New York: Academic Press, 1973.

Oster, H. "Recognition" of emotional expression in infancy? In. M. E. Lamb & L. R. Sherrod (Eds.), *Infant social cognition: Empirical and theoretical considerations*. Hillsdale, N.J.: Erlbaum, 1981.

Pannabecker, B. J., Emde, R. N., Johnson, W., Stenberg, C., & Davis, M. *Maternal perceptions of infant emotions from birth to 18 months: A preliminary report*. Paper presented at the International Conference of Infant Studies, New Haven, Conn., April 1980.

Russell, J. A., & Ridgeway, D. Dimensions underlying children's emotion concepts. *Developmental Psychology*, 1983, *19*, 795–804.

Shantz, C. U. The development of social cognition. In E. M. Hetherington (Ed.), *Review of child development research*. Chicago: University of Chicago Press, 1975.

Tagiuri, R. Person perception. In G. Lindzey & E. Aronson (Eds.), *The handbook of social psychology*. Reading, Mass.: Addison-Wesley, 1969.

Tomkins, S. S. *Affect, imagery, consciousness* (2 vols.). New York: Springer, 1962, 1963.

Wolman, R. N., Lewis, W. C., & King, M. The development of the language of emotions: I. Theoretical and methodological introduction. *Journal of Genetic Psychology*, 1972, *120*, 167–176. (a)

Wolman, R. N., Lewis, W. C., & King, M. The development of the language of emotions: IV. Bodily referents and the experience of affect. *Journal of Genetic Psychology*, 1972, *121*, 65–81. (b)

Young-Browne, G., Rosenfeld, H. M., & Horowitz, F. Infant discrimination of facial expressions. *Child Development*, 1977, *48*, 555–562.

Zahn-Waxler, C., Radke-Yarrow, M., & King, R. Child rearing and children's prosocial initiations towards victims of distress. *Child Development*, 1979, *50*, 319–330.

7

Socialization of Affect Communication

Linda A. Camras

The investigation of affect communication constitutes an ideal domain in which to study the interaction of biological and social factors in the genesis of complex human behavior. Facial expressions of emotion are among the few socially relevant actions for which strong evidence exists to support claims of species specificity. Research conducted in both Western and non-Western societies (Ekman, 1972, 1977; Ekman & Friesen, 1971; Izard, 1971) shows significant agreement in the identification of facial expressions for at least six emotions: happiness, sadness, anger, fear, disgust, and surprise. At the same time, anthropologists (Birdwhistell, 1970; Eibl-Eibesfeldt, 1972; Ekman, 1972, 1976; Klineberg, 1938; LaBarre, 1947) have provided numerous examples of cross-cultural variability in the use of these facial expressions. This variability suggests that environmental factors also have an important influence on affect expression. Thus, to understand the development of emotion communication, one must consider how it is socialized or shaped in the course of the child's interactions with other members of society.

Socialization of affect communication may include many constituent processes and outcomes (Lewis & Michalson, 1982a). For example, the child may learn what emotions are appropriate in particular situations and what are the socially acceptable means of displaying these emotions. In addition, the child may learn how to recognize affects in others and how to respond to them. Indeed, one might argue that any

LINDA A. CAMRAS • Psychology Department, DePaul University, 2323 North Seminary, Chicago, Illinois 60614.

investigation of the socialization process cannot fail to touch on some facet of emotion communication.

This chapter examines three aspects of socialization relevant to the communication of affect: (a) parents' role in the development of children's ability to recognize facial expressions of emotion; (b) the role of peers in the development of this ability; and (c) the development of children's capacity to recognize and express affect by nonfacial means, in particular by the use of polite or impolite language. The chapter focuses on a line of investigation initiated even prior to Darwin (1872/ 1965), that is, the investigation of affective facial expressions. However, in addition, an attempt is made to demonstrate that emotion communication is not confined to the nonverbal channel. The intricacy and complexity of human language enable the verbal channel to perform a multiplicity of functions simultaneously, including the communication of attitude and feeling. Thus, the development of affect communication involves the socialization of both facial and linguistic behavior.

RECOGNITION OF AFFECTIVE FACIAL EXPRESSIONS

Current research suggests that the ability to recognize the facial expressions of emotion is acquired or at least refined during the course of development. Although the imitation of some emotional expressions by neonates has recently been reported (Field, Woodson, Greenberg, & Cohen, 1982), most studies suggest that differential responding to facial expressions before age 4–6 months does not involve an understanding of their affective content (see review by Oster, 1981). A few investigators have produced ambiguous evidence of appropriate responses to affective expressions by infants in the middle of their first year. However, in the most successful of these studies (Kreutzer & Charlesworth, 1973; Lelwica & Haviland, cited in Malestesta & Izard, 1984), infants were presented with both a facial and a vocal stimulus and could have been responding to either or both of these.

Studies with older infants have produced stronger evidence for the recognition of *facial* expressions of emotion *per se*. For example, Sorce, Emde, and Klinnert (1981) showed that 1-year-olds produced different and appropriate action responses to facial expressions of fear versus happiness. In their experiment, infants were placed on a visual cliff and were found to cross it more often when their mothers produced a smile rather than when they produced a fearful expression. Thus, by the end of the first year, facial expressions of emotion may be understood, at least with respect to their positive versus their negative affective tone.

Consistent with this view, Davidson and Fox (1982) reported that 10-month-old infants showed different patterns of EEG response when viewing videotapes of a happy versus a sad expression.

Although infants may thus have some limited understanding of emotional facial expressions, research with older children shows that further development occurs during early and middle childhood. Children aged 4 usually can correctly identify smiles as an expression of happiness but very often confuse expressions of different negative emotions with one another (Green & Ekman, 1973). By age 5 or 6, negative affects are confused less often, and expressions of anger, sadness, fear, disgust, surprise, and happiness can all be identified with significant accuracy. Performance in emotion identification tasks improves even further during the next several years (Izard, 1971; Odom & Lemond, 1972).

The gradual improvement in children's recognition of emotional expressions suggests that this ability depends importantly on the child's backlog of experience with the social world. Yet, few researchers have studied the factors and processes that contribute to the development of emotion recognition skills. A notable exception is a recent study by Daly, Abramovitch, and Pliner (1980). Using the encoding–decoding paradigm developed by Buck (1975), Daly et al. videotaped mothers as they viewed a set of slides designed to elicit pleasant, disgusted, or neutral expressions of affect. The mothers were classified as good or poor encoders based on the performance of undergraduate students who were shown the videotapes and asked to guess which slides the mothers were viewing. The children of these mothers were also shown the videotapes and were asked to identify the slides viewed by their own mother, another mother who was classed as a poor encoder, and another mother who was classed as a good encoder. Data analysis showed a relationship between the mother's encoding performance and her child's decoding skill. The children of good encoders were themselves good decoders, but their superiority was manifested only when they viewed mothers who had been classed as good encoders. Although Daly et al. acknowledged that their findings might reflect genetic variation in decoding ability, they believed that a learning process was more likely involved. They suggested that children of good encoders receive extensive experience with easily identifiable facial cues and thus themselves become skilled at decoding.

One limitation of the Daly et al. study is its failure to specify the morphology of the facial expressions produced by the mothers and recognized by the children. Thus, one cannot determine whether the emotion cues utilized were or were not the universally recognizable facial expressions described by Darwin (1872/1965), Ekman and Friesen (1975),

Izard (1971), Tomkins (1963), and others. Furthermore, interesting questions about the expressive behavior remain unanswered. Did good encoders produce more intense emotional expressions, or did they simply use a greater number of expressions? Did the children recognize the disgusted nature of their mother's response to the disgust slides, or did they simply perceive the response as negative in emotional tone? Such questions illustrate the need for a more refined analysis of expressive behavior produced in this and other encoding–decoding studies.

In one respect, the approach taken by Daly *et al.* exemplifies an established, almost conventional, strategy for studying developmental processes. That is, an attempt was made to relate individual differences in ability to individual differences in presumably relevant experiences. Here, individual differences were studied among children from normal home environments, children whose development might be assumed to be normal with respect to emotion recognition abilities. A variant of this approach might involve the study of individuals whose backgrounds are deviant in a way that may affect the development of their emotion recognition skills. If such children indeed were deficient or delayed in development, the hypothesis that children learn to recognize emotional facial expressions through social experience in the home would receive support. A subsequent detailed comparison of the social environments of delayed versus nondelayed children might suggest the specific processes and factors involved in learning to recognize emotional expressions.

Recent research suggests that physically abused children are delayed in their development of emotional recognition skills, and thus, their experiences with others' emotional expressions might be profitably investigated. In a recent study, Barahal, Waterman, and Martin (1981) showed that abused children were inferior to nonabused children in recognition of emotions presented in the form of audiotaped scenarios. Even after the investigators partialed out IQ (as a covariate), they found abused children to be less accurate than nonabused children in identifying emotion. This finding suggests that abused children may have similar difficulties in recognizing the emotions manifested by facial expressions.

A Study of Expression Recognition by Abused Children

Such difficulties in the recognition of emotional facial expressions by abused children were demonstrated in an investigation by Camras, Grow, and Ribordy (1983). The subjects in this study were 17 (11 male and 6 female) physically abused children and 17 (11 male and 6 female) nonabused children ranging from 3½ to 6½ years of age. All children attended day-care centers having programs in child abuse prevention services serving a largely lower-class population. The abused subjects generally had experienced moderate levels of abuse; hospitalization rarely had been required. However, many children also were thought to have experienced neglect. The abused and the nonabused children were matched on the variables of sex, race, and age.

The subjects were presented with 12 brief stories, each representing a child experiencing one of the following six emotions: happiness, sadness, anger, fear, surprise, or disgust. With each story were displayed three photographs of a child showing different facial expressions of emotion. The subject was asked to choose the facial expression that would be appropriate for the child in the story. Of the 12 stories, 11 had been used in one or more previous studies of emotion recognition by normal children (Camras, 1980; Ekman & Friesen, 1971; Green & Ekman, 1973). Examples of these stories are:

1. "It is his/her birthday and he/she is happy."
2. "He/she has just been told that his/her new puppy is sick and is going to die. He/she is sad."

Two brief stories were told for each of the six emotions.

The facial expressions were presented to the subjects in the form of 5 × 7 inch glossy black-and-white photographs. Each showed the face of a child model posing a facial expression of one of the emotions studied. Two models were used: a 12-year-old boy and a 13-year-old girl. To obtain the expression photographs, the models were instructed about the facial muscle movements involved in each of the emotional expressions. The models were photographed while producing these muscle movements. Inspection of the photographs by two persons trained to use the Facial Action Coding System (Ekman & Friesen, 1978) confirmed that the models had produced the specified muscle movements. The expressions posed were described by Ekman and Friesen (1975) and are considered cross-culturally recognizable expressions of emotion.

Our data analysis showed that the abused children were significantly less accurate in their overall identification of emotional expressions than were the nonabused children. In addition, some emotions were recognized more easily than others by all subjects. An inspection of the data suggested that the expressions of happiness, sadness, and anger were identified more readily than the expressions of fear, surprise, and disgust.

These results point to the potential value of studying abused children further to determine the source of the difficulties. In particular, one might compare them to nonabused children in terms of their experiences with the expressive behavior produced by their parents. The

Daly *et al.* study suggests that children learn to recognize facial expressions in part by observing these expressions appropriately displayed by their mothers in emotional situations. Perhaps abusing parents do not adequately provide their children with appropriate displays of emotional expression. This might be a critical factor in their children's relatively undeveloped emotion-recognition skills.

The facial behavior of abusing parents may deviate from the behavior of nonabusing parents in several important ways. First, abusing parents may be facially inexpressive; they may tend to use fewer facial expressions than other persons when placed in an emotional situation. In addition (or alternatively), abusing parents may be inappropriate or inconsistent in their use of facial expressions; for example, they may smile when scolding their children, rather than frown. A third possibility is that abusing parents are not atypical in their use of facial expressions, but that they are atypical with regard to their frequency of parent–child interactions. Thus, their children do not get adequate experience with facial expressions because they engage in fewer social exchanges with their parents overall.

Some circumstantial evidence supporting this last possibility can be found by combining the results of Camras *et al.*'s study with an earlier investigation by Burgess and Conger (1978) of family interaction in abusive, neglectful, and normal families. Although Camras *et al.* collected few data on each of their individual facial expressions, they found a nonsignificant trend suggesting that the difference between abuse and nonabused children was greater for some emotions than for others. In particular, their data showed greater differences in the recognition of happiness than for the recognition of anger and sadness. According to the third hypothesis presented above, one would therefore expect abused children and their parents to engage in fewer pleasant or happy social exchanges in comparison to nonabused children and parents. However, their frequency of angry and sad exchanges should not differ. Consistent with this prediction, Burgess and Conger reported that abusive parents had significantly fewer positive interactions with their children than nonabusing parents, but approximately the same number of negative interactions. Burgess and Conger relied in part on facial and vocal cues to classify their positive versus negative interactions but did not describe the specific expressive behaviors they observed. Nevertheless, their findings, along with those of Camras *et al.*, suggest that a more detailed investigation of the relationship between parents' facial expressions and children's expression-recognition abilities may be profitable. Such a study would enable us to arrive at a clearer understanding of parents' role in the development of both abused and nonabused children's capacity to recognize facial expressions of emotion.

PROCESSES IN THE DEVELOPMENT OF CHILDREN'S
ABILITY TO RECOGNIZE EMOTIONAL EXPRESSIONS

As suggested in the preceding section, the development of expression recognition abilities is likely to depend on appropriate social experience, that is, experience with other persons' expressive behavior. However, to fully understand the development of expression recognition, one also must understand how children process the relevant experiences that they have. Although virtually no research has addressed this issue directly, several hypotheses can be advanced that would merit future investigation. Two of these hypotheses are considered here.

One process possibly involved in the acquisition of emotion recognition skills is concept formation. That is, based on their experiences with other persons' expressive behavior, children may develop emotion concepts related to emotional facial expressions. The development of expression recognition skills thus might be viewed as being somewhat analogous to semantic development. In the case of semantic development, children are often presented with various exemplars of word referents during the course of their daily experiences. Thus, children hear a word used to refer to a number of objects and/or in a variety of circumstances. Based on their experiences with word usage by those around them, children formulate a concept that constitutes the meaning of the word to them. Subsequently, the word comes to be recognized and used as a sign for the concept.

Similarly, in the course of their daily experience, children encounter exemplars of emotional facial expressions. Each emotional expression is observed in a variety of circumstances. For example, an anger expression might be used when the mother is scolding the child, when she is arguing with a neighbor, and/or when she is interrupted by an unsolicited salesperson's call. Based on his or her observations of emotional expression usage, the child may develop a concept of the expression similar to the type of concept that he or she may develop for a word. Thus, the facial expression comes to be recognized as an index of the emotion, and its meaning is the emotion concept (see Lewis & Michalson, 1982b, for a related discussion of emotions and scripts).

In investigating the development of emotion expression concepts, one would expect to consider questions similar to those currently being debated with regard to the development of word meanings and the processes of categorization and concept formation in general (Anglin, 1977, 1978; Bowerman, 1978; Hupp & Mervis, 1982; Macnamara, 1982; Mervis & Pani, 1980; Nelson, Rescorla, Gruendel, & Benedict, 1978; Oviatt, 1982). What dimensions of experience provide the basis for children's early concepts? How are children's word (expression) concepts modified during the course of development? Do children match words (or facial expressions) to previously developed concepts, or do children formulate new concepts organized around a word (or facial expression)? Answers to these questions would provide information about children's understanding of the social and nonsocial world as well as about the acquisition of expression recognition skills. Thus, the concept formation hypothesis may provide one fruitful avenue for future research.

A second process that may be involved in learning to recognize emotional facial expressions is empathic responding. That is, when children see an emotional expression, they may experience the associated subjective feeling state as a consequence. The evidence of early empathic responding to affective facial expressions is primarily circumstantial. However, empathy may be invoked to explain infants' responses to facial expressions reported in the recent literature. As indicated previously, several studies (Klinnert, 1981; Sorce et al., 1981) have shown that 1-year-old children alter their behavior in response to their mother's expressions. For example, in the Sorce et al. study, infants crossed a visual cliff more often when their mothers smiled than when they showed a fearful facial expression. This finding suggests that infants may have empathically responded with fear to their mothers' fear expressions and with pleasure to their mothers' smiles. Although Sorce et al.'s data provide no direct support for this interpretation, more convincing evidence could be obtained in future studies, for example, by observing the infants' own emotional facial expressions in Sorce's visual-cliff experiment.

Although empathy and concept formation may both contribute to the development of affect recognition skills, the two processes could be associated with qualitatively different "recognition" experiences. Recognition based on empathy may be restricted to the subjective feeling aspect of emotion and may involve no understanding of other components, for example, likely emotion elicitors and predictable action responses. Furthermore, an empathizing child may not clearly distinguish between her or his own emotional state and that of the expresser. Her or his recognition of emotion may be egocentric in nature; because she or he is experiencing the subjective feeling state herself or himself, she or he also attributes it to the other person.

In the course of development, empathy-based emotion recognition may be combined with the more cognitive concept-based form of emotion recognition discussed above. In fact, children's first emotion-expression concepts may involve both facial expression and subjective feeling as defining criteria. Subsequently, the child would become aware of other aspects of emotion that generally are associated with particular feeling states and facial expressions. Thus, his or her emotion concept

would gradually expand to include an understanding of emotion elicitors, associated action responses, and so on. At the same time, strong
empathic (i.e., feeling) responses to other persons' facial expressions
may diminish over the course of development. However, the older child
or adult would still be able to recall the subjective feeling associated
with the expression and thus to "recognize" the expression as indicating
the corresponding feeling state.

Regarding the origins of empathic responses to facial expressions,
one possible source would be the social exchanges of mothers and infants.
Recent studies of mother–infant interaction suggest that maternal
responses to young infants are closely tied to the infants' own behavior
(Brazelton, Koswolski, & Main, 1974; Gottman & Ringland, 1981; Kaye,
1977; Kaye & Fogel, 1980; Kaye & Wells, 1980; Tronick, Als, & Adamson,
1979). Mothers' responses often involve imitation of the infant (Pawlby,
1977) and sometimes include the imitation of emotional facial expressions
(Malatesta & Haviland, 1982; Malatesta & Izard, 1984; Pawlby, 1977). By
imitating their infants' facial behavior, mothers display the expression
that corresponds to the infant's emotional state. This response tendency
by mothers may serve to establish an association between facial expression and subjective feeling and thus may provide the basis for a subsequent empathic response by the infant to the sight of the emotional
facial expression.

PEER INTERACTION AND AFFECT COMMUNICATION

Thus far the discussion of affect communication has focused on
the role of the parent and the home experience in the development of
children's ability to recognize facial expression of emotion. Yet, recognition of affective facial expressions is a generalized capacity that is used
in interactions with all persons, not just with family members. Starting
at a relatively early age, most children acquire experience with expressive
behavior produced by other children as well as by their parents. Children
may reasonably be expected to draw on these experiences with peers in
the course of learning to recognize affect cues. Certainly, the proposed
contributing processes of empathic responding and concept formation
could operate during peer social interactions as well as during parent–
child interactions. Nonetheless, virtually no research has investigated
possible peer influences on the development of affect recognition skills.

Some data do exist that indicate that young children attend and
respond to other children's facial expressions. The data also show that
sensitivity to peer expressions is justified because such expressions can

be informative; they bear regular relationships to certain aspects of the expresser's subsequent behavior. Evidence of systematic production and response to facial expressions was obtained by studying children's communication during mild conflicts over object possession.

A Study of Children's Facial Expressions in a Conflict Situation

In this study (Camras, 1977), same-sexed pairs of unacquainted kindergarten children were given brief play sessions involving an object with which only one child could play at a time. The children were seated at a table on which was placed a box containing a pair of live gerbils. The box could be passed back and forth across the table through an opening in the transparent plexiglass screen that bisected the table. When a child pulled the box over to his or her side of the table, she or he was able to engage in a number of play activities (e.g., feeding the gerbil or giving it a ride on a "merry-go-round"). The children were told that they might play with the gerbils while the experimenter left the room for a short while. No instructions were given about sharing or competing for access to the box. However, the children were asked to remain in their seats and to pull the box over to their own side of the table when they wished to play.

Periodically during the course of these play sessions, the children came into conflict over possession of the gerbil box. Conflicts arose when the child who was playing with the box resisted an attempt by his or her partner to obtain it. Data analysis focused on the facial expressions used by the playing child as he or she defended the possession of the gerbil box. In particular, a set of *target* expressions was identified, and children's use and response to these target expressions was compared to their use and response to other (i.e., nontarget) expressions.

The target expressions were facial expressions that had been described in previous ethological studies of children's naturally occurring social behavior. Grant (1969) and Blurton-Jones (1972) had both observed these expressions in association with aggressive acts such as hitting, kicking, and biting. Briefly described, the expressions were lowered brows, stare, lips pressed together (several forms), both lips thrust forward, face thrust forward, nose wrinkle, and lower lip dropped and accompanied by a jaw thrust (intention to bite). Although Grant and Blurton-Jones both considered these expressions aggressive, their conclusions regarding motivational underpinnings were judged to be premature and were not automatically assumed in the present study.

Data analysis indicated relationships between the target expressions and the subsequent behavior of both expresser and recipient. When a child used a target expression while defending possession of the gerbil box, she or he was more likely to continue to resist her or his partner than if she or he used only nontarget expressions. That is, the target expressions were associated with a continued defense of the gerbil box by the expresser. In addition, when the children observed their partner using a target expression, they appeared to become more hesitant about taking the disputed object. That is, after observing a target expression, the child tended to give up the current attempt to get the box and waited longer before making a new attempt than he or she waited after observing only nontarget expressions.

The relationship between the target expressions and the expresser behavior indicates that facial expression can be used as a source of information about the expresser during peer conflicts. For example, in this study, the target expressions appeared to indicate that the expresser was very unwilling to give up possession of the gerbil box. In general, facial expressions may be used to infer how intensely the expresser will pursue the goals in a conflict situation. The relationship observed in this study between the target expressions and the recipient's behavior suggests that children do respond to facial expressions produced during conflicts between peers. For example, in the present study, the recipients may have interpreted the target expressions as indicating that the expresser was highly invested in retaining possession of the gerbil box. Thus, these recipients hesitated before renewing their attempt to obtain the desired object (see Camras, 1982, for a further discussion of this issue).

Special Contribution of Peers to the Development of Emotion Recognition Skills

The Camras (1977) study indicates that there are regular relationships between children's expressions and other aspects of their behavior. Thus, peers may provide experiences with appropriate use of emotional expressions that facilitate the development of emotion concepts and recognition skills. To this extent, peers and parents may be seen to serve similar functions. However, one might also argue that the child's experience with facial expressions used by other children has a special importance of its own.

In the course of peer interactions, children are likely to see emotional expressions produced in circumstances that are quite different from those in which they have observed their parents' facial behavior. Thus, the children are introduced to new examples of relationships between facial expression and nonexpressive aspects of emotion, for example, between angry expressions and anger-eliciting situations or anger-motivated actions. These new examples of emotion expression usage could contribute in two important ways to the development of affect recognition abilities. First, they may facilitate the development of a broader, more general emotional expression concept. Second, they may encourage the child to make context-dependent interpretations of facial expressions.

The importance of context in the interpretation of facial expressions can be illustrated by again drawing an analogy between facial expressions and words. As any brief perusal of the dictionary will show, a single word often has a number of definitions or meanings. A person hearing the word must rely on its context of occurence in order to interpret it correctly. Thus, semantic development must sometimes include the development of several word-related concepts (i.e., several alternative "definitions"), and interpretations of each word token (i.e., instance of word use) must involve a context-dependent inference about what the speaker "means" to convey when she or he produces the word.

Similarly, many facial expressions must be interpreted in terms of their context of occurrence. This is particularly true of the target expressions studied by Camras (1977, 1980). Most of these expressions have different meanings, depending on the circumstances of their use. For example, lowered brows are a component of the complete facial expression of anger and may be interpreted as indicating anger when occurring in a conflict interaction (Camras, 1980). However, lowered brows also occur in many situations in which it would be unreasonable to infer that the expresser is angry. According to Darwin (1872/1965), lowered brows may follow "from the sense of anything difficult or displeasing together with concentration of mind" (p. 235). Thus, Darwin contended that lowered brows sometimes indicate reflection or deep thought instead of anger. Similarly, Darwin observed that lips pressed together (another target expression) sometimes indicates anger and sometimes "fixed determination" (p. 239). Thus, a correct interpretation of these expressions must involve a consideration of their context of occurrence.

Two unresolved questions regarding the contextual interpretation of facial expressions should be briefly mentioned because of their potential relevance to the development of emotion recognition skills by children. First is the question of relationships between alternative interpretations of facial expressions. Smith (1965, 1977) argued that the meaning of nonverbal signals (both human and animal) may vary with context, but that a common thread or "message" runs through all instances of a signal's use. This may be true of some expressions (e.g., lowered brows as discussed in Camras, 1980). However, whether a common thread or message can be identified for all human facial expressions remains to be empirically determined.

A second issue regarding contextual interpretation involves a possible difference between complete facial expressions of emotion (e.g., the lowered brows, the widened eyes, and the compressed lips of anger) and components of these complete expressions (e.g., lowered brows displayed alone). Possibly, components of emotion expressions have context-dependent meanings, but complete emotional expressions do not. For example, one might argue that lowered brows may sometimes mean anger and sometimes mean deep thought, but that there are no instances when the complete expression of anger can be interpreted as anything but angry. A brief consideration of the nonverbal communication literature, however, indicates that fixed meaning is not characteristic of all complete expressions of emotion. For example, smiles are well known to have many meanings (e.g., happiness or deference). In addition, the nose wrinkle (a complete expression of disgust) may sometimes be interpreted as indicating anger or aggression (Grant, 1969).

To summarize, as recognized by many investigators (e.g., Camras, 1980, 1982; Lewis & Michalson, 1982b; Smith, 1965, 1977), context plays an important role in the interpretation of human facial expressions. Children probably learn to make contextual interpretations in the course of social interactions with both parents and peers. Peer interaction may also contribute to the development of affect recognition skills by giving the child a broader range of experiences in which to observe the use of emotional facial expressions. This variety may be important to the development of the child's emotion-expression concepts.

AFFECT EXPRESSION BY LINGUISTIC MEANS

Although emotional expression almost traditionally has been relegated to the nonverbal channel and propositional communication to the verbal channel, recent theoretical analyses of language suggest that the distinction may be less clear-cut than previously imagined. In particular, speech act theory (Austin, 1962; Searle, 1969, 1976) provides the basis for hypotheses regarding emotional expression by linguistic means. Communication of emotion via choice of language could be particularly important in situations where display rules (Ekman, 1972, 1977; Saarni, 1979, 1982) militate against the use of emotional facial expressions.

According to the speech act theory, verbal statements may be categorized according to the action that is conventionally performed when the statement is produced (e.g., commanding, promising, or describing). Of particular interest, speakers may perform a speech act (e.g., directing the listener to carry out a particular action) utilizing any one of several linguistic forms (Searle, 1975). Thus, a directive may be expressed directly as an imperative ("Give me $100") or indirectly as an interrogative ("Would you give me $100?") or a declarative ("I wish you would give me $100").

According to Ervin-Tripp (1976a, b), the speaker's choice of directive form depends on situational variables (e.g., the difficulty of the requested act, the likelihood of compliance, the obligation of the listener to perform the act) and relationship variables (e.g., the familiarity and the relative status of speaker and listener). In addition, directive forms can vary in politeness (Clark & Schunk, 1980; Lakoff, 1973). For example, interrogative statements ("Would you shut the door?") are usually considered more polite than imperatives ("Shut the door").

Although psycholinguists have commented only casually on the affective implications of directive choice (Ervin-Tripp, 1976a, 1977; Lakoff, 1973), emotion may be an important variable influencing the individual's selection among statements that vary in politeness. In studying children's comprehension of polite directive forms, at least one investigator (Bates, 1976; Bates & Silvern, 1977) has used *nice* as a synonym for *polite*, suggesting a relationship between positive affect and politeness and perhaps between negative affect and impoliteness. Thus, directive choice may serve in part as a display of feeling analogous in some sense to a facial expression.

A Study of Affect, Situation, and Directive Choice

The relationship between affect, situation, and the politeness of children's directives was recently investigated in a study by Camras, Pristo, and Brown (in press). As part of this study, first-grade children were presented with stories, were shown pictures of the main character's facial expression of emotion, and were asked to supply the directive that would be used by the story character.

Three stories presented situations having features that Ervin-Tripp (1977) described as being associated with the use of imperatives as directives. In these stories, the speakers were of higher status than the listeners and made requests with which compliance would be expected. An example of an *imperative* story was the following:

> My friend Johnny has a little brother who wanted to go outside and play in the snow. Johnny saw his little brother go outside without his jacket or boots. What did Johnny say to his little brother if Johnny wanted his brother to put on his boots and jacket?

Three stories presented situations having features that Ervin-Tripp described as being associated with the use of indirect directives, particularly embedded imperatives. In these stories the speakers were of lower status thanj the listeners and made requests with which compliance would not necessarily be expected. An example of an *indirect directive* story was the following:

One day my friend Julie was playing the piano. She was in the middle of playing a song when she heard someone ringing the doorbell. Julie knew her mom was somewhere downstairs. What did Julie say to her mom if Julie wanted her mom to answer the bell?

The story characters were presented as being either happy, angry, or neutral in affect. The character's emotional state was indicated by showing a facial expression photograph similar to those used in Camras et al.'s study (1983) of emotion recognition by abused children. For the experimental procedure, the subjects were told each story and were simultaneously shown the appropriate facial-expression photograph. The subjects then were asked to produce a verbal statement (directive) that would be used by the child in the story.

The children varied their directives according to both affect and situation. When presented with happy or neutral story characters, the subjects usually produced imperatives for the imperative stories and indirect directives for the indirect directive stories. Thus, Ervin-Tripp's predictions were confirmed in these two emotion conditions. However, portraying the story character as being angry radically altered the subjects' responses. For both the imperative and the indirect directive stories, the subjects produced imperative statements for angry speakers 90% of the time. Thus, the effect of the angry emotion on the directive choice was even more powerful than the effect of those situational variables described by Ervin-Tripp.

An additional politeness-oriented analysis of the subjects' directives yielded similar results. For this analysis, the directives were scored for politeness by means of an empirically derived scale developed by James (1975). Each directive was assigned a politeness score that depended both on the syntactic structure of the statement (e.g., imperative or interrogative) and on other linguistic features (e.g., the choice of an auxiliary verb or the use of *please*). Analysis of these scores showed that the politeness of the children's directives varied with both situation and emotion. Overall, the children produced politer directives for happy and neutral speakers than for angry ones and politer directives for indirect directive stories than for imperative stories (see Figure 1). However, when producing directives for angry speakers, children were not significantly more polite in response to the indirect directive stories. Thus again the effect of the angry emotion on directive choice was found to be preeminently important.

The results of this study indicate that children expect there to be relationships between speaker affect and directive choice. In particular, angry speakers are expected to be less polite than happy or neutral speakers. Based on these findings, one might argue that adults and children sometimes make inferences about the speaker's emotion based on his or her use of polite or impolite directives. Although this claim

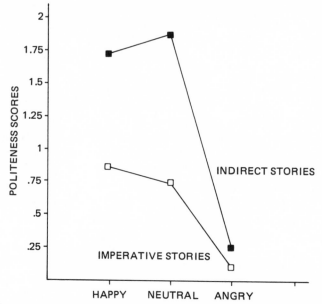

FIG. 1. Politeness scores for subjects' responses to imperative stories and indirect directive stories.

must be subjected to more direct empirical investigation, it seems reasonable to propose that directive choice can indeed provide emotion information indicating at least a generally positive or negative affective tone.

Socialization of Affect Expression through Language

Learning to express emotion via linguistic politeness presumably would be part of a broader language socialization process. This process would involve both learning the social meaning of politeness and learning politeness-relevant linguistic distinctions. That is, the child must come to know what linguistic forms are considered polite, when one is expected to use polite forms (to ask "nicely"), and how variations in linguistic politeness may be related to affect.

How do children learn the principles governing politeness and language use? For example, how do they learn to make an appropriate choice of directives? As indicated above, directive choice depends on a number of factors, including the speakers' emotion, speaker–listener relationship, and the difficulty of the requested action. Children must learn how directive choice is related to all these variables.

As a first step in the learning process, children may become aware that directive choice is not random but varies systematically with one or more aspects of the situation. Possibly, affect is the first component of the situation that children notice as varying with directive choice. Some data consistent with this hypothesis were found in Camras et al.'s investigation (in press). Here, children attributed imperative statements to angry speakers in the indirect directive stories. These stories described situations in which imperatives would normally not be the type of directive used. This finding suggests that emotion is considered a more important determinant of directive choice than other situational factors. Possibly, this finding reflects emotion's ontogenetic priority as a determining variable.

CONCLUDING REMARKS

This chapter has examined several diverse aspects of emotion communication, focusing on facial expression and language choice. As yet, little is known about the processes and mechanisms involved in the socialization of affect communication. However, several fruitful avenues of investigation can be identified. Of particular interest, the research strategies proposed in this chapter involve a consideration of the relationships between emotion communication and children's conceptual development, language development, empathy, and social interaction. Thus, the socialization of affect communication can be understood only when considered in relation to developments in many social and cognitive domains. Affect communication, like other complex forms of human behavior, involves the integration of many factors that operate during the course of development.

REFERENCES

Anglin, J. M. *Word, object and conceptual development*. New York: Norton, 1977.
Anglin, J. From reference to meaning. *Child Development*, 1978, 49(4), 969–976.
Austin, J. *How to do things with words*. Cambridge: Harvard University Press, 1962.
Barahal, R., Waterman, J., & Martin, H. The social-cognitive development of abused children. *Journal of Consulting and Clinical Psychology*, 1981, 49, 508–16.
Bates, E. *Language and context*. New York: Academic Press, 1976.
Bates, E., & Silvern, L. Sociolinguistic development in children: How much of it is social? *Program on Cognitive and Perceptual Factors in Human Development Report No. 10*. Boulder: Institute for the Study of Intellectual Behavior, University of Colorado, 1977.
Birdwhistell, R. *Kinesics and context*. Philadelphia: University of Pennsylvania Press, 1970.
Blurton-Jones, N. G. Categories of child-child interaction. In N. G. Blurton-Jones (Ed.), *Ethological studies of child behavior*. London: Cambridge University Press, 1972.

Bowerman, M. Systematizing semantic knowledge: Changes over time in the child's organization of word meaning. *Child Development*, 1978, *49*(4), 977–987.

Brazelton, T., Koslowski, B., & Main, M. The origins of reciprocity: The early mother–infant interaction. In M. Lewis & L. Rosenblum (Eds.), *The effect of the infant on its caregiver*. New York: Wiley, 1974.

Buck, R. Nonverbal communication of affect in children. *Journal of Personality and Social Psychology*, 1975, *31*(4), 644–653.

Burgess, R., & Conger, R. Family interaction in abusive, neglectful and normal families. *Child Development*, 1978, *49*, 1163–1173.

Camras, L. Facial expressions used by children in a conflict situation. *Child Development*, 1977, *48*, 1431–1435.

Camras, L. A. Children's understanding of facial expressions used during conflict encounters. *Child Development*, 1980, *51*, 879–885.

Camras, L. A. Ethological approaches to nonverbal communication. In R. S. Feldman (Ed.), *Development of nonverbal communication*. New York: Springer-Verlag, 1982.

Camras, L. A., Grow, G., & Ribordy, S. C. Recognition of emotional expressions by abused children. *Journal of Clinical and Child Psychology*, 1983, *12*(3), 325–328.

Camras, L. A., Pristo, T. M., & Brown, M. Social use of language by children and adults: Affect, situation and directive choice. *Merrill-Palmer Quarterly*, in press.

Clark, H., & Schunk, D. Polite responses to polite requests. *Cognition*, 1980, *8*, 111–143.

Daly, E., Abramovitch, R., & Pliner, P. The relationship between mothers' encoding and their children's decoding of facial expressions of emotion. *Merrill-Palmer Quarterly*, 1980, *26*(1), 25–33.

Darwin, C. *The expression of the emotions in man and animals*. London: John Murray, 1872. (Reprinted Chicago: University of Chicago Press, 1965.)

Davidson, R., & Fox, N. Asymmetrical brain activity discriminates between positive and negative affective stimuli in human infants. *Science*, 1982, *218*, 1235–1237.

Eibl-Eibesfeldt, I. Similarities and differences between cultures in expressive movements. In R. A. Hinde (Ed.), *Non-verbal communication*. London: Cambridge University Press, 1972.

Ekman, P. Universals and cultural differences in facial expressions of emotion. In J. Cole (Ed.), *Nebraska Symposium on Motivation, 1971*. Lincoln: University of Nebraska Press, 1972.

Ekman, P. Movements with precise meaning. *Journal of Communication*, 1976, *26*(3), 14–26.

Ekman, P. Biological and cultural contributions to body and facial movement. In J. Blacking (Ed.), *The anthropology of the body*. New York: Academic Press, 1977.

Ekman, P., & Friesen, W. Constants across cultures in the face and emotion. *Journal of Personality and Social Psychology*, 1971, *17*(2), 124–129.

Ekman, P., & Friesen, W. *Unmasking the face*. Englewood Cliffs, N.J.: Prentice-Hall, 1975.

Ekman, P., & Friesen, W. *Facial action coding system: A technique for the measurement of facial movement*. Palo Alto, Calif.: Consulting Psychologists Press, 1978.

Ervin-Tripp, S. Is Sybil there?: The structure of some American English directives. *Language in Society*, 1976, *5*, 25–66.(a)

Ervin-Tripp, S. Speech acts and social learning. In K. Basso & H. Selby (Eds.), *Meaning in anthropology*. Albuquerque: University of New Mexico, 1976. (b)

Ervin-Tripp, S. Wait for me, rollerskate! In S. Ervin-Tripp & C. Mitchell-Kernan (Eds.), *Child discourse*. New York: Academic Press, 1977.

Field, T., Woodson, R., Greenberg, R., & Cohen, D. Discrimination and imitation of facial expressions by neonates. *Science*, 1982, *218*, 179–181.

Gottman, J., & Ringland, J. The analysis of dominance and bidirectionality in social development. *Child Development*, 1981, 52(2), 525–536.

Grant, E. C. Human facial expression. *Man*, 1969, 4, 525–536.

Green, J., & Ekman, P. *Age and the recognition of facial expressions of emotion.* Unpublished manuscript, 1973.

Hupp, S., & Mervis, C. Acquisition of basic object categories by severely handicapped children. *Child Development*, 1982, 53, 760–767.

Izard, C. E. *The face of emotion.* New York: Appleton-Century-Crofts, 1971.

James, S. *The effect of listener and situation on the politeness of preschool children's directive speech.* Unpublished doctoral dissertation, University of Wisconsin, 1975.

Kaye, K. Toward the origin of dialogue. In H. Schaffer (Ed.), *Studies in mother–infant interaction.* New York: Academic Press, 1977.

Kaye, K., & Fogel, A. The temporal structure of face-to-face communication between mothers and infants. *Developmental Psychology*, 1980, 16(5), 454–464.

Kaye, K., & Wells, A. Mothers' jiggling and the burst-pause pattern in neonatal feeding, *Infant Behavior and Development*, 1980, 3, 29–46.

Klineberg, O. Emotional expression in Chinese literature. *Journal of Abnormal and Social Psychology*, 1938, 33, 517–520.

Klinnert, M. *Infants' use of mothers' facial expressions for regulating their own behavior.* Paper presented at the meeting of the Society for Research in Child Development, Boston, April 1981.

Kreutzer, M., & Charlesworth, W. *Infants' reactions to different expressions of emotions.* Paper presented at the meeting of the Society for Research in Child Development, Philadelphia, March 1973.

LaBarre, W. The cultural basis of emotions and gestures. *Journal of Personality*, 1947, 16, 49–68.

Lakoff, R. The logic of politeness: Or minding your p's and q's. In C. Corum, T. Smith-Stark, & A. Weiser (Eds.), *Papers from the 9th regional meeting, Chicago Linguistic Society.* Chicago: Chicago Linguistic Society, 1973.

Lelwica, M., & Haviland, J. *Ten-week-old infants' reactions to mothers' emotional expressions.* Paper presented at the meeting of the Society for Research in Child Development, Detroit, 1983.

Lewis, M., & Michalson, L. *Emotions and moods: Theory and measurement.* New York: Plenum Press, 1982. (a)

Lewis, M., & Michalson, L. The measurement of emotional state. In C. Izard (Ed.), *Measuring emotions in infants and children.* New York: Cambridge University Press, 1982. (b)

Macnamara, J. *Names for things: A study of human learning.* Cambridge: MIT Press, 1982.

Malatesta, C., & Haviland, J. Learning display rules: The socialization of emotion expression in infancy. *Child Development*, 1982, 53(4), 991–1003.

Malatesta, C., & Izard, C. Human social signals in ontogenesis: From biological imperative to symbol utilization. In N. Fox & R. J. Davidson (Eds.), *Affective development: A psychobiological perspective.* Hillsdale, N.J.: Erlbaum, 1984.

Mervis, C., & Pani, J. Acquisition of basic object categories. *Cognitive Psychology*, 1980, 12, 496–522.

Nelson, K., Rescorla, L., Gruendel, J., & Benedict, H. Early lexicons: What do they mean? *Child Development*, 1978, 49(4), 960–968.

Odom, R., & Lemond, C. Developmental differences in the perception and production of facial expressions. *Child Development*, 1972, 43, 359–369.

Oster, H. "Recognition" of emotional expression in infancy? In M. Lamb & L. Sherrod (Eds.), *Infant social cognition.* Hillsdale, N.J.: Erlbaum, 1981.

Oviatt, S. Inferring what words mean: Early development in infants' comprehension of common object names. *Child Development*, 1982, *53*, 274–277.

Pawlby, J. S. Imitative interaction. In H. Schaffer (Ed.), *Studies in mother-infant interaction*. New York: Academic Press, 1977.

Saarni, C. Children's understanding of display rules for expressive behavior. *Developmental Psychology*, 1979, *15*(4), 424–429.

Saarni, C. Social and affective functions of nonverbal behavior: Developmental concerns. In R. S. Feldman (Ed.), *Development of nonverbal communication*. New York: Springer Verlag, 1982.

Searle, J. *Speech acts*. Cambridge: Cambridge University Press, 1969.

Searle, J. Indirect speech acts. In P. Cole & J. Morgan (Eds.), *Syntax and semantics. Vol. 3: Speech acts*. New York: Academic Press, 1975.

Searle, J. A classification of illocutionary acts. *Language in Society*, 1976, *5*, 1–23.

Smith, W. J. Message, meaning, and context in ethology. *The American Naturalist*, 1965, *99*(908), 405–409.

Smith, W. J. *The behavior of communicating*. Cambridge: Harvard University Press, 1977.

Sorce, J., Emde, R., & Klinnert, M. *Maternal emotional signaling: Its effect on the visual cliff behavior of one-year-olds*. Paper presented at the meeting of the Society for Research in Child Development, Boston, April 1981.

Tomkins, S. S. *Affect, imagery, and consciousness* (Vols. 1 and 2). New York: Springer, 1963.

Tronick, E., Als, H., & Adamson, L. Structure of early face-to-face communicative interactions. In M. Bullowa (Ed.), *Before speech: The beginnings of human communication*. Cambridge: Cambridge University Press, 1979.

8

What Children Know about the Situations That Provoke Emotion

Paul L. Harris

Introduction

There are several good reasons for studying children's insight into their emotional processes. We occasionally think of an emotional reaction as being more-or-less involuntary, but it is obvious that, in certain respects, we can exercise control over our emotions. We can be taught to hide our emotions or we can be taught to exaggerate them. Indeed, some cultures expect their members to inhibit displays of emotion, and others encourage lavish displays. These cultures presumably teach their children both explicitly and implicitly what is acceptable. We also, as most psychotherapies presuppose, try to exercise control, not just over the outward display of our feelings but over the actual experience of emotion. We put anxiety-provoking thoughts out of our mind. Alternatively, we dwell on an emotionally charged episode in an effort to prolong the emotion. Thus, both our outward display of emotion and our emotional experience can be redirected and controlled. By analogy with the development of memory (Flavell & Wellman, 1977), therefore, we might expect the developing child to gradually acquire insight into such strategies for self-control and put them into practice.

PAUL L. HARRIS • Department of Experimental Psychology, Oxford University, South Parks Road, Oxford OX1 340, England.

A second reason for looking at children's understanding of emotion is that such understanding clearly enters into their relationships with others, be they fictitious characters or real people. To the extent that children know something about the situations that distress other people and about the signs of that distress, they are capable of reacting sympathetically to a friend or a parent. Similarly, most stories and films require that the child empathize with the protagonist. Empathy requires that the child be able to grasp what provokes love and fear, and to interpret its sometimes covert signals.

A third reason for looking at children's understanding of emotion is less obvious but deserves spelling out. Many of our decisions and choices depend not on our actual emotional reactions to a current situation, but on an anticipation of the way that we will feel in some future situation. A child's readiness to go to school, to brave the dentist, to seek out a new friend, or to run away from punishment is based on an appraisal of how he or she will feel when facing these situations. We cannot understand children's behavior if we ignore their expectations about how each of these situations will affect them. We may also help children to make more mature decisions, if we come to an understanding of the biases and distortions that enter into such expectations.

In adults, of course, this appraisal process is crucial, because many important decisions about the future are usually taken without a trial run; we marry, choose careers, and decide to become parents not on the basis of our past emotional reactions but on the basis of an estimate of how these relatively unfamiliar situations are likely to make us feel in the future. The fact that we are often quite wrong about how we feel is of considerable psychological interest. We may fail to conjure up the relevant aspect of the course that we are about to embark on, dwelling in our imagination on the wedding day itself, rather than on the lifetime thereafter. Alternatively, we may conjure up the relevant aspects but be very bad at gauging our future emotions. We may envisage a lifetime partnership but underestimate our emotional vicissitudes. Whatever the exact explanation, it is clear that both as a child and as an adult, we act and choose on the basis of an implicit theory about our feelings that may or may not correspond to reality. My aim is to give a sketch of the early development of that theory.

The plan of the chapter is as follows. First, I describe some of our early findings indicating that children's concept of emotion changes markedly somewhere between the ages of 6 and 11. Then, I describe some more recent findings that focus on the child's developing conception of the link between situation and emotion. I conclude by attempting to draw together the two sets of findings.

A Changing Concept of Emotion

A simple way to investigate children's understanding of emotion is to give them a set of questions about situations in which emotion would be provoked and to ask about their reactions to these situations. This was the method adopted by Harris, Olthof, and Meerum Terwogt (1981). They asked questions about three aspects of emotion (its identification, its control, and its effect on other psychological processes) and then put these questions to three quite widely spaced groups of children aged, 6, 11, and 15 years. The idea was to try to get a broad picture of the changes that take place in the child's knowledge and to fill in the details later.

As it turned out, a consistent picture did emerge from the various questions. Six-year-old children adopt what might be called a situation–response theory of emotion. They know what kinds of situations are linked to particular emotional responses. They know that a quarrel provokes anger in the form of an angry facial expression, stamping of the feet, fighting, and so forth. Although children continue to acknowledge these situation–response relationships at the age of 11, they are much more likely to refer to the mental processes that accompany and even engender an emotional reaction.

This age change emerged with regard to each of these three aspects of emotion that we studied: identification, control strategies, and effects. For example, in answering questions about the identification of emotion, 6-year-old children said that they knew how they felt because of the situations that they found themselves in: "I'm happy when it's my birthday"; "I get angry when my little brother messes up my toys." In contrast, the two older groups of children, the 11- and 15-year-olds, were much more likely to claim that they identified their emotions by reference to inner mental states: "I'm happy when I feel good inside"; "I'm sad when I think about bad things."

A related difference emerged when the children were asked about strategies for the control of emotion. With regard to the control of the display of emotion, most children, young and old alike, claimed that you could pretend to be happy when you really were not or could pretend not to be afraid when you really were, and they mentioned the kind of facial expression and behavior that you would have to display in order to pretend. However, the younger children had a less complex notion of pretense than the older children. For the younger children, pretense consisted simply in acting in a way that was not appropriate to the situation: laughing after a quarrel or smiling when you were on your way to the dentist. The older children, in contrast, were much more likely to mention the mismatch that would result from such pretense, the mismatch, that is, between what one would actually feel inside and what one would display outside. They talked of trying to hide their feelings or admitted that their feelings would still show through anyway. Going back to the difference in the implicit theory of the two age groups, we can make sense of this age change. If the younger children describe emotion in terms of overt emotional reactions, then pretense involves not a mismatch between inner and outer, but a mismatch between situation and overt reaction. For the older children, on the other hand, the mismatch between inner and outer is also likely to be mentioned because they acknowledge that one's reaction to a situation is mediated by an inner mental state.

With regard to the control of emotion itself rather than its display, the younger children again differed from the older children. Consistent with their situation–response model, the younger children suggested that it is possible to change one's emotion by changing the situation: if you feel fed up, you should go out to play with your friends. The older children, on the other hand, although they, too, often recommended a change of situation, also offered another more mentalistic strategy: they proposed that one redirect one's thought processes by thinking about nice things or by not thinking about what was making one unhappy. Again, then, we see that the older children, but not the younger children, talked about emotion as partly engendered from within.[1]

Finally, there was an age change in the way in which the children interpreted the effects of emotion. Although all three age groups claimed that life went better when one was happy, that you were nicer to other people, and that you did better work, the youngest children were at a loss to explain these effects. In contrast, the two older groups offered a plausible mentalistic explanation. They claimed—for example, in the case of making a drawing at school—that they would think of more things to draw if they were cheerful, but that if they were upset, their unhappy thoughts would distract them from their task.

Reviewing these results, Harris and Olthof (1982) came to the conclusion that, at around the age of 6 years, the child thinks that there is a direct one-to-one link between the situation that one is in and the emotional response that one makes. For older children, on the other

---

[1]There was a hint in our data (Harris et al., 1981) that the oldest group of subjects, aged 15 years, were more skeptical than the 11-year-olds about the efficacy of such mentalistic strategies. Paula Levin (personal communication, 1983) has also noted that Tahitian adolescents talk about the more-or-less inevitable persistence of some emotions. It may be that, although insight into strategies for controlling emotion emerges in middle childhood, higher order reflection on the limitation of those strategies emerges in adolescence. This is an intriguing issue for further research.

hand, this link is not so direct: it needs to be mediated by an inner mental process that gives rise to the outward behaviors that we associate with emotion. This account also ties in with results reported by Saarni (1979). She told children of the ages 6, 8, and 10 about various situations in which it would be appropriate to hide one's feelings. For example, she told children a story about receiving a present from a relative, opening it up, and finding that the present inside was very disappointing. When questioned about how one would look in such a situation, the 10-year-olds were likely to claim that one would still look happy, and to explain that this would avoid hurting the relative's feelings. The two younger groups, in contrast, rarely mentioned such strategies for hiding one's true feelings. This age change makes sense in terms of the proposal made by Harris and Olthof (1982). If the younger children think that one's current situation is linked in a direct fashion to how one responds, they should find it difficult to conceive of how one's inner mental reaction could fit the situation, but one's facial expression and behavior would convey a different emotion. These complicated relationships should be easier for older children to conceptualize because they make a three-fold distinction between situation, inner mental feelings, and overt reaction.

Below, I take up three issues that arose out of these initial findings. Each issue is concerned with the way in which children conceive of the link between a situation and the emotional reaction that it provokes. First, if 6-year-old children already know a good deal about which situations provoke particular emotions, how early does this knowledge develop? Second, how is such knowledge organized? Do children acknowledge, for example, that situations are sometimes not linked in a one-to-one fashion with a single emotion? Some situations provoke more than one emotion, and some situations can even arouse both positive and negative emotions. Finally, when do children admit that one's current emotional state is not always in correspondence with the current situation? Certain emotions, particularly intense emotions, persist well beyond the precipitating situation, so that one's current emotional state can be understood only in the light of past as well as current events.

THE EARLY EMERGENCE OF SITUATIONAL KNOWLEDGE

Several recent studies have shown that, even at 2–3 years of age, children know some of the links between situations and the emotional reaction that they provoke. One of the earliest studies was carried out by Borke (1971). She presented children with stories describing various simple situations: attending a birthday party, losing a toy, being lost, and so forth. The child's task was to say how the story protagonist would feel by selecting from one of several facial expressions. The main finding was that even from 3–3½ years of age, most children correctly picked out the happy face for the happy situations, and were less accurate but better than chance for the "angry" and "sad" stories. Only for the "afraid" stories were their choices unsystematic.

One possible conclusion from these results is that children learn to empathize with some emotions before others, and this is, in fact, the conclusion that Borke drew: "Improvement in ability to react on an empathic basis varies greatly with the emotional response being identified" (p. 268). I doubt that this conclusion is warranted. What the results do show is that children find it easier to predict the impact of some situations than of others. It is easy to conceive, for example, of a happy situation that would be difficult for 3- to 4-year-olds to understand (e.g., getting tenure). Conversely, their difficulties with the fear-provoking situation that Borke used (getting lost in the woods at night) might have been reduced if a more familiar situation, such as going into a dark room, had been used instead. Thus, we may conclude that children can predict the emotional consequences of some situations from an early age. The evidence suggesting that such predictions vary in difficulty depending on the emotional response that is provoked can also be interpreted as showing simply that some situations are more familiar than others.

Bretherton and Beeghly (1982) interviewed the mothers of children aged 28 months about their children's use of various psychological terms concerned with perception, physiology, affect, volition and ability, cognition, and morality. I concentrate here on the affect terms. The terms *happy, sad, mad,* and *scared* were among those that a high percentage of children used (57%–73%), and terms such as *proud, surprised,* and *angry* were used by a minority (13%–27%). To what extent did the children's usage of these terms reflect their knowledge of the situations that provoke the emotion in question? Bretherton and Beeghly reported statements that do indicate some causal knowledge. For example, the children made statements like "Grandma mad. I wrote on wall." Or "It's dark. I'm scared." Note that these findings reinforce the suggestion made earlier that young children know about certain fear-provoking situations, even if they do not know about the particular one used by Borke (1971).

Bretherton and Beeghly concluded that the children probably used the terms to refer to mental states rather than behavior. They cited two sources of evidence to support this conclusion. First, the children typically used each term more frequently to refer to themselves, but they also extended the terms to other people. Second, they used the terms to refer to nonpresent states, as in questions, denials, or statements about the future. Interesting though such extensions are, they do not clearly demonstrate that the children were referring to mental states rather than behavior. The children could presumably detect similarities between other people's behavior and their own just as readily as they could infer similarities between other people's mental states and their own. Similarly, behavior can be anticipated or denied just as readily as mental states. Thus, both of the extensions observed by Bretherton and Beeghly could have been based simply on observations of behavior rather than on inferences about inner mental states. The safest conclusion, therefore, is that young children begin to know and comment on the links between certain situations and certain emotions from the age of 2–3 years. How they conceive of emotions at that age is difficult to diagnose from their spontaneous utterances.[2]

Children have access to several potential sources of information about the link between situations and emotion. They can observe and remember what produces a particular emotion in themselves. They can observe and remember what produces a particular emotion in other people.[3] Finally, they are provided with verbal reports of varying accuracy on what people feel or will feel in a given situation. At present, we simply do not know which of these three sources children use and extrapolate from, but some hints provided by Dunn and Kendrick (1982) suggest that children's knowledge about the link between situation and emotion is not based exclusively on self-observation. These authors reported the following comment by Bruce when he was not yet 3 years old about his younger sibling, who was playing with a balloon: "He going to pop it in a minute. And he'll cry. And he'll be frightened of me too. I like the pop."

In this example, Bruce distinguished quite explicitly between his younger sibling's reaction to the bursting of the balloon and his own. Nevertheless, inaccuracy, bordering on projection, was also apparent in other comments. For example, one mother said to Ian, her 3-year-old, who was playing a rough physical game with his younger brother, "I don't think he likes that." Ian insisted, "He do. He do."

In summary, three recent studies using quite disparate techniques—children's story judgment, mothers' reports of their children's vocabulary, and direct observation—all indicate that children aged 2 and upward know what emotions particular situations would provoke

---

[2]The claim that adults, let alone children, are referring to inner mental states when they use emotion terms is not uncontroversial (Wittgenstein, 1953).
[3]Recent research on "social referencing" has documented the readiness with which infants in the first year of life observe and are even guided by the emotional reaction that a given situation elicits in significant adults such as their mothers (Klinnert, Campos, Sorce, Emde, & Svejda, 1982).

and can refer by name to the emotions in question. Their references tend to be restricted to emotions falling within the basic set described by Ekman (1973), but there are no convincing data showing that children find certain emotions within this set easier to diagnose than others. Children's knowledge of the link between situations and emotions is not restricted to those that they themselves have experienced. They are able to correctly diagnose links in others that do not obtain in their own case, although they are also prone to projection.

THE ORGANIZATION OF SITUATIONAL KNOWLEDGE

If children rapidly link particular situations with particular emotions, how do they organize such knowledge? Several recent studies have looked at the extent to which children treat certain emotions as having similar situational causes. Trabasso, Stein, and Johnson (1981) told children aged 3 to 4½ years about a story character who felt one of six emotions (angry, sad, scared, happy, excited, or surprised). The children were asked to think of a possible cause for the emotion, or a possible consequence. Their responses were analyzed by means of a cluster analysis that indicated the degree to which each of the six emotions was thought to share with the others either the same causes or the same consequences. The results showed first that the children replied differently when asked about causes as opposed to consequences, and in each case, their replies were usually judged as appropriate by adult raters (72% for causes; 73% for consequences). Thus, there was little indication that children at this age confuse cause and effect, notwithstanding Piaget's assertions to the contrary (Piaget, 1928/1969). Second, the children offered different causes and effects for the three positive emotions (happy, excited, and surprised) as compared to the three negative emotions (angry, sad, and scared). They rarely, if ever, mentioned the same situation in connection with both a positive and a negative emotion. Thus, the negative-positive dimension is, by this criterion, well established at 3–4 years of age. Third, and finally, the children distinguished much less sharply among the three positive emotions and the three negative emotions. For example, they tended to offer similar causal explanations for why the story character was happy or excited, or to suggest similar consequences if a story character was sad or angry.

Harris and his colleagues have carried out two similar studies. Harris, Olthof, and Meerum Terwogt (1984) presented Dutch and English children with a wide range of emotions and asked them to think of situations that would be likely to provoke each of them. Their analyses corroborate and extend the findings of Trabasso *et al.* (1981). The 5-year-olds, the youngest age group tested, showed the same clear differentiation between positive and negative emotions. Thus, distinct situations were offered for positive terms such as *excited, happy,* and *proud* as compared to negative terms such as *sad, angry, shy,* and *afraid*. In addition, among the older children, subclusters or pairings emerged within these large clusters (e.g., ashamed/guilty; afraid/worried). Harris and Hardman (1984) also asked whether a similar organization could be found among children living in a non-Western culture. They tested children aged 6–14 in an isolated Himalayan community of Eastern Nepal, the Lohorung Rai (for ethnographic information, see Hardman, 1981). Again, it was found that subdivisions emerged within two larger clusters of positive emotions on the one hand and negative emotions on the other.

Lutz (1982) studied the use of emotion terms by adult members of the Ifaluk, a Malayo-Polynesian community inhabiting a small coral atoll in the Western Pacific. Her technique was somewhat different from that employed by Trabasso, Harris, and their colleagues. The informants were not asked to supply situations likely to provoke a particular emotion. Instead, they were simply asked to sort emotion words into groups depending on their similarity. As it turned out, however, Lutz found that her informants tended to justify the fact that they had sorted certain terms together, on the grounds that they were associated with the same situation. Thus, despite the differences in method, her results are comparable to those reported above. Two distinct clusters again emerged, one associated with positive, and the other with negative, emotions. Lutz also found that subclusters emerged, particularly within the large cluster of negative emotions. Such subclusters seemed to emerge around certain themes, such as danger (associated with the emotions of disappointment, fear, panic, discomfort, and shame) or loss (associated with the emotions of compassion, loneliness, longing, homesickness, and insecurity).

Taken together, these diverse studies yield the following conclusions. First, to a greater or lesser extent, particular situations are not uniquely tied to a single emotion. In all the age groups studied, whether 3-year-old Western children or adults in the Western Pacific, a single situation could be cited with reference to one, two, or several emotions. Second, certain emotions come together in subclusters by dint of their being provoked by the same situations. These clusters can be seen in children even at the age of 3–4 years; by adulthood, they have been considerably elaborated and organized around themes that, to some extent, are culture-specific. Third, when subjects think about the situational determinants of emotion, two over-arching clusters emerge, one composed of negative emotions, the other of positive emotions. Thus, although a given situation may be linked with two or more negative emotions, or two or more positive emotions, it is not linked with both a negative and a positive emotion. The importance of the negative-positive dimension can be seen in Western children even at the age of 3–4 years, and it can be seen in children and adults alike, living in communities relatively isolated from Western culture. Below, these three conclusions are discussed in more detail.

One Situation Can Provoke Several Emotions

How do children come to associate emotion terms with particular situations? One possible model may be borrowed from recent work on early object naming. An emotion term is associated, at first, with a particular situation that serves as a prototype or an exemplar. Thereafter, the child extends the term to other situations that have some similarity to the prototypical instance, but the range of situations over which the child extends the term need not have any features that are common to the entire range of situations. Such an account fits quite well with what we know of children's early naming of objects (Harris, 1983b; Kay & Anglin, 1982). It implies that prototypical situations that are frequently cited for one emotion should be rarely cited in connection with a second emotion. In the same way, a prototypical red will rarely be picked out as an instance of blue (although a borderline red, such as purple, may be picked out as a blue).

However, the results reported above for emotion terms appear to be different. One situation is often cited in connection with two or more emotions. Moreover, such situations cannot easily be dismissed as borderline or peripheral instances of one emotion that could be readily assimilated to a second. They included situations that were frequently cited in connection with two given situations. For example, children in Nepal often said that encountering a fight or a quarrel would provoke unhappiness, but they also often mentioned such an episode in connection with both anger and fear. Similarly, many children mentioned that they became unhappy when something went wrong in a task that they were expected to do for their parents (Rai children work every day either in the home, or in the field, or minding cattle and goats), but they also said that they would be worried.

One possible explanation of such multiple citations is that young children are simply muddled about what situation provokes what emotion, mentioning the same situation first in connection with one situation, and then in connection with a second. Gradually, they will come to classify situations on a more exclusive basis. I doubt that this explanation is correct. The results obtained by Lutz (1982) indicate that adults also claim that one situation provokes several emotions, and Schwartz and Weinberger (1980) reported that when adults ruminate about certain emotionally charged episodes, they frequently claim to experience more than one emotion.

These various observations suggest that, for children and adults alike, current approaches to object classification and early object naming (Kay & Anglin, 1982; Rosch, 1978; Smith & Medin, 1981) cannot be extended to the classification of emotion-inducing situations. At a given level of classification, objects tend to be assigned to mutually exclusive categories. A dog is rarely assigned to the category of birds, and a bird is rarely assigned to the category of dogs. Similarly, red and blue are not readily confused with one another. It is only occasionally, when dealing with peripheral instances—platypuses or purples—that we misclassify. In contrast, situations do not fall neatly into mutually exclusive emotion categories. A situation that is likely to provoke sadness is also a good candidate for anger. It looks as if we often have several emotional reactions to a given situation, and our classification system reflects this multiplicity.

How, then, is the appropriate emotional reaction to a situation assessed and the appropriate emotion term selected to describe it? A tentative answer is that situations are analyzed for their various implications, and not simply for their immediately identifiable characteristics. To spell this point out more clearly, the Nepalese children who spoke of being unhappy and worried when something went wrong in their work were probably focusing on two different implications. On the one hand, work that is not finished prevents the child from doing something more enjoyable, and this makes the child unhappy. Indeed, another frequently mentioned cause of unhappiness was being prevented from going on an outing or going to a ritual by one's parents because of illness or the need to work. On the other hand, work that is not finished is likely to anger one's parents and make the child worried. The most frequently mentioned cause of worry was, in fact, being told off, or running the risk of being told off.

This interpretation is plausible, but it is based on inference supplemented by ethnographic information. Is there more direct evidence that children assess emotional reactions in terms of the various implications of a situation rather than in terms of its immediate identity? Gnepp (1983) has offered some suggestive evidence. She presented children aged 3–12 years with pictures depicting a child in an emotionally charged situation. In one condition, the facial expression of the child in the picture was congruent with the picture; in another condition, it was incongruent. For example, a child with a fearful expression (congruent) or a sad expression (incongruent) might be looking at a big spider. For the incongruent condition, the children were asked to gloss the picture with a story, and Gnepp looked at the various strategies that the children adopted for resolving the incongruence. The most frequently adopted strategy for all age groups was an elaboration of the situation. Thus, pursuing the above example, one boy said, "Maybe the boy had a pet fly, and it flew into the spider's web, and the spider ate him up." Among preschoolers, this strategy accounted for almost one half of all resolutions, and among 7- and 12-year-olds, it accounted for about three quarters of all resolutions. Thus, Gnepp's study suggests that, from an early age, children can embed any specific sutiation in a wider context and gauge the protagonist's emotional reaction in terms of this wider context, rather than in terms of the specific situation.

This account draws attention to an interesting irony. Schacter and Singer (1962) stressed that physiological changes are ambiguous cues for emotion because no distinct physiological changes are tied to particular emotions. Schacter and Singer's assumption was that situational cues could serve a disambiguating role. Subjects could assess their current emotional state by noting their current situation. The results reviewed above, however, suggest that situations also carry a great deal of ambiguity, for children and adults alike. The solution to this problem is not to search for some further source of disambiguating information, but to admit that one situation can provoke several emotions. Alternatively, the same situation can provoke different emotions at different times, depending on the implication that is most apparent.[4]

The Emergence of Subclusters

Because certain situations provoke more than one emotion, it is possible, as was noted earlier, to identify subclusters of emotion. Terms like *excited* and *happy*, or *afraid* and *worried*, cluster together because similar situations are mentioned as likely to provoke each emotion.

How are such subclusters related to one another? One possibility is that the basic emotions, as described by Ekman (1973)—namely, fear, happiness, anger, sadness, surprise, and disgust—serve as anchor points for the various subclusters, and the relationships among anchor points remain constant throughout development and universal across cultures. For example, one can envisage that, at all stages of development and in

[4]One potent factor that is likely to influence what is most apparent is the mood or the emotion that the subject brings to the situation, rather than any change in the situation itself (Bower, 1981).

all cultures, "anger" is more closely related to "sadness" than to "happiness." The elaboration of subclusters could occur within such a model, but only around the relatively fixed anchor points of the basic emotions.

However, it is also conceivable that a different type of organization emerges. Harris and Hardman (1984) found that the situations that provoke emotion are rapidly appraised in culturally specific terms. For example, one 6-year-old in Nepal, when asked what would make him proud, replied, "Being able to study [at school]." Such a reply makes sense when it is noted that many Rai children do not get the opportunity to go to school or are forced to leave school early to help their parents, especially if their parents are poor. Among Western children, where schooling is not regarded as a privilege, such a reply is hard to imagine. Similarly, many Nepalese children said that they would be shy if they met important or respected people, such as any elder of the village. Children in England and Holland, on the other hand, mentioned shyness in connection with strangers or unfamiliar people. The replies of the Nepalese children can be attributed to the fact that they are expected to show some respectful hesitation in front of all adults, even when those adults are highly familiar to them. Geertz (1959) described a similar phenomenon among Javanese children.

Given that the situations that provoke emotion are so rapidly appraised in culturally specific terms, one can imagine that the subclusters that emerge will also be defined in culturally specific terms and will reflect particular themes important to the culture. Such themes might eventually produce alignments or realignments of the basic emotions that would not be at all congruent with Western expectations. One example of such a culturally specified theme was described by Gerber (1975). Her adolescent informants in Samoa tended to cluster "fed up," "lazy," "reluctant," and "suppressed anger" together because they were all associated with the obligation to work for one's parents, an obligation that was resented and was perceived as onerous. This particular cultural theme does not necessarily result in a culturally specific realignment of the basic set of emotions, but a second example, from Rosaldo (1980), does suggest that this can occur. She pointed out that anger among the Ilongot was seen, at least in part, as a positive emotion; their headhunting rituals celebrated the expression of anger, which is associated with the strength and vigor of youth. In this culture, then, one can envisage a much closer alignment of "happiness" and "anger" than we would expect.

In summary, the data available at present suggest that, once a child is beyond infancy, the lens through which he or she perceives a situation, and its implications, is strongly influenced by the culture of the society.

An important research task for the future is to learn about the effects of this lens. Does it lead the child to realign the basic emotions in ways that are culturally specific? Alternatively, does the child elaborate cultural themes around a set of basic emotions, whose relationship to one another remains fixed throughout development and across cultures?

Ambivalence

The various cluster analyses described earlier suggest that children rapidly make a sharp distinction between situations that give rise to negative emotions and those that give rise to positive emotions. Although children and adults alike refer to situations that can give rise to one or more positive emotions, they rarely, if ever, refer to situations that can provoke both a positive and a negative emotion. Hence, we might expect children to have some difficulty in admitting that certain situations can actually provoke such ambivalent feelings. Harter (1982) reported an interesting set of findings on this issue. She asked children aged 3 to 12 years to describe situations that would be likely to provoke a mixture of feelings. Young children found this task virtually impossible. At a somewhat later age, children were able to describe two successive situations, rather than a single episode. For example, they might say, "I was *mad* when my brother Peter got into my stuff and wrecked it—very mad—and then I was very *happy* when Peter put the stuff back into shape." Responses such as these typically emerged at around age 7. Finally, at around 9 years of age, the children began to describe situations that would be likely to provoke two simultaneous feelings, one positive, the other negative. For example, "When I went horseback riding by myself, I was glad 'cause it was good to be away from my brothers and sisters, but I was *lonesome* all by myself 'cause there was no-one to talk to." Harter's results are very intriguing. However, there is one serious objection to the technique that she used. It could be argued that even young children appreciate that one situation can provoke conflicting feelings; they simply find it difficult to remember or to invent such situations. Harter's developmental findings may therefore reflect the fact that childen get better at remembering or inventing illustrative situations, rather than at developing insight into ambivalence.

One solution to this problem is to present children with situations to judge rather than to get them to invent their own. This was the procedure adopted by Oosterhoff and Meerum Terwogt (1982) and, with certain additional controls, by Harris (1983a). In this latter study, children aged 6 and 10 were told stories and had to decide how the main character in the story would feel. The stories contained situations that would be likely to engender an emotional conflict. For example, in one story, the protagonist hears a dog barking just as he is falling asleep. He goes downstairs, opens the door, and there he discovers his dog Lassie. Lassie has been lost all day. Now she has come home, but her ear has been cut in a fight. This story is intended to describe a situation likely to provoke both happiness—that the dog has now come home—and also sadness because the dog has been hurt in a fight. After listening to the story, children were asked to say which of four emotions they would feel: happiness, sadness, anger, or fear. It was stressed that they could say yes to as many or as few of these emotions as they wished. Both age groups were often likely to focus on only one component of the stories: either the positive component or the negative component. Thus, if they said that the events in the story would make them feel happy, they denied that they would feel any of the three negative emotions, and vice versa. Nevertheless, the tendency to ignore either the positive emotion or the negative emotions was much stronger in the younger children. The older children were more likely to mention both a positive and a negative emotion.

These results show that children of 6–10 years, and especially 6-year-olds, do not readily admit a conflict of feelings; they stress either their positive or their negative feelings, but not both. Other explanations of the results can be ruled out on the basis of various control procedures. First, the children's memory of the stories was assessed to make sure that they remembered each component of the conflict and were not simply forgetting half the story. The recall protocols showed that younger and older children alike found it very easy to remember the entire story, even though they appeared to be ignoring part of it in describing their emotional reactions. Second, the stories were also presented in a different format so that the conflict between the two components was eliminated. For example, in the case of the story about Lassie, the children were told one version in which Lassie comes home after being lost and another version in which Lassie has not been lost but arrives with a cut ear. Under these circumstances, younger and older children alike admitted that the positive version (i.e., Lassie coming home after being lost) would make them feel happy, whereas the other version would make them feel sad. Thus, we can be sure that, when the children considered each component in isolation, they admitted that opposing feelings would be aroused by the two components. However, when the two components were embedded in the same story, one of the conflicting feelings was ignored. Finally, it is worth mentioning that the children were asked explicitly at the end of the experiment whether one could feel happy and sad at the same time. Many of them, especially the younger children, said that this was impossible: "You can't make your mouth go up and down at the same time," explained one child. "They're the opposite of one another," said another. Those children who did admit that it was possible often justified their assertion by offering a convincing example. For example, one child said, " 'Cos I feel happy and sad at the same time like at the dinner table—when I can eat but they're quarrelling." Another child recalled what had happened a few days before we spoke to him: "You're happy because you're going to the fair but you're sad because President Sadat has been shot."

These results confirm and extend the basic findings of Harter (1982). Whether they are asked to offer situations likely to provoke mixed feelings, are asked to identify the feelings that would be provoked in a conflict situation, or are asked explicitly about the possibility of simultaneously feeling a positive and a negative emotion, children of approximately 6 years are loath to admit the existence of ambivalence. In contrast, older children, of 10 years, are more ready to do this.

Are there circumstances in which 6-year-olds will admit to the existence of both positive and negative feelings? This is an important issue, because if we can find circumstances in which young children do acknowledge the existence of such mixed feelings, we will be helped to formulate an account of their denial in the situations described above. Harris (Experiment 3, 1983a) made use of a task devised by Olthof, van Eck, and Meerum Terwogt (1982) and was able to get 6-year-olds to admit to both positive and negative feelings. The children were told stories that invoked two successive episodes, the first negative and the second positive, such as having a quarrel on the way home from school, and then getting an unexpected gift at home afterward.[5] These stories did not confront the child with two conflicting components embedded in the same event, as in the story about Lassie described earlier; rather, the conflict was created by two successive episodes. Simple though it appears, the admission of emotional conflict in this task involves quite a lot of knowledge on the part of the child. First, it requires that children understand that an emotion can persist even when the situation that prompted it is over. Second, they must be able to conceive of two concurrent emotions—one connected with the earlier episode and one connected with the later episode—and grasp that one's emotional reaction to the first situation will not be replaced by one's reaction to the second. The results showed that both age groups, 6- and 10-year-old alike, were quite good at appreciating that such successive episodes would engender a conflict of emotions. This appreciation came out in several ways. First,

---

[5]In order to simplify a somewhat complex study, the order of the two episodes was not counterbalanced. Hence, the data pertain only to negative episodes followed by positive episodes. Intuitively, it seems likely that negative emotion colors positive emotion more strongly than the reverse.

when the children were asked at the end of the stories how they would feel (happy, sad, or both happy and sad), most of them said that they would feel both happy and sad. The children were also asked to say how they would feel using a nonverbal scale. They were shown a row of nine circles running from left to right. The left-most circle had a schematic sad facial expression drawn in it, with a down-turned mouth and drooping eyebrows, and the right-most circle had a schematic happy facial expression, with a suitably upturned mouth. The circles in between were blank, but the children were told that they represented increasing happiness in one direction (i.e., toward the right) and increasing sadness in the other (i.e., toward the left). The children frequently chose the middle circles to indicate how they would feel after the two episodes, again providing graphic evidence that they appreciated that one would feel neither completely sad nor completely happy. Finally, asked to explain their choice, many children referred to each of the two episodes. For example, they would say, "Well, you'd feel sad 'cos the cat died, but happy 'cos your Dad reads you a nice story." Or, "You'd be happy playing marbles, but you'd still think about the mirror you broke." The tendency to admit the persisting influence of the first episode was weaker in the 6-year-olds than in the 10-year-olds, just as Olthof et al. (1982) had reported; nevertheless, the majority of children in each age group did admit its influence.

These data show that the conclusion of Harris and Olthof (1982) was premature. Even at 6 years of age, most children realize that one's emotional state need not be congruent with the current situation; it can be a residue of some earlier situation that persists despite encounters with later events, even events that provoke an emotion opposite to the earlier reaction. This conclusion is important because it suggests that, from an early age, children may be sophisticated in diagnosing the cause of their own emotional state or that of another person. They do not confine their attention to the immediate situation but can look appropriately beyond it. In concrete terms, therefore, they can understand that their mother's irritation may have been caused not by their current behavior, but by some incident earlier in the day. In the final section, children's insight into the persistence of emotion is discussed in more detail. The last experiment also shows that 6- and 10-year-olds do admit that one would have mixed or ambivalent feelings after two successive episodes, one negative and the other positive. Apparently, children find it easier to admit ambivalence about two successive episodes than about a single event with two conflicting components, a conclusion that Harter (1982) has proposed.

Why do 6-year-olds admit to mixed feelings when confronted by two successive episodes, but not when confronted by a single episode simultaneously combining two conflicting components? The most plausible account is one that focuses on how the child goes about analyzing emotionally charged episodes. Suppose the child examines all the episodes in a story, but each episode is examined only until a single emotional reaction has been identified. In other words, there is an exhaustive search across all episodes but not within each episode. Such a process of analysis would predict the current pattern of results quite readily. Faced with two discrete and successive episodes, the child would examine each, identifying the emotional reaction appropriate to one and then the other. On the other hand, if two conflicting components are embedded in the same episode, the child should discontinue the search process as soon as one emotional reaction has been identified, thereby denying any mixed feelings.

This account makes several clear predictions. As long as the conflicting components of a single episode are intertwined (i.e., they involve the same actions by the same person or agent at one moment in time), an exhaustive analysis should be very difficult, and so the acknowledgment of mixed feelings should be unlikely. On the other hand, if the conflicting components involve different actions carried out by different people that are unrelated but coincident, the process of exhaustive analysis should be facilitated. Equally, to the extent that an adult is able to encourage an exhaustive search by calling the child's attention first to one conflicting component then to the other component, the child should be more ready to admit to mixed feelings. Such a process of guided search is, of course, reminiscent of certain clinical procedures: the patient is asked to recall an emotionally charged episode and to dwell on its potentially multiple implications, under the guidance of the therapist.

In summary, the results presented in this section suggest three conclusions. First, 10-year-olds spontaneously acknowledge the existence of mixed feelings, but 6-year-olds rarely do so. Second, 6-year-olds can be prompted to admit to the existence of mixed feelings if they are confronted by two quite distinct episodes. Third, to the extent that the 6-year-old's difficulty resides in his or her disinclination to exhaustively analyze a situation for its emotional implications, it seems likely that a parent or a therapist could help the child toward greater awareness by prompting the child to scrutinize those multiple implications.

THE DURATION OF EMOTION

How much weight do young children attach to the current situation in assessing what emotion someone is feeling? Do they appreciate that emotion sometimes persists for hours or days? Harris and Olthof (1982) concluded that young children think that the current situation rather than any earlier episode is likely to dictate one's emotion. In the previous section, data were reported that cast doubt on this conclusion. Although young children were sometimes apt to ignore the enduring impact of an earlier episode, as noted by Olthof *et al.* (1982), for the most part they could acknowledge that an earlier emotion would persist. We have now carried out several studies in which children have been questioned explicitly about the persistence of emotion. The studies have involved children aged 4, 6, and 10, and a clear pattern can be observed across the various studies (Harris, Guz, Lipian, & Man-Shu, in press). The children were told a story about either a positive episode (e.g., being given a new bicycle) or a negative episode (e.g., having a bicycle stolen). They were then shown a set of pictures depicting facial expressions ranging from very happy to very sad and were asked to pick out a facial expression to indicate how the story protagonist would feel immediately after the episode. They went on to indicate the facial expression that would be appropriate at various points in time after the episode. Once they had made their choice, they were asked to explain why they had chosen different expressions at different points in time.

The results can be best described by looking at each of the three age groups in turn. The 4-year-olds judged that an emotional reaction wanes gradually over time. Figure 1 illustrates their choice of an appropriate facial expression for the story protagonist at three points in time following either a positive or a negative story episode. The 4-year-olds

FIG. 1. Four-year-olds' judgment of emotional state at three points in time following either a positive or negative story episode.

typically explained their patterns of choice in situational terms. They described some change in the original situation, or they described some entirely new situation. In either case, they introduced facts that had not been mentioned or implied by the experimenter. For example, following the episode about the pet dog that has died, children might explain their choice by saying that at first the story character would be very unhappy, but later on, he or she would be given another dog or would be doing something else like going out to play. A minority of children, on the other hand, offered mentalistic explanations. They referred to the possibility that the story character might forget or stop thinking about the initial episode.

The data for the 6-year-old children are given in Figure 2. They, too, thought that happiness and sadness wane gradually. These results essentially confirm those reported by Taylor and Harris (1983) and by Harris (Experiment 1, 1983a) but extend these earlier results by showing that our 6-year-olds judged that emotion wanes gradually after positive as well as negative episodes. The 6-year-olds also gave mentalistic explanations somewhat more often than the 4-year-olds, but even for the 6-year-olds, situational explanations were the most popular.

The results for the 10-year-olds are given in Figure 3. Like the 6-year-olds, they judged that emotion wanes gradually over time, but most of their explanations (66%) focused on mentalistic factors, whereas only a minority (approximately 30%) invoked situational factors.

FIG. 2. Six-year-olds' judgment of emotional state at three points in time following either a positive or negative story episode.

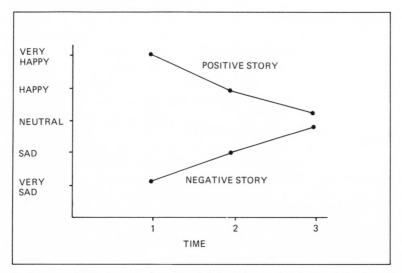

FIG. 3. Ten-year-olds' judgment of emotional state at three points in time following either a positive or negative story episode.

Across the three age groups, therefore, two different patterns are apparent: the younger children and the older children alike judged that an emotional reaction wanes gradually over time. On the other hand, whereas the younger children explained changes in emotion predominantly in terms of external situational factors, the older children increasingly cited mentalistic factors. On a speculative note, these data can be explained in the following way. We need to distinguish between two hypothetical components: a measuring instrument and a theoretical component. An analogy may be helpful in clarifying this distinction. In order to study heat, physicists need to have a measuring instrument, such as a thermometer, and a theory with which to explain the measurements that they record. Conceptual progress can be brought about either by a refinement in the measuring instrument that leads to more accurate data-collection, or by a theoretical insight that highlights or reinterprets existing data.

The child who is trying to make sense of his or her emotional experience also needs these two components: (a) an emotional "thermometer" to record the intensity of a felt emotion at different points in time and (b) a theory to account for the changes that are observed. Our results suggest that even the 4-year-old can make fairly accurate recordings on his or her emotional thermometer but is less inclined than the 10-year-old to conceptualize those variations as being attributable to internal psychological processes.

CONCLUSIONS

Pulling together the results of the various experiments, we are now in a position to try to state just what young children do know about their emotional life and what remains for them to learn. The proposal made by Harris and Olthof (1982) was that young children think of emotion as being a direct and unique response to a given situation. In contrast, older children were said to regard emotion as being mediated by an inner mental state that allows them to conceive of a mismatch between one's private feelings and one's public display, and to appreciate how that inner experience can be redirected by thinking about something else.

I will first review the major findings of the chapter and then ask to what extent they require a revision of the framework offered by Harris and Olthof (1982). First, we have seen that young children rapidly learn some of the links that exist between situations and emotions. Such knowledge is additional testimony to the claim that young children have a good deal of causal knowledge (Bullock & Gelman, 1979) and are not confused about the relationship between cause and effect. Although there have been some claims to the contrary (e.g., Bretherton & Beeghly, 1982), I find no indication in young children's use of emotion terms that they have a truly mentalistic conception of emotion. The comments may be provoked by and may be intended to refer to the purely behavioral manifestations of emotion that young children can observe and anticipate. Such precocious knowledge can be readily assimilated by the framework offered by Harris and Olthof (1982).

The second set of data reviewed showed that children and adults alike, whether they live in Western urban communities or remote, non-Western rural communities, mention certain situations in connection with the provocation of not just one but several emotions. These several emotions tend to be of the same valence. For example, in our data from Nepal, a single situation—namely, failing to complete a task for one's parents—was mentioned in connection with two negative emotions: fear and sadness. It seems likely that children and adults are focusing on different implications of the same situation in such cases. An important research task for the future is to discover how children come to understand that different implications are associated with different emotions.[6]

Because situations that provoke both positive and negative emotion are rarely mentioned, a basic division emerges for all age groups between positive and negative emotions. However, when children are asked

---

[6]Stein and Jewett (in press) reported an interesting study showing how young children identify distinct determinants of sadness, anger, and fear within the same situation.

explicitly about situations likely to provoke both a positive and a negative emotion, this developmentally invariant picture is replaced by a clear picture of developmental change. According to a variety of measures, younger children, age 6, tend to deny or ignore the existence of emotional conflict, focusing on either the positive or the negative aspect of the conflict, but not on both. In contrast, older children, age 10, although sometimes focusing on only one component, typically do acknowledge that a conflict between positive and negative emotions is likely and can identify the two emotions appropriately. How well do these conclusions fit into the framework suggested by Harris and Olthof (1982)? For the most part, the fit is a reasonable one. If young children assume that there is a direct one-to-one relationship between a situation and an emotion, they would indeed have difficulty in acknowledging the way in which one's mental appraisal of a situation can focus on two different components, each giving rise to a different and potentially conflicting emotion. On the other hand, to the extent that older children do acknowledge the role of such cognitive processes, they should be much more willing to admit the possibility of ambivalence. However, it must also be admitted that, as yet, we have no established explanation for children's increasing willingness with age to admit the existence of mixed emotions. It might be attributable to their greater appreciation of the role of cognitive processes in emotion, but other explanations are possible (Harris, 1983a).

The findings on children's insight into the duration of emotion indicate two things. First, children from 4 to 10 years of age judge that happiness and sadness wane gradually in intensity over time. Second, younger children explain emotional change in terms of an alteration in the external situation, not in terms of inner mental processes, whereas older children are more likely to focus on mental processes rather than on the external situation. These findings indicate that the developmental change proposed by Harris and Olthof (1982) is partially correct: although young children can appreciate that emotion persists beyond the current situation and wanes gradually over time, their explanation of that time course differs from that typically offered by older children.

A final cautionary remark is warranted. The research that we have carried out—and, indeed, most of the research that has been reviewed in this chapter—examines children's knowledge about hypothetical situations, or about situations recalled from their own past. At no point have children been questioned about any emotion that they are currently experiencing. We should not assume that their knowledge remains constant across these two cases. A current emotional experience may help or hinder emotional insight. An important research task for the future is to investigate these possibilities.

ACKNOWLEDGMENTS

I thank Gabrielle Guz, Paula Levin, Nadja Reissland, Dale Tiller, and Andrew Tolmie for their helpful comments on the manuscript.

REFERENCES

Borke, H. Interpersonal perception of young children: Egocentricism or empathy. *Developmental Psychology*, 1971, 5, 263–269.
Bower, G. H. Mood and memory. *American Psychologist*, 1981, 36, 129–148.
Bretherton, I., & Beeghly, M. Talking about internal states: The acquisition of an explicit theory of mind. *Developmental Psychology*, 1982, 18, 906–921.
Bullock, M., & Gelman, R. Preschool children's assumptions about cause and effect: Temporal ordering. *Child Development*, 1979, 50, 89–96.
Dunn, J., & Kendrick, C. *Siblings*. Cambridge: Harvard University Press, 1982.
Ekman, P. *Darwin and facial expression: A century of research in review*. New York: Academic Press, 1973.
Flavell, J. H., & Wellman, H. M. Metamemory. In R. V. Kail & J. W. Hagen (Eds.), *Perspectives on the development of memory and cognition*. Hillsdale, N.J.: Erlbaum, 1977.
Geertz, H. The vocabulary of emotion: A study in Javanese socialization processes. *Psychiatry*, 1959, 22, 225–237.
Gerber, E. *The cultural patterning of emotion in Samoa*. Unpublished doctoral dissertation, Anthropology Department, University of California, San Diego, 1975.
Gnepp, J. Children's social sensitivity: Inferring emotions from conflicting cues. *Developmental Psychology*, 1983, 19, 805–814.
Hardman, C. E. The psychology of conformity and self-expression among the Lohorung Rai of East Nepal. In P. Heelas & A. Lock (Eds.), *Indigenous psychologies*. London: Academic Press, 1981.
Harris, P. L. Children's understanding of the link between situation and emotion. *Journal of Experimental Child Psychology*, 1983, 36, 490–509. (a)
Harris, P. L. Infant cognition. In P. M. Mussen (Ed.), *Carmichael's manual of child psychology. Vol. 2: Infancy* (ed. by M. M. Haith & J. J. Campos). New York: Wiley, 1983. (b)
Harris, P. L. *The child's insight into emotion*. Paper presented at the Conference on the Social Psychology of Emotion, Oxford University, June 23, 1984.
Harris, P. L., & Hardman, C. E. *Children's knowledge of the situations that provoke emotion in a remote Himalayan community*. Unpublished manuscript, Department of Experimental Psychology, Oxford University, 1984.
Harris, P. L., & Olthof, T. The child's concept of emotion. In G. Butterworth & P. Light (Eds.), *The individual and the social in cognitive development*. Sussex, U.K.: Harvester, 1982.
Harris, P. L., Olthof, T., & Meerum Terwogt, M. Children's knowledge of emotion. *Journal of Child Psychology and Psychiatry*, 1981, 22, 247–261.
Harris, P. L., Guz, G. R., Lipian, M. S., & Man-Shu, Z. Insight into the time-course of emotion among Western and Chinese children. *Child Development*, in press.
Harris, P. L., Olthof, T., & Meerum Terwogt, M. *Children's knowledge of the situations that provoke emotion*. Unpublished manuscript, Department of Experimental Psychology, Oxford University, 1984.
Harter, S. Children's understanding of multiple emotions: A cognitive developmental approach. In A. Collins (Ed.), *Proceedings of the Piaget Society, June 1979*. Hillsdale, N.J.: Erlbaum, 1982.

Kay, D. A., & Anglin, J. M. Overextension and underextension in the child's expressive and receptive speech. *Journal of Child Language*, 1982, *9*, 83–98.

Klinnert, M. D., Campos, J. J., Sorce, J. F., Emde, R. N., & Svejda, M. Emotions as behavior regulators: Social referencing in infancy. In R. Plutchik & H. Kellerman (Eds.), *Emotions in early development*. New York: Academic Press, 1982.

Lutz, C. The domain of emotion words on Ifaluk Atoll. *American Ethnologist*, 1982, *9*, 113–128.

Olthof, T., van Eck, O., & Meerum Terwogt, M. *Children's knowledge of the integration of successive emotions*. Unpublished manuscript, Department of Developmental Psychology, Free University, Amsterdam, Holland, 1982.

Oosterhoff, T., & Meerum Terwogt, M. *Development in the processing of multiple emotions*. Unpublished manuscript, Department of Developmental Psychology, Free University, Amsterdam, Holland, 1982.

Piaget, J. *Judgment and reasoning in the child*. Totowa, N.J.: Littlefield, Adams, 1969. (Originally published, 1928.)

Rosaldo, M. Z. *Knowledge and passion*. Cambridge: Cambridge University Press, 1980.

Rosch, E. Principles of categorization. In E. Rosch & B. Lloyd (Eds.), *Cognition and categorization*. Hillsdale, N.J.: Erlbaum, 1978.

Saarni, C. Children's understanding of display rules for expressive behavior. *Developmental Psychology*, 1979, *15*, 424–429.

Schacter, S., & Singer, J. E. Cognitive, social and physiological determinants of emotional state. *Psychological Review*, 1962, *69*, 379–399.

Schwartz, G. E., & Weinberger, D. A. Patterns of emotional responses to affective situations: Relations among happiness, sadness, anger, fear, depression and anxiety. *Motivation and Emotion*, 1980, *4*, 175–191.

Smith, E. E., & Medin, D. L. *Categories and concepts*. Cambridge: Harvard University Press, 1981.

Stein, N. L., & Jewett, J. L. A conceptual analysis of the meaning of negative: Implications for a theory of development. In C. E. Izard & P. Read (Eds.), *Measuring emotion*. Cambridge: Cambridge University Press, in press.

Taylor, D. A., & Harris, P. L. Knowledge of the link between emotion and memory among normal and maladjusted boys. *Developmental Psychology*, 1983, *19*, 832–838.

Trabasso, T., Stein, N. L., & Johnson, L. R. Children's knowledge of events: A causal analysis of story structure. In G. Bower (Ed.), *Advances in learning and motivation* (Vol. 15). New York: Academic Press, 1981.

Wittgenstein, L. *Philosophical investigations*. Oxford: Blackwell, 1953.

9

Indirect Processes in Affect Socialization

CAROLYN SAARNI

The vast majority of socialization studies and most of socialization theory have been guided by social learning tenets of observational learning and instrumental conditioning. The emphasis in this chapter is not on these direct methods of socialization but on *indirect* processes that influence the form and course of emotional development. These indirect processes are embedded in interpersonal relations, verbal and nonverbal communication, and organismic constraints imposed by the developmental level (or complexity) of the individuals involved. The kinds of indirect processes examined here emphasize how expectancies are acquired for determining how one is to feel and how one is to express one's feelings "appropriately."

It should also be pointed out to the reader that much of the material presented here is a rather suppositional and personally arbitrary attempt to raise and clarify issues in affect socialization. To facilitate the reader's bearing in mind this personal construction of affect socialization, I shall freely use the first person pronoun throughout this chapter.

The notion that emotional socialization may be quite sensitive to expectations rather than being primarily or only shaped by observing models of emotional behavior is a perspective that is also shared by some researchers in sex-role socialization (e.g., Lueptow, 1980) and in children's behavioral conduct (e.g., Chapman, 1981). Attribution theorists also focus on the role that expectation plays in focusing our attention

CAROLYN SAARNI • Department of Counseling, Sonoma State University, Rohnert Park, California 94928.

on certain "causes" of behavior and choices of action. In clinical contexts, cognitive therapists emphasize how distorted expectations contribute substantially to maladaptive mood states. Anthropologists also stress the significance of expectations held by a culture about emotional states and displays (for example, see Chapter 2 by Harkness and Super in this book). Even more emphatically, Hochschild (1979), from a sociological perspective, has contended that we actually create some of our emotional states through the use of *feeling rules*, which function as cultural (or subcultural) expectations for normative emotional responses in assorted situations. What we see here is an increasing convergence on the importance of belief systems, which function as expectations, which mediate what we feel and how and whether we express our feelings.

Children clearly develop expectancies about emotions, that is, beliefs about what to feel in assorted situations and beliefs about how and whether to show what one feels to others. What is remarkably missing from the research on affect development is *how* these beliefs are acquired. The social learning theorist might respond with "This acquisition is obviously due to observational learning and patterns of reinforcement." But is it? Perhaps a cognitive developmentalist would respond with "An expectancy is a generalized scheme, and therefore, its developmental course would be similar to the acquisition of any other cognitive scheme." Finally, a hypnotherapist might assert, "Suggestions are internalized as expectancies only when they stimulate the child's imaginal involvement and appear to offer useful ways of coping." I am not about to argue the relative merits of these three or other possible positions on how expectancies are developed in children about emotional experience; however, I am intrigued by some of the notions that hypnotherapy might provide us in trying to understand how outside "influence" does, indeed, become influential and is eventually internalized as a personal expectancy. Attribution theory also has much to offer in this regard, although little work has been done with children wherein the very process of expectancy *formation* was examined.

It might be useful at this point to try to distinguish three related concepts: expectation, suggestion, and expectancy, especially as they may be related to emotional development. Somewhat arbitrarily, I am going to propose that *expectations* be thought of as initially having their source outside the child. For example, Mother expects Mary to feel angry at her when Daddy is asked to move out of the house, or in a less extreme example, Mother expects Mary to inhibit her disgust for Grandma's unappetizing-looking casserole. If the expectation is attended to by the child and is experienced as meaningful, it becomes a *suggestion*. Thus, expectations are held by others about Mary, but only if she responds to the expectation as a *credible* perspective for making sense of her experience will the expectation be responded to as a suggestion. The point in interjecting the notion of *suggestion* here is to emphasize that others' expectations are often not attended to or not processed as meaningful. Obviously, children and adults also resist and defy others' suggestions, but such rejection means that the expectation was first comprehended, appraised as a suggestion, and then rejected. An irrelevant expectation is experienced as simply tangential; it is not credible. The individual neither assimilates it nor accommodates to it. (The maturation of attentional processes, especially within interpersonal contexts, may well be involved here as well.)

If the suggestion is accepted, the process of expectancy formation begins. I propose that the formation of an expectancy, which is essentially an internalized suggestion, is an accommodative act, whereas once the expectancy is "in place," it functions assimilatively, that is, via generalizability to novel, albeit similar, situations. But how does a suggestion become internalized as an expectancy? What accommodative process does the child go through?

To clarify this murk, I examined the hypnosis literature and was impressed by the work done on therapeutic metaphor (cf. Gordon, 1978). What a number of hypnosis researchers have proposed is that the hypnotist's suggestion stimulates a "transderivational search" within the subject. What this means is that we respond to the suggestion by checking through our recall of experiences to find something that seems to fit the suggestion, at least in part. We may indeed find something in our memory that is related to the suggestion, thereby rendering the suggestion credible, but we can still reject, resist, or defy the suggestion. For the suggestion to be accepted, it has to be motivating: it has to offer some notion of gain, of improved coping, of mastery, or of self-validation, and so forth. However, the acceptance or desirability of the suggestion as being a credible perspective for making sense of our experience still does not indicate internalization of the suggestion into an expectancy. That occurs after the accepted situation has been tried out and found to be *valid* in making sense of our experience and after the motivational source is indeed satisfied (e.g., self-confirmation or gaining approval).

To summarize, an individual attends to someone's expectation about her or his anticipated emotional experience, sees that it credibly fits with some of her or his own associations, and then responds to the other's expectation as a suggestion. The suggestion is scanned for its "value": Why should it be adopted? If it is adopted or accepted, the person applies the suggestion to the emotional situation to see if, indeed, the emotional experience can be made congruent with the suggestion. This "making the emotional experience congruent with the suggestion" is perhaps the crux of the accommodative process that the individual goes through in the course of acquiring an expectancy. If the emotional experience can be confirmed as being congruent with the suggestion, what has occurred is both a validation process and the first step in internalizing the suggestion as a personal expectancy. Repeated confirmations of the suggestion as congruent with how one is now making sense of one's emotional experience consolidate the personal expectancy, and it becomes an increasingly assimilative feature of the individual's emotional repertoire.

At this point, I need to clarify some assumptions embedded in the preceding hypothesized sequence of how something originating from the "outside" becomes incorporated into the "inside." First, I assume that communication is occurring in either or both the verbal and the nonverbal channels, although the expectation may not be consciously or intentionally communicated. (This may be particularly true of the nonverbal channels of communication.) Second, this sequence is not posed as being somehow mutually exclusive of direct modes of socializing influence as in social learning and instrumental conditioning. Indeed, the proposed sequence might well also occur as part of why a model is observed and imitated or why a particular contingency is found to be gratifying.

A third assumption has to do with the phrase used previously: "emotional repertoire." I am assuming that human emotions follow a developmental course and become increasingly differentiated and integrated systems by which experience is organized. Implicated here is the integration of affect and cognition, which reciprocally elaborate one another. The result is that even as the individual acquires more complex cognitions, which permit more complex emotions, more complex emotions, in turn, provoke more complex cognitions. This dynamic of reciprocal elaboration may be seen in the acquisition process of a personal expectancy: a more complex expectation, if ultimately internalized as a personal expectancy, leads to more finely tuned emotional responses that accommodate to variable contextual and attributional nuances. The more finely tuned emotional responses not only accommodate to the context, but they also subtlely alter it, thus necessitating increasing complexity of cognition.

A concrete illustration of the above, rather abstract presuppositions is as follows:

> Heather (3 years, 11 months) had been informed for some time before her mother's departure that her mother would be gone a long time (three weeks) but then would return. Several days before the departure, Heather's

grandmother suggested to Heather that she would be feeling sad during her mother's absence. Clinging to her mother, crying, and general distress abruptly escalated, only to be followed a couple of days later by anger that manifested itself as an imperial reserve and detachment. When questioned about why she was staying away from Mommy, Heather answered, "My mommy shouldn't make me sad, so she's bad."

(As the reader may have already surmised, this transaction involved the author and her daughter.) The example illustrates how an expectation was communicated ("She would feel sad"), which was responded to as a credible and valid suggestion (she had felt sad during other, shorter absences). She adopted the suggestion and applied it to the anticipated emotional experience; however, she created almost immediate considerable distress for herself (and for her mother). The termination of the distress and its replacement by angry withdrawal appears to show how the configuration of distressed affective state and behaviors stimulated further reflection on the circumstances of her emotional experience, leading to a more complex appraisal of the emotion-inducing situation. The new attribution (Mommy is bad for making her daughter sad) entails not only a new affect (self-righteous anger) but also new and more subtle assumptions about interpersonal relations.

SELF-GENERATED SUGGESTIONS

In addition to others' being the source of suggestions for how to make sense of one's emotional experience, I also propose that, with the acquisition of self-awareness and some degree of skill in affect labeling, the self can generate suggestions about the self. (Thinking about the self as both agent and object may be useful here.) However, these self-generated suggestions are transformed into genuine self-expectancies only if the conditions of credibility, desirability, and validity are met. I think it also likely that self-generated suggestions about how one is to feel emerge later than responding to externally communicated suggestions about how to feel. Self-generated suggestions may also represent elaborations of earlier internalizations of external suggestions, but the self-generated suggestions are more integrated with the psychological needs and the developmental level of the child, the adolescent, or the adult.

Support is implicit only for the notion that affect labeling and self-awareness are fundamental prerequisites for the development of self-generated suggestions about how one expects to feel. Empirical research has not been undertaken to explore this topic developmentally. There would also appear to be different levels of complexity involved in how one suggests to oneself that one feel or that one express one's affective state in a particular way. The youngster who "tells" herself or himself that roller coasters are not really scary and that she or he will be feeling terrific while swooping around sharp curves at breakneck speeds is using a simpler level of self-suggestion about how to feel than an adolescent or an adult who contemplates a complex intimacy conflict, wherein resolution requires nondefensiveness.

Research, as well as clinical descriptions of self-hypnosis, also implies that one can generate suggestions to oneself that meet the criteria of credibility, desirability, and validity, and that, indeed, one's affective state or observable expressive behavior does appear to be changed (regarding adults, see Hilgard, 1977; regarding children, see Gardner & Olness, 1981).

In these two examples and in the self-hypnosis work, the desirability component of self-suggestions about how to feel appears to represent attempts at coping (or protecting one's intrapsychic adjustment). Elsewhere, I have discussed how personal display rules serve a similar function by affecting expressive displays (Saarni, 1982). Personal display rules appear to function as coping strategies that allow the individual to regulate self-perceived affective equilibrium by altering affective expressive behavior. Personal display rules may be motivated by the need to relieve the discomfort of negative emotions by transforming their behavioral expression.

Also relevant here is Hochschild's (1979) discussion of feeling rules, in which she contends that we can actually create our emotional state by using assorted strategies for modifying our current feelings (e.g., by altering our breathing rate, by using secondary appraisal of the situation, and so on). I distinguish self-generated suggestions about how to feel from both Hochschild's feeling rules and personal display rules, in that the self-generated suggestions can structure emotional response (including state and behavior) in *future* or anticipated situations. Hochschild's feeling rules apply to that moment of discrepancy between what one is *currently* feeling and what one thinks one "ought" to feel—the latter referring usually to normative, customary affective responses, as in airline hostesses' "automatically" functioning in an agreeable, gracious manner. (Hochschild studied this particular group of employees.) Personal display rules also affect current expressive behavior and are provoked when one's "vulnerability barometer" signals too great a discomfort with some present affective state (e.g., as in smiling during excruciating anxiety). (See Saarni, 1982, for further distinctions among feeling rules, personal display rules, cultural display rules, and direct deception.)

HOW EXPECTANCIES MAY BE ACQUIRED IN ADULTHOOD

Looking at the "end product" in adulthood, so to speak, may be a suitable way to generate hypotheses or reinterpretations of child data for how expectancies influence subsequent emotional experience. From the attribution perspective, Jones and McGillis (1976) suggested that expectancies are formed with different rationales. They specified the following classification of expectancies, which are in the context of attributions about another's behavior or about one's own:

1. Category-based expectancies, which mean that the inferential generalizations attributed to the target person (self or other) stem from her or his membership in a social category (e.g., gender, ethnic group, or astrological sign).
2. Target-based expectancies, which are the inferences attributed to a target person (or self) that are based on particular information, about the target person or the self, that one has had access to.

Relative to self-directed expectancies, Baumeister and Cooper (1981) extended Jones and McGillis's classification by hypothesizing that the more an individual perceives an expectancy as unique to him or her (i.e., as target-based), the more likely it is that he or she will fulfill the expectancy. Likewise, if membership in a category is perceived to be a function of choice (e.g., choosing to be a member of a political party), then an expectancy based on this intentionally chosen category will also be more likely to be fulfilled. More specifically, Baumeister and Cooper examined how expectancies could be manipulated in order to determine whether the public expectation of an emotion "caused" the emotion subsequently experienced. They suggested to subjects three different expectancy rationales regarding why they would experience inhibition (i.e., anxiety) in their subsequent singing performance. There was also a fourth, control group who received no suggestions about emotional experience. What was manipulated here was the rationale for the expectancy of inhibition: (a) personal knowledge about the subject that would be likely to produce inhibition (target-based expectancy as earlier defined); (b) knowledge about others who are similar to the subject, which would be likely to produce inhibition (intentional category-based expectancy); and (c) information about one's coincidental, nonintentional membership in a category that would allegedly produce inhibition (i.e., one's birth order was the "basis" for the expectancy inhibition). Only the first two expectancy manipulations resulted in a significant effect on the emotional response of the subjects, namely, experiencing inhibiting anxiety over their singing performance.

Baumeister and Cooper reasoned about their results that expectancy rationales that implied that the person's own actions or personality were the justification for the expectancy were most likely to affect the individual's subsequent emotional behavior. Thus, if Person A attributes to Person B an expectation for some particular display of emotional behavior and also indicates that something about B (or people like B), over which B has some volitional control, is the alleged basis for the expectation, then the circumstances are most likely created in which B will indeed experience the subsequent emotional behavior.

This sounds remarkably like a "transderivational search," wherein we search our experience for something that relates to the suggestion (in this case, an attribution), and if something fits (which is also under our control), we are most likely to internalize the suggestion as an expectancy. The motivational source here may be the prospect of self-validation or self-confirmation. Baumeister and Cooper (1981) stated that "subjects were presumably best able to identify with an image of themselves having the expected emotional response when this image was supposedly based on their prior choice behavior" (p. 58). This interpretation seems congruent with a self-validation motive for accepting the suggestion as a credible and valid perspective for anticipated emotional response.

CHILDREN'S ACQUISITION OF EXPECTANCIES ABOUT EMOTIONAL EXPERIENCE

If my model for how expectancies are formed from internalized suggestions is assumed for the time being to be adequate for adults, how do we account for children's acquisition of expectancies about emotional experience? Several studies clearly document that children have such emotional expectancies. For example, Barden, Zelko, Duncan, and Masters (1980) studied grade-school children's consensual knowledge about the emotions most likely to occur in assorted situations (the latter provided by the authors in vignette form). They concluded that

> children four years of age and older show numerous consensuses in their expectancies regarding emotional responses to a wide variety of experiences. Furthermore, the consensus reached regarding such expectancies is a function of the nature of the experience category considered as well as the age of the child. (p. 975)

From a somewhat more complex perspective about emotional expectancies, Saarni (1979b) asked children (Grades 1, 3, and 5) about when they would expect (a) to mask or hide their feelings; (b) to dissimulate them by substituting other affective expressive behavior; and

(c) to allow their feelings to be openly expressed. That study indicated significant age effects in that older children clearly expected affective expressive behavior to be regulated. All the children could cite instances when masking and dissimulation would occur in their emotional experience, and the older children's proposed situations and rationales for such emotional regulation were predictably more subtle and more numerous.

Harris's research on children's understanding of emotion (see his chapter in this book) indicates further subtlety in children's beliefs about their emotional experience. In a set of recent studies (Harris, 1983), he determined that children as young as 6 years old clearly do have beliefs about emotions as persisting over time and as potentially being in conflict with subsequent affective responses.

Harter's work on children's understanding of multiple emotions (i.e., Harter, 1982; Harter & Buddin, 1983) suggests the kinds of developmental constraints that may limit what sorts of expectations about emotions a child can respond to. As an illustration, consider the previously mentioned example of Heather's distress becoming anger at her mother's anticipated departure. The two affects were experienced sequentially and not simultaneously, as would be predicted by Harter for this age group. Had Heather's grandmother further suggested that Heather would feel sad during her mother's absence but would also feel happy to have her daddy all to herself, Heather (according to Harter's research) would have been constrained by her developmental level to respond to only one of the suggested emotions as credible. At best, she might view as credible each of the two suggested emotions, but they would occur at different times and in different contexts in her anticipated emotional experience (perhaps in the form of feeling sad at the airport right at the time of her mother's departure and later feeling happy at home with her father).

The significance of Harter's research on children's expectancies about emotional experience lies in her cognitive-skills analysis of the progressive levels of understanding of multiple emotions, including the dilemmas presented to the child when the valence of two emotions are in opposition or when two different feelings are provoked by the same target or event (e.g., ambivalence). According to her analysis, what children extrapolate from others' expectations is predicated on what they can cognitively assimilate (e.g., can one experience ambivalence, or is one limited to sequential emotional states?).

It is my opinion that this sort of multiple-emotion dilemma is parallel to the dilemma that a child feels when showing his or her genuine affective state would be "inappropriate," and he or she must dissociate affective state from expressive behavior. In successfully carrying out this dissociation (as in personal or cultural display-rule usage), the child has to cope simultaneously with at least two different sets of emotional information that may be at odds with one another: internal affective cues and his or her beliefs about what constitutes appropriate affective expressive behavior in the situation at hand. Although my own research suggests that many 6-year-olds can reason about this dissociation of two sets of affective information (Saarni, 1979, b), and, indeed, some even spontaneously display it (Saarni, 1984), Harter's work suggests that only in later childhood do children articulate their understanding that two sets of affective information (in this case, two emotional states) may co-occur. Coordinating these two problem areas of how children deal with multiple facets of emotional experience is a rich area for future research. Both problem areas are clearly affected by socialization, but we have virtually no empirical demonstration of how socializing agents affect these complex features of emotional development. A possible exception may be the research discussed in the next section.

Current Research on Children's Expectancies about Emotional Experience

I would like to move beyond theoretical discussion at this point and describe a recent study of children aged 7–13 that examined (a) their *justifications* for why affective expressive behavior "should" be regulated; (b) their expectations about the interpersonal *consequences* of regulated affective expressive behavior; and (c) their beliefs about how they achieve a *balance* in showing their genuine feelings or regulating their expression. It was assumed that justifications, expected consequences, and beliefs about how to balance showing or not showing one's feelings would be isomorphic to internalized expectancies held by children (or adults, for that matter). Such internalized justifications and consequences of an action were also presumed to be more readily traced back to expectations communicated by socializing agents.

The children's expectancies were also examined in conjunction with their parents' (a) attitudes toward children's expressive behavior; (b) perception of their own self-monitoring; and (c) perception of their families' "social climate." This study was limited to a descriptive and inferential approach in attempting to investigate parental influence on children's internalized expectancies. Such parental influence was assumed to be communicated via verbal and nonverbal behavior, which, in turn, functioned in a socializing manner by means of expectations/suggestions and social learning mechanisms.

Finally, developmental differentiation, as indexed by age, was presumed to have a major impact on how children constructed justifications and consequences for regulated affective expressive behavior and on how children believed they achieved a balance in regulated versus spontaneous affective expressive behavior. However, the effects of the parent variables were hypothesized to contribute further unique information about children's beliefs about these aspects of emotional experience, over and beyond what would be explained by development alone.

Sample

The participants were 32 children in Grades 2, 5, and 8 from an urban West Coast parochial school and their parents. The age and sex distribution were nearly equal in this sample. All the subjects gave written informed consent for their participation. No deception was involved.

Procedure for Children

The children were seen individually and interviewed; the stimuli used were four photographed scenarios of children involved in conflicts in which the target child in the scenario could respond with a facial expression that was discrepant from internal affect. This procedure had been followed in an earlier study (Saarni, 1979a) and had yielded significant age differences in reasoning about the dissociation of affect and expressive behavior. In the present study, the children were additionally asked about (a) the rationale or justification for the target child's regulation of expressive behavior; (b) the interpersonal consequences of the regulation of expressive behavior (i.e., what would the interactant think about the target child's expressive behavior in the scenario?); and (c) the child's own rationale for how she or he personally figured out the balance between showing or not showing her or his real feelings to others. (These variables are hereafter referred to as [a] justification, [b] consequences, and [c] balance. Note that the first two refer to the child's responses to the photographed scenarios, and the last refers to the child's belief about her or his own emotional experience.)

Procedure for Parents

The parents individually responded to the author-developed questionnaire, Parent Attitude toward Child Expressiveness Scale (PACES); to Snyder's Self-Monitoring Scale (SMS; Snyder, 1974); and to Moos's Family Environment Scale (FES; Moos, 1974).

A score on PACES provides a measure of the respondent's degree of permissiveness-control allowed toward a child's hypothetical emotional expressive behavior. All items begin with "if my child . . . ," the intent being to elicit the parents' expectations about their response to their own child's expressive behavior. The affective expressive behavior sampled in PACES includes anger (four items), distress (three items), fear (three items), anxiety or nervousness (three items), interest or curiosity (three items), happiness (three items), and disgust (one item). A copy of the PACE Scale appears at the end of this chapter, with additional information on test–retest reliability, interrater reliability of the weights assigned to the multiple-choice options, and validity as assessed by contrasted groups.

The other two measures, FES and SMS, are either commercially available (FES; Moos, 1974) or frequently used research instruments (SMS; Snyder, 1974, 1979). Their reliability is high, and their construct validity may be considered adequate, although challengeable. The SMS yields a single score indicating the degree to which the respondent monitors her or his interactional behavior, including expressiveness. The score appears to index both the facility and the motivation with which the individual manages her or his impression on others.

The FES subscales used in this study were Expressiveness, Independence, and Control. Higher scores indicate the relatively greater salience of these dimensions in the family's "social climate." Control is somewhat negatively correlated with the other two subscales ($r = -.27$ and $-.26$), whereas the other two subscales are somewhat positively correlated ($r = .28$). Moos (1974) defined these three subscales as follows:

> Expressiveness: The extent to which family members are allowed and encouraged to act openly and to express their feelings directly.

> Independence: The extent to which family members are encouraged to be assertive, self-sufficient, to make their own decisions, and to think things out for themselves.

> Control: Assesses the extent to which the family is organized in a hierarchical manner, the rigidity of family rules and procedures, and the extent to which family members order each other around. (p. 4)

Coding of Child Data

The first variable examined (the children's justification for the scenario-target-child's regulation of expressive behavior) used the four categories of justification developed in the earlier study (Saarni, 1979a). These four categories, when ranked, indicate increasing subtlety and implicitly increasing complexity of social perspective-taking. In order of increasing complexity, the children's justification responses were rated as follows:

1 = trouble-avoiding set (e.g., "She doesn't want to get caught")
2 = qualifying factors of a relationship (e.g., "He doesn't want to hurt his aunt's feelings by showing he doesn't like the gift")
3 = maintenance of self-esteem (e.g., "She doesn't want to look dumb in the other girl's eyes")
4 = maintenance of norms (e.g., "It's not polite to react that way")

The children's justification ratings, summed across the four scenarios, yielded a final score.

The second variable, the children's expectations about the interpersonal consequences for the target child's having regulated his or her expressive behavior, was coded by means of five ranked categories. This consequences variable was also intended to indicate increasing subtlety and perspective-taking with higher ratings. The category ratings were as follows:

1 = child says she or he does not know or gives a tangential response
2 = child says there can be no dissemblance in expressive behavior, despite interviewer suggestions to the contrary
3 = child contends that the facial expression adopted by the target child will not influence the interactant's reaction to the target child
4 = child says that the target child's intent in dissembling is congruent with how the interactant interprets the facial expression (i.e., the sender is successful in achieving his or her purposes and is taken at "face value")
5 = the child thinks that the interactant is likely to see past the dissemblance and realize that the target child's facial expression is a "false front"

This variable was also summed across all four scenarios, the sum being the final score.

The third variable examined children's beliefs or expectancies about how they personally "decide" when to reveal their genuine feelings or not. This variable, labeled *balance*, was coded according to the following ranked categories:

1 = child does not know or gives a tangential response
2 = child cites a concrete instance in which she or he concealed her or his feelings but does not generalize (e.g., "Once I fell off my bike and it hurt bad but I didn't cry")

3 = child gives an unelaborated response that it depends on the situation, or that she or he just uses common sense about when she or he shows feelings or not

4 = child gives an elaborated and generalizable response, either situation- or relationship-oriented, with which she or he balances revealing or not revealing feelings (e.g., "I wouldn't show my feelings when people are in a bad mood. I'd show my feelings if people are in a good mood and feel like listening and talking to someone")

5 = child gives an elaborated and generalizable response about relying on own self-perception of how she or he feels *about* the feeling itself and on other-perception of how another person may evaluate the "appropriateness" of these feelings if they are revealed. (e.g., "Well, it would depend on how important the feeling was to me and how I'd think the people I was with would react to my showing how I really felt; probably if I felt embarrassed about the feeling, I wouldn't show it, or I'd try to smile")

Buss's discussion (1980) of private and public self-awareness is relevant here: this last category was reserved for children's responses that *integrated* both private and public self-awareness. Clearly, this variable also indicates greater subtlety and complex perspective-taking with higher ratings. Because this question about balance was asked only once (i.e., "How do you figure out for yourself the balance between when to show your real feelings and when not to?"), there was obviously no summation involved as there was for the other two variables.

Results

The data were analyzed by means of stepwise regression analyses for each of the three child variables. The acceptance p value was set at .005 because of the number of multiple comparisons. Eleven predictor variables were entered: the child's age, the mother's PACES, the father's PACES, the three FES subscales for mother and for father, the mother's SMS, and the father's SMS. The outcome for each child variable is discussed in turn.

Justification

Two of the predictor variables contributed significantly to the variation in this child variable. Age, as expected, accounted for the most variation ($r = .40$), but additionally, the father's Self-Monitoring Scale was a significant contributor. Together, they accounted for .26 (R^2) of the variation in the children's justification responses.

Consequences

Again, age was the major significant predictor of this child variable ($r = .70$), but the father's SMS and the father's PACES also contributed significantly, yielding an $R^2 = .65$. Interestingly, the two father variables obtained negative regression coefficients, a result suggesting that lower scores on the father's PACES (i.e., more permissive) and on the father's SMS (i.e., less concerned with self-monitoring) were associated with higher, more complex, and more subtle child perceptions of the interpersonal consequences of regulated expressive behavior.

Balance

Predictably, age was again the major contributor to this child variable ($r = .74$). In addition, three maternal variables proved to be significant contributors to the variation in this child variable. They were (in order) the mother's SMS, the mother's PACES, and the mother's FES Expressiveness. Together, all four variables obtained a robust $R^2 = .74$. All regression coefficients were positive, in contrast to the finding for the two father variables in the regression analysis on the consequences variable.

No sex differences were found for the child variables, a finding that is consistent with the outcome of several studies on children's comprehension of emotional experience (e.g., Barden *et al.*, 1980; Saarni, 1979a).

Discussion

The data from this study appear, in part, to be congruent with those of several other socialization studies in which the mothers' controlling or "corrective" behaviors (or style) predicted their children's higher level rationales, whereas the fathers' behavior typically did not have readily detectable influence (see Hoffman's review, 1970; see also Johnson & McGillicuddy-Delisi, 1983). However, Gardner (1982) contended that "mothers highlight the caretaking response and *the control of inner feelings*, while fathers initiate vigorous play and model the oscillation *from greater to less self-control*" (p. 48; italics mine). Although Gardner's conclusion regards young children, it also appears to be relevant to interpreting the seemingly contradictory effects in this study that the mothers' and the fathers' attitudes apparently had on their children's emotional beliefs. However, it should be noted that, although the mothers of the children who gave higher level rationales (for the balance variable) professed more controlling attitudes, they also perceived a greater degree of expressiveness in their families. Perhaps, the two more controlling measures (PACES and SMS) derived from the mothers' perception that because there was a high degree of family expressiveness, there was likewise a higher need for regulation and monitoring of affective displays. The result was that their children acquired a more complex understanding of the need to work out a balance between controlling the display of one's own feelings and openly expressing them.

On the other hand, the fathers of the children who gave higher level rationales for the consequences variable were significantly more permissive in their attitudes toward affective expressiveness, vis-à-vis both their children's (PACES) and their own behavior (SMS). It should be recalled that the consequences variable is about hypothetical characters in a story that the child is asked to reason about out loud. The orientation is toward how *others* think, whereas the balance variable emphasized *self-reflection*. It should also be noted that (in addition to age) only the fathers' SMS predicted the justification variable, which also represented the child's attributions about *others'* emotional experiences. However, in contrast to the consequences variable, the fathers' SMS was in the direction of more *self*-control in predicting higher level justification rationales. This finding is again suggestive of Gardner's notion that fathers may model the oscillation from greater to less self-control. Attitudes toward children's expressiveness, as indexed by PACES, did not influence this variable.

Although I am not comfortable with the simplified notion that fathers represent the instrumental, allocentric socializing pole, whereas mothers represent the expressive, autocentric pole within the family, this viewpoint may be useful for understanding the present pattern of results (see Guttman, 1965; Lueptow, 1980; Weitz, 1977; Zelditch, 1955). The fathers mediated expectancies about *others'* responses, whereas the mothers mediated expectancies about *personal* responses toward emotional experience.

Interestingly, although the mothers' and the fathers' perceptions of independence and control in their families' social climate (FES) correlated .42 and .63, respectively, for expressiveness, the parents' correlation coefficient was only $r = .12$. The parental PACES scores correlated only .15, and the parental SMS scores correlated only .05. These negligible correlations among the parental measures most directly related to beliefs about regulated expressiveness account for the divergent paths that the fathers and the mothers appear to have traversed in the socialization of their children's beliefs about regulated affective expressive behavior.

Conclusion

The data presented here do appear to confirm the argument that expectations held by others about emotional experience eventually do influence the formation of expectancies held by the individual about her or his own and others' emotional experience. The present study also illustrates how different socializing agents' expectations (i.e., mothers versus fathers) may have a differential impact on the child's expectancies or beliefs. This "differential impact" may reflect how the child responds to some expectations as valid, credible, and desirable suggestions and thus more readily incorporates them into her or his own belief structure. Clearly, the role of suggestion (as defined here) as the mediator of this process of internalization can only be hypothesized at this point and awaits further empirical (preferably observational) research.

APPENDIX A

Parent Attitude toward Children's Expressiveness Scale (PACES)

Scoring of PACES

The scoring weights for the multiple-choice format used in PACES range from 1 to 4, where 1 = most permissive attitude endorsed by the respondent about a child's emotional expressiveness and 4 = the most controlling or restrictive attitude. In the following table, each scale item number is represented by the number in parentheses; the numbers following are the weights assigned to the multiple-choice options a, b, c, and d. The total score is obtained by adding the number of weighted options endorsed by the respondent. The higher the score, the more controlling the attitude held by the respondent toward children's expressive behavior.

(1) 4, 3, 1, 2	(6) 1, 4, 3, 2	(11) 4, 1, 2, 3	(16) 4, 1, 2, 3
(2) 4, 2, 3, 1	(7) 1, 4, 2, 3	(12) 1, 2, 4, 3	(17) 3, 2, 1, 4
(3) 1, 3, 4, 2	(8) 3, 1, 2, 4	(13) 4, 1, 3, 2	(18) 4, 1, 3, 2
(4) 4, 1, 3, 2	(9) 3, 1, 2, 4	(14) 1, 4, 2, 3	(19) 1, 4, 2, 3
(5) 2, 1, 3, 4	(10) 3, 2, 1, 4	(15) 2, 1, 4, 3	(20) 2, 4, 1, 3

Psychometric Properties of PACES

The percentage of agreement on the preceding scoring weights, based on the ratings of 24 graduate students in a child clinical seminar and those of the author, was 71%.

The test–retest reliability, over a four-week interval, was calculated on 36 respondents (half of whom were, in fact, parents) who were graduate students enrolled in a psychological assessment class. The correlation coefficient was $r = .77$. The first mean was 33.5, $sd = 4.9$; the second mean was 33.7, $sd = 5.7$.

The construct validity of PACES receives some substantiation from the scores obtained by contrasted groups: 50 parents of middle-class parochial-school children obtained a mean of 41.26 and a standard deviation of 4.63, whereas the above-mentioned 36 graduate students in a counseling department obtained a mean of 33.5, $sd = 4.9$. This difference is both significant ($p < .05$) and conceptually expected (i.e., it can be expected that adult graduate students in a counseling program would espouse a more permissive attitude toward children's affective expressive behavior than adults who are parents of children sent to parochial school).

The construct validity of PACES receives some further support from the correlation coefficient ($r = .50$) between the Control scores obtained by the fathers of parochial-school children on the Family Environment Scale (Moos, 1974) and their PACES scores. However, for the mothers, this coefficient was only .33. Whether this parent difference was due to sampling variability or to the nature of the scales involved is unknown.

Parent Attitude Questionnaire[1]

Instructions: In the following multiple-choice questions please circle only the *one* response that seems most similar to what you would be likely to do in the situation described.

1. If my school-age child is bragging about his/her skill in some activity to another child, proceeds to goof up and hurt him/herself, and then comes to me for aid, I would
   a. tell him/her that he/she looks foolish being so upset after bragging.
   b. attend to him/her a little, but with some annoyance.
   c. comfort him/her about the injury and ignore the bragging.
   d. give comfort but also mildly chide him/her about the bragging.

2. If my school-age child receives an undesirable birthday gift from a family friend or relative and looks obviously disappointed, even annoyed, after opening it in the presence of the person giving the gift, I would

---

[1]Copyright 1982, by Carolyn Saarni.

   a. be annoyed with my child for being rude.
   b. look the other way.
   c. remind my child to say thank you.
   d. say that it really was too bad she/he didn't get what she/he wanted.

3. If my school-age child is very shy around adults who come to visit our home and prefers to stay in the bedroom during the visit, I would
   a. let my child do as he/she pleases.
   b. reproach my child about behaving like a mouse.
   c. tell my child that he/she must stay in the living room and visit with the guest.
   d. remind my child to be polite.

4. If during a bus ride my school-age child continues to look intently at someone whose whole head is covered with scar tissue, I would
   a. nudge my child and tell him/her to mind his/her own business.
   b. permit the looking.
   c. tell my child it is impolite to stare.
   d. ask what he/she is doing.

5. If my school-age child starts to giggle during a funeral, I would
   a. ignore it.
   b. smile understandingly at my child.
   c. frown at my child.
   d. frown and also tell my child to be quiet.

6. If my school-age child is afraid of injections and becomes a bit shaky while waiting for his/her turn for a shot, I would
   a. comfort him/her before and after the shot.
   b. tell him/her not to embarrass me by crying while getting the shot.
   c. tell him/her to try to get more under control.
   d. tell him/her that the pain lies more in the fear than in the actual shot.

7. If my school-age child shouts at me in anger after I accidentally throw away his/her favorite comic book, I would
   a. apologize.
   b. give him/her a piece of my mind about the disrespect shown to me and tell him/her to go to his/her room.
   c. apologize but tell him/her to stop yelling at me.
   d. send him/her to his/her room to cool off, then apologize later.

8. If my school-age child carelessly loses some prized (but inexpensive) possession and reacts with tears, I would
   a. tell her/him not to get so upset about it.
   b. tell her/him how unhappy I am about the loss, too.
   c. remind her/him to be more careful next time.
   d. say that she/he should not feel so sorry for her/himself because she/he was so careless as to lose it in the first place.

9. If my school-age child is about to appear on a local television program and

inquires with visible nervousness about how many people will be watching the show, I would
a. say to get control of her/himself and try not to show her/his nervousness.
b. reassure and comfort my child.
c. suggest thinking about something relaxing so that the nervousness will not be so obvious.
d. tell my child to get a grip on him/herself if he/she wants a good performance.

10. If my school-age child attends a family birthday dinner in a nice restaurant and exuberantly jumps out of his/her chair and shouts, "Happy birthday!" I would
a. smile but also tell my child to try not to be so rambunctious.
b. say nothing.
c. smile understandingly about my child's feelings so happy.
d. say that proper restaurant behavior requires sitting down and speaking quietly, despite feeling happy and excited.

11. If my school-age child becomes very angry at his/her sibling and begins to shout and stomp around the room, and if I am nearby, I would
a. tell my child to speak civilly and apologize as well.
b. not intervene.
c. try to find out what the altercation was all about.
d. tell my child to cool down.

12. If my school-age child has some unfounded fear (e.g., of the dark or of dogs) and gets panicky in the feared situation, I would
a. reach out with a touch and assure her/him that I was there to help.
b. give assurance that I was there to help but that it was time for her/him to realize that she/he had no real reason to be afraid.
c. tell the child that she/he is being silly and will embarrass her/himself someday by being so afraid.
d. tell her/him to control her/himself better so that she/he will feel less afraid.

13. If my school-age child is teased and called names by another youngster on the way home from school and arrives home trembling and tearful, I would
a. say, "If you don't want to be a sissy, scaredy-cat, or whatever, you should stick up more for yourself."
b. feel concerned myself and also comfort and reassure my child.
c. tell my child to keep a stiff upper lip and not let the other child see him/her so upset.
d. reassure my child but also say that showing one's fear to others sometimes causes problems.

14. If my school-age child rather obviously watches a mentally retarded person as we ride the bus, I would
a. permit the staring.
b. nudge my child and say to mind his/her own business.
c. ask what he/she is doing.
d. tell my child that it is impolite to stare.

15. If my school-age child wins a race in a track meet and after receiving everyone's congratulations continues to jump around gleefully and exclaim over the victory, I would
   a. say nothing but would begin to feel uncomfortable.
   b. smile approvingly and offer more congratulations.
   c. frown at the display and say that real winners do not keep "crowing."
   d. suggest she/he is overdoing it and to calm down.

16. If my school-age child appears to be quite afraid during an amusement park ride and other accompanying youngsters do not seem to be afraid, I would
   a. tell my child to shape up or he/she will be teased by the other kids.
   b. comfort and reassure my child.
   c. let him/her cope with the fear without my intervening.
   d. tell my child to try to get better control of him/herself.

17. If my school-age child is in a recital (e.g., dance, music, or gymnastics) and during a solo makes an error and proceeds to look as if on the verge of tears, afterward I would
   a. say that the performance was fine, but it would have been better if he/she had not looked so upset about the mistake.
   b. compliment the performance and saying nothing about the mistake.
   c. compliment the performance and say that the concern on his/her face after the mistake showed the audience that he/she really wanted to do well.
   d. say that no one would have paid attention to the mistake if he/she had not acted so babyish about it.

18. If my school-age child comes home from school very angry about something the teacher has done and proceeds to slam doors, mutter dire threats, and scowl fiercely, I would
   a. reprimand my child for being so out of control and behaving inappropriately in the house.
   b. ask what happened.
   c. tell my child that his/her behavior is disruptive.
   d. tell my child that I just hope he/she doesn't act this way at school.

19. If my school-age child is staring with interest at a woman breast-feeding her baby, I would
   a. permit the looking.
   b. nudge my child and say to mind his/her own business.
   c. ask my child what he/she is doing.
   d. tell my child that staring is impolite.

20. If my school-age child mutters "yecchh" and grimaces when Grandma serves some of her casserole on his/her plate, I would
   a. remind my child to be more polite.
   b. tell my child to apologize and shape up immediately or leave the table.
   c. smile rather nervously and ask my child, "Well, what do you think it is?"
   d. frown at my child while asking him/her to apologize for the poor manners.

REFERENCES

Barden, R. C., Zelko, F., Duncan, S. W., & Masters, J. C. Children's consensual knowledge about the experiential determinants of emotion. *Journal of Personality and Social Psychology*, 1980, *39*, 968–976.

Baumeister, R., & Cooper, J. Can the public expectation of emotion cause that emotion? *Journal of Personality*, 1981, *49*, 49–59.

Buss, A. *Self-consciousness and social anxiety.* San Francisco: Freeman, 1980.

Chapman, M. Isolating causal effects through experimental changes in parent-child interaction. *Journal of Abnormal Child Psychology*, 1981, *9*, 321–327.

Gardner, H. *Developmental psychology* (2nd ed.). Boston: Little, Brown, 1982.

Gardner, K., & Olness, G. *Hypnosis and hypnotherapy with children.* New York: Grune and Stratton, 1981.

Gordon, D. *Therapeutic metaphors.* Cupertino, Ca.: Meta Publications, 1978.

Guttman, D. Women and the conception of ego strength. *Merrill-Palmer Quarterly*, 1965, *11*, 229–240.

Harris, P. Children's understanding of the link between situation and emotion. *Journal of Experimental Child Psychology*, 1983, *36*, 490–509.

Harter, S. Children's understanding of multiple emotions: A cognitive-developmental approach. In W. Overton (Ed.), *The relationship between social and cognitive development.* Hillsdale, N.J.: Erlbaum, 1982.

Harter, S., & Buddin, B. *Children's understanding of the simultaneity of two emotions: A developmental acquisition sequence.* Paper presented at the meeting of the Society for Research in Child Development, Detroit, April 1983.

Hilgard, E. R. *Divided consciousness: Multiple controls in human thought and action.* New York: Wiley, 1977.

Hochschild, A. Emotion work, feeling rules, and social structure. *American Journal of Sociology*, 1979, *85*, 551–575.

Hoffman, M. Moral development. In P. H. Mussen (Ed.), *Carmichael's manual of child psychology.* New York: Wiley, 1970.

Johnson, J., & McGillicuddy-Delisi, A. Family environment factors and children's knowledge of rules and conventions. *Child Development*, 1983, *54*, 218–226.

Jones, J., & McGillis, D. Correspondent inferences and the attribution cube: A comparative reappraisal. In H. Harvey, W. Ickes, & R. Kidd (Eds.), *New directions in attribution research* (Vol. 1). New York: Erlbaum, 1976.

Lueptow, L. Social structure, social change and parental influence in adolescent sex-role socialization: 1964–1975. *Journal of Marriage and the Family*, February 1980, pp. 93–103.

Moos, R. *The family environment scale.* Palo Alto, Calif.: Consulting Psychologists Press, 1974.

Saarni, C. Cognitive and communicative features of emotional experience, or do you show what you think you feel? In M. Lewis & L. Rosenblum (Eds.), *The development of affect.* New York: Plenum Press, 1978.

Saarni, C. Children's understanding of display rules for expressive behavior. *Developmental Psychology*, 1979, *15*, 424–429. (a)

Saarni, C. *When not to show what you think you feel: Children's understanding of relations between emotional experience and expressive behavior.* Paper presented at the meeting of the Society for Research in Child Development, San Francisco, March 1979. (b)

Saarni, C. Social and affective functions of nonverbal behavior. In R. Feldman (Ed.), *Development of nonverbal behavior in children.* New York: Springer, 1982.

Saarni, C. An observational study of children's attempts to monitor their expressive behavior. *Child Development*, 1984, *55*, 1504–1513.

Snyder, M. The self-monitoring of expressive behavior. *Journal of Personality and Social Psychology*, 1974, *30*, 526–537.

Snyder, M. Self-monitoring processes. In L. Berkowitz (Ed.), *Advances in experimental social psychology* (Vol. 12). New York: Academic Press, 1979.

Weitz, S. *Sex roles*. New York: Oxford University Press, 1977.

Zelditch, M., Jr. Role differentiation in the nuclear family: A comparative study. In T. Parsons & R. Bales (Eds.), *Family, socialization and interaction process*. Glencoe, Ill.: Free Press, 1955.

III

Regulation of Behavior and Emotional States

10

Behavioral Consequences of Affect

BERT S. MOORE

Michael Lewis introduced his volume *The Development of Affect* (1978) with the following quote:

> Douglas, a 13-month-old, sits quietly playing with blocks. Carefully, with a rapt expression, he places one block on top of another until a tower of four blocks is made. As the last block reaches the top, he laughs out loud and claps his hands. His mother calls out, "Good, Doug. It is a ta-l-l-l tower. Don't you feel good!" Returning to the tower, Doug tries one more block, and as he places it on top, the tower falls. Doug bursts into tears and vigorously scatters the blocks before him. His crying brings his mother, who, while holding him on her lap and wiping his tears, says softly, "Don't feel bad. I know you're angry. It's frustrating trying to build such a tall tower. There, there, try again." (p. 3)

This quote also provides an appropriate illustration of the concerns of this book.

The focus here is the socialization of affect: how it is that children acquire the capacity to differentiate among the various feeling states that populate and color their and our lives. However, the quote stops before the next step in the drama is played out, how Douglas's affect influences his subsequent behavior. The focus of this chapter is how links are made between affective states and behavior. Whereas most of the other chapters focus on the labeling and categorizing of emotions, the topic here is the relationships that have been observed between affect and behavior. We summarize a large number of studies that have been conducted recently (primarily during the past decade) and that have examined how mood influences behavior, and we try to derive some general inferences about the socialization process. These inferences are tentative because almost none of this work has been done from a developmental perspective. We shall switch blithely from child to adult studies in our

---

BERT S. MOORE • Department of Psychology, University of Texas at Dallas, Richardson, Texas 75080.

attempt to come to some conclusions regarding those relationships and noting the different findings and processes where possible. Because much of the research on affect has been focused on the dependent variable end (e.g., work relating mood to altruism), there have been few attempts to integrate the findings from various areas. Our goal is to do a selective review of the literature relating affect to social behaviors and to derive some general principles about how mood may moderate these processes. In general, we focus on research employing induced mood states because of the interpretational problems that arise with research that employs clinical moods such as depression. However, we draw on this literature to highlight comparable processes.

INVESTIGATING AFFECT

That our behavior, our reactions to our world, is colored by our affect requires only a moment's introspection. We can point to numerous ways in which we respond differently to ourselves and to others depending on our mood, and in fact, the defining characteristics of some affective states often include the behavioral concomitants of these states. We are all aware that our moods may be potent determiners of how we respond to ourselves. We have all felt the flush of buoyancy and self-approbation that accompanies a "high"; we are also well acquainted with the self-abnegations and the self-doubt that may accompany our depressions. Of course, our affective states are subtle and multifaceted. Different shades of affects seem to be accompanied by specific forms of reaction to experience. Melancholy, guilt, nostalgia, exuberance, and joy all seem to produce, to some extent, specific reactions. It is not critical for our purposes to go into the issues regarding the directionality of these associations, for doubtless they are bidirectional, with the affective state engendering certain types of cognitive activity and cognitions leading to distinctive affective experiences. For a comprehensive examination of these issues, the reader may examine Izard's *Human Emotions* (1977) and Mandler's *Mind and Emotion* (1975). What is important for us is to see whether these relationships form any comprehensible statement about how affect regulates behavior.

MANIPULATION OF EMOTIONS AND MOODS

Children learn very early what we mean when we use an emotional label. If you ask children of age 2 to make a happy face and a sad face, they can usually do it. Although 2-year-olds are less adept at describing what makes them happy or sad, by age 3, children can readily come up with some examples for you. Doubtless, this early development of a shared meaning system regarding what is a subtle and complex private experience derives partially from the shared biological experiences tied to emotional states. Also doubtless, as is discussed elsewhere in this book, emotional states have certain cultural specificities, and the expression—and we surmise the experience—of certain emotions is differentially socialized across cultures. Therefore, part of a child's developmental task is to learn the appropriate emotional "repertoire" appropriate to her or his culture. On the other hand, because of our different wirings and different experiences, we have idiosyncratic emotional experiences. While acknowledging the individual nature of affective experiences, investigators have frequently tried to bring the study of mood into the laboratory. They have used a variety of methods for manipulating affect that are briefly outlined here.

The design used in most mood-manipulation research is typically simple. One treatment group of subjects undergoes a short induction experience designed to elicit positive mood. Another group experiences a negative mood induction, and a third group is given a suitable control experience. A behavioral characteristic is assessed *immediately* following the induction phase, and analyses are computed for the group differences on this characteristic attributable to the induction variable.

The use of this design entails the assumption that mood levels can be somewhat readily manipulated within the person. Indeed, mood is conceived of as a within-person variable; that is, it is assumed that an individual can be in a relatively happier or sadder state, perhaps relative to a neutral-affect balancing point, from moment to moment. Furthermore, it is assumed that shifts in mood level are predictably related to the nature of current experiences.

Experimental studies of affect manipulations have generally used one of four recognized procedures: the Velten technique (Velten, 1968); the success-or-failure experience (e.g., Fry, 1977); the reminiscence interview (Moore, Underwood, & Rosenhan, 1973); and the unexpected gift (e.g., Isen & Levin, 1972). Although different techniques are plainly more suited to different subject populations, the assumption is made that the different techniques achieve similar psychological consequences, that is, changes in a positive-to-negative mood dimension.

The *Velten technique* involves allocating subjects to either elation, depression, or control treatments. The subjects are asked to read aloud 50 statements, each one being typed on a separate small card. The statements used in the elation treatment have positive self-referring connotations (e.g., "If my attitude is good, then things go better"). The depression treatment statements have a negative self-referring bias (e.g., "There are too many bad things in my life"). The control group statements are designed to have neutral connotations (e.g., "Peanuts are grown in Georgia"). Obviously, the Velten procedures are most suited to work with adults.

The *success-or-failure experience* involves subjects' receiving information about success, failure, or a control experience applied to a task on which the subjects are unable to judge their own performance level or, alternatively, on a task on which a predictable outcome is assured. For example, suitable tasks for young children include Matching Familiar Figures problems, the "ray-gun" test, and the ubiquitous bowling game.

The *reminiscence procedure* consists of a short interview between a subject and an experimenter. The subject is asked to describe some experience(s) that has happy or sad connotations, or that has a neutral affect content. In a typical study, for example, the experimenter instructs the positive induction subjects, "I want you to tell me of something that really makes you happy, that makes you feel good." Negative induction subjects are asked about something that makes them feel unhappy and sad. Control group subjects could be asked to verbalize some innocuous content, such as counting to 10 three times; to describe a scene in a picture; or to list the names of other children in their classroom. In the case of the positive and negative induction treatment, the subjects are asked to dwell on the relevant experience for perhaps 20 or 30 seconds. A typical induction is thus likely to last about a minute.

An unexpected gift is simply one that a subject receives unexpectedly. The gift need not be one of great value; indeed, several studies have used items of merchandise valued at around 30 cents.

Additionally, some investigators have used stories whose affective tone is varied, movies, audiotapes, or even hypnotic inductions in attempts to create different moods within their subjects.

Although these manipulations probably do not evoke profound emotional experiences very frequently, there is evidence that they can reliably alter mood. Moore *et al.* (1973) videotaped their second- and third-grade subjects' faces during the reminiscence affect induction. They then had blind judges rate the faces for emotional state. The judges were able to reliably discriminate among the affect groups.

Bugental and Moore (1979) used a different approach to assess the validity of an affect manipulation. They recorded the voices of their elementary-school subjects, then used a pass-band filter that removes verbal content while maintaining vocal quality. Again, the raters were able to distinguish among the affect and the control conditions. A variety of more prosaic manipulation checks (e.g., using adjective checklists and having children indicate the face closest to their mood) have been used with children and adults; generally, differences have been found among conditions. In summary, it does appear that at least transient affective states can be successfully induced in both children and adults; so we can proceed with our examination of the consequences of those results.

It must be said, as a caveat, that we are well aware that we are tapping complicated affective complexes when we call on subjects to generate a specific affective state. Indeed, it has been demonstrated recently by Polivy (1981) and by Underwood, Froming, and Moore (1982) that laboratory inductions designed to influence a single affective state, such as sadness, anger, or fear, can actually cause significant alterations in all those states simultaneously. All of this suggests that any procedure designed to validate a mood induction should attempt to measure multiple affective states so as to give a more complex and realistic picture of the effects of emotion.

OVERVIEW OF EMPIRICAL RELATIONS

We have commented on the intuitive rationales for expecting there to be important relationships between affect and behavior. Numerous theoretical arguments have also been advanced for such relationships (cf. Izard, 1977). However, most of the empirical work done in the past decade has not grown out of any specific theoretical position. Indeed, most of the research has been rather piecemeal, and there have been very few attempts to come up with an undergirding conceptual framework. Yet, there is, of course, at least some sort of implicit framework that leads investigators to the topic in the first place.

The most general form of the framework (somehow, *theory* seems far too highblown a term for what is applied in this area) is that affective states have their behavioral concomitants. This does not mean that moods have necessary behavioral products, but rather that, when individuals encounter certain types of situations, their affective state moderates how they respond to that situation. Now, this does not seem like a terribly startling revelation, but what becomes interesting is what we can induce about the affect–behavior–cognition links from the observed behavior patterns.

Psychodynamic theory sees behavior as "solutions" to emotional states. Although we do not accept most of the trappings of the analytic position, much of the work that has emerged from our laboratory and that will be reported here has found this notion of affect a useful guideline. Affect is an important guide for behavior in that it influences the selection among the behavioral opportunities. That selection process is doubtless idiosyncratically organized, but to the extent that we can uncover affect–behavior links that have some generality, we can look at how those links may be socialized and how they act as "solutions" for different moods.

One way to categorize the diverse work that has been conducted on mood is to examine separately how it influences reactions to self and reactions to others. Naturally, some of the research on affect (e.g., state-dependent memory) does not lend itself to such categories, but they will do for the bulk of our review.

Why should affect function as a setting condition for self- and other-oriented behavior? Negative affect, by definition, increases the psychological distance between self and other. It creates, in Tomkins's colorful expression (1962), a "sociophobe." Under negative affect, we suspect that natural tendencies arise to comfort the self, by heightening self-reward, and by punishing others by decreasing their reward. If this view holds, what is striking about it is the tendency of negative affect to generalize: to displace from its original source (the reminiscence) to the "generalized other." Positive affect, in contrast, decreases psychological distance, making one feel good about the self and others. Again in Tomkins's terms, positive affect creates a "sociophile." And again, one sees a high degree of generalization from the original source of the affect. Because the psychological distance between self and others is decreased, one feels about others as one does about oneself. To the extent that one is generous to oneself, one will predictably be generous to others. What we want to do now is to describe a number of studies that examine the affects of happiness and sadness, or reactions to the self and others.

AFFECT AND REACTIONS TO SELF

What we do wish to examine in this section is some representative research on the self-oriented cognitive and behavioral consequences of affect. We use these arbitrarily selected categories of cognitive and behavioral consequences, fully recognizing their inseperable nature.

Cognitive Consequences of Affect

Some theorists (e.g., Duvall & Wicklund, 1972; Tomkins, 1962) have argued that emotions play a central role in the emergence of consciousness and are an integral component of the development and maintenance of the self-concept.

This idea is most fully developed in work by Izard. Izard (1977) discussed assumptions of his differential emotions theory that he considered especially relevant to emotional development. The central proposition is that emotions emerge as they become adaptive in the life of the infant. Some other key assumptions are that emerging emotions increase the infant's information-processing and responding capabilities and add to his or her complexity of consciousness; provide social signals (via facial expressions) that are important to infant–caregiver relationships; and help to set the stage for particular types of learning and development. Izard filled his conceptual framework with descriptions of the emergence of fundamental emotions (interest, joy, surprise, distress, anger, disgust, contempt, fear, shame, and guilt) in terms of their facilitation of a number of crucial developmental processes, including (a) survival and healthy development (e.g., from birth, the distress cry is a signal to the caretaker that help is needed); (b) infant–environment interreactions (e.g., beginning at about 2½ months, the social smile helps to bond the caretaker to the infant); (c) differentiation of self and others (e.g., shame facilitates the development of self-awareness); (d) expanding the sphere of activity (e.g., at around the age of 5 months, interests increasingly motivate exploration); and (e) self-cognitions and self-control (e.g., fear emerges sometime after 6 months, engendering cognitions about the self concerning threat and helping to set boundaries on action). Also, around the last quarter of the first year, the infant begins to link particular affects with particular images and symbols to form affective-cognitive structures. Such structures soon become the "predominant motivational features in consciousness" (Izard, 1977, p. 411).

It is our view that, as the child becomes more emotionally differentiated, certain forms of self-reaction become tied to affective states. One form of self-reaction that has been investigated is self-reward.

Self-Reward

We are using the term *self-reward* very broadly and really see it as a prototype of a number of ways in which we respond to ourselves, in that we have found that there are a number of correlations between self-reward and other forms of self-response, such as estimation of task performance, social comparisons, and even state self-concept.

Some early work by Mischel, Coates, and Raskoff (1968) suggested that the momentary experience of success appears to increase noncontingent self-reward. There were several other studies in this vein (e.g., Feather, 1968). Much of this early work attributed the mechanism by which success and failure influences behavior to the affective concomitants of those experiences; however, there are a number of additional components of the success–failure experience beyond the affective that make the generalization to other forms of mood difficult. Also, the finding that commonly emerged that there was no difference between failure and control subjects did not make intuitive sense to those of us who have stared failure in the face more often than we might have liked.

A study by Underwood, Moore and Rosenhan (1973) is represen-tative of the paradigm that has been used in much of the research to be described here, so we describe it in a little greater detail. Basically, the intent of the research is to try to find a vehicle that would allow for the "direct" altering of children's affective state without the accompanying by-products of the success–failure manipulations. This study utilized the reminiscence procedure, in which children are asked to generate positive and negative events from their own life and are then asked to focus on those events for about 90 seconds, with a few reminders to keep at it.

However, the children were asked to do this prior to being given an opportunity of self-reward from a treasure chest full of pennies. We felt certain that this would be a situation where one could expect to find unbridled self-indulgence—and, indeed, we did. We found through pi-loting that we had to run subjects very quickly because rumors swept through the school that "they were giving free money" over at our research trailer. Also, we discovered one of those variables that are rarely anticipated before the piloting of a study: envelope size. We gave the children envelopes in which they could put their money. However, after the second pilot subject was able to cram $8.78 into the envelope, we decided that, if this research was going to be conducted, the size of the envelopes would have to be reduced.

Even though we had created a situation where children were able to self-reward at will, their tendency to do so was influenced by the affective state that had been induced prior to the self-reward. It was found that both the happy and the sad children self-rewarded more than the controls. Although there was no significant sex-by-condition inter-action in the parametric analysis, the use of the Mann–Whitney showed different patterns for males and females: the females, both positive and negative affect subjects, were not different from each other but were different from the controls, whereas the males showed differences between positive and negative affect, with the positive affect subjects self-gratifying more.

The more interesting finding was that the positive and the negative affect subjects showed similarly high levels of self-reward as compared to the controls. However, we suspected that different processes might be producing the self-gratifications in the positive and the negative affect conditions, and that possibility will be examined shortly.

An interesting ancillary result was that the negative-mood male subjects seemed to conjure up primarily angering thoughts, whereas the females came up with more depressive thoughts. This finding may reflect different socialization patterns in the expression and/or the experience of negative affect in males and females.

Two further studies that were conducted suggest that there are some other complicating factors in the relationship between mood and self-reward. The first to be discussed is a study by Moore and Underwood (1982) that used self-gratification as a measure and compared children at two age levels under contingent and noncontingent self-reward conditions. The noncontingent self-gratification was essentially as described in Underwood et al., 1973, except that, in the Moore and Underwood study, the children played a bowling game and then were told that they could take tokens that could be turned in for a prize at the end of the session. The contingent condition subjects were told to award themselves tokens in accordance with how they thought they had performed on the bowling game. The outcome of the game could be controlled by the experimenter, and all the subjects received a score of 6 out of 10.

There were no main effects for age; the affect condition subjects differed from controls in self-reward; and the contingency differed from noncontingency. Additionally, affect interacted with age and contingency. The younger children (4–5) in both the positive and the negative affect conditions self-rewarded more than the control subjects. The contingency did not influence their self-reward. However, the older children (8–9) did show different patterns under the contingent and the noncontingent conditions. The older positive-affect subjects self-rewarded more than the control subjects under the higher contingent-reward conditions. Under sadness, the subjects did not differ from the control subjects in their self-reward. Under the noncontingent reward conditions, both affect groups showed higher levels of self-reward than did the controls.

The results of this study are complicated but do suggest that mood effects on self-gratification come to be associated with issues of deservingness as children get older. This finding ties in with some of the research that we shall review indicating that negative affect leads to more stringent self-evaluations.

The second relevant study was by Jones and Thelen (1978), who studied adult subjects and used the Velten statements to induce mood in an investigation of self-reward. One half of the subjects were asked to reward themselves with points when they were satisfied with their performance on a word association task, and the other half (the self-criticism group) were asked to allocate points indicating dissatisfaction. Under the self-reward conditions, the happy subjects rewarded themselves more than the control subjects and the sad subjects. Under self-criticism, the number of points allocated by the sad subjects exceeded the number allocated by the controls, who, in turn, exceeded the positive affect group.

This study again suggests that mood influences our response to ourselves and that deservingness becomes an important process by which such judgments are made. There are still some ambiguities about the relationship between affect and self-reward. Generally, across ages, we have found differences between both positive and negative affect conditions and control subjects but not necessarily any differences *between* affect groups under conditions of noncontingent self-reward. Yet, intuitively and theoretically, we suspect that the self-reward functions in different ways in happiness and sadness, as witness the different performances under contingent conditions. The role of self-gratification under happiness and sadness may be partially clarified by some additional studies that have examined different aspects of self-reward.

An issue related to the above discussion of self-reinforcement processes is how affective state influences delay of gratification. Delay of gratification has been extensively researched by a number of investigators during the past 20 years. Delay of gratification has been seen as a basic mechanism of self-control processes and has been found to be influenced by a number of situational and dispositional factors.

The delay-of-gratification situation has been construed as having two separate components: (a) the decision to choose between an immediate and delayed reward and (b), once the decision is made to wait for a delayed reward, the length of the waiting interval itself. These separate components are seen as being governed by different mechanisms and have generally been investigated in separate experiments.

Moore, Clyburn, and Underwood (1976) examined the relationship between affective state and delay choice. They investigated preferences for immediate, smaller rewards versus preferences for delayed, larger rewards. They contended that delay choice might be a productive area for exploring the previously observed tendency for both positive and negative affect subjects to show increased rates of noncontingent self-gratification. If, as Underwood *et al.* (1973) argued, these tendencies are produced by different processes, then the delay choice paradigm may differentiate between these processes. Moore *et al.* contended that, if sad people are acting to terminate an aversive emotional state, they would show a preference for the smaller but immediately available rewards. Happy subjects should show a preference for delayed, larger rewards in that they are seen as not having as much felt need for immediate reward and therefore should opt for a reward-maximizing choice. Moore *et al.* used nursery-school children who were asked to think about happy, sad, or neutral events and then were given a choice between rewards that had been pretested for preferences. The preferred reward (a lollipop) was offered as being available at the end of the day, whereas the less preferred reward (a pretzel) was presented as being immediately available. Moore *et al.* found the predicted relationships: the happy affect subjects showed more delayed-reward choices.

These results are buttressed by a study by Seeman and Schwartz (1974) using success and failure as an affect-inducing procedure. They used 9-year-olds who were given feedback that a drawing had been accepted or rejected for an art show. The subjects were then given a choice between immediate rewards and large, delayed rewards. The success subjects chose the delayed, larger rewards more often than did the failure subjects.

Finally, a study by Mischel, Ebbesen, and Zeiss (1973) investigated, among other things, the role that affect played in children's ability to successfully delay gratification once a choice had been made to wait for a larger, delayed reward. They found that nursery-school children who "thought happy thoughts" waited dramatically longer than those thinking sad thoughts. It would appear that focusing on positive affect events helps to bridge the aversive delay interval, whereas, not surprisingly, focusing on sad thoughts made the delay interval more aversive and produced short waiting times.

Both delay choice and delay behavior were influenced by affective state. The results of these studies appear to be consistent with an emerging picture of the relationship between affect and self-gratification that finds positive affect subjects and negative affect subjects differing in their patterns of contingent self-reward but showing similar amounts of noncontingent self-reward. However, findings from several areas suggest that the mechanisms underlying noncontingent self-reward differ for positive and negative affect subjects and therefore give some picture of the psychological properties of these affective states.

The conclusions arrived at regarding sadness must be tempered in view of a study by Sacco and Hokanson (1982), who examined depressed and nondepressed subjects on a 22-trial skill task in which the success rate was experimentally controlled, and all subjects received either an initially high rate of success, followed by a low rate of success, or a low rate followed by a high rate. The subjects self-reinforced in either a public or a private situation. It was found that the depression level interacted with the sequence of feedback and public or private reward conditions. The most interesting result for our purposes was found among the depressed, private, high-low-sequence subjects, who rewarded themselves significantly more highly than did the nondepressed subjects in the same condition. These results were discussed in terms of previously obtained tendencies for depressives to be more stringent in terms of standards for self-reward. Sacco and Hokanson speculated that some of these previous conclusions may have been produced by the public nature of the determination of the reinforcers and that, in private conditions (at least, in conditions where some sense of deservingness has been created, as was the case here, where the subjects received initially high levels of success feedback), depressives may act in a "self-therapeutic" fashion. Clearly, these relationships are complicated and require further investigation. Additionally, we feel compelled to remind ourselves and the reader of the caution that must be exercised in drawing conclusions where studies are based on diverse methodologies such as these, where success-failure, mood inductions, and individual differences in affect have been discussed as tapping similar affective processes.

Research by Baumann, Cialdini, and Kenrick (1981) supports the notion that, at least under some conditions, self-gratification does operate in negative affect subjects in order to terminate the unpleasant experience of negative mood. They induced happy, sad, or neutral affect in college students using the reminiscence procedures and then offered the subjects an opportunity to self-gratify noncontingently from tokens that the subjects would later be able to turn in for a prize. Some subjects self-rewarded immediately after the affect condition, whereas others had an interpolated task that Baumann *et al.* assumed produced positive affect. When there was no interpolated task, the positive and negative affect subjects showed increased levels of self-reward as compared to the control subjects. However, when there was a positive-affect interpolated task, the tendency for sad subjects to show increased self-reward disappeared. The interpolated task had no effect on the positive affect subjects' tendency to self-reward. We shall return to this issue when we look at the relationship between reactions to self and reactions to others.

We have seen that self-reward seems to be influenced by affective state and that it interacts with the perceived contingency of the rewards. What other forms of self-reaction seem to be influenced by affect?

Task Performance and Feedback

Masters, Barden and Ford (1979) had children perform a learning task, using the reminiscence procedure described previously. Masters *et al.* asked 4-year-old children to discriminate different shapes. The length of time it took them to learn the discrimination, the latency of response, and the number of errors were measured. Masters *et al.* found a significant relationship between affect and task performance with both positive- and negative-affect subjects being different from the controls.

Positive affect increased the rate of learning and lowered the latency at response. Negative affect produced an opposite pattern.

These findings are buttressed by work by Moore (1982), who found on an anagram solution task that, although overall main effects were not obtained, the time-to-solve for the initial trials did differ among the affect groups, the negative affect subjects differing from the positive affect subjects and the controls. Using adult subjects, Leight and Ellis (1981) found that subjects in a negative affect condition were less efficient in using an available strategy in a problem-solving task. It may be that, under some conditions, task performance itself is influenced by affective state, which may, in turn, influence both affect and self-reward. It may also be that we then become differentially sensitive to certain kinds of information.

Moore, Underwood, Doyle, Heberlein, and Litzie (1979) had college students perform two tasks. One group performed a second task that was highly similar to the initial task, and the other half performed a dissimilar task. Additionally, the subjects received either success, failure, or neutral feedback on the initial task. On the second task, performance feedback was delivered via a tone that the subjects heard over headphones, high tones denoting success and lower tones marking failure. Actually, on half the trials, the subjects received an ambiguous tone that was halfway in between the success and failure tones. The dependent measure then became how the subjects would interpret the ambiguous tones. Moore *et al.* found that, in general, the subjects made interpretations congruent with previously received feedback. They also discriminated between whether the tasks were similar or dissimilar, having a greater tendency to interpret ambiguous stimuli as consistent with prior feedback on the similar task. Perhaps the most interesting finding was that failure seemed to have a greater impact on the interpretation of ambiguous feedback than did success. Although data directly measuring the subjects' attributions were not obtained, it appears that the failure subjects made more stable, internal attributions on the basis of the feedback of the initial task. This result is, of course, inconsistent with a number of findings in the attribution literature, which indicate an "egocentric bias" in attributions whereby people tend to attribute failure to external, unstable factors. An important difference between the Moore *et al.* results and those studies is that the Moore *et al.* study looked at the actual interpretation of performance feedback rather than attributions about postperformance. Moore *et al.* stated in their discussion, "our findings [greater generalizability of failure] are in accord with at least the authors' subjective feelings that it is our failures that color our vision in a more pervasive way than our successes" (p. 379). This same principle may apply as well to our sadnesses.

Locus of Control

Another issue relating to the self-cognition consequences of affective states is mood's effect on an individual's perception of locus of control. Locus of control has been one of the heavily researched dimensions in the past 15 years, and in spite of its having been used in a broader fashion than was originally intended (Rotter, 1975), it has been found to be an important predictor of a number of behaviors. Natale (1978) examined the effects of induced affect on individuals' generalized expectancies regarding internality and externality. Based on the previous research that we have reviewed, we would expect that positive affect is associated with the internal control of reinforcers. Natale's results supported this hypothesis. We used the Velten statements to induce elation, neutral affect, or sadness, and our subjects filled out Rotter's locus-of-control scale before and after the affect-induction procedure. Elation caused an increased sense of internality, whereas sadness caused an increased sense of externality. These findings are partially supported by a study by Masters and Furman (1976), who found that the induction of positive affect led to a greater expectancy of noncontingent success on a task. Masters and Furman, however, did not find a difference between neutral and sad conditions.

Alloy, Abramson, and Viscusi (1981) examined the effects of mood on subjects' perceptions of personal control. Previous work (e.g., Alloy *et al.*, 1981) had suggested that depressed people may accurately judge their personal control, whereas nondepressed subjects succumb to an "illusion of control," whereby they overestimate their impact on objectively uncontrollable circumstances. Alloy *et al.* (1981) induced a depressive mood in nondepressed college students and an elated mood in naturally depressed students and assessed the effects of these transient mood states on the subjects' sense of personal control. They found that the nondepressed women who were made transiently sad became more like chronically depressed women in that they gave *more* accurate assessments of contingencies. Naturally, the depressed subjects who experienced a positive mood induction overestimated their control over contingencies.

Self-Concept

Underwood, Froming, and Moore (1980, 1982) have reported a series of studies relevant to the question of how affective state influences self-concept. The initial study (1980) used a reminiscence-based induction of happiness and sadness, with a series of personality measures serving as the dependent variables. Although the manipulation succeeded in altering self-reported states of happiness and sadness (and, interestingly, none of the other moods measured by Nowlis's Mood Adjective Checklist), none of the personality measures varied significantly across the experimental conditions. This result would certainly seem to indicate that personality descriptions did not differ as a function of changes in happiness or sadness, but there are at least two different explanations of why this might be so. One explanation suggests that self-concept is simply not affected by changes in happy and sad moods. The other, more indirect explanation suggests that happy and sad moods are causally related to self-concept, but that this causal relationship holds only for momentary self-concept and not for the more stable trait measures used in the study.

If the second explanation is correct, it should be possible to find a significant effect of a mood manipulation on measures of momentary—or "state" rather than "trait"—self-concept. This possibility was the focus of later studies, the first of which used both a questionnaire on which the instructions had been changed from traitlike ("Describe yourself as you usually or typically feel and behave") to statelike ("Describe yourself as you think you would feel or behave right now") and an adjective checklist Mood Adjective Checklist (MACL) to which items related to competence and self-esteem (skillful, competent, proficient, and successful) had been added. The mood manipulation consisted of films designed to induce feelings of happiness and sadness, and the subjects' responses to the mood items on the MACL indicated that the films had had the desired effect. The MACL responses also indicated that the "sad" film had made the subjects more anxious, as well as sadder. The films did not have any differential effect on the questionnaire, but the "state" self-esteem scale added to the MACL was significantly higher in the happy-film condition than in the control or in the sad-film conditions.

Buoyed by this initial success with the MACL, Underwood et al. (1982) added still more descriptive adjectives to the MACL to form positive-sociability (sociable, outgoing, and friendly) and negative-sociability (shy, alienated, and rejected) subscales. They used this measure as the dependent variable in another study that employed a success–failure manipulation to induce moods. The responses to the mood items on the MACL indicated that the failure manipulation made the subjects both sadder and more anxious, and that the success manipulation failed to produce a significant difference from the control levels on any of the mood scales. Furthermore, the subjects in the failure condition scored higher on the added negative-sociability items but lower on the added self-esteem items of the MACL. An examination of the within-condition correlations ruled out anxiety as a possible mediator of the effect on self-esteem. If we consider the results of the three studies together, it seems likely that certain kinds of mood changes do have a causal influence on at least state self-concept.

Summary

It appears that a variety of self-reactions are influenced by the affective state that we are in. Positive mood seems to produce a number of positive benefits: We tend to be generous to ourselves, in both contingent and noncontingent circumstances; we tend to recall more positive self-attributes; and we attribute success to ourselves. Our expectations for future performance are more positive, and we tend to set fairly high standards for our behavior and expect to achieve them. Predictably, the consequences of sadness are more complex. We tend to engage in some behaviors that are "self-therapeutic"; that is, we show more noncontingent self-gratification and take perhaps a lesser reward in order to have it immediately. We also tend to show greater recall of negative self-attributes and to have more trouble delaying gratification. Our recall of past performance is more negative, and our expectancy for future performance is lower. We also tend to generalize to novel situations on the basis of our failures.

As to the socialization of these processes, there is little direct evidence; however, the pattern of results often has the flavor of the precursors of those tendencies that are found in younger children and that develop over the early years. For instance, Yates (1982) found that nursery-school-aged children were not more likely to delay gratification when told to think happy thoughts, whereas 8-year-olds were. However, when instructions were given that were specifically designed to keep the child attending to the happy thoughts, the nursery-school children acted like 8-year-olds.

Another interesting finding is by Glasberg and Aboud (1981), who noted that young children seem to have more difficulty differentiating sadness and anger, although children as young as 3 had no difficulty identifying happy-making situations. They went on to find that younger (kindergarten) children did not attach negative self-evaluations to sadness. However, 8-year-old children evaluated sad others, as well as themselves, in a negative light. Indeed, it is only when children are older that they recognize sadness as being a component of their experience and makeup.

So it may be that part of what we learn is that sadness is vaguely inappropriate and serves as a cue for negative self-reactions. Indeed, some of the behavioral data described here support this idea.

Younger children were more likely to label anger as being like sadness. It may be that we socialize sadness into children. Glasberg and Aboud (1981) reported that kindergarteners were reluctant to view themselves as sad. One cannot help but be reminded of Freud's formulation of depression as anger turned inward.

AFFECT AND REACTIONS TO OTHERS

We have seen a number of consequences of mood in self-reaction, but as we try to get a more complete picture of affect's influences, we need to examine the other side of the picture: how our reactions to others are shaped by affect. As might be expected, the literature on this topic is much more limited. After all, because emotion is a private experience, the bulk of the behavioral correlates that have been investigated have been individual ones. However, it is intuitively persuasive that the manner in which we respond to other people is partially determined by our moods. We summarize here literature from several areas that has focused on the examination of reactions to others that are influenced by mood.

Altruism

A major domain for the investigations of mood's influence on our reactions to others has been prosocial behavior. Altruism provides an interesting example for the investigation of the role of moods, for it provides a case where there are not external, ostensible rewards for the behavior, so that the most parsimonious assumption is that it is sensitivity to the needs of others that promotes the act. A number of studies examined the role that affect plays in the maintenance of prosocial behavior. We shall discuss a few representative studies in this important area.

The earliest laboratory finding in this area is by Berkowitz and Connor (1966), who induced success experiences in adults and found them to be more willing to help a supervisor to make envelopes than were controls or those who failed. Isen (1970), using less constrained tasks, found that adults were more helpful and more charitable following a success induction. Both investigators were struck by the emotional overtones of such experiences with success. Berkowitz and Connor explained their results in terms of the "glow of goodwill" that is generated by success and that makes people more tolerant of the costs of helping. Isen's "warm glow of success" similarly emphasizes the emotional aspects of a success experience.

The "feel good, do good" phenomenon is not limited to success, by any means. Kazdin and Bryan (1971) varied perceived competence and found that subjects who believed themselves more competent were more willing to donate blood in an ongoing drive than were those who felt less competent. Similar findings were obtained by Midlarsky and Midlarsky (1973).

Simple, even accidental, good fortune of the most trivial sort apparently has effects that are similar to those of success and competence. Receiving a cookie for no apparent reason other than spontaneous kindness, finding a dime in a telephone booth (Isen & Levin, 1972), or being given free stationery (Isen, Clark, & Schwartz, 1976) predisposes people to help. Such helpfulness, it should be noted, is not directed toward the cookie or stationery donor—that would be a *quid pro quo*—but toward third parties who were not involved in the gift giving, a matter to which we must return shortly.

Success, competence, and good luck are complex mixtures of cognition and emotion. Yet, until recently, investigators in this area believed that it was the affective aspects of these experiences that were significant for altruism.

Moore *et al.* (1973) attempted a direct examination of the effects of affective state on children's prosocial behavior. They asked second- and third-grade children to recall events from their lives that had made them particularly happy or particularly sad. Children assigned to a control condition spent the same amount of time doing nothing or counting slowly while the experimenter listened. After the mood manipulation, the subjects were given an opportunity to donate some of the 25 pennies that they had received for participating in the experiment to other children who would not have an opportunity to participate. The experimenter emphasized to the children that the donating was entirely voluntary. The child was then left alone and allowed to make a donation.

The child's affective state had a potent effect on the child's tendency to donate some of his or her resources. The children who had focused on happy thoughts gave significantly more than did the control or the "sad" subjects. The children who had recalled unhappy events contributed significantly less than the control subjects. Moore *et al.* (1973) concluded that even the transient affective states tapped in this experiment may have influenced the child's orientation toward others' needs. Positive affect may generate a general expansiveness to the external world—a feeling of more than adequate resources. Negative affect may generate the opposite sense: a turning inward emotionally and perhaps even perceptually. A subsequent unpublished study by the same authors extended these findings by demonstrating the same relationship with a measure of helpfulness toward an anonymous other child.

Underwood, Froming, and Moore (1977) tested the idea that what might be happening under conditions of negative affect is that subjects are less attentive to external cues and thus less aware of the needs of others. These investigators used an experimental situation almost identical to that of Moore et al., except they included in the room a bulletin board containing a number of pictures. Underwood et al. hypothesized that, if negative affect produces decreased attention to external information, the negative affect subjects should be less able to report what was on the bulletin board. They found, however, that, although they replicated the previously obtained difference in donation between the positive and the negative affect subjects, there was no difference in the subjects' ability to recall the items on the bulletin board. So it appears it is not mere attentional deficit that produces the reduced sharing under negative affect.

We shall discuss possible mechanisms shortly, but first, we must add a few complexities to the issue. To begin with, Cialdini and Kenrick (1976) raised a number of questions regarding the effects of negative mood on altruism. They contended that, as the child matures, he or she increasingly internalizes social norms regarding the desirability of exhibiting prosocial behavior. Because prosocial action is valued by society, we are able to feel good about ourselves when we help others. Thus, one would expect that people in a negative mood to be more helpful to others than people in a neutral mood, as the people in a negative mood should want to improve their mood by doing something as socially desirable and reinforcing as altruism. Cialdini and Kenrick, therefore, contended that, although negative mood may inhibit prosocial action in young children prior to the internalization of norms regarding such behavior, in adult subjects the relationship should reverse.

To test their explanation, Cialdini and Kenrick replicated the procedures used by Moore and his colleagues, but with subjects at three different age levels, in order to see if negative affect had different consequences for altruistic behavior at different ages. They found that younger children tended to donate less money after reminiscing about sad experiences; however, with tenth- and twelfth-grade subjects, negative affect led to increased rates of donation as compared to the neutral affect of the controls. The authors interpreted these results as supporting their ideas regarding the acquired reinforcing value of prosocial action.

Unfortunately, for the sake of theoretical parsimony, two studies using adult subjects (McMillen, Sanders, & Solomon, 1977; Underwood, Berenson, Berenson, Cheng, Wilson, Kulik, Moore, & Wenzel, 1977) point out the need for further clarification of this issue. Underwood et al., using movies prerated for affective content, and McMillen et al., using negative personality feedback, found lower donation rates and helping, respectively, under conditions of negative affect. So although the general results are fairly consistent regarding the facilitative effects of positive moods on prosocial behavior, the role of negative affect is less certain and may involve counteracting tendencies.

This confusion may be partially reconciled by looking at work that shows that negative mood can result in increased helping when the costs of helping are low and the potential benefits are high (Kenrick, Bauman, & Cialdini, 1979; Weyant, 1978). This work suggests, however, that we must not perceive the costs of helping as too great if we are to help, and that we need to expect to derive some benefits in terms of recognition and feeling good about ourselves.

Another important issue that has grown out of research relating mood to altruism is the focus of attention of the mood. As we noted earlier, speaking of positive or negative mood is clearly too general a conceptualization of the subtle shades of affect that may be experienced. Recent work has begun to explore the differences.

Rosenhan, Salovey, and Hargis (1981) induced joy in two groups of subjects. The first experienced joy for themselves, an egocentric joy. The second experienced empathic joy for a close friend. Those who experienced egocentric joy were markedly more altruistic toward a third party than those who experienced empathic joy. Indeed, the latter were less altruistic than a comparable control group, which experienced neither of these affects.

Attention, to the self or to the other (and that is what is involved in egocentric or empathic experiences), is surely significant for cognition. Thinking of another's joy simply does not signal cognitions about the other's needs: obviously, if someone is joyful, she or he cannot simultaneously be attending to the other's experiences.

Thompson, Cowan, and Rosenhan (1980) also examined the issue of focus of attention. They tested this hypothesis by manipulating subjects' focus of attention while they were experiencing negative affect. The subjects listened to a tape that solemnly described their friend's tragic death from cancer. The subjects were directed to attend either to the worry, the anxiety, and the intense pain of the dying friend or to their own pain and sorrow caused by their friend's death. The subjects in the control condition listened to a boring, emotionally "neutral" tape. Both the other- and the self-oriented subjects were much sadder than the controls (but did not differ from each other). However, as predicted, the subjects who attended to the thoughts and feelings of their friend were significantly more helpful than the self-focused or control subjects. Thus, Thompson et al. stated, "negative moods . . . facilitate altruism only among people who are attending to the problems of others, but not among people who attend to their own needs, concerns and losses" (p. 297).

Barnett, King, and Howard (1979) also argued that the focus of the negative affect is likely to have a pronounced effect on what sort of behavior is produced. Barnett *et al.* had children focus on happy, neutral, or sad events that had been experienced either by themselves or by another child. Following the affect induction, the children were given the opportunity to share their experimental earnings with some less fortunate children. It was found that, when the children focused on their own sad events, they were less likely to share their earnings than were neutral subjects, but that their focusing on the sad events of others promoted sharing. This finding, of course, is consistent with Hoffman's ideas regarding empathy and emphasizes the necessity of explicitness when discussing the role of "negative affect" as a mediator of prosocial action. That is, it is not some generalized negative affect that promotes altruism but a fairly specific subvariety of negative affect.

This point is accented if one examines the literature on the effects of another negative affective state, guilt, on prosocial behavior. A review of this diverse literature is not possible here (see Rosenhan, Karylowski, Salovey, & Hargis, 1981, for a review), but it should be noted that, although the relationships are complex, the experience of guilt often appears to promote prosocial behavior.

Distribution of Rewards

A paradigm related to, but differing in significant ways from, the altruism situation has been used for an investigation of the relationship between reactions to self and others. Moore, Underwood, and Litzie (1982) placed elementary-school children in a situation where they had control over the distribution of rewards to themselves and to another child.

Elementary-school children were brought individually to a research trailer and were asked to perform a simple task. They were told that another child would be working on the same task elsewhere. Following completion of the task, the children were assigned randomly to one of three mood conditions: happy, sad, and neutral, or control, by means of the reminiscence procedure. Following the manipulation, the children were given 40 pennies to divide anonymously between themselves and the other child. The children were told either that they had performed better (positive social comparison) or worse than the other child (negative social comparison).

Not surprisingly, the children who had been told that they performed better than the other child kept more pennies for themselves than did the children who had been told that they performed worse. If we examine only the positive social-comparison condition, there was a significant linear increase from happy to neutral to sad conditions in the number of pennies that the children kept for themselves. The quadratic trend was not significant. The pattern was quite different for the negative social-comparison condition. There, the control children kept significantly more pennies for themselves than did the children in the happy and sad mood conditions, who did not differ significantly from each other.

Examining the data, one notes that five of the six conditions are very much in accord with the linear trend found in prior research on altruism. The condition that does not fit with that trend is the sad mood, a negative social-comparison condition in which the children kept fewer pennies for themselves than would have been anticipated from the linear trend. One might speculate that the sad mood, although increasing the children's motivation to keep more pennies for themselves, also sensitized them to the negative information about their performance (and therefore their deservingness). Hence, they kept fewer pennies for themselves because of the enhanced impact of the negative social comparison. Thus, it appears that, although happy children behave in a manner consistent with the "altruism" findings of previous research, negative affect children self-reward in a selective fashion, depending on whether they "deserve" the reward or not. This finding suggests the importance of examining the various effects of negative affect on the perception of the self and the other.

One final piece of data highlights the different processes that may be engendered by mood. Rosenhan, Underwood, and Moore (1974) examined donations and self-rewards under different affective states within the context of a single experiment. They found that, under positive mood, children showed a positive correlation between generosity to self and generosity to others. Under negative moods, the correlation was negative. These data suggest that negative affect does produce a conserving of resources through both self-gratification and lack of sharing with others. Happy mood states encouraged a generosity inwardly and outwardly. Thus, the mechanisms for the promotion of responsiveness to oneself under positive and negative moods appear to be quite different. Generosity to others also appears to be produced by different motives, depending on one's affective state.

In this brief review, we have tried to highlight some of the consequences that affect has for our behavior. There are a number of domains, such as influences on social attraction, memory, and aggression, that there was not the space to explore. Additionally, we have barely mentioned the enormous literature on clinical moods such as depression. It is interesting to note that there are many parallels between the findings in studies of laboratory-induced sadness and research using subjects who scored high on a depression inventory. What does seem clear is that a number of important ways in which we respond to ourselves and to others are influenced by our affective state.

The role that socialization plays in these processes has not received any significant attention. However, we do find some evidence of age changes in such things as the relationship between affect and altruism, delay of gratification, and children's understanding of affect–behavior relationships. Clinical evidence also suggests that there may be some long-term continuities in the sorts of behavioral patterns that people engage in in relation to affective events. One possibility that seems to be emerging (or reemerging) in psychology is that affect is an important contextual element in people's learning (Bower, 1981), and that we retrieve information that is tied to affect when that same or a similar affect is reinstated. If this is the case, then the socialization of affect may be a particularly potent and pervasive kind of learning. The behaviors that become attached to those affects are to some degree idiosyncratic but, as evidenced by some of the research reviewed here, show some degree of generality.

The challenge is to try to extrapolate some general theoretical organization that gives coherence to these diverse findings. The way to that theory(ies) that today (we hedge our bets) seems most promising is in terms of a better understanding of the relationship between affect and memory and perception (Gilligan & Bower, 1983). We are a long way from a comprehensive view of the complex interrelations of affect and behavior but the past decade has also seen impressive advances. Before long, we may be in a better position to understand the experience and the processes that were described in Douglas's behavior at the start of this chapter.

REFERENCES

Alloy, I. B., Abramson, L. Y., & Viscusi, D. Induced mood and the illusion of control. *Journal of Personality and Social Psychology*, 1981, 41, 1129–1140.

Barnett, M., King, L. M., & Howard, J. A. Inducing affect about self and other: Effects on generosity in children. *Developmental Psychology*, 1979, 15, 164–167.

Baumann, D. J., Cialdini, R., & Kenrick, D. Altruism as hedonism: Helping and self-gratification as equivalent processes. *Journal of Personality and Social Psychology*, 1981, 41, 1039–1046.

Berkowitz, L., & Connor, W. H. Success, failure and social responsibility. *Journal of Personality and Social Psychology*, 1966, 4, 664–669.

Bower, G. Mood and memory. *American Psychologist*, 1981, 36, 120–148.

Bugental, D. B., & Moore, B. S. Effects of induced moods on voice affect. *Developmental Psychology*, 1979, 15, 664–665.

Cialdini, R. B., & Kenrick, D. T. Altruism as hedonism: A social development perspective on the relationship of negative mood state and helping. *Journal of Personality and Social Psychology*, 1976, *34*, 907–914.

Duvall, S., & Wicklund, R. A. *A theory of objective self-awareness*. New York: Academic Press, 1972.

Feather, N. T. Change in confidence following success or failure as a predictor of subsequent performance. *Journal of Personality and Social Psychology*, 1968, 39–46.

Fry, P. S. Success, failure and resistance to temptation. *Developmental Psychology*, 1977, *15*, 519–520.

Gilligan, S. G., & Bower, G. How mood biases cognition. In C. Izard, J. Kagan & R. Zajonc (Eds.), *Emotion, cognition, and behavior*. New York: Cambridge University Press, 1983.

Glasberg, R., & Aboud, F. E. A developmental perspective on the study of depression: Children's evaluative reactions to sadness. *Developmental Psychology*, 1981, *17*, 195–202.

Hoffman, M. Developmental synthesis of affect and cognition and its implications for altruistic behavior. *Developmental Psychology*, 1975, 607–612.

Isen, A. M. Success, failure, attention and reaction to others: The warm glow of success. *Journal of Personality and Social Psychology*, 1970, *15*, 294–301.

Isen, A. M., & Levin, P. F. The effects of feeling good on helping: Cookies and kindness. *Journal of Personality and Social Psychology*, 1972, *21*, 384–388.

Isen, A. M., Clark, M., & Schwartz, M. F. Duration of the effect of good mood on helping: Footprints on the sands of time. *Journal of Personality and Social Psychology*, 1976, *34*, 385–393.

Izard, C. *Human emotions*. New York: Plenum Press, 1977.

Jones, G. F., & Thelen, M. H. The effects of induced mood states on self-reinforcement behavior. *Journal of Psychology*, 1978, *98*, 249–252.

Kazdin, A. E., & Bryan, J. H. Competence and volunteering. *Journal of Experimental Social Psychology*, 1971, *7*, 87–97.

Kenrick, D. T., Bauman, D. J., & Cialdini, R. B. A step in the socialization of altruism as hedonism: Effect of negative mood on children's generosity under public and private conditions. *Journal of Personality and Social Psychology*, 1979, *37*, 747–755.

Leight, K. E., & Ellis, W. C. Emotional mood states, strategies, and state-dependency in memory. *Journal of Verbal Learning and Verbal Behavior*, 1981, *20*, 251–266.

Mandler, G. *Mind and emotions*. New York: Wiley, 1975.

Masters, J. C., Barden, R. C., & Ford, M. E. Affect states, expressive behavior and learning in children. *Journal of Personality and Social Psychology*, 1979, *37*, 380–390.

Masters, J. W., & Furman, W. Effects of affective states on noncontingent outcome expectancies and beliefs in internal and external control. *Developmental Psychology*, 1976, *12*, 481–482.

McMillen, D. S., Sanders, D. Y., & Solomon, G. S. Self-esteem, attentiveness, and helping behavior. *Personality and Social Psychology Bulletin*, 1977, *3*, 257–262.

Midlarsky, E., & Midlarsky, M. Some determinants of aiding under experimentally induced stress. *Journal of Personality*, 1973, *41*, 305–327.

Mischel, W., Coates, B., & Raskoff, A. Effects of success and failure on self-gratification. *Journal of Personality and Social Psychology*, 1968, *10*, 381–390.

Mischel, W., Ebbesen, E., & Zeiss, A. Cognitive and attentional mechanisms in delay of gratification. *Journal of Personality and Social Psychology*, 1973, *21*, 204–218.

Moore, B. *Mood and anagram solution*. Unpublished manuscript, 1982.

Moore, B., & Underwood, B. *Affect, age and self-reward*. Unpublished manuscript, 1982.

Moore, B. S., Underwood, B., & Rosenhan, D. L. Affect and altruism. *Developmental Psychology*, 1973, *8*, 99–104.

Moore, B. S., Clyburn, A., & Underwood, B. The role of affect in the delay of gratification. *Child Development*, 1976, *47*, 237–276.

Moore, B. S., Underwood, B., Doyle, L., Heberlein, P., & Litzie, K. Generalization of feedback about performance. *Cognitive Therapy and Research*, 1979, *3*, 371–380.

Moore, B. S., Underwood, B., & Litzie, K. *Affect and distribution of rewards*. Unpublished manuscript, 1982.

Natale, M. Effect of induced elation and depression on internal external locus of control. *Journal of Psychology*, 1978, *100*, 315–321.

Polivy, J. On the induction of emotion in the laboratory: Discrete moods or multiple affect states. *Journal of Personality and Social Psychology*, 1981, *41*, 803–817.

Rosenhan, D. L., Underwood, B., & Moore, B. S. Affect moderates self-gratification and altruism. *Journal of Personality and Social Psychology*, 1974, *30*, 546–552.

Rosenhan, D. L., Karylowski, J., Salovey, P., & Hargis, K. Emotion and altruism. In J. P. Rushton & R. M. Sorrentino (Eds.), *Altruism and helping behavior*. Hillsdale, N.J.: Erlbaum, 1981.

Rosenhan, D. L., Salovey, P., & Hargis, K. The joys of helping: Focus of attention mediates the impact of positive affect on altruism. *Journal of Personality and Social Psychology*, 1981, *40*, 899–905.

Rotter, J. Some problems and misconceptions related to the construct of internal versus external control of reinforcement. *Journal of Consulting and Clinical Psychology*, 1975, *43*, 55–67.

Sacco, W. P., & Hokanson, J. E. Depression and self-reinforcement in a public and private setting. *Journal of Personality and Social Psychology*, 1982, *42*, 377–385.

Seeman, G., & Schwartz, J. C. Affective state and preference for immediate versus delayed reward. *Journal of Research in Personality*, 1974, *4*, 384–394.

Thompson, W. C., Cowan, C. L., & Rosenhan, D. L. Focus of attention mediates the impact of negative affect on altruism. *Journal of Personality and Social Psychology*, 1980, *48*, 291–300.

Tompkins, S. S. *Affect, imagery, consciousness* (Vol. 1). New York: Springer, 1962.

Underwood, B., Moore, B. S., & Rosenhan, D. L. Affect and self-gratification. *Developmental Psychology*, 1973, *9*, 320–326.

Underwood, B., Berenson, J. F., Berenson, R. J., Cheng, K. K., Wilson, D., Kulik, J., Moore, B. S., & Wenzel, G. Attention, negative affect and altruism: An ecological validation. *Personality and Social Psychology Bulletin*, 1977, *7*, 221–226.

Underwood, B., Froming, W. J., & Moore, B. S. Mood, attention, and altruism: A search for mediating variable. *Developmental Psychology*, 1977, *13*, 541–542.

Underwood, B., Froming, W. J., & Moore, B. S. Mood and personality: A search for the causal relationship. *Journal of Personality*, 1980, *48*, 331–339.

Underwood, B., Froming, W., & Moore, B. S. *Dimensions of affect*. Unpublished manuscript, University of Texas at Dallas, 1982.

Velten, E. A laboratory task for induction of mood states. *Behavior Research and Therapy*, 1968, *6*, 473–482.

Weyant, J. M. Effects of mood states, costs and benefits on helping. *Journal of Personality and Social Psychology*, 1978, *36*, 1169–1176.

Yates, L. *Affect age and self-control*. Unpublished doctoral dissertation, 1982.

11

Unresponsive Children and Powerless Adults
Cocreators of Affectively Uncertain Caregiving Environments

Daphne Blunt Bugental

Picture a common scene in a pediatrician's office. The waiting room is filled with an assortment of parents and children engaged in a variety of interactions. One set of parents is absorbed in magazines while their 4-year-old wanders through the room talking to everyone. A mother has her daughter close at her side as she points out magazine pictures to the child. Another mother is engaged in active combat with a 7-year-old boy who appears intent on touching every object in the room and getting onto or under every piece of furniture. "Johnny, leave that alone," she implores plaintively in a weak voice. Johnny glances at her briefly but ignores her. She smiles nervously and comments to the woman in the next chair, "Boys. You can't do anything with them. You're lucky you have a girl. She sits there so nice and quiet."

This everyday vignette allows for many different interpretations. One might focus on differences in parental behavior as causal determiners of their children's behavior. One might make the interpretation that termperamental differences between the children are acting to elicit different parental behavior. Or one might note the mother's expressed beliefs about children and parenting and make the inference that these

Daphne Blunt Bugental • Psychology Department, University of California, Santa Barbara, California 93111.

cognitions act as basic underlying causes of caregiving sequences. In this chapter, we want to describe and present empirical evidence to support a transactional model of caregiving in which we are concerned with all of these causal agents. This model will be applied to unresponsive children, the affectively negative and weak socialization environments that they tend to induce, and the subsequent maintenance of an aversive childhood behavioral style. We are concerned with the interaction of children's behavior, parental behavior, and parental beliefs. And in looking at the caregiving environments created by various pairings of adults and children, we are particularly interested in *complex adult communication patterns that occur in response to and that, in turn, influence children's behavior.* Measures are reported not only for direct paraental messages of affect, but also for their subtle messages of power—cues that suggest how much importance should be assigned to the caregiver's affective reactions. In order to determine the full range of communicated affect and power, we are concerned here not only with what parents say, but with how they say it, and with what they look like when they say it.

In considering the history of developmental psychology, it is easy to see the primacy of the view that the child's emerging emotions and behaviors are determined by the child's socialization. What the child becomes as an adult has been seen as a product of socializing agents—parents, peers, and the broader culture. This causal relationship appeals to common experience and has a history of empirical support. Within this book, for example, the child's developing affective expression is typically interpreted in terms of socialization. What is debatable, however, is the relative weight assigned to socializing agents and the variability in the extent to which socializing agents act as causal components. Early behaviorists, like primiparous parents, placed enormous stock in the importance of parental behavior as a causal factor. Just as parents are likely to attempt to control their first child's behavior at every turn, early behaviorists assigned a central role to the parents as shapers of the child's behavior.

As the years went by—within psychology, just as for more experienced parents—greater attention has been paid to the contribution of the child to his or her own socialization. Parents are often surprised to discover that what worked with their first child has little effect on their second child, and the emerging possibility looms that perhaps they are not the all-powerful "molders" and "shapers" that they thought they were. Perhaps there are initial temperamental differences in their children. Bell (1966) pulled together evidence from a variety of sources to support the argument that we have historically underemphasized the extent to which a child's behavior and a child's characteristics influence the socialization that she or he receives. Not only do parents influence children. Children influence parents.

Implicit in the emerging consideration of "child effects" has been the assumption of sequential *two-way* effects between children and socializing agents. Children influence caregivers, who alter their behavior so as to present a different socializing environment to the children, who in turn alter their behavior, and so on. Most research, however, has been concerned with unidirectional rather than bidirectional effects. Some of the best evidence for reciprocal sequential effects has come from careful observations of ongoing family interaction. Patterson (1976), from a behavioral standpoint, pointed out the extent to which the behavior of family members can act to maintain (or remediate) a dysfunctional system. Aggressive children, for example, may ignore initially reasonable maternal control efforts—behavior that leads to escalating and more negative control eforts—which are eventually terminated when the mother "gives up"—a reaction that allows the child control over his or her environment. Within clinical psychology (Haley, 1976; Minuchin, 1974; Mishler & Waxler, 1965), there has also been an emerging interest in self-sustaining transactional systems. "Enmeshed" families behave in such a way as to maintain malfunctioning family systems. What appears to be needed to support these observations of natural family systems is greater experimental evidence for these implicit transactional sequences.

Of particular interest to us here is the extent to which "difficult" or "aversive" behavior patterns of the child act as major contributors to socializing environments. A number of individual differences in children's dispositions have been found to be present even in early infancy—differences that may set the stage for later development. Some young children demonstrate behaviors that are interpretable as manifestations of negative affect. They may be "cranky." Their cries may sound "demanding." They may seem "rejecting" as a function of their unresponsiveness or "noncuddliness." A low smile rate may make a child seem "depressed" or "indifferent." In short, children produce behaviors that a caregiver may easily interpret as reflecting negative affective states. These apparent negative affective expressions on the part of a child may—in some caregivers—elicit matched affective responses. And from there, a series of escalating negative encounters may ensue. We are proposing here that the socialization of affect often begins with original individual differences in the child's real or apparent emotional expression. And differences in the caregiver's perception and interpretation of these behaviors will determine the extent to which the child sets the initial course for his or her subsequent affective development.

PARENTAL ATTRIBUTIONS: MODERATOR VARIABLES IN TRANSACTIONAL SYSTEMS

In our original vignette, we alluded to one mother's belief about children and about parenting. What role can we assign to parental beliefs in caregiving transactions? As Bell (1979) observed, children interact with *thinking* parents. Family interactions are not just a matter of the behavior of individuals impacting on each other. Not every adult responds in the same way to identical child behavior (nor do different children respond in the same way to identical parental behavior). A highly active child may be perceived as "out of control" and as needing discipline by one adult; yet, another adult may perceive the same child behavior as perfectly acceptable and as an indication of "high spirits" and healthy energy. Adults come to caregiving relationships with different beliefs about children and different beliefs about the causes of successful caregiving. One might expect (and many researchers have devoted years in an effort to demonstrate) that these well-entrenched parental belief systems act as underlying determiners of adult behavior and subsequent child behavior. And yet, the history of research exploring parental attitudes and beliefs in interviews and questionnaires has been notably weak in demonstrating strong relationships with socialization practices and outcomes (Becker & Krug, 1965). To some extent, the reason is the reactive nature of the measurement procedures employed. But it may also be that we have been placing these cognitive factors in the wrong position within the caregiving system. We have been looking at the *direct* role of cognitions as elicitors of adult behavior and subsequent child behavior. We have proposed in our research (Bugental, Caporael, & Shennum, 1980; Bugental & Shennum, 1984) that parental beliefs act in a *moderator* role within caregiving systems. Specifically, parental beliefs about the causes of caregiving outcomes act as selective filters in determining the impact of different types of child behavior on adult behavior. Stated simply, particular child behaviors have more impact on some adults than on others.

The general model of socialization that we have proposed can be conceptualized as follows:

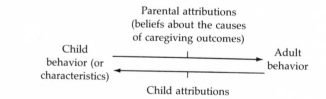

The effect of the child's behavior is seen as *moderated* by the adult's beliefs about the causes of successful and unsuccessful caregiving outcomes. If, for example, the parent believes that he or she can effect successful interaction as a function of his or her caregiving ability, he or she is likely to present a stable, self-confident behavioral pattern that is not readily eroded by behavior demonstrated by difficult children. As another example, the parent who believes that children contribute significantly to their own socialization is likely to monitor and to be reactive to the capabilities and competencies of different children. We are suggesting that parental attributions (regarding their own influence *and* the child's influence of caregiving outcomes) act as differential *sensitizers* to different kinds of child behavior.

Adult behavioral responses to children are seen here to occur as an interactive function of child behavior and adult attributions. The impact of certain types of child behavior is heightened for adults whose attributions sensitize them to that particular child behavior. Their response is predicted, in turn, as *eliciting or maintaining child behavior supportive of their belief system*. If, for example, the adult believes that she or he has little power or competence as a caregiver *and* the child is, in fact, hard to control, the adult will behave in such a way as to maintain the child's unresponsive behavior and thus to support the adult's beliefs. Just as adult expectations of children have been found to act in a self-fulfilling fashion (Rosenthal & Jacobson, 1968; Zanna, Sheras, Cooper, & Shaw, 1975), we have predicted that parental causal attributions about caregiving outcomes act in a self-fulfilling fashion. The extent to which adult responses act back to influence child behavior will, in turn, be moderated by the complexity and the nature of the child's attributions.

APPLICATION OF TRANSACTIONAL MODEL TO UNRESPONSIVE CHILDREN

The general transactional model proposed here can be applied to a variety of interactive systems. The focus of attention in this paper is upon caregiving transactions involving child unresponsiveness. Unresponsive children are seen as eliciting relatively "uncertain" affective responses from caregivers who believe they have little control over caregiving outcomes:

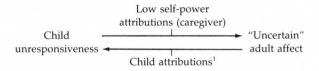

[1]Although a test of the full model requires the assessment of the role of child attributions, the research reported here was concerned only with adult attributions (because of an insufficient number and heterogeneity of children).

Unresponsive Children

In applying our transactional model to unresponsive children, we are concerned with what kinds of socializing environments that such children are likely to create for themselves and what kinds of adults are likely to respond adversely to them. In considering child unresponsiveness, we are dealing with a variable that has received considerable popular, clinical, educational, and research attention—under the various labels of *out-of-control, impulsive,* or *hyperactive behavior.* Unresponsive children form a high percentage of those targeted for special clinical interventions, educational remediation, and psychoactive medication. They are also more likely to come to the attention of social service agencies in that they are at risk for abuse (Solomon, 1973) and are overrepresented among those children available for adoption or foster placement (Menlove, 1965). Additionally, hyperactivity is one of the most common symptoms among children referred to mental health clinics (Patterson, 1975). Those who provide care or service to unresponsive children often appear to feel it particularly urgent that something be done to alter their behavior.

Unresponsive child behavior has also reached considerable *research* attention. Systematic observations of unresponsive children have revealed that they have a negative impact on the interaction patterns of their parents (e.g., Campbell, 1973); teachers (e.g., Whalen, Henker, & Dotemoto, 1981); and peers (e.g., Campbell, Endman, & Bernfeld, 1977). In our own initial research with "disturbed" children (characteristically described as "hard to control" or unresponsive), we observed a number of parental communication patterns not found in well-functioning families. For example, there was more affective inconsistency across communication channels (Bugental, Kaswan, Love, & April, 1971). Additionally, the mothers of "disturbed" children showed an interesting combination of affect and power cues: their verbal content expressing approval or disapproval was accompanied by relatively weak vocal intonation (Bugental & Love, 1975). When the mother made an affective statement to the child, there was a relative drop (from baseline) in her subtle communication of power. In short, messages delivered to "difficult" children were inconsistent or lacking in potency. The affective reactions of parents were packaged in such a way that it was not clear what message was being conveyed or with what conviction. These findings were similar to the "double-bind" communication patterns posited as operating in more severely disturbed family systems (Bateson, Jackson, Haley, & Weakland, 1956).

Correlational studies of unresponsive children are, of course, subject to problems in determining the direction of effect. That is, do unresponsive children adversely influence caregivers, or do incompetent caregivers cause child unresponsiveness? A recent strategy that has been employed to unscramble the direction of effects has been the experimental manipulation of the real or apparent behavior of children in interaction with parents or strangers. Within this general research paradigm, it has been demonstrated that (a) responsive children are more likely to elicit reasoning strategies from adults, whereas unresponsive children elicit more bargaining strategies (Keller & Bell, 1979); (b) responsive children are reacted to with greater positive affect than are unresponsive children (Bates, 1975); (c) responsive children receive more adult help and attention than do unresponsive children (Cantor & Gelfand, 1977); and (d) increasing child unresponsiveness elicits from adults an increased use of negative controls (Vasta & Copitch, 1981). In short, it appears that adults are likely to respond with more negative affect and more extreme control tactics when confronted with an unresponsive child.

Caregiver Attributions as Moderators of the Effects of Unresponsive Children

Given the fact that unresponsive children elicit negative adult reactions, it may nonetheless be anticipated that there is considerable individual variation among caregivers. Just as uncontrollable stimuli are responded to negatively by most people, it is nonetheless true that some individuals are more adversely affected than others. And as suggested earlier, individuals with low self-perceived power are likely to be particularly susceptible to the debilitating effects of hard-to-control or uncontrollable situations. It is reasonable to suppose that caregivers with a low belief in their ability as caregivers are more likely to react negatively to unresponsive children. Intractable child behavior poses a greater threat to caregivers who lack a stable belief in their own competence.

We are specifically concerned here with caregiver beliefs concerning the extent to which caregiving outcomes are under their own control or are subject to the vagaries of chance. This attributional variable has been conceptualized within social psychology in terms of "personal causation" (DeCharms, 1972), "internal" versus "external" locus of control (Rotter, 1966), or a combination of the dimensions of locus, stability, and intentionality (Weiner, 1974). We refer to this construct in terms of a dimension of self-perceived power or competence. Specifically, we are interested in assessing the extent to which high importance is attributed to internal, stable factors versus external, unstable factors as causes of caregiving success.

In considering the behavioral reactions of parents as a function of their attributional style, one may think in terms of both self-presentation strategies and the unaware leakage of attitudes. That is, their communication patterns will reflect some composite of the image that they wish to convey and their actual affective responses. Baumeister (1982) proposed that the two main self-presentational motives are (a) to please the audience, and (b) to construct one's public self so that it is congruent with one's ideal. Although Baumeister did not specifically note the relevance of self-presentational motives to individual differences in attributional style, such a conceptualization would seem to be appropriate. Individuals with low self-perceived power (externals) have characteristically been found to be more attentive and responsive to social cues (Baron & Ganz, 1972; Baron, Cowan, Ganz, & McDonald, 1974; Lefcourt, Hogg, Struthers, & Holmes, 1975; Phares, 1976; Rajecki, Ickes, & Tanford, 1981); correspondingly, their dominant self-presentation motive appears to be that of "pleasing an audience." In contrast, individuals with high self-perceived power (internals) are more likely to resist social influence and, in turn, to be more effective as sources of influence. These individuals appear to have a self-presentation style characterized by more of a need to meet their own standards more than to meet those of others.

It was our expectation here that adults who have low self-perceived competence as caregivers would monitor every new situation for social expectations. In the absence of any stable belief that they are competent caregivers, it is necessary to be constantly vigilant regarding the characteristics of the child and the setting. The apparent responsiveness or tractability of the child acts as a particularly salient cue to such individuals. Unresponsive or uncontrollable child behavior can be thought of as one example of environmental uncontrollability. And we know from the learned-helplessness literature that "external" individuals react with greater manifested helplessness to hard-to-control or uncontrollable situations (e.g., Dweck & Repucci, 1973; Gregory, Chartier, & Wright, 1979; Hiroto, 1974; Lefcourt, Hogg, Struthers, & Holmes, 1975: Pittman & Pittman, 1979).

In a pilot study, we explored the extent to which the parental communication patterns that we had observed earlier in natural family interaction could be elicited experimentally in a synthetic family analogue. In particular, we wanted to determine the extent to which "weak" caregiver affect was elicited by child unresponsiveness, by "weak" adult attributions, or by some interaction of the two. We trained elementary-school-aged children to act either in a responsive or an unresponsive fashion when interacting with unfamiliar women. We observed that a particular pattern of adult communication (more assertively voiced neutral content and relatively less assertively voiced affective content) occurred as an interactive function of unresponsive child behavior and low self-perceived adult power ("external" locus of control). Shifting patterns of vocal assertion were characteristic of women with an external locus of control—but only in interaction with impulsive, unresponsive children.

Child Response to Adult Communication Patterns

The final leg of the posited transactional system involves the child's response to adult communication patterns. Developmental analyses of children's decoding processes suggest that young children (at the pre-operational age) respond to confused or inconsistent messages by a discounting process (Bugental, Kaswan, & Love, 1970). That is, instead of integrating or synthesizing the incompatible components of a message, they discount any positive affect and interpret the message as affectively negative. And even among older children and adult decoders, affective inconsistency within the *audio* channel (content versus intonation) appears to be resolved by a discounting process; that is, the more affectively negative of the two components is given greater credibility (Bugental, 1974). No information is available on children's interpretation of the assertiveness of adult messages. But there does seem to be a very general tendency to assign greater weight to vocal intonation (the channel we found to "leak" cues to powerlessness) than to verbal content when messages are inconsistent (Mehrabian & Weiner, 1967) or potentially deceptive (Zuckerman, DePaulo, & Rosenthal, 1981).

EMPIRICAL TEST OF TRANSACTIONAL MODEL

Method

In a more complete test of our transactional model, we conducted a second study in which we systematically varied child responsiveness. We conducted a two-part study in which children were either *trained* to role-play responsive versus unresponsive behavior or were *selected* on the basis of their dispositional responsiveness. This strategy allowed greater generalization capability; that is, the adult behavior elicited reliably by both "acting" and "dispositionally" unresponsive children could be safely assumed to be causally connected to unresponsive child behavior. Again, the children were paired with unfamiliar women (all of whom were mothers of school-aged children). These women were initially given the Parent Attribution Test (PAT), an instrument that measures the importance assigned to internal versus external, and stable versus unstable, factors as causes of caregiving success.[2] The adults and the children were videotaped interacting in (a) a purely social interaction in which they were simply told to "get to know something about each other" and (b) a game-playing situation, in which they worked together building things with Tinkertoys. Analyses were made of the caregiver's verbal content, facial expression and head movement, and vocal intonation.[3]

The communication patterns demonstrated by the mothers were analyzed in verbal (content), vocal (content-filtered voice intonation), and visual (head/face) channels. Each channel was judged independently on three relatively orthogonal dimensions:

1. Affect (the extent to which the messages were pleasant and friendly versus unpleasant and unfriendly).
2. Self-power (the extent to which the messages were strong and assertive versus weak and unassertive)
3. Referred power (the assumed age and competence of the addressee)

The first two dimensions are the familiar variables of evaluation and potency (Mehrabian, 1971). The third variable has been observed less commonly and refers to the extent to which a speaker engaged in a "maternal," "baby-talking," or condescending style of interaction. This third dimension was included so that we could assess not only the manifested power of the speaker but the "respect" (referred power or competence) that was demonstrated for the child. "Referred power" was assessed by asking the judges to rate the extent to which a message appeared to be addressed to a young child versus an adult peer.

In addition to obtaining global impressions of the communication characteristics of the three channels, we also obtained ratings and behavior counts on more specific behaviors, for example, the prosodic properties of speech (pitch, pitch variability, and so on); the characteristics of smiling behavior (frequency, intensity, and so on); head movements and postural symmetry; and specific verbal-content categories (the frequency of conversational initiations, answers, and so on). Regression analyses were conducted to determine the relationship of specific communication components to global judgments of channels.

---

[2]Up to this point, only attributions for caregiving success have proved to be significantly related to caregiver communication patterns. The PAT does include attributions for caregiving failure, however.

[3]Vocal intonation was separate from verbal content by routing audiotapes through a bandpass filter that effectively eliminated the intelligible portions of speech.

In the remainder of this chapter, we will summarize some of the findings[4] from this investigation.

Results and Discussion

1. *The mothers with low self-perceived power rated child "difficulty" more differentially than did the mothers with high self-perceived power.* Following the interactions, the adult subjects were asked to rate how much they liked the child and how difficult they found the interaction to be. The caregivers with low self-perceived power (S+) appeared to be significantly and sizably more reactive to child responsiveness than were the caregivers with high self-perceived power. As can be seen in Figure 1, they rated responsive children as "easier" and unresponsive children as

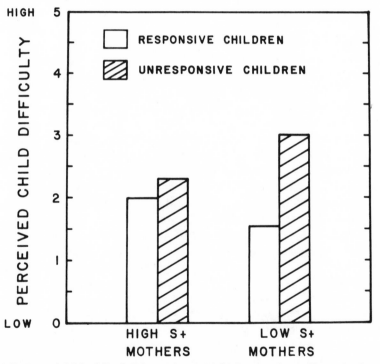

FIG. 1. Ratings of child "difficulty" by mothers with high versus low self-perceived power (on a 7-point scale where 1 = "easy" and 7 = "difficult").

___
[4]Findings are reported only for those caregiver patterns elicited as a function of *both* enacted child responsiveness and dispositional child responsiveness.

more "difficult" than did the mothers with high self-perceived power. High S+ mothers showed little distinction in their ratings of responsive and unresponsive children (their expressed "liking" of the children was unaffected by child behavior or parental attribution).

So, in support of our general prediction, caregivers with low self-perceived power or competence are much more *reactive* to gradations (or *create* greater gradations) in child responsiveness. And, in particular, they rate unresponsive children as relatively "difficult."

2. *The mothers with low self-perceived power were behaviorally more reactive to child responsiveness than were the mothers with high self-perceived power.* In support of our predictions (and past research), significant interactions were obtained between child behavior and adult attribution on all three dimensions. The first general characteristic of the observed interaction patterns was that of *differential reactivity.* The women with low self-perceived parental power responded somewhat more differentially to the responsive and the unresponsive children than did the women with high self-perceived power. As suggested earlier, they appeared to modify their self-presentation to fit the characteristics of the "audience." To some extent, this modification may have been directed toward pleasing the experimenter (low S+ mothers were significantly more likely to look at the experimenter when being introduced to a child who was behaving in an unattentive fashion; Cruzcosa, 1982). Alternately (or additionally), their behavior may reflect their high level of reactivity to the social stimulus posed by the child. The mothers with relatively high self-perceived power, on the other hand, did not show any significant variation in their behavior as a function of the child's responsiveness. They maintained relatively moderate levels of affect, assertion, and "respect."

The significance of the differential behavior patterns shown by the low S+ mothers to responsive and unresponsive children can be determined by noting what was communicated in different channels. Quite different messages were given in communication components that are prone to "leakage" versus components that are readily subject to deliberate management (and are thus not good sources of "leakage").

3. *The mothers with low self-perceived power "leaked" their beliefs and attitudes through their vocal intonation.* Vocal intonation, a "high-leakage" communication channel, yielded important differences in maternal reactions to responsive versus unresponsive children. The low S+ mothers appeared to "leak" their beliefs about the children through their vocal intonation. With the responsive children, their voice intonation was relatively pleasant (high pitch variability and smooth quality); with the unresponsive children, their intonation was neutral or slightly unpleasant (monotone in pitch and relatively rough in quality). Second, their

vocal intonation (during affective messages) was relatively assertive (loud, resonant) with the responsive children and relatively weak (soft, thin) with the unresponsive children. It appears that the differential reaction to the unresponsive children by the low S+ mothers was directly reflected in their vocal intonation, a channel over which speakers have relatively low control (Holzman & Rousey, 1966). Thus, support is offered for the "leakage" of underlying attitudes through communication channels not easily subjected to monitoring and control (Ekman & Friesen, 1969).

4. *The mothers with low self-perceived power played a role reciprocal to the child's role through their visual behavior.* The low S+ mothers were also differentially reactive to the responsive and the unresponsive children in their visual behavior. When interacting with a responsive child, they demonstrated "respectful" visual behavior (i.e., facial expressions and head movements judged to be characteristic of adult speech to a peer). When interacting with an unresponsive child, however, they manifested a "condescending" communication style (i.e., their visual behavior was judged to be characteristic of speech to a young child). This condescending or baby-talking pattern included such specific visual behaviors as:

1. High duration of smiling
2. Head and body asymmetry (e.g., many head tilts)
3. "Ducking" head movements (moving the head lower and toward the child)

This total visual pattern is depicted in Figure 2 by actors simulating the behavior shown by sample low S+ mothers.

The observed visual behavior may be thought of as being more under speaker control than vocal intonation. Visual behavior, as a whole, cannot be firmly identified as being a high-leakage or a low-leakage channel. Most body behaviors have been found to be good sources of leakage concerning unexpressed affect (Ekman & Friesen, 1974). Micro-momentary facial expressions (Haggard & Isaacs, 1966) have been posited as leaking unexpressed emotion. Alternately, many longer duration facial expressions are a primary source of "managed" affect and "display behavior." Smiling, for example, appears to be highly subject to control in self-presentation management (e.g., Bugental, Love, & Gianetto, 1971). We have no information on the self-monitoring and management of the other two visual behaviors (head or body tilts and head "ducking") characteristic of "condescending" speech. One might suspect that they are under communicator control. Observers of the total pattern of "condescending" visual behavior commented on the "effortful" nature of the behavior, for example, "She looks like she's on a first date"; "She's doing her darnedest to get something out of that kid."

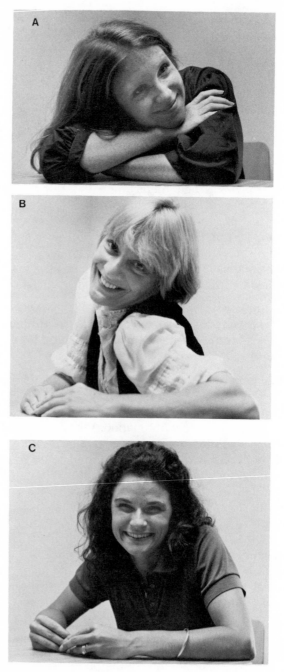

FIG. 2. Actor simulations of visual appearance shown by three low S+ mothers interacting with unresponsive children.

A couple of interpretations may be offered concerning the significance of the low-power mother's visual self-presentation with responsive versus unresponsive children. Her "condescending" style with unresponsive children may be directed toward defusing the "power" or "threat" posed by the child. Alternately, her behavior may be that of playing a role reciprocal to the part portrayed by the child. The child is allowed to direct her role. If he is acting in a "mature" (responsive) fashion, she reciprocates by acting as if she is talking to an adult. If he is "immature" (unresponsive), she acts as if she is talking to a small child. (It should be noted that the behavioral reactivity of low-power mothers was selective. We did not find, for example [Bugental & Shennum, 1984], that they were differentially reactive to shy versus assertive children. They appeared to respond selectively to child behavior that had implications for *their own* potential for successful influence.)

5. *No important differences were found in the mothers' verbal content.* In the framework of this particular observation setting, the *verbal content* of maternal communication was of little interest. The mothers appeared to have a rather standard "script" in interacting with an unfamiliar child ("How old are you?" "Where do you go to school?" "Is this the first time you've been here?")

6. *The total communication pattern shown by the mothers with low self-perceived power in interaction with unresponsive children was affectively inconsistent.* The total multichannel pattern of adult communication (low S + mothers with unresponsive children) was an inconsistent one. It included a rather fixed smile (high smile duration) together with a somewhat unpleasant voice. The mother's head movements suggested that she was "in charge" and the child was very small—but her voice revealed that she did not feel very confident (at least during her affective messages). The composite picture was one of inconsistent affect accompanied by uncertain power. If the smile was to be believed, she was being pleasant; if the voice quality was heard, she was being unpleasant. If the "condescending" head movements were noted, she appeared to be talking to a very small child. But at the same time, she unwittingly revealed that she felt weak. In short, she and the child, together, created an affectively uncertain caregiving environment.

7. *The children behaved differently with the mothers with high versus low self-perceived power.* The next step in assessing the adequacy of our transactional model was to determine the counterinfluence of the mothers on the children. Specifically, we wanted to determine (a) whether the mothers with high versus low self-perceived power had a differential impact on child responsiveness and (b) which maternal behavior(s) appeared to account for any shift in child behavior.

In answering the first question (the effects of maternal attributional style), the changes in child responsiveness were assessed across the course of the interaction. Child responsiveness was measured by two behaviors found to reliably distinguish the responsive versus the unresponsive children (both for the children who were dispositionally responsive versus unresponsive *and* for the children who were acting out responsive versus unresponsive roles):

1. Response latency
2. Responsive quality of verbal content (relative frequency of messages that acknowledged statements made by the mother or followed up on her conversational leads)

The children were found to react differentially to high S+ and low S+ mothers on the dimension of response delay.[5] Specifically, the responsive and the unresponsive children acted very differently from each other when interacting with low S+ mothers. Just as the low S+ mothers showed differential behavior with the two groupings of children, the behavior of the children themselves was polarized. The responsive children responded quickly, whereas the unresponsive children responded slowly. With the high S+ mothers, on the other hand, the two groups of children showed very slight (and significantly lower) differences in behavioral responsiveness. The behavior ratings of the children are shown in Figure 3. The differences in the children's behavior paralleled the differences found in the adults' ratings of the child's "difficulty." This leads one to suspect that the postratings made by the adults may have reflected the reality that they created; that is, their behavioral reactions to the children influenced how "difficult" or "easy" the child's behavior actually became.

8. *The mothers with a "condescending" visual appearance induced more behavioral unresponsiveness in the children.* The second question concerns the mediating adult behaviors that produced "caregiver effects." Limiting ourselves to those adult communication patterns that shifted in response to the child's responsiveness, we performed regression analyses to determine their counterinfluence on child behavior (using adult behaviors in initial time periods to predict child behavior in later time periods, and controlling for initial differences in child behavior). Only one adult communication pattern significantly predicted child responsiveness. Specifically, the more the adult demonstrated a "condescending" visual appearance (smiling, asymmetrical head or body, and head

[5]It should be recalled that the *same* children interacted with high versus low self-power mothers. Therefore, preexisting differences in the children is not a viable alternate hypothesis.

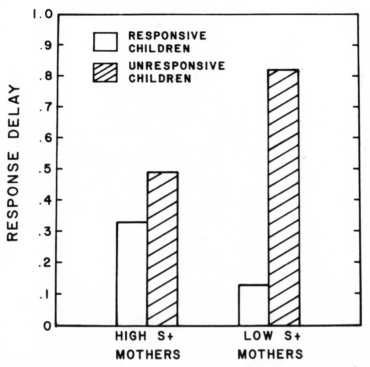

FIG. 3. Child response delay with high and low S+ mothers (on a 3-point scale where 0 = immediate response, 1 = slow response [≤ 3 sec], and 2 = no response).

"ducking") early in the interaction, the more unresponsive (long response latency) the child was in the last part of the interaction. This finding would appear to support the notion of video primary, but the significance of the child's reaction is subject to alternate interpretations. Increased or maintained unresponsiveness in the face of the mother's "condescending" style may have reflected either (a) reactance against her style of control or (b) acceptance of his role as being "very little" and, therefore, not needing to behave in a responsible, responsive fashion.

The children did not respond significantly to maternal vocal intonation (affect, assertion). This finding is somewhat surprising in view of the reliance that listeners place on vocal quality—in particular in "suspect" messages. It appears that vocal intonation revealed important information about the mother's unexpressed attitudes and beliefs, but that this information did not have a direct impact on the child's behavior in this setting. It may be that vocal intonation provides an interpretive anchor for the mother's facial message. Her "maternal" style may alternately be interpreted as reassuring or as an implicit putdown; and her voice indicates what inference should be made. Future research is necessary in which adult vocal quality is systematically varied, and adult effect is measured as a function of *child* attribution.

Summary and Conclusions

In summarizing our findings, it appears that we have a fair amount of support for the proposed transactional model of socialization. The feedback loop that we observed is depicted in Figure 4. Unresponsive children—when paired with women with low self-perceived power—elicited an affectively "unconvincing" and inconsistent adult communication style, components of which acted to *maintain* the child's unresponsiveness.

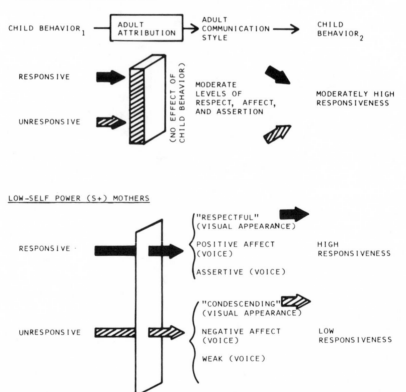

FIG 4. Feedback loops reflecting child unresponsiveness, maternal attributions, and maternal communication patterns.

We can see from this "minitransaction" how real-life family transactions may occur. Poorly functioning family systems often include parents who express reservations about their own competence and children
who demonstrate "out-of-control" behavior. It is easy to see how such
systems may trace back to the child's first introduction to the family.
Behaviors that appear early in infancy have been found to place the child
"at risk" for later problems. Impulsivity, for example, has early manifestations; it may be influenced by genetic factors (Buss & Plomin, 1975)
in terms of its origins, but it is also subject to environmental effects.
Infants who show aversive or unresponsive behavior (e.g., premature
infants) elicit negative affect on a short-term basis (Frodi, Lamb, Leavitt,
Donovan, Neff, & Sherry, 1978) and may even precipitate parental abuse
on a long-term basis (Elmer & Gregg, 1966; Klein & Stern, 1971). If a
"difficult" infant is born to certain kinds of parents, the stage is set for
a downward spiraling transactional system. To Thomas, Chess, and
Birch's long-term analysis of mismatched adult-child pairings (1968),
we have added information concerning (a) nonverbal mediators and
(b) attributional moderators.

The contribution of *adults* to this malfunctioning social system can
be traced back to their beliefs about caregiving relationships. Adults who
believe that caregiving success is due to uncontrollable, unpredictable
situational factors are "set to fail" if they have to deal with a "difficult"
child. Their "externality" influences their behavior differentially with
responsive and with unresponsive children. We may conjecture that
because of their belief in the importance of unstable external factors,
they are reactive to social cues regarding the demands and characteristics
of each new interaction. The behavior of the low-power mother acts to
place the child in control, and correspondingly the child's behavior stays
unchanged. Conversely, the "high-power" adult, who can be thought
of as expecting caregiving success (because of her or his own stable
ability), need not be very concerned by any "threat" posed by a given
child. High-power adults do not alter their behavior in reaction to differences in a child's responsiveness. The child's behavior, in turn, becomes
more modal. That is, when mothers fail to be reactive to the child's
responsiveness or unresponsiveness, children act more alike. One could
think of this adult behavior as "extinguishing" extremes of child behavior.

Adult attributions, in short, appear to act in a self-fulfilling fashion.
For the low-power adults whom we observed here, the outcome *was*
under the control of external forces. It worked out to be a pleasant or
an unpleasant interaction according to the dictates of the actions taken
by the child. For high-power adults, the outcome was under the control
of the adult. Child behavior had little effect. It appears that child effects,

or at least the effects of this type of child behavior, are greater for low-power adults. The moderating effects of self-perceived control extend findings from the learned-helplessness research to adult–child interactions. Just as individuals with low self-perceived control are more reactive to very difficult or negative events as a whole (Lefcourt, Miller, Ware, & Sherk, 1981), caregivers with low self-perceived control are more reactive to difficult children. Their attributional style leads to a behavior pattern that ultimately has the consequence of maintaining their subjective and real helplessness.

To the extent that our findings can be generalized to a broader class of aversive child behaviors, we have shown support for our suppositions concerning the relative contributions of adult and child to the socialization of affect. Child behaviors that appear to be affectively negative act to determine the subsequent caregiving that they receive—*if* the adult's belief system leads him or her to be reactive to these behavior patterns. It may be that child behaviors that suggest negative affective states or negative reactions to a caregiver regularly elicit negative affect (and "helplessness") from adults who have low expectations concerning their own caregiving ability. In contrast, the effects of apparent child negativity are much reduced for adults who have high initial expectations concerning their caregiving ability.

There are applied implications in our results for the pairing of adults and children in a variety of caregiving settings. It appears that some adults are better suited to "withstand" unresponsive (hyperactive, impulsive) child behavior. To the extent that caregivers are selected or matched with children in remedial or caregiving settings, an assessment of caregiver attributions could be employed to potentially predict interaction success. In naturally constituted families, on the other hand, it is important to determine the particular dyadic combination that creates an at-risk situation for later problems. The early identification of parent–child pairings that represent "mismatches" is increasingly being used to target families in need of special assistance. For example, a temperamentally "difficult" infant born following an unwanted pregnancy to a teenage mother is likely to be at risk for a variety of later problems (e.g., child abuse). Our findings suggest that new mothers with low self-perceived parental power are likely to be particularly mismatched with unresponsive children. Remediations for such mismatches lie in many directions: parental education, attribution training, assertiveness training, economic and social changes that give greater power to families, and so on. The unresponsive child may be an initial elicitor of his or her own affectively undesirable caregiving environment, but these effects can be curtailed if the child's caregivers have secure beliefs about their own ability to successfully enact a parental role.

REFERENCES

Baron, R. M., & Ganz, R. L. Effects of locus of control and type of feedback on the task performance of lower-class Black children. *Journal of Personality and Social Psychology*, 1972, *21*, 124–130.

Baron, R. M., Cowan, G., Ganz, R. L., & McDonald, M. Interaction of locus of control and type of performance feedback: Considerations of external validity. *Journal of Personality and Social Psychology*, 1974, *30*, 285–292.

Bates, J. E. The effects of a child's imitation versus nonimitation on adult's verbal and nonverbal positivity. *Journal of Personality and Social Psychology*, 1975, *31*, 840–851.

Bateson, G., Jackson, D., Haley, J., & Weakland, J. Toward a theory of schizophrenia. *Behavior Science*, 1956, *1*, 251–264.

Baumeister, R. F. A self-presentational view of social phenomena. *Psychological Bulletin*, 1982, *91*, 3–26.

Becker, W. C., & Krug, R. S. The Parent Attitude Research Instrument—A research review. *Child Development*, 1965, *36*, 329–365.

Bell, R. Q. A reinterpretation of the direction of effects in studies of socialization. *Psychological Review*, 1966, *75*, 81–95.

Bell, R. Q. Parent, child, and reciprocal influences. *American Psychologist*, 1979, *10*, 821–826.

Bugental, D. B. Interpretation of naturally-occurring discrepancies between words and intonation: Modes of inconsistency resolution. *Journal of Personality and Social Psychology*, 1974, *30*, 125–133.

Bugental, D. B., & Love, L. R. Nonassertive expression of parental approval and disapproval and its relationship to child disturbance. *Child Development*, 1975, *46*, 747–752.

Bugental, D. B., & Shennum, W. A. "Difficult" children as elicitors and targets of adult communication patterns: An attributional-behavioral transactional analysis. *Monographs of the Society for Research in Child Development*, 1983, 1984, *49* (1, Serial No. 205).

Bugental, D. B., Kaswan, J. W., & Love, L. R. Perception of contradictory messages conveyed by verbal and nonverbal channels. *Journal of Personality and Social Psychology*, 1970, *16*, 647–655.

Bugental, D. B., Kaswan, J. W., Love, L. R., & April, C. Verbal-nonverbal conflict in parental messages to nornal and disturbed children. *Journal of Abnormal Psychology*, 1971, *77*, 6–10.

Bugental, D. B., Love, L. R., & Gianetto, R. M. Perfidious feminine faces. *Journal of Personality and Social Psychology*, 1971, *17*, 314–318.

Bugental, D. B., Caporael, L., & Shennum, W. A. Experimentally-produced child uncontrollability: Effects on the potency of adult communication patterns. *Child Development*, 1980, *51*, 520–528.

Buss, A. M., & Plomin, R. A. *A temperament theory of personality development.* New York: Wiley-Interscience, 1975.

Campbell, S. B. Mother-child interaction in reflective, impulsive, and hyperactive children. *Developmental Psychology*, 1973, *8*, 341–349.

Campbell, S. B., Endman, M. W., & Bernfeld, G. A three-year follow-up of hyperactive preschoolers into elementary school. *Journal of Child Psychology and Psychiatry*, 1977, *18*, 239–249.

Cantor, N., & Gelfand, D. Effects of responsiveness and sex of children on adult's behavior. *Child Development*, 1977, *48*, 232–238.

Cruzcosa, M. M. *Adult effect on child responsiveness as a function of adult locus of control.* Unpublished master's thesis, University of California, Santa Barbara, 1982.

DeCharms, R. Personal causation training in the schools. *Journal of Applied Social Psychology,* 1972, 2, 95–113.

Dweck, C. S., & Repucci, D. Learned helplessness and reinforcement responsibility in children. *Journal of Personality and Social Psychology,* 1973, 25, 109–116.

Ekman, P., & Friesen, W. V. Nonverbal leakage and clues to deception. *Psychiatry,* 1969, 32, 88–106.

Ekman, P., & Friesen, W. V. Detecting deception from the body or face. *Journal of Personality and Social Psychology,* 1974, 29, 288–296.

Elmer, E., & Gregg, G. S. Developmental characteristics of abused children. *Pediatrics,* 1966, 40, 596–602.

Frodi, A. M., Lamb, M. E., Leavitt, L. A., Donovon, W. L., Neff, C. N., & Sherry, D. Fathers' and mothers' responses to the faces and cries of normal and premature infants. *Developmental Psychology,* 1978, 14, 490–498.

Gregory, W. L., Chartier, G. M., & Wright, M. H. Learned helplessness and learned effectiveness: Effects of explicit response cues on individuals differing in personal central experiences. *Journal of Personality and Social Psychology,* 1979, 37, 1982–1982.

Haggard, E. A., & Isaacs, K. S. Micro-momentary facial expressions as indicators of ego mechanisms in psychotherapy. In L. A. Gottschalk & A. H. Auerbach (Eds.), *Methods of research in psychotherapy.* New York: Appleton-Century-Crofts, 1966.

Haley, J. Development of a theory: A history of a research project. In C. E. Sluzki & D. C. Ransom (Eds.), *Double bind: The foundation of a communication approach to the family.* New York: Grune and Stratton, 1976.

Hiroto, D. S. Locus of control and learned helplessness. *Journal of Experimental Psychology,* 1974, 102, 187–193.

Holzman, P. S., & Rousey, C. The voice as a percept. *Journal of Personality and Social Psychology,* 1966, 4, 78–86.

Keller, B. B., & Bell, R. O. Child effects on adult's method of eliciting altruistic behavior. *Child Development,* 1979, 50, 1004–1009.

Klein, M., & Stern, L. Low birth weight and the battered child syndrome. *American Journal of Diseases of Childhood,* 1971, 122, 15–18.

Lefcourt, H. M., Hogg, E., Struthers, S., & Holmes, C. Causal attributions as a function of locus of control, initial confidence, and performance outcomes. *Journal of Personality and Social Psychology,* 1975, 32, 391–397.

Lefcourt, H. M., Miller, R. S., Ware, E. E., & Sherk, D. Locus of control as a modifier of the relationship between stressors and moods. *Journal of Personality and Social Psychology,* 1981, 41, 357–369.

Mehrabian, A. Nonverbal communication. In J. K. Cole (Ed.), *Nebraska Symposium on Motivation.* Lincoln: University of Nebraska Press, 1971.

Mehrabian, A., & Weiner, M. Decoding of inconsistent communication. *Journal of Personality and Social Psychology,* 1967, 6, 109–114.

Menlove, F. I. Aggressive symptoms in emotionally disturbed adopted children. *Child Development,* 1965, 36, 519–532.

Minuchin, S. *Families and family therapy.* Cambridge: Harvard University Press, 1974.

Mishler, E. G., & Waxler, N. E. Family interaction processes and schizophrenia: A review of current theories. *Merrill-Palmer Quarterly of Behavior and Development,* 1965, 11, 269–315.

Patterson, G. R. The aggressive child: Victim or architect of a coercive system. In L. A. Hamerlynck, L. C. Handy, & E. J. Mash (Eds.), *Behavior modification and families. Vol. 1: Theory and research.* New York: Brunner/Mazel, 1965.

Phares, E. J. *Locus of control in personality*. Morristown, N.J.: General Learning Press, 1976.

Pittman, N. L., & Pittman, T. S. Effects of amount of helplessness training and internal-external locus of control on mood and performance. *Journal of Personality and Social Psychology*, 1979, *37*, 39–47.

Rajecki, D. W., Ickes, W., & Tanford, S. Locus of control and reactions to strangers. *Personality and Social Psychology Bulletin*, 1981, *7*, 282–289.

Rosenthal, R., & Jacobson, L. *Pygmalion in the classroom*. New York: Holt, Rinehart and Winston, 1968.

Rotter, J. B. Generalized expectancies for internal versus external control of reinforcement. *Psychological Monographs*, 1966, *80* (1, Whole No. 609).

Solomon, T. History and demography of child abuse. *Pediatrics*, 1973, *51*, 773–776.

Thomas, A., Chess, S., & Birch, H. G. *Temperament and behavior disorders in children*. New York: New York University Press, 1968.

Vasta, R., & Copitch, P. Simulating conditions of child abuse in the laboratory. *Child Development*, 1981, *52*, 164–170.

Weiner, B. (Ed.). *Achievement motivation and attribution theory*. Morristown, N.J.: General Learning Press, 1974.

Whalen, C. K., Henker, B., & Dotemoto, S. Teacher response to the methylphenidate (Ritalin) versus placebo status of hyperactive boys in the classroom. *Child Development*, 1981, *52*, 1005–1014.

Zanna, M. P., Sheras, P., Cooper, J., & Shaw, C. Pygmalion and Galatea: The interactive effect of teacher and student expectancies. *Journal of Experimental Social Psychology*, 1975, *11*, 279–287.

Zuckerman, M., De Paulo, B. M., & Rosenthal, R. Verbal and nonverbal communication of deception. In L. Berkowitz (Ed.), *Advances in experimental social psychology* (Vol. 14). New York: Academic Press, 1981.

12

Coping with Stress and Frustration
Origins, Nature, and Development

SUZANNE M. MILLER AND MARGOT L. GREEN

When Johnny last visited the dentist, he was greeted in the waiting room by the dental assistant, who explained the forthcoming procedures to him in great detail. As she described the equipment, the sensations, and the sequence of events, Johnny became tense, wide-eyed, and quiet. During the examination itself, he squirmed in the dentist's chair and winced when the dentist warned him that he was about to feel pain. Johnny also suffered for several days after the procedure, complaining that his teeth were sore and that he was afraid of having a new cavity filled the following week. Craig's experience at the dentist was quite the opposite. In his case, the assistant gave him a coloring book and crayons to occupy him while he waited. He happily played with these toys, humming softly to himself. Throughout the examination, Craig listened carefully to the dentist's stories about fishing and swimming and remained cheerful. He never mentioned the dentist or his teeth to his mother after the examination and seemed nonplussed at the prospect of having another cavity filled.

This example raises several intriguing questions. Both youngsters experienced the identical aversive dental procedure, yet the child who

SUZANNE M. MILLER AND MARGOT L. GREEN • Department of Psychology, Temple University, Philadelphia, Pennsylvania 19122. This research was partially supported by the Robert Wood Johnson Foundation and by Temple University Research Incentive Fund Grant 700-950-43 and Temple University Biomedical Science Research Grant and Temple University Grant in Aid of Research to Suzanne M. Miller.

was exposed to voluminous preparatory information was more anxious and afraid before, during, and after the procedure than the child who was distracted from threat-relevant information. What accounts for this differential arousal? Are there situational and/or individual differences that moderate such effects? How do these alternative coping patterns hold over time and across different affective contexts?

The selection or avoidance of particular kinds of information while coping with aversive events is one of the most enduring issues in our attempt to understand the nature and development of self-regulation and its implications for dealing with stress. Freud recognized the importance of these phenomena and dealt with them in terms of repression and sensitization, concepts that underlie the entire structure of psychodynamic thought. Indeed, attention to a coping dimension of this kind has preoccupied personality psychology throughout its history (Mischel, 1981a). Yet, despite previous research into individual differences, little is known about the basic processes that determine informational choice under threat. Even less is known about the developmental course and coherences of these self-regulatory patterns. For example, the processes of coping with threat (impending aversive outcomes) and frustration (delay of positive outcomes) have traditionally been treated as distinct, nonoverlapping domains. Yet, there may be some important (but heretofore unexamined) links between self-regulatory patterns under threat and information-seeking or avoidance during delay of gratification. That is, when children distract themselves from reward-relevant cues, it may be easier for them to wait for a preferred but desired outcome than when they monitor and tune into information about the outcome.

Recent theoretical advances recommend viewing the coping process in interactional terms (Mischel, 1973, 1979), suggesting that it is best analyzed by taking simultaneous account of relevant personal dispositions and the specific properties of the situation. This view proposes an explicitly cognitive analysis of personality variables, for example, cognitive competencies, encoding strategies, and plans for self-regulation. In this chapter, we attempt to shed some light on the processes underlying effective self-regulation in youngsters, from the perspective of such an interactional framework. The overarching aim is to begin to forge some integration between these self-regulatory issues and developmental considerations.

We begin by detailing this theoretical perspective as it applies first to the process of coping with threat and then to the process of coping with frustration. The available evidence in each domain is also reviewed, and its fit to this framework is examined. Methodological inadequacies in existing studies are outlined, revealing empirical gaps and confounds in the literature. Next, we attempt some degree of integration between the findings on threat and those on frustration, highlighting areas of empirical and conceptual convergence between them. Finally, we briefly discuss the clinical implications of these self-regulatory patterns.

COPING WITH THREAT

Conceptualization

Classically, the evidence on the effects of threat-relevant cues on human stress has been as confusing as it is voluminous, with a morass of studies yielding conflicting results. The major experimentally based theories all predict that information and knowledge about threat should be preferred and stress-reducing (see Miller, 1981b). Psychodynamically based theories agree to the extent of considering repression a primitive mode of coping.

However, the literature shows that distraction is often chosen and can have stress-*red*ucing effects. In addition, information often has been found to be stress-*ind*ucing. It has been difficult to find a theoretical formulation that makes sense of these inconsistencies. One unifying theme that seems to be emerging suggests not one but *two* basic modes of coping. The first mode, "monitoring," involves being alert for and sensitized to the negative aspects of an experience. An alternative mode, "blunting," involves distraction from and cognitively shielding oneself from objective sources of danger. So there are two competing forces at work in the coping process: orienting toward or away from threat-relevant cues. The main thrust of our work has been to investigate, for each mode, when it is engaged and when it is stress-reducing (see also Lazarus, Cohen, Folkman, Kanner, & Schaefer, 1980; Leventhal, Brown, Sacham, & Engquist, 1979).

Here is a brief outline of the basic conceptual framework proposed by the "blunting hypothesis" (Miller, 1979b, 1980b, 1981b; Miller & Grant, 1979). When an individual is in an aversive situation, she or he is anxious and aroused to the extent that she or he is monitoring the negative aspects of the situation. Arousal is reduced when she or he can cognitively avoid and psychologically blunt objective sources of danger. When an aversive event is controllable, monitoring is the main coping modality. Although it heightens arousal, it enables the individual to execute controlling actions. When an aversive event is uncontrollable, monitoring (which heightens arousal) has little instrumental value. Therefore, blunting becomes the main coping mode because an individual without the option to execute controlling actions can reduce stress more effectively by tuning out and engaging in distraction and similar psychological techniques. In this case, information (predictability) is arousal-inducing and hence is often shunned because it would force the individual back into the psychological presence of danger that she or he cannot avoid. Consider a dental patient whose dentist warns him every time the drill goes on. He will be listening for the dentist's warning; and the dentist's voice itself will become invasive and intrusive. In contrast, if he were to receive no warning, threat-relevant information would be more diluted and less psychologically invasive and intrusive. Thus, it would be easier for the individual to distract. Previous work bears out this prediction (Geer & Maisel, 1972; Miller, 1979b; Miller & Mangan, 1983; Monat, 1976; Monat, Averill, & Lazarus, 1972; see also Garber, Miller, & Abramson, 1980; Miller, 1979a, 1980c, for a more thorough discussion of the construct of control).

In addition to distraction, there are other cognitive blunting strategies that are conducive to psychological withdrawal from cues about danger and that thereby reduce stress. For example, individuals who are exposed to aversive films depicting gory and painful scenes can be induced to intellectualize about the film (e.g., "As you can see, the operation is formal, and the surgical technique, although crude, is very carefully followed"); or to deny its stressful aspects (e.g., "You will see that the words of encouragement offered by the older men have their effect, and the boy begins to look forward to the happy conclusion of the ceremony") (Lazarus & Alfert, 1966; Lazarus, Opton, Nomikos, & Rankin, 1965; Speisman, Lazarus, Mordkoff, & Davison, 1964). Additionally, in dental and surgical populations, the induction of blunting strategies such as reinterpretation has been shown to reduce psychological and subjective arousal and to facilitate the recovery process (e.g., "Focus on the positive aspects of the experience") (Langer, Janis, & Wolfer, 1975; Mead, 1970; see also Barber & Hahn, 1962; Blitz & Dinnerstein, 1971; Bloom, Houston, Holmes, & Burish, 1977; Holmes & Houston, 1974; Neufeld, 1970).

Two main conditions may make it difficult or inappropriate for the individual to distract himself or herself. The first is situational; that is, the threat may be too intense to allow distraction. For example, when it is high-level, high-probability, of long duration, or imminent, it is harder to distract than when it is low-level, low-probability, of short duration, or remote (Averill & Rosenn, 1972; Klemp & Rodin, 1976). In addition, providing subjects with explicit instructions that they should not or are not permitted to distract inhibits their ability to distract (see Miller, 1980b, 1981b; Miller & Grant, 1979). The second moderating condition involves individual differences in the ability and the inclination to distract oneself. When situational factors permit distraction as a mode of coping, some individuals choose to distract themselves. However, in these very same situations, others do not. They find it undesirable or too difficult to distract themselves. For this latter group, it is information that is preferred and stress-reducing, because information provides them at least with external cues that reduce uncertainty and signal periods of safety. For example, if the dentist always provides a warning before the drill goes on, then the monitoring individual can relax when the dentist is silent.

In order to demonstrate the existence of such informational dispositions, and to explore their nature, breadth, and coherences, we devised a scale to identify the "blunters" (information avoiders) and the "monitors" (information seekers), an approach that circumvents the problems of earlier scales. The Monitor-Blunter Style Scale (MBSS) divides individuals into monitors and blunters based on their self-reported preferences for information or distraction in stressful situations, and it has been validated in both laboratory and field settings (Chorney, Efran, Ascher, & Lukens, 1981; Miller, 1980a, 1981a; Miller & Mischel, 1985).

With the MBSS, it became possible to investigate the interacting effects of dispositional and situational factors in the coping process. To do that in settings as naturalistic as possible, we have been studying a variety of patients about to undergo diagnostic and surgical procedures. The patients are first divided into monitors or blunters based on our scale (Chorney et al., 1981; Miller, 1980a, 1981a; Miller & Mischel, 1983). Half of each group is then given voluminous information about the forthcoming procedure and its effects; the other half receives minimal information. The patient's responses are measured before, during, and after the procedure, by means of psychophysiological reactions, subjective report, and behavioral measures (Miller & Mangan, 1983; Miller, Mangan, & Wagner, 1980; Taylor, Odegaard, & Watkins, 1983).

These studies have yielded three principals results. First, voluminous preparatory information appears to exacerbate patient distress, both subjectively and behaviorally, before, during, and in the days following the procedure. The second conclusion concerns the effects of coping style on stress. In these uncontrollable settings, monitors are more aroused than blunters, both behaviorally and subjectively, before and during the procedure. Finally, the results show that variations in coping style interact with and determine the impact of information, particularly on the physiological level; specifically, blunters are less aroused with low information and monitors are less aroused, at least eventually, with high information. These results are consistent with the coping-style preferences of these groups. Because blunters prefer to deal with threat by not dealing with it, they show reduced arousal with low information, which allows them cognitively to avoid and transform threat-relevant cues. Conversely, monitors, who cannot or do not choose to distract themselves, eventually derive some benefit from being exposed to voluminous preparatory information.

The Process of Coping with Threat: Children Facing Hospital and Dental Procedures

In contrast to extensive evidence on coping patterns in adults, relatively little is known about the analogous process of coping in children. Research on adults has been guided primarily by theoretical considerations and thus has tended to be characterized by conceptually cleaner manipulations and multimodal response measures. Corresponding work with children has been less concerned with delineating the mechanisms underlying effective coping. Instead, it has tended to be guided primarily by practical considerations, such as how best to prepare children for aversive procedures. Studies to date suggest that various cognitive factors do indeed alter the nature of the stress response in children (see Haggerty, 1983). However, it is difficult to untangle conceptually the various components that contribute to successful stress-reduction.

Early Investigations

Studies exploring the coping process in children have most often looked at youngsters about to undergo aversive dental or hospital procedures (cf. Kendall & Watson, 1981). Early field observations suggested that much of the distress associated with being in the hospital is attributable to its unfamiliar environment and to poor procedures for disseminating information and providing support (Leonard, Skipper, & Woolridge, 1967; Skipper & Leonard, 1965; see also Gellert, 1958; Jackson, Winkley, Faust, & Cermack, 1952; Jessner, Blom, & Waldfogel, 1952; Landes, 1973; Mellish, 1969; Prugh, Staub, Sands, Kirschbaum, & Lenihan, 1953). This evidence led to investigations of how to alleviate stress in hospitalized children and their families. Although these studies do not make explicit comparisons of increased information versus distraction (as does the analogous adult research), they do compare the effects of receiving some kind of extra preparation to the effects of receiving the usual minimal preparatory information.

For example, Skipper and Leonard (1968) explored the effects of providing information and support from trained personnel to the mothers of children about to undergo routine surgery. These researchers hypothesized that, because a mother's affective state may be communicated and may thus produce changes in her child's level of stress, children of well-informed and emotionally supported mothers would be less stressed than would children whose mothers had received the usual hospital-preparatory information. A specially trained nurse gave clear information and provided emotional support to the mothers of children in the experimental group. Their children, in turn, showed reduced stress (pre- and postoperatively) relative to a control group that received the usual minimal preparation, as measured by lower blood pressure, temperature, and pulse rate; greater intake of fluids and voiding, higher staff evaluations of adaptation to the hospital; subjective reports of less fear of hospitals; less crying; and less disturbed sleep.

Unfortunately, it is unclear why the extra information given to the parents decreased stress in their children. Perhaps, as hypothesized, the children were less stressed while in the hospital because their parents were less stressed. However, it is still unclear whether the reduced stress in the parents was due to the fact that they had received increased information or to having received increased attention. Yet a third possibility is that the parents who received information (and support) communicated this information to their children, which, in turn, reduced the youngsters' level of distress.

A study by Cassell (1965) more directly explored the effects of preparatory information on children themselves in the form of a puppet show for youngsters about to undergo cardiac catheterization. The rationale for choosing a puppet show was that it would give the children the opportunity to master vicariously the experience of cardiac catheterization by familiarizing themselves with the procedure and by observing it to be less fearsome than they may have anticipated (see Bandura & Menlove, 1968). This opportunity, in turn, should reduce postoperative distress. The puppet show, presented by the hospital staff, was a miniature mock-up of the catheterization procedure and involved a cast of doctors, nurses, and the child. The instruments and the surrounding equipment used during the actual cardiac catheterization were included in the presentation, and the children were invited to participate, if they wished, by holding the puppets representing their parents. The youngsters who viewed the puppet show were less emotionally disturbed (as measured by behavioral observations of the hospital staff) during the invasive procedure. Furthermore, they expressed more willingness to return to the hospital than did the children who received minimal preparatory information. These results were supported by a further study (Johnson & Stockdale, 1975) that demonstrated that puppet therapy was more effective than the usual hospital minimal-preparatory information in reducing anticipatory and postoperative palmar sweat in a group of surgical and dental patients.

Unfortunately, it is difficult to interpret these results. First, the children who viewed the puppet shows spent more time with the experimenters and the hospital staff than did the control subjects. Therefore, the reduced stress may simply have been a function of this additional attention. Furthermore, a puppet show involves many diverse elements. Beyond providing voluminous information about the nature of the upcoming procedure, the show also may have reframed the threatening event as less aversive, may have demonstrated a standard of behavior for the children to imitate, may have taught the children methods of distracting themselves from the threat, and so forth.

Filmed Modeling

Follow-up studies introduced the medium of filmed peer modeling as a convenient means of preparing children for aversive procedures. This approach involves the observation of a peer model who experiences the same events as the children themselves are about to undergo. Pioneering studies (Vernon, 1973; Vernon & Bailey, 1974) found that exposure to filmed peer modeling reduced children's anticipatory and preoperative uncooperative behavior and observed stress, relative to the usual minimal preparatory information (see also Ferguson, 1979). However, the children's observable mood during the operation was unaffected. Stronger results were found by Melamed and Siegel (1975), in that exposure to filmed peer modeling reduced pre- and postoperative palmar sweat, and self-reports of fear, as well as follow-up ratings of behavioral disturbances, relative to exposure to an irrelevant (control) film.

In addition, work by Melamed and her colleagues in a dental setting showed that children exposed to a peer modeling film engaged in fewer disruptive and anxious behaviors immediately following the film directly before the procedure) and during the treatment itself than did those who saw an irrelevant control film (Melamed, Hawes, Heiby, & Glick, 1975; Melamed, Weinstein, Hawes, & Katin-Borland, 1975; see also Machen & Johnson, 1974).

Overall, in seven out of seven studies, youngsters who were exposed to a filmed peer model showed less anxiety across a variety of measures before, during, and after the aversive procedure than youngsters who viewed an irrelevant film or who received the usual minimal preparatory information. Unfortunately, the filmed-peer-modeling studies are difficult to interpret because the procedure involves as many confounding factors as the puppet modeling intervention; if not more of them. For example, the film used in several studies, "Ethan Has an Operation," shows a pleasant 7-year-old boy experiencing a variety of situations generally encountered by children who are hospitalized for elective surgery. Various scenes are narrated by Ethan, who describes his feelings, thoughts, and concerns at each stage of his hospital experience. Although he exhibits some visible apprehension at the outset, Ethan is a "coping model" (Anderson & Masur, 1983; Meichenbaum, 1977; Ross, 1981), who then overcomes his anxiety and, without further distress, successfully completes his operation.

Given the complexity of the factors involved in the peer modeling films, it is difficult to tease out the crucial stress-reducing elements. Simple procedural information alone may reduce uncertainty and may account for decreased stress. Alternatively, the films may reduce the anticipated aversiveness of the procedure by portraying it as less traumatic than the child has imagined it to be. They may also teach children to selectively filter information about the procedure by engaging in cognitive avoidance and blunting strategies ("See Ethan's pleasant expression and hear his comforting thoughts as he awaits a painful injection"). Furthermore, filmed peer modeling may provide an opportunity for vicarious mastery of the prospective hospital procedure or, finally, may demonstrate a standard for the child's behavior ("Like Ethan, I can handle this, no matter how scary it is").

Filmed Peer Modeling versus Increased Information

Further work has helped to rule out at least one possibility. The effectiveness of peer modeling treatments seems to be due not to receiving additional information, but to some other component of the manipulation. Ferguson (1979) compared exposure to filmed peer modeling to pure information delivered in a pre-hospital-admission home visit from a nurse. The children who viewed the filmed model showed reduced anticipatory, preop, and follow-up EMG responses, as well as less observable disruptive behavior at follow-up. In contrast, the children who received the preadmission information visit maintained higher arousal on all of these measures.[1] Other research further supports the idea that the efficacy of filmed peer modeling is probably not due to receiving additional information, but rather to providing the child with an altered cognitive perspective on the forthcoming event. Melamed, Yurcheson, Fleece, Hutcherson, and Hawes (1978) compared a peer modeling film to a videotaped demonstration in which a dentist explained the procedure. The critical difference between these treatments was that the demonstration film involved the simple dissemination of information, whereas the modeling film included the additional component of a peer "mastering" the experience. The children exposed to the peer modeling film were observed to be less disruptive during the actual dental treatment and reported

---

[1] It is interesting to note that, although children actually benefited more from filmed modeling, their parents were more satisfied with the prehospital admission visit. Because both adults and children were included in the preadmission visit, and only the children themselves were included in the modeling condition, it is likely that the parents' increased satisfaction with the preadmission visit was attributable to the increased personal attention that they received.

fewer fears postoperatively than did the children who viewed the demonstration film. Thus, although exposure to a filmed peer model is clearly stress-reducing, it appears to operate through some mechanism other than the provision of increased procedural information.

Additional results showed that the children who were exposed to the modeling film showed decreased cardiac arousal following the film, relative to the children who viewed the filmed demonstration (Melamed *et al.*, 1978; cf. Melamed, 1982). Following Lacey's hypothesis (1967), the authors interpreted the cardiac deceleration that occurred with peer modeling as an indication that these subjects were processing and absorbing the information at an increased rate, presumably because they were more functionally attentive and better able to assimilate incoming cues. The fact that they processed more of the information in turn would have modified their expectancies about the forthcoming procedure and would thus have reduced their subsequent distress. If we view these results within a cognitive framework, although the children in both groups received information about the threatening event, those who watched the demonstration alone were also induced to focus on procedural aspects of the event (e.g., the sequence of events, the equipment, and the steps that could cause pain), which simply alerted them to possible negative outcomes and sensitized them to the unpleasant features of the procedure. In contrast, the youngsters who viewed the peer modeling film were induced to focus selectively on less threatening aspects of the event, such as the model's behavior and the reduced aversiveness of the actual procedure for the model relative to the child's expectations. Therefore, the information contained in the modeling film may have framed the event in a more attenuated form and thus would have made the film more arousal-reducing than the demonstration.

In two out of two studies, then, exposure to a filmed peer model resulted in less stress than did exposure to increased procedural information, as reflected in behavioral, physiological, and observational measures across various measurement times.[2] Thus, the effectiveness of filmed modeling appears to be due not to the additional information

---

[2]An exception to this pattern is one relatively early investigation (Machen & Johnson, 1974). These researchers compared filmed modeling to procedural information presented in the form of a hierarchy of increasingly anxiety-inducing stimuli relevant to the impending procedure (see also Sawtell, Simon, & Simeonsson, 1974). Both groups showed equally reduced negative behaviors during the dental procedure, but not beforehand, as measured by observer ratings. However, because the information was presented initially in a degraded form, it could have progressively desensitized the child to the stressful situation. Peterson and Shigetomi (1981) also found no differences between filmed modeling and information. However, the information was presented in the context of a puppet show, and this fact may account for the lack of a significant difference.

that it provides, but to the fact that it allows for and encourages selective filtering of the information.

Cognitive Coping Techniques

More recent work with children has attempted to clarify the cognitive factors underlying adaptive coping wih threat. Wolfer and Visintainer (1975, 1979) found that a variety of cognitive strategies, such as receiving descriptions of sensory experiences (e.g., the smell of alcohol), engaging in play therapy techniques, and providing supportive care, were more effective in reducing children's observed distress at anticipatory, preoperative, and follow-up measurement times than was receiving no pretreatment. Furthermore, these cognitive procedures reduced children's resistance to anesthetic inductions during surgery, increased their fluid intake after surgery, reduced their parents' postoperative ratings of anxiety, and raised their satisfaction with the care and the information that they had received relative to the no-treatment control group (see also Visintainer & Wolfer, 1975).

A study by Peterson and Shigetomi (1981) compared the efficacy of filmed peer modeling with a more purely cognitive coping manipulation, which involved engaging in cue-controlled deep-muscle relaxation, distracting and pleasant mental imagery (such as imagining a beach scene), and comforting self-talk (such as "Everything will be all right"). Four groups of children received either filmed peer modeling alone, cognitive coping techniques alone, both treatments, or a control condition in which neither treatment was administered but procedural information was given (in the form of a puppet show). The group that received the combination of coping plus modeling was the most calm and cooperative during the invasive procedure, as measured by behavioral observations from a variety of staff members. The authors suggest that both treatments may be necessary to facilitate optimal coping, as modeling provides the child with information that reduces uncertainty, whereas cognitive distraction strategies teach the child to relax and reduce arousal.

However, the combination coping-plus-modeling group also spent a significantly longer time with trained experimenters than did the other group, and this may have accounted for the combination's superior effectiveness. Where differential length of exposure was not a factor, the children in the cognitive-behavioral coping group generally exhibited less distress than did the filmed-modeling and control groups, which generally did not differ. Specifically, the group that received cognitive coping strategies had lower observed levels of pre- and postoperative anxiety than did the modeling-alone group or the control group. In addition, the coping group showed a trend toward greater consumption of foods and fluids in the hours following surgery, an indication of physical resilience and adaptiveness.

These results support the view that, when filmed modeling works, it does so by inducing the child to distract from or transform threat-relevant cues. Furthermore, engaging in an adaptive cognitive coping strategy may best be accomplished in the absence of the increased procedural information contained in the peer modeling procedure. Unfortunately, this study did not include a group that received increased preparatory information alone (in an unattenuated form), so the efficacy of such a manipulation compared to a purely cognitive distraction manipulation remains unknown. Future studies should compare directly the effects of increased information alone, cognitive distraction alone, and a combination of these two treatments.

Finally, a study by Siegel and Peterson (1980) compared the differential effectiveness of two cognitive manipulations: the first involved training in cognitive blunting and the avoidance of threat-relevant information, and the second involved providing sensory information about the impending threat. Children about to undergo dental treatment were assigned to one of three conditions: (a) Coping-skills training, which involved the use of body relaxation, pleasant imagery (e.g., "Imagine a favorite place"), and self-talk (e.g., "Everything will be all right"); (b) Sensory information, which was a description of the sights, sounds, and sensations associated with the experience (e.g., "Your tooth will feel tingly and warm"); and (c) A no-treatment control group. Both treatment groups showed fewer disruptive responses, less observable anxiety and distress, and lower pulse rates during the procedure than did the control children. The only difference between the treatment groups was that the children who received coping-skills training showed lower pulse rates immediately after the intervention and before the dental treatment. The authors suggest that the children in the coping group may actually have used the relaxation techniques that they had been taught, thereby directly reducing their physiological arousal.

Although the presumed mechanism underlying these manipulations is different, there may be some degree of conceptual overlap between them. Coping-skills training teaches children cognitively to distract themselves from threat-relevant cues. In contrast, sensory information presumably provides information that prepares individuals with a detailed preview of the tactile, thermal, and visual changes that they will experience. However, such information may actually induce children cognitively to encode the event in less threatening terms because it focuses them on objective features of the experience, such as coolness, numbness, and pins and needles, rather than focusing them on the more aversive aspects of the impact, such as pain, fear, and uncertainty. Conversely, procedural information may induce the child to encode the event in more threatening terms because it focuses them on emotional aspects of the procedure.

Other evidence is consistent with this interpretation of sensory versus procedural information. In a study by Johnson, Kirchhoff, and Endress (1975), children who received sensory information about the forthcoming removal of a cast (e.g., "You will feel vibrations and tingling warmth") showed fewer overt signs of distress during cast removal than did those who received voluminous procedural information (e.g., "We will use a scissors and spreaders") or a control group who received the usual minimal preparation. Thus, the stress-reducing effects of receiving sensory information may be attributable not to increased information, but to inducing children to process the event in more benign, less frightening ways. Like cognitive distraction strategies, sensory information may divert children's attention away from the more threatening aspects of the procedure, in this case by focusing them on its more abstract, personal, and experiential components.

Individual Differences in Children

The studies described above simply manipulated the amount and type of information given to children facing aversive procedures. They did not take into account individual differences in information-seeking style, age, or gender, which may affect the impact of these manipulations (for a discussion of these and related issues, see Mechanic, 1980; Melamed, 1982; Melamed, Robbins, & Graves, 1981).

Two investigations by Melamed and her colleagues suggest that such factors are indeed important, and that not all children benefit equally from preparatory pretreatments. In one study (Melamed *et al.*, 1978), the children's age and level of previous experiences were found to interact with the type of pretreatment. Older children benefited more from filmed peer modeling than from a filmed demonstration of the procedure by the dentist and were less fearful when they were presented with a shorter videotape. Conversely, younger children were not differentially affected by the type of presentation (i.e., modeling versus dentist's demonstration) but were less fearful when they were presented with a longer videotape. The authors suggest that the similarity in age between the older children and the child in the film may have facilitated their learning from the model, whereas the younger children found it difficult to learn from the dissimilar model (hence, they did not benefit from exposure to the filmed peer model as did the older children).

Additional results showed that the level of previous experience affected children's behavior during the dental treatment (see also Klorman, Hilpert, Michael, LaGana, & Sveen, 1980). Children with no previous dental experience became significantly more disruptive during restorative treatment than did experienced children. In addition, they did not benefit from exposure to a peer model and needed a longer demonstration (in the absence of a peer model) to reduce their fears about restorative treatment. The authors suggested that children who have never undergone treatment may become sensitized unless they view a lengthy and explicit demonstration, whereas experienced children can benefit even from an abbreviated presentation.

In a further study (Melamed, Dearborn, & Hermecz, 1983) among younger children (ages 4–8) those who had previous experience with surgery were rated as overall more anxious than those without previous experience. Moreover, younger children and older children (ages 8–17) who had had previous experience were generally more aroused than older, less experienced children, on behavioral and self-report indices. In addition, younger children who viewed a film that presented information about the hospital procedure (but did not involve a peer model) were observed to be more anxious than those who saw a film unrelated to the hospital procedure. Thus, children who are younger, particularly if they have had previous dental experience, are especially vulnerable to the possible negative effects of receiving voluminous information, which appears to sensitize rather than to relax them.

In one final study (Burstein & Meichenbaum, 1979), children's styles of responding to the stress of surgery were measured without manipulating the level of information administered. One group of children scored low on a prehospitalization questionnaire assessing their level of defensiveness (e.g., they did not deny having common weaknesses) and were more willing to play with toys that were relevant to their stressful surgery. In contrast, a second group scored high on the prehospitalization defensiveness scale and were less willing to play with threat-relevant toys. The less defensive children recovered more quickly from surgery than did the highly defensive children. The authors conclude that there are two main modes of coping with the stress of surgery: So-called less defensive children are disposed to focus on their fears while under stress and so engage in the "work of worrying," which reduces their subsequent distress. In contrast, so-called high-defensive children are less willing to attend to threat-relevant information while under stress and do not engage in the "work of worrying," and thus, their arousal remains high.

This pattern of results contradicts findings with adults, which show that those who attend to and seek threat-relevant information generally exhibit more stress than do those who can cognitively avoid such information (e.g., Cohen & Lazarus, 1973; Miller & Mangan, 1983). Moreover, results with adults typically show an interaction between their preferred coping style and the amount of preparatory information: Individuals who are disposed to monitor for information show reduced anxiety when they receive maximal information regarding aversive procedures. Conversely, adults who are disposed to distract from threat-relevant cues adapt best to aversive medical procedures when provided with minimal information. It is difficult to reconcile these two sets of findings. It is possible that children show distinct patterns of coping with threat that do not correspond to those observed in adults. Alternatively, the anxiety manifested by high-defensive children in the study by Burstein and Meichenbaum (1979) may have been an artifact of having received the standard (and rather high) hospital-information package as preparation for surgery. If so, although low-defensive children would have received a level of information that was consistent with their coping preference, the high defensives would have received more information than they typically preferred. Further studies should both measure children's dispositions toward voluminous or minimal information and simultaneously manipulate the actual amount of information available.

Evaluation of the Evidence

Although almost no evidence exists on how children cope with controllable threats, some conclusions can be drawn about how they respond to uncontrollable threats such as dental restorative treatment and elective surgery. Table 1 presents a summary of this evidence. As can be seen, children do not benefit from the effects of increased information alone. In two out of two studies, increased information was generally found to be more stress-inducing for the child than the usual minimal preparatory information (Ferguson, 1979; Johnson *et al.*, 1975).

When children do benefit from preparatory information, it is under conditions in which that information is delivered in an attenuated form, such as occurs in viewing a puppet show or filmed peer modeling. In contrast to generally weak support for the effects of receiving procedural information alone, information embedded within the context of a modeling demonstration (usually with a "coping" model) is clearly beneficial. In nine out of nine studies, puppet or filmed peer modeling was found to be more stress-reducing than minimal preparation (Cassell, 1965; Ferguson, 1979; Johnson & Stockdale, 1975; Machen & Johnson, 1974; Melamed & Siegel, 1975; Melamed, Hawes, *et al.*, 1975; Melamed, Weinstein, *et al.*, 1975; Vernon, 1973; Vernon & Bailey, 1974). This effect was consistent across a variety of anxiety measures (physiological, subjective,

Table 1. Evidence on Preparatory Treatments for Children Facing Aversive Procedures

Treatment	Comparison	Reference (no. and age)	Outcome measures	Results[a]
I. a. Increased information	Usual minimal preparation (unrelated film)	Ferguson (1979) N = 82; age: 3–7 yrs. Setting: hospital	Self-report anxiety	←
			Self-report maternal anxiety	←
			Self-report maternal satisfaction	↑
			Observation of anxiety-related behavior	↑
			EMG	←
			Posthospital behavior ratings by parents	←
Increased information	Usual minimal preparation	Johnson, Kirchhoff, and Endress (1975) N = 84; age: 6–11 yrs. Setting: hospital.	Observed distress	↑
			Pulse rates	↑
b. Puppet modeling	Usual minimal preparation	Cassell (1965) N = 40; age: 3–11 yrs. Setting: hospital.	Behavioral observations during catheterization	←
			Ward observations	↑
			Parental questionnaire	↑
			Posthospital parental questionnaire	←
Puppet modeling	Usual minimal preparation	Johnson and Stockdale (1975) N = 43; ages: 5–8 yrs. Setting: hospital	Palmar Sweat Index	←
c. Filmed peer modeling	Usual minimal preparation (unrelated film)	Ferguson (1979) N = 82; age: 3–7 yrs. Setting: hospital	Self-report anxiety	↑
			Self-report maternal anxiety	←
			Self-report maternal satisfaction	↑
			Observation of anxiety-related behavior	←
			EMG	←
			Posthospital behavior ratings by parents	←

Technique	Comparison	Study	Measures	Outcome
Filmed peer modeling	Usual minimal preparation	Machen and Johnson (1974) N = 31; ages: 3–5.5 yrs. Setting: dental	Behavioral ratings during treatment	↑
Filmed peer modeling	Usual minimal preparation (unrelated film)	Melamed, Hawes, et al., (1975b) N = 48; ages: 5–11 yrs. Setting: dental	Self-report anxiety / Observation of disruption / Observation anxiety-related behavior / Palmar Sweat Index	↑ ← ← ←
Filmed peer modeling	Usual minimal preparation (unrelated task)	Melamed, Weinstein et al., (1975a) N = 16; ages: 5–9 yrs. Setting: dental	Self-report general fears / Observation of disruption / Observation of cooperation and anxiety / Self-report maternal anxiety	↑ / ↑ ← ←
Filmed peer modeling	Usual minimal preparation (unrelated film)	Melamed and Siegel (1975) N = 60; ages: 4–12 yrs. Setting: hospital	Self-report anxiety / Self-report medical concerns / Observation of anxiety-related behaviors / Trait anxiety / Projective drawings / Palmar Sweat Index / Postoperative behavior ratings by parents	↑ / ← ← ← / ↑ ↑ ← ←
Filmed peer modeling	Usual minimal preparation	Vernon (1973) N = 38; ages: 4–9 yrs. Setting: hospital	Observed mood / Projective Anxiety Test / Posthospital behavioral ratings by parents	← ↑ ←
Filmed peer modeling	Usual minimal preparation	Vernon and Bailey (1974) N = 38; ages: 4–9 yrs. Setting: hospital	Observed mood	←
d. Cognitive distraction	Usual minimal preparation	Siegel and Peterson (1980) N = 42; ages: 3.5–6 yrs. Setting: dental	Self-report anxiety / Observed anxious behavior / Observed cooperation and distress / Pulse rate	↑ ← ← / ←

Continued

TABLE 1. (*Cont.*)

Treatment	Comparison	Reference (no. and age)	Outcome measures	Results[a]
e. Sensory information	Usual minimal preparation	Johnson et al. (1975) N = 84; ages: 6–11 yrs. Setting: hospital	Observed distress Pulse rates	← →
Sensory information	Usual minimal preparation	Siegel and Peterson (1980) N = 42; ages 3.5–6 yrs. Setting: dental	Self-report anxiety Observed anxious behavior Observed cooperation and distress Pulse rate	↑ ← ← ←
Sensory information (and other supportive care)	Usual minimal preparation	Wolfer and Visintainer (1975) N = 80; ages: 3–14 yrs. Setting: hospital	Self-report parental satisfaction and anxiety Observed cooperation and distress Fluid intake Pulse rate Resistance to anesthetic induction Recovery-room dosage Time to first voiding Posthospital behavior ratings by parents	← ← ← ← ← ↑ ↑ ←
Sensory information (and other supportive care)	Usual minimal preparation	Wolfer and Visintainer (1979) N = 63; ages: 3–12 yrs. Setting: hospital	Self-report parental anxiety Self-report parental satisfaction Observed cooperation and distress Resistance to anesthetic induction Fluid intake Time to first voiding Posthospital behavior ratings by parents	← ← ← ← ↑ ↑ ↑

Sensory information (and other supportive care)	Usual minimal preparation	Visintainer and Wolfer (1975) N = 84; ages 3–12 yrs. Setting: hospital	Self-report parental anxiety	←
			Self-report parental satisfaction	←
			Observed cooperation and distress	←
			Recovery-room dosage	↑
			Resistance to anesthetic induction	←
			Fluid intake	↑
			Time to first voiding	←
			Posthospital behavior ratings by parents	←
f. Emotional support (alone)	Usual minimal preparation	Visintainer and Wolfer (1975) N = 84; ages: 3–12 yrs. Setting: hospital	Self-report parental anxiety	↑
			Self-report parental satisfaction	←
			Observed cooperation and distress	↑
			Recovery-room dosage	↑
			Resistance to anesthetic induction	↑
			Fluid intake	↑
			Time to first voiding	↑
			Posthospital behavior ratings by parents	↑
II. a. Filmed peer modeling	Increased information (preadmission visit)	Ferguson (1979) N = 82; ages: 3–7 yrs. Setting: hospital	Self-reported anxiety	↑
			Self-reported maternal anxiety	→
			Self-reported maternal satisfaction	→
			Observation of anxiety-related behavior	←
			EMG	←
			Posthospital behavior ratings by parents	←

Continued

Table 1.(*Cont.*)

Treatment	Comparison	Reference (no. and age)	Outcome measures	Results[a]
Filmed peer modeling	Increased information (taped demonstration with no model)	Melamed et al. (1978) N = 80; ages 4–11 yrs. Setting: dental	Self-report anxiety	↑
			Observed disruptive behavior during treatment	←
			Observed anxiety and cooperation	↑
			Self-report maternal anxiety	↑
			Heart rate changes	←
			Palmar Sweat Index	↑
			Galvanic skin response	↑
b. Filmed peer modeling (plus puppet information)	Puppet information (only)	Peterson and Shigetomi (1981) N = 66; ages: 2.5–10.5 yrs. Setting: hospital	Self-report anxiety	↑
			Parental self-report anxiety and confidence	↑
			Parental satisfaction with hospital experience	↑
			Observed maladaptive behavior	↑
			Observed anxiety and cooperation	↑
			Pulse rate	↑
			Temperature	↑
			Latency to void	↑
			Food and fluid consumption	↑
c. Cognitive distraction (plus puppet information)	Puppet information (only)	Peterson and Shigetomi (1981) N = 66; ages: 2.5–10.5 Setting: hospital	Self-report anxiety	↑
			Parental self-report anxiety and confidence	←
			Parental satisfaction with hospital experience	←
			Observed maladaptive behavior	↑
			Observed anxiety and cooperation	←
			Pulse rate	↑
			Temperature	↑
			Latency to void	↑
			Food and fluid consumption	↑

	Comparison	Study	Measure	Result
d. Sensory information	Increased information	Johnson et al. (1975) N = 84; ages: 6–11 yrs. Setting: hospital	Observed distress	←
			Pulse rate	↑
III. Cognitive distraction (plus puppet information)	Filmed peer modeling (plus puppet information)	Peterson and Shigetomi (1981) N = 66; ages: 2.5–10.5 yrs. Setting: hospital	Self-report anxiety	↑
			Parental self-report of anxiety and confidence	←
			Parental satisfaction with hospital experience	←
			Observed maladaptive behavior	↑
			Observed anxiety and cooperation	←
			Pulse rate	↑
			Temperature	↑
			Latency to void	↑
			Food and fluid consumption	↑
IV. Sensory information	Cognitive distraction	Siegel and Peterson (1980) N = 42; ages: 3.5–6 yrs. Setting: dental	Self-report anxiety	↑
			Observed anxious behavior	↑
			Observed cooperation and distress	↑
			Pulse rate	↑

[a] (↑) Indicates that the treatment group did significantly better than the comparison.
(↓) Indicates that the treatment group did significantly worse than the comparison.
(→) The treatment and comparison groups did not differ.

and behavioral) obtained at various points in time (before, during, and after the procedure). Indeed, when filmed peer modeling was compared directly to increased information, modeling was found overall to be more stress-reducing (Ferguson, 1979; Melamed *et al.*, 1978; Peterson & Shigetomi, 1981). Although modeling involves an informational component, its efficacy appears not to be due to the increased information that it provides, as information alone is not an effective preparatory strategy. However, it is not yet entirely clear what components of the modeling procedure do account for its effectiveness. In general terms, viewing a model appears to alter the way in which the child selectively attends to and cognitively filters the threatening event (Melamed *et al.*, 1978; Peterson & Shigetomi, 1981).

Two main attentional strategies have been explored in the literature. The first strategy entails teaching techniques such as muscle relaxation, pleasant imagery, and comforting self-talk, which divert the child's attention away from aversive cues and onto more affectively pleasant imagery. The second strategy is to expose children to sensory information about the event and thereby to focus their attention onto its more benign, less negative aspects. Engaging in cognitive distraction has been found to be more stress-reducing than exposure to the usual minimal preparation (Siegel & Peterson, 1980) and than exposure to increased procedural information and filmed peer modeling (Peterson & Shigetomi, 1981). Similarly, receiving sensory information has been shown to reduce anxiety more effectively than receiving either minimal preparation (Johnson *et al.*, 1975; Siegel & Peterson, 1980; Visintainer & Wolfer, 1975; Wolfer & Visintainer, 1975, 1979) or increased procedural information (Johnson *et al.*, 1975). Both sets of techniques appear to reduce stress by psychologically attenuating the oncoming threat, either by distracting the child from the event (e.g., as in relaxation or pleasant imagery) or by transforming how he or she processes it (e.g., as in sensory information).

Which of these main types of cognitive strategies (attention diversion vs. transformation) is optimal for stress reduction is as yet undetermined. Only one study directly compared these two cognitive techniques and it found both to be equally effective in minimizing distress (Siegel & Peterson, 1980). However, it is also possible that sensory information is not the most direct means of inducing the child to transform the aversive event cognitively. A more direct manipulation might be explicitly to induce the child to attend to its nonarousing aspects while cognitively avoiding its more frightening aspects (e.g., "The gas mask is like one you might wear on Halloween"). This approach may yield different results and should be explored in future work.

These findings are consistent with evidence on coping in adults, which clearly shows that cognitive avoidance and blunting are the strategies of choice for dealing with uncontrollable threats. However, the adult literature also shows clearly that information seeking and monitoring are strategies of choice for coping with controllable threats. This finding makes sense because only by monitoring an outcome can an individual be prepared to execute the appropriate controlling actions. For example, in order to avoid a potential disaster when crossing a busy intersection, one can and should scan for oncoming vehicles (see Miller & Grant, 1979). It seems reasonable to expect that children may learn to discriminate controllable from uncontrollable situations and to switch to an information-seeking mode when faced with controllable outcomes. However, no data currently address whether the informational preferences of youngsters vary as a function of the controllability of an impending aversive outcome.

The adult literature further shows that even when dealing with uncontrollable aversive events, various situational factors interfere with the ability to distract psychologically and to transform threat-relevant cues. When such cues are psychologically invasive and intrusive (e.g., when the event is predictable or intense, as when it is of high likelihood, high frequency, high level and/or is imminent), adults may find it difficult or inappropriate to distract themselves. Under these conditions, information is often preferred and stress-reducing because it at least provides the monitoring individual with external cues that signal safety or reduce uncertainty. Conversely, the presence of external distractors (e.g., Muzak at the dentist's office) or explicit ideational instructions to distract oneself from threatening cues facilitate distraction. There is as yet no research on coping in children that systematically bears on these issues. Therefore, it is not now known how these situational factors alter children's coping patterns. Future work should explore whether the information-seeking preferences of children are affected when selected parameters of the aversive events are varied, for example, when information is imposed or withheld, or when the event is of high or low intensity. Because it is known how these situational factors influence the information seeking of adults, one could investigate whether there is continuity in this pattern over various stages of development.

Finally, in addition to the effects of situational factors, the adult literature shows that there are individual differences in information-seeking or blunting preferences that interact with and moderate the effects of exposure to information (see Miller, 1981b; Miller & Mangan, 1983). Some individuals actually prefer to receive increased information and are less anxious when they are exposed to such information than when such information is withheld. In contrast, some individuals prefer to blunt threat-relevant information and are less anxious when unwanted information is not imposed on them.

To date, some work with children has suggested that individual differences such as age and level of experience affect responses to threat (e.g., Melamed *et al.*, 1978, 1983). Younger children and those with previous experience may be generally more fearful of aversive procedures than those who are older or inexperienced. Additionally, more experienced children, especially if they are young, may be adversely affected when they receive increased information. Preliminary work now also suggests that individual differences in children's cognitive informational preferences do indeed exist (cf. Burstein & Meichenbaum, 1979). Future work should investigate how these individual differences in informational preferences interact with relevant situational factors (e.g., the amount of threat-relevant information actually available) to determine stress.

In sum, contrary to traditional theoretical formulations, the evidence on children's (and adults') coping patterns is consistent with a view that emphasizes the stress-reducing effects of the cognitive blunting of threat-relevant information. Therefore, simply providing children with increased information about an upcoming aversive hospital or dental procedure probably is not an effective stress-reducing strategy. In contrast, exposure to either puppet or filmed peer modeling is clearly an effective means of alleviating anxiety, as is inducing children to engage in muscle relaxation and pleasant imagery or providing them with sensory information. Although some kind of attentional filtering, such as cognitive avoidance or transformation, appears to underlie the efficacy of these diverse treatments, the specifics of this mechanism have yet to be isolated. Finally, the adult literature further suggests that situational factors (e.g., the amount of information actually available) interact with dispositional factors (e.g., information-seeking preferences) to determine the effectiveness of cognitive blunting. This issue has not yet been explored in research with children.

COPING WITH FRUSTRATION

Conceptualization

The ability to postpone immediate gratification for the sake of future consequences, and to tolerate the frustration of waiting for deferred outcomes, is a central aspect of the socialization process. (The issues and findings in this section are presented more fully in Mischel, 1974,

1983, on which the present summary draws extensively.) From the most elementary to the most complex chains of socialized behaviors, the individual is required to delay impulses and to limit their expression to certain specific situatons. Indeed, eligibility for most of society's important rewards and other "goodies" is dependent on such delay of gratification. The developing individual therefore must learn to impose restraint on himself or herself and to inhibit immediate action for the sake of attaining his or her more long-term, future-oriented goals.

Freud emphasized the theoretical importance of self-control, especially in the form of the voluntary postponement of immediate gratifications for the sake of more distant, long-term gains. Early views, based on psychodynamic theorizing, speculated that the ability to wait for more valued but deferred outcomes rests on the facility to substitute satisfactions derived from hallucinatory and other compensatory thought processes for the unobtainable gratification (e.g., Freud, 1911/1959; Singer, 1955). Similarly, related views of impulse control suggested that the capacity to bridge the delay of gratification hinges on self-instructional processes through which the individual increases the salience of the deferred outcome (Jones & Gerard, 1967). According to these theoretical approaches, delay behavior should be facilitated by attention to the anticipated reward. Therefore, conditions that increase the psychological salience of deferred outcomes should facilitate attention to the rewards and thereby should enhance tolerance of frustration. Conversely, conditions that decrease the salience of rewards and thereby impede attention should decrease tolerance of frustration.

More recent perspectives on self-control (Mischel, 1973, 1974) view delay behavior as a basic person variable that constitutes a central feature of cognitive and social competence. This research is guided by a concern with how the growing child increasingly is able to free himself or herself from the constraints and demands of ongoing events and to act instead in anticipation of future consequences. This view highlights the processes through which these competencies are acquired as well as the motivational and cognitive considerations that influence the child's selection and execution of acquired behaviors (see also Bandura, 1977). The aim of the research is both to delineate the conditions under which consistency in self-control behavior can be found (e.g., Mischel & Peake, 1982) and to specify the situational factors that determine the discriminativeness of such behaviors (Mischel, 1973; see also Jenkins, 1974).

In the analysis of delay behavior, the research has emphasized the reciprocal interaction between cognitive processes and the situational factors that enhance or impair the individual's ability to tolerate frustration (Mischel, 1973, 1977, 1979). It suggests that delay is enhanced when individuals are able to attenuate cognitively the appetitive qualities of the anticipated outcome, either by distracting themselves from it or by reframing the event in less emotional terms. Situational factors that promote such processing, such as waiting in the absence of the anticipated reward, should facilitate delay. Conversely, situational factors that impede such processing, such as waiting in the presence of the anticipated reward, should interfere with delay. In addition, delay should be enhanced when individuals are explicitly instructed or induced to engage in these cognitive strategies. Finally, individuals who are disposed to cognitively avoid or to transform reward-relevant cues should cope better with the frustration of waiting than those who are disposed to monitor the appetitive qualities of the outcome.

The Process of Coping with Frustration: Children Waiting for Preferred but Delayed Rewards

Most of the work on delay of gratification has been conducted with children, particularly with preschoolers (Mischel, 1983). Little evidence exists on the analogous process of coping in adults. In earlier phases of this work, the main thrust was to delineate the social and personal antecedents and correlates of the preference for an immediate, lesser reward versus the preference for a delayed but greater reward (e.g., Mischel, 1966, 1974; Mischel & Staub, 1965). Currently, interest has shifted to elucidating the processes underlying effective delay behavior (e.g., Mischel, 1974, 1981b). Among the conditions varied are the presence or absence of the anticipated reward, the availability of external or cognitive distractions during the delay interval, and the introduction of external or cognitive strategies for enhancing or hindering the ability to delay (e.g., Mischel & Ebbesen, 1970; Mischel, Ebbesen, & Zeiss, 1972).

In the standard delay-of-gratification paradigm, children are faced with the prospect of opting for a smaller but more immediate reward or waiting for a larger and more desirable but delayed reward (e.g., one marshmallow now versus three marshmallows later). The child can choose to wait for the experimenter to return of her or his own accord and thereby obtain the larger, preferred outcome at that time. Alternatively, the child can terminate the delay period at any point (usually by ringing a bell) and thereby obtain the lesser reward immediately. In investigations of children's spontaneous cognitions and focus of attention during delay, children wait in the presence of a "Mr. Talk Box," which contains a microphone and a tape recorder hidden behind the facade of a brightly painted clown face. Mr. Talk Box encourages the children to "fill his big ears with all the things they think and feel, no matter what." Children typically engage in elaborate discussions with Mr. Talk Box and appear to treat him as an extension of themselves (Mischel, 1974).

Information about the Reward

In order to vary systematically the salience of rewards, pioneering work manipulated the physical presence or absence of the anticipated outcome during the delay interval (Mischel & Ebbesen, 1970). While they were waiting, the children in one group were presented with both the immediate (less preferred) reward and the deferred (but more desirable) reward. For a second group, neither reward was available for attention. In two additional groups, either the delayed reward only or the immediate reward only was left facing the child. The length of time that the child was willing to wait for the deferred outcome was used to index her or his frustration tolerance. The children who waited in the absence of either reward showed substantially increased delay time in comparison to the children who waited in the presence of either or both of the rewards. These latter three groups did not differ in voluntary delay time. Thus, decreasing the salience of a desired outcome increased the ability to tolerate frustration, whereas increasing the salience of a desired outcome decreased the ability to tolerate frustration.

According to psychodynamic views, children should wait longest when the delayed reward is present and visually available because its presence enhances their ability to attend to it. Children should find it harder to delay in the absence of either reward because its absence reduces their ability to attend to the anticipated outcome. However, attending to the potential reward (either immediate or deferred) appeared to increase the frustration of waiting and thereby inhibited effective delay. Thus, conditions that *decreased* attention to the desired rewards and *distracted* the children from the frustration of waiting for the more positive outcome appeared to reduce the aversiveness of the waiting interval. These results are contrary to Freudian and other early theorizing but are consistent with a social learning framework.

Cognitive Distraction from the Reward

Just as the absence of a reward appears to decrease the frustration of waiting, presumably by allowing the child to distract from it, so should techniques that explicitly instruct the child to distract from the deferred outcome. To explore this possibility, Mischel *et al.* (1972) conducted a series of experiments that manipulated children's cognitive and attentional strategies during delay. In the first study, preschool children were assigned to one of three relevant conditions during a standard delay procedure: (a) external distraction, in which an attractive toy was provided to keep the youngsters distracted; (b) ideation distraction, in which the children were instructed beforehand to think "fun" and pleasant distracting thoughts (e.g., "Think about playing with toys or singing songs"); and (c) neither distracting objects nor any ideation instructions. In addition, there were two control groups that simply experienced the external or ideation distraction condition without the delay-of-reward contingency. In all conditions, both the less preferred outcome (e.g., a hand-operated toy) and the more preferred outcome (e.g., a marshmallow and a pretzel) were present during the delay interval. The children who were instructed to distract from the anticipated outcome, by either external or cognitive avoidance mechanisms, waited longer than did those who did not receive any special instructions. These findings support the view that delay of gratification is enhanced, not hindered, by cognitively avoiding and suppressing a desired but deferred outcome. An intriguing finding was that the children who were induced to distract via fun thoughts showed greater frustration tolerance than did those who distracted themselves with toys and other external activities.

To examine this further, a second study instructed one group of children to think fun thoughts. A second group was instructed to think unhappy or sad thoughts (e.g., "Think about falling down and hurting your knee"), and a third group was told to think about the rewards (e.g., "Think about the marshmallow and the pretzel"). As in the first study, both rewards were present during the delay interval. The first group of children, who distracted themselves cognitively by engaging in affectively pleasant cognitions, waited longer than did the children who were induced to engage in affectively unpleasant thoughts or who were instructed to think about a reward (these latter two groups did not differ).

In a third study, the effects of cognitive ideation were examined when children waited in the absence of the desired objects. One third of the subjects were told to think fun thoughts, and one third were told to think about the rewards. Rather than "Think sad" instructions, the control subjects were given no specific cognition ideation instructions (parallel to the control group in Experiment I). Again, the group instructed to "Think fun" waited longer than did the "Think reward" group. Thus, engaging in affectively pleasant ideation appears to be an effective strategy for distracting oneself from the frustration of waiting. Interestingly, the control group given no particular preparatory instructions to think distracting thoughts also waited longer than did the group instructed to think about the rewards.

This result contradicts the findings from Experiment I, where the group given no special instructions was just as ineffective at delay as the group told to think about the rewards. This difference can be reconciled by considering the interaction between the situational variations (i.e., reward present versus absent) and the cognitive strategy. When the rewards are absent, and hence less salient, it appears to be easier for children spontaneously to distract themselves and thereby to reduce the frustration of waiting. When the rewards are present, and hence more salient, children may find it harder to suppress thoughts about the delayed outcome and may benefit from instructions that explicitly induce them to distract.

Taken together, these studies suggest that cognitive factors are of prime importance in determining successful delay behavior. Situational and attentional manipulations that enhance the cognitive salience of the outcome (e.g., looking at or thinking about it) greatly impede delay. Conversely, situational and attentional manipulations that decrease the cognitive salience of the outcome (e.g., waiting in the absence of the outcome or thinking about something else) facilitate delay. These findings further undermine theories that predict that attention to rewards will decrease frustration and thus enhance delay behavior. Instead, they lend support to a view that emphasizes the frustration-reducing effects of engaging in distraction and other cognitive avoidance techniques.

Abstract Representation of the Reward

Interestingly, casual observation of children in the delay studies revealed subtleties in their waiting behavior that indicated that engaging in cognitive distraction may not explain entirely the mechanism underlying effective frustration tolerance (Mischel & Moore, 1973). For example, although many of the children spontaneously sang or performed other distracting behaviors while they were waiting, they also occasionally attended to the desired rewards by reminding themselves of the contingencies for delay (e.g., "When he comes back, I'll get my candy"). This finding suggests that children may briefly "flash themselves" an image of the reward, as an aid to remembering the goal of and the reasons for waiting, but that they terminate this imagery before it becomes too aversive and frustrating and so are able to maintain goal-directed waiting.

These observations are consistent with views that distinguish between the informational (cue) function of a stimulus and its motivational or arousal function (e.g., Berlyne, 1960). As this principle is applied to the present context, a visible reward can be said to have properties that serve an informational or cue function (e.g., it reminds the child about the contingencies for delay) as well as properties that serve a motivating and arousing function (e.g., it depicts the appearance, taste, smell, and so on of the reward object). Therefore, when an anticipated reward is physically present during the delay interval, not only does it remind the child of the reward contingency, but its very presence is also arousing and frustrating ("If I reached out my hand, I could grab it and eat it or play with it right now"). Here, the arousal function may swamp the cue function and thus impede waiting. In contrast, a reward presented in a more symbolic form (e.g., as in a neutral or pictorial image) is a more abstract, intangible representation of the outcome, and so its arousal function may not be as powerful as the presence of the actual reward (e.g., "It's not really there . . . I can't eat a picture"). Therefore, a representation of the reward may serve the cue function of reminding a child of the contingencies for waiting without simultaneously inducing frustration. Thus, although exposure to the reward itself impedes delay, exposure to a symbolic representation of the reward may actually enhance delay.

To explore this possibility, Mischel and Moore (1973) presented children with slides of the anticipated outcome (the "relevant reward") or showed them slides that depicted images of similar but "irrelevant rewards" during the delay interval. Two control groups received either a blank slide or no slide during the delay interval.[3] Exposure to the images of the relevant rewards facilitated delay behavior more effectively than exposure to comparable but distracting images. Thus, abstract representation of an anticipated reward appears to enhance delay even more effectively than does distraction, presumably because children are reminded of the reasons for waiting but do not become overly aroused or frustrated by these reminders. In contrast, exposure to the actual rewards or instructions to attend cognitively to the rewards produces a strong frustrative arousal that interferes with delay.

Cognitive Filtering of the Reward

The results summarized so far suggest that it is not the presence or the absence of a reward (or its symbolic representation) that accounts for effective delay of gratification. Rather, the way in which the child attends to the anticipated outcome appears to determine his or her ability to tolerate the frustration of waiting for it. Attending to the more informative cue properties of a reward stimulus, whether real or symbolic, should decrease the frustration of waiting and should effectively sustain goal-directed delay. Conversely, attending to arousing or consummatory

---

[3]Half of the subjects then received slide presentations on a continuous basis (analogous to incessant mental imagery), and the remaining half were exposed to the slides at a periodic fixed interval of 30 seconds. The children were then further divided into a group for which the delay situation was structured as a passive, waiting task and a group for which it was structured as an active, working task. The results showed no significant effects of the schedule of the slides or the structure of the task.

qualities of a reward should increase frustration and thereby impede delay.

To investigate the primacy of cognitive attentional factors, Mischel and Baker (1975) varied ideation instructions about a forthcoming (not visually available) reward. Children were induced to think either about relevant rewards or about comparable but irrelevant rewards (the latter group was a control similar to that in Mischel & Moore, 1973). Additionally, half of each group were instructed to think about consummatory ("hot") aspects of the reward (e.g., they were told to focus on its taste and texture, such as "Marshmallows are sweet and sticky"), and half of each group were instructed to think about nonconsummatory ("cool") features of the reward (e.g., they were told to emphasize less arousing and more associative properties of the objects, such as "Marshmallows look like puffy clouds"). When the children focused cognitively on the consummatory qualities of the deferred reward, it was difficult for them to delay. In contrast, delay was facilitated when they focused on nonconsummatory qualities of the reward. Thus, when children think "cool," they can transform cognitively an anticipated outcome and reduce its arousing properties. In contrast, when children focus on the "hot" aspects of an anticipated outcome, they intensify its arousing properties.

Surprisingly, although nonconsummatory ideation about a reward that actually was forthcoming increased delay, nonconsummatory ideation about an irrelevant reward *impaired* delay. The children who thought about an object irrelevant to the delay waited longer when they fantasized about its consummatory qualities than when they focused on its cool or nonconsummatory qualities. Apparently, ideation about irrelevant rewards can work as an effective distractor, but only when such thoughts are absorbing and hot enough to sustain the child's attention. Engaging in such thoughts is not frustrating, as is consummatory ideation about an outcome that is actually anticipated, as the object is not potentially obtainable. Thus, the attentional strategy of choice appears to differ depending on whether the object of attention is actually imminently available. Cognitively transforming the outcome, by focusing on its cue properties, is an effective strategy when the child is attending to the reward; cognitively distracting oneself from the outcome, by focusing on the arousing properties of an irrelevant outcome, is an effective strategy when the child is not attending to the reward.

These results suggest that the cognitive processing of a reward is more important than its mode of presentation in determining delay of gratification. To test this, Moore, Mischel, and Zeiss (1976) exposed preschool children to either the real reward or a symbolic representation of the reward (e.g., a slide) and further divided them into a group that was told to imagine the reward as real and a group that was told to imagine the reward as a picture. Regardless of the actual mode of presentation, the children's cognitive representation of the anticipated reward determined their tolerance of frustration. The children who pretended that the reward was real could not wait as long as those who pretended that the reward was a picture (whether they viewed the slide or the reward itself). Thus, *how* a child cognitively construes a deferred outcome, rather than how the outcome is actually presented, appears to be crucial in determining the child's ability to sustain goal-directed waiting. Children can transform actual objects into abstract images (and thereby facilitate delay) or transform pictorial images into "real" objects (and thereby impede delay) simply by pretending through imagination.

Given these findings, Mischel and Moore (1980) speculated that the effects found for the mode of presentation of the reward stimuli in earlier research (Mischel & Moore, 1973) occurred because the symbolic representation of a reward encouraged the children to think about it in a less arousing way than did the actual physical presence of the reward. To explore directly whether the mode of reward presentation or the child's ideation about the outcome was more important, Mischel and Moore (1980) assigned children either to a group that viewed a slide of the relevant reward or to a group that viewed a slide of an irrelevant but rewarding object. The subjects were then further divided into a group instructed to fantasize about the consummatory aspects of the deferred reward ("consummatory-relevant") or a group told to ideate about the consummatory features of a comparable but irrelevant food object ("consummatory-irrelevant"). A third group was given no special ideation instructions. Exposure to the symbolically presented (relevant) rewards greatly enhanced delay, whereas exposure to the symbolic representations of irrelevant rewards did not. This result parallels earlier findings (Mischel & Moore, 1973). However, this effect was undermined by instructions to focus on the consummatory qualities of the reward. Specifically, the children who were instructed to focus on consummatory aspects of the relevant reward delayed for a shorter time than did those who were told to focus on consummatory aspects of a reward irrelevant to the delay contingency, regardless of whether they viewed a relevant or an irrelevant slide.

Thus, how the individual ideates about a reward appears to be the primary determinant of effective delay behavior, completely overriding the availability of the reward. Engaging in consummatory ideation about the reward prevents the effective delay of gratification, whether the reward is symbolically present or is absent. This finding suggests that the symbolic presentation of a reward enhances delay by enabling the child to transform the outcome and to ideate about it in a nonconsummatory fashion.

Overall, then, frustration tolerance depends on the way in which the child processes and ideates about a reward object, rather than on its physical mode of presentation or the content depicted. Consummatory cognitions generate arousal and impede delay, whereas non-consummatory cognitions provide a reminder for waiting and facilitate delay.

Individual Differences

Early studies on coping with frustration explored the personality correlates of preference for immediate, lesser rewards or delayed, larger rewards. The preference for delayed but more valuable outcomes was found to be correlated positively with age, level of cognitive development, achievement motivation, resistance to temptation, sociocultural and rearing conditions (e.g., the father's presence in the home), and general intelligence (see, for example, Grim, Kohlberg, & White, 1968; Klineburg, 1968; Mischel, 1974; Mischel & Gilligan, 1964). Specifically, the individual who typically prefers delayed outcomes is likely to be oriented toward the future, to score high on ego-control measures, and to be high in level of aspiration (Klineburg, 1968; Mischel, 1966, 1971). Conversely, the individual who prefers immediate gratification over waiting or working for more valuable but delayed outcomes is characterized by greater concern about the immediate, greater impulsivity, lower socioeconomic status, membership in cultures with less emphasis on achievement, and less competence on measures of social and cognitive capacity.

Evaluation of the Evidence

A summary of the evidence on delay gratification is presented in Table 2. As can be seen, information about or attention to an anticipated but deferred outcome appears to impede frustration tolerance relative to no information (Mischel & Ebbesen, 1970; Mischel et al., 1972). In contrast, manipulations that distract the child from the reward promote frustration tolerance (Mischel & Ebbesen, 1970; Mischel et al., 1972). Distracting through an external means, such as playing with a toy, is one important strategy for enhancing delay (Mischel et al., 1972). Ideational distractors, such as engaging in affectively pleasant imagery, appear to be even more effective (Mischel et al., 1972). Finally, distracting oneself from a deferred outcome by viewing an abstract (e.g., slide) representation of an irrelevant reward also appears to be an effective (if not the best) cognitive avoidance technique, as long as the individual focuses

TABLE 2. Evidence on Delay of Gratification in Children

Condition	Comparison	Reference (N and age)	Outcome measure	Results[a]
Rewards physically present	Rewards physically absent	Mischel and Ebbesen (1970) N = 32; ages: 3.5–5.67 yrs.	Time waited	→
External distraction (rewards present)	No distraction (rewards present)	Mischel, Ebbesen and Zeiss (1972) Exp. I N = 50; ages: 3.5–5.5 yrs.	Time waited	←
Ideation distraction (rewards present)	External distraction (rewards present)	Mischel, Ebbesen and Zeiss (1972) Exp. I N = 50; ages 3.5–5.5 yrs.	Time waited	←
Think rewards (rewards present)	Think sad (rewards present)	Mischel, Ebbesen and Zeiss (1972) Exp. II N = 26; ages: 3.75–5.25 yrs.	Time waited	↑
Think fun (rewards present)	Think rewards (rewards present)	Mischel, Ebbesen and Zeiss (1972) Exp. II N = 26; ages: 3.75–5.25 yrs.	Time waited	←
Think rewards (rewards absent)	No ideation (rewards absent)	Mischel, Ebbesen and Zeiss (1972) Exp. III N = 16; ages: 3.4–5.5 yrs.	Time waited	→

Think fun (rewards absent)	No ideation (rewards absent)	Mischel, Ebbesen, and Zeiss (1972) Exp. III $N = 16$; ages: 3.4–5.5 yrs.	Time waited	↑
Symbolic rewards (relevant)	Symbolic rewards (irrelevant)	Mischel and Moore (1973) $N = 123$; 3.5–5.4 yrs.	Time waited	←
Symbolic rewards (relevant)	Symbolic rewards (irrelevant)	Mischel and Moore (1980) $N = 90$; age: 3.75–5.1 yrs.	Time waited	←
Cool ideation (relevant rewards)	Hot ideation (relevant rewards)	Mischel and Baker (1975) $N = 60$; age: 3.3–5.4 yrs.	Time waited	←
Cool ideation (irrelevant rewards)	Hot ideation (irrelevant rewards)	Mischel and Baker (1975) $N = 60$; age: 3.3–5.4 yrs.	Time waited	→
Imagine rewards as a picture (viewing slide or real reward)	Imagine rewards as real (viewing slide or real reward)	Moore, Mischel, and Zeiss (1976) $N = 48$; age: 4–5.6 yrs.	Time waited	←
Consummatory ideation irrelevant rewards (symbolic presentation of any rewards)	Consummatory ideation relevant rewards (symbolic presentation of any rewards)	Mischel and Moore (1980) $N = 90$; age: 3.75–5.1 yrs.	Time waited	←

[a] (↑) Experimental condition group delayed significantly longer than the comparison.
(↓) Experimental condition group delayed significantly less time than the comparison.
(→) Experimental and comparison groups did not differ in delay time.

on its hot affective properties (Mischel & Moore, 1980). However, these three distraction strategies have not yet been compared directly to one another (e.g., symbolic representation vs. external or ideational distraction).

In addition to distraction, cognitively reframing the deferred outcome appears to be a fundamental delay-enhancing strategy (Mischel & Baker, 1975; Mischel & Moore, 1980; Moore et al., 1976). For example, when individuals view a symbolic representation (e.g., a slide) of the outcome itself, it is easier for them to delay than when they view a slide of an irrelevant (distracting) reward (Mischel & Moore, 1973, 1980). Focusing on a symbolic representation of the reward appears to highlight its cue properties (thereby reminding the child of the contingencies of delay) while blunting its more appetitive qualities (thereby minimizing arousal). It is not yet known whether focusing on a symbolic representation of the reward is superior to other forms of distraction (external or ideational) as a means of promoting delay.

Similar to symbolic representation, cognitively transforming a delayed outcome by focusing on its cool or nonconsummatory qualities while cognitively avoiding its hot or consummatory qualities is an effective technique for reducing arousal and providing cues for delay. The evidence shows that inducing a child to fantasize about the reward in nonaffective terms is more delay-enhancing than inducing the child to fantasize about an irrelevant (distracting) outcome in nonconsummatory terms (Mischel & Baker, 1975). The evidence further suggests that cognitive transformation may be a more effective strategy than other forms of distraction (e.g., focusing on the arousing properties of an irrelevant reward). However, conclusive comparisons of these strategies are lacking.

Although cognitive avoidance and transformation are effective frustration-reducing strategies, there are situational factors that interfere with the young child's ability to engage in such strategies. When the reward is psychologically invasive and intrusive, as when it is physically present or when the child is instructed to think about it, it becomes difficult for the child to engage spontaneously in distraction (Mischel & Ebbesen, 1970; Mischel et al., 1972). Under these conditions, explicitly instructing the child to distract facilitates effective delay (Mischel & Ebbesen, 1970; Mischel et al., 1972). It is not yet known whether manipulations that increase the psychological salience of an anticipated outcome (e.g., its physical presence) similarly impair the child's ability to transform the reward spontaneously or to benefit from viewing a symbolic representation of it. However, it is clear that the way in which children are induced to represent or focus cognitively on an anticipated outcome affects their ability to wait for it. Instructing a child to imagine the reward as a picture (rather than as real) facilitates delay, whereas instructing the child to imagine the reward as real impedes delay, whether the child is actually exposed to the real reward or to a symbolic representation of the reward (Moore *et al.*, 1976). Similarly, delay is impaired by explicit instructions to ideate about the reward itself in consummatory terms. Again, this effect is obtained whether the child is exposed to a slide of an irrelevant reward or to a slide of the reward itself (Mischel & Moore, 1980). It is not yet known whether the child would be able to override stimulus constraints if he or she were induced to focus on nonconsummatory or cool ideation. For example, would delay be enhanced if the child were to fantasize about a relevant reward in nonconsummatory terms, regardless of the content (relevance) of the slide that he or she is actually viewing?

Finally, although certain individuals appear to be generally more inclined to wait for preferred but delayed rewards (see Mischel, 1974), studies have not yet explicitly explored dispositional differences in the inclination or ability to seek or avoid information during delay. Further studies should investigate how such preferences interact with relevant situational factors (such as increased versus decreased reward salience) to determine frustration tolerance.

To summarize, contrary to early theorizing which emphasized the role of attention to forthcoming rewards as a means of tolerating frustration, children cope best when they can cognitively avoid or transform the preferred but delayed outcome. Consistent with this pattern, conditions that decrease the salience of an anticipated reward clearly promote frustration tolerance, whereas conditions that increase the salience of the reward impede frustration tolerance. However, even when situational constraints make it difficult to distract from or transform the forthcoming outcome, inducing the child to engage in cognitive strategies overrides these factors and enhances delay of gratification. Preliminary evidence also suggests that there are dispositional factors (e.g., informational preferences) that predict children's attentional strategies during delay. Further research should explore how these individual differences interact with relevant situational factors to determine frustration tolerance.

THE COPING PROCESS: SUMMARY AND INTEGRATION

In this section, we briefly summarize the evidence on coping with threat and frustration, identifying empirical gaps and confounds and distilling the theoretical implications of these findings. Then, we attempt to integrate the two literatures, emphasizing the areas of their conceptual and empirical convergence.

Impending Threat: Brief Summary of the Evidence

Clearly, the way in which a child is prepared to face aversive hospital or dental procedures affects his or her response to the event. Voluminous procedural information alone is at best ineffective and at worst actually detrimental to adaptive coping (Ferguson, 1979; Johnson *et al.*, 1975; Melamed *et al.*, 1978). Treatments such as puppet and filmed peer modeling appear to facilitate stress reduction, apparently because they enable the child to selectively filter information about the impending event (Cassell, 1965; Ferguson, 1979; Johnson & Stockdale, 1975; Machen & Johnson, 1974; Melamed & Siegel, 1975; Melamed, Hawes, Heiby, & Glick, 1975; Melamed, Weinstein, Hawes, & Katin-Borland, 1975; Vernon, 1973; Vernon & Bailey, 1974). Manipulations that explicitly distract children from salient aversive cues or divert their attention to less threatening cues are most effective in reducing stress (Peterson & Shigetomi, 1981; Siegel & Peterson, 1980). These include engaging in muscle relaxation, affectively pleasant imagery, and calming self-talk. Exposure to sensory information may also be an effective stress-reducing technique (Johnson *et al.*, 1975; Siegel & Peterson, 1980; Visintainer & Wolfer, 1975; Wolfer & Visintainer, 1975, 1979). No studies of children have compared directly the effects of receiving increased procedural information to the induction of cognitive distraction strategies. However, the evidence shows that exposure to sensory information that may cognitively transform the event for the child is superior to exposure to increased procedural information (Johnson *et al.*, 1975). Future research should attempt to clarify the mechanisms underlying the efficacy of these procedures and the conditions under which these techniques do and do not reduce stress.

Unfortunately, studies of children's coping patterns have generally collapsed across age, gender, experience, and relevant individual dispositions. Therefore, it is not known whether children, like adults, exhibit consistent differences in *styles* of information seeking; nor is it known whether such informational preferences interact with relevant situational factors, or how such preferences evolve over different stages of cognitive development.

Frustration Tolerance: Brief Summary of the Evidence

Clearly, cognitive attentional manipulations affect the way in which a child responds to the frustration of waiting for a preferred but delayed reward. Increasing the salience of a delayed outcome (e.g., by making the child wait in its presence) increases frustration, whereas decreasing the salience of a delayed outcome decreases frustration (Mischel &

Ebbesen, 1970). Indeed, providing a child with an external distractor (such as a toy) further enhances the ability to delay gratification (Mischel *et al.*, 1972). Cognitive strategies that facilitate distraction, such as engaging in affectively pleasant imagery, are even more effective techniques for promoting delay than are external distractors (Mischel *et al.*, 1972). The most successful strategy for enhancing frustration tolerance demonstrated so far is to induce the child cognitively to transform the forthcoming reward, for example, by instructing the child to focus on its nonconsummatory features while selectively filtering out its arousing and appetitive features (Mischel & Baker, 1975). This strategy appears to help the child concentrate on the contingencies for waiting while simultaneously reducing the frustration of doing so. Even under conditions that hinder delay, such as being in the physical presence of a deferred reward, cognitive attentional mechanisms can override these constraints and promote tolerance of frustration (Moore *et al.*, 1976). Future research should investigate whether these findings hold when the relevant parameters of the deferred outcome are varied (such as by manipulating its desirability or the likelihood of its actually being received). Unfortunately, studies on children's patterns of coping with frustration have generally collapsed across age, gender, and relevant dispositions. Therefore, it is not yet known whether children show consistent *styles* of attentional preferences during delay of gratification nor how such preferences interact with relevant situational variables. Furthermore, it is not yet clear whether these individual patterns of cognitive coping mechanisms may change as a function of the child's stage of cognitive development.

Integration of Theory and Evidence

Research on the processes of coping with threat and frustration suggests some striking coherences, at both the conceptual and the empirical levels. More specifically, attentional processes underlying effective coping strategies appear to be remarkably similar in both contexts. Inducing individuals to engage in such cognitive techniques appears to help them overcome the (aversive) arousal associated with both anticipated negative and delayed positive outcomes. In addition, there may be parallels in the situational and dispositional factors that impinge on an individual's ability to engage in effective cognitive coping strategies when dealing with threat and with frustration.

Theories in both areas initially emphasized the arousal-reducing value of attending to information about the forthcoming event. Information relevant to the outcome was presumed to reduce uncertainty and signal periods of safety (in the case of threat) and to facilitate hallucinatory satisfactions and other thought processes that bind time and assist in resisting temptation (in the case of frustration). Contrary to these early formulations, evidence on children's and adults' coping with uncontrollable threat and deferred gratification has shown that increased information about or attention to the event actually increases anxiety and frustration. Conversely, cognitive avoidance and the transformation of outcome-relevant cues reduce anxiety and frustration. Accordingly, current theories focus on delineating the cognitive mechanisms underlying adaptive coping, and they highlight the interplay between situational factors and dispositional preferences in promoting adaptive coping.

On the empirical level, the evidence shows that, when dealing with both positively and negatively valenced affective events, techniques that distract and divert attention have been found to be more arousal-reducing than techniques that increase the salience of or information about such outcomes. In coping with threat, engaging in strategies such as distraction, pleasant imagery, calming self-talk, and muscle relaxation are more stress-reducing than either exposure to minimal information (Siegel & Peterson, 1980), increased information, or modeling (Peterson & Shigetomi, 1981). Similarly, in coping with frustration, distracting from the reward through external means or, better yet, through engaging in pleasant or hot imagery about an irrelevant reward is more effective in promoting frustration tolerance than either attending to the outcome (Mischel & Ebbesen, 1970), waiting for the outcome without an external means of distraction (Mischel et al., 1972), or engaging in affectively unpleasant ideation. Thus, in both affective contexts, distraction is the coping mode of choice. The frustration literature further suggests that distracting oneself through cognitive ideation or symbolic representation is superior to distracting oneself through external means (Mischel et al., 1972). The differential effectiveness of these modes of distraction has not yet been investigated in the literature on threat.

In addition to cognitively distracting oneself, cognitively reframing or transforming the threatening or frustrating nature of an impending event appears to be an important arousal-reducing strategy. One technique for psychologically reframing a delayed reward is to attend to a symbolic representation of it. This appears to highlight its cue properties while filtering out its affectively arousing features, and it has been shown to be even more effective in enhancing delay than focusing on a slide of an irrelevant reward (Mischel & Moore, 1973). A related technique for engaging in psychological transformation is to focus the child on the cool or nonconsummatory features of the reward (e.g., its appearance in metaphorical terms) while diverting attention from its hotter, more appetitive aspects (e.g., its taste and texture). Some evidence suggests that inducing a child to filter an appetitive outcome in less arousing terms may be more effective in promoting frustration tolerance than simply distracting her or him from thoughts about the reward (Mischel & Baker, 1975). Engaging in cognitive avoidance enables the child to block out the appetitive qualities of the reward and thus to reduce arousal. Engaging in cognitive transformation enables the child to filter selectively information so that he or she both reduces arousal (by avoiding ideation about the event's consummatory properties), and is reminded of the contingencies of delay (by focusing on its cue, nonconsummatory properties).

In the domain of aversive events, one technique for cognitively transforming the outcome may be to receive sensory information about it (see, for example, Visintainer & Wolfer, 1975; Wolfer & Visintainer, 1975, 1979). Sensory information appears to focus the child on the experiential and personal aspects of an impending procedure (e.g., how it will feel, in metaphorical terms, and how it will smell and sound), which mute its more affectively toned aversive qualities (e.g., the details of the procedure that cause pain). Direct comparisons of the efficacy of cognitive avoidance versus cognitive transformation in children or adults have yet to be conclusive. The one study that compared these two strategies in children found them to be equally stress-reducing (Siegel & Peterson, 1980). However, as has been noted above, giving sensory information may not be the most potent procedure for inducing a child cognitively to transform an aversive outcome. Consistent with the suggestive findings on delay, it seems plausible that cognitively transforming threat-relevant cues may be superior to simply distracting oneself from this information.

Cognitively transforming an impending threat seems to share some of the arousal-reducing properties of cognitively distracting oneself from the outcome. However, whereas distraction suppresses *all* thoughts about an impending stressful event, the cognitive transformation of threat-relevant cues may not have the consequences of turning the individual's attention so far afield. That is, such techniques may combine some degree of reduced arousal (as in cognitive avoidance) but may still allow for continued processing of external threat-relevant information. One advantage that an individual gains from engaging in threat-relevant information-processing is that he or she is able to discriminate changes in the external situation. For example, when a formerly uncontrollable event becomes controllable, the monitoring child inputs that information and therefore is in a position to execute the appropriate controlling response. In contrast, an individual who has completely "tuned out" does not input new information and therefore is not responsive to changes in the situation. Moreover, engaging in certain cognitive transformation strategies (e.g., reinterpretation) may be more adequate for this purpose than others (e.g., sensory information). Indeed, an explanation for the relative efficacy of filmed peer modeling may be that it lends itself easily to cognitively reframing the aversive outcome (as does the symbolic representation of a forthcoming positive outcome during delay).

No evidence bears directly on the differential efficacy of these cognitive modes in children or adults, but the issue is an important one. In chronically uncontrollable or high-intensity situations, the strategy of choice may be the one that most effectively reduces the level of arousal and the concomitant processing of threat-relevant information, such as distraction. However, in situations that may be subject to change (e.g., that may progress from uncontrollable to controllable or from more intense to less intense), the use of a strategy that accomplishes some degree of arousal reduction but does not impede completely external processing of threat-relevant information may be optimal (see also Lazarus, 1983). It will be interesting to determine whether the role of cognitive transformation in reducing arousal and enhancing self-regulation is a further coherence between the processes of coping with threat and frustration.

Although the cognitive blunting of cues relevant to impending uncontrollable threats and delayed rewards is an effective strategy, there appear to be situational factors that impair the individual's ability to engage in such strategies (see Table 3). When affective *cues* are psychologically salient, such as being in the presence of signals that predict the onset of the outcome (in the case of threat) or being in the presence of a physically visible outcome (in the case of deferred reward), it is more difficult to engage in distraction and similar psychological techniques (see Miller, 1980c, 1981b; Mischel & Ebbesen, 1970; Mischel *et al.*, 1972). Conversely, when the salience of threat- and reward-relevant cues is decreased (e.g., by reducing the predictability of a threatening event or by physically removing an anticipated reward), it is easier to engage in such strategies and thereby to reduce arousal. These effects clearly are borne out by the evidence on children's attempts to distract from frustrating stimuli and on adults' patterns of coping with threat. However, there are no data that directly explore the role of these situational factors in children's responses to the symbolic representation and transformation of frustrating stimuli nor are there any data on children's patterns of coping with threat.

In addition to the importance of outcome-relevant cues, the evidence shows that when the outcome itself is psychologically invasive, individuals may find it more difficult to distract themselves. Adults facing an aversive event that is psychologically intense (e.g., when it is highly likely, has a high frequency, or is imminent) generally find it

TABLE 3. Situational Factors That Facilitate or Impair Cognitive Blunting

Cognitive blunting of arousing stimuli[a]	
Facilitated	Impaired
Cues not salient (unpredictability) Threat: anxiety ↓ Geer and Maisel (1972) Miller (1980c, 1981b) Miller and Grant (1979) Monat (1976)	Cues salient (predictability) Threat: anxiety ↑ Geer and Maisel (1972) Miller (1980c, 1981b) Miller and Grant (1979) Monat (1976)
Deferred rewards: frustration ↓ Mischel and Ebbesen (1970) Mischel, Ebbesen, and Zeiss (1972)	Deferred rewards: frustration ↑ Mischel and Ebbesen (1970) Mischel, Ebbesen, and Zeiss (1972)
Outcomes not salient (uncertain irrelevant) Threat: anxiety ↓ Garber, Miller, and Abramson (1980) Miller (1981b) Deferred rewards: frustration ↓ Mischel and Baker (1975) Mischel and Moore (1973, 1980)	Outcomes salient (certain, relevant) Threat: anxiety ↑ Garber, Miller, and Abramson (1980) Miller (1981b) Deferred rewards: frustration ↑ Mischel and Baker (1975) Mischel and Moore (1973, 1980)
Presence of external distractors Threat: anxiety ↓ Miller (1981b) Miller and Grant (1979) Deferred rewards: frustration ↓ Mischel, Ebbesen, and Zeiss (1972)	Absence of external distractors Threat: anxiety ↑ Miller (1981) Miller and Grant (1979) Deferred rewards: frustration ↑ Mischel, Ebbesen, and Zeiss (1972)
Induced ideational distraction Threat: anxiety ↓ Miller (1981b) Peterson and Shigetomi (1981) Siegel and Peterson (1980) Deferred rewards: frustration ↓ Mischel, Ebbesen, and Zeiss (1972) Mischel and Moore (1973, 1980)	No ideational distraction Threat: anxiety ↑ Miller (1981) Peterson and Shigetomi (1981) Siegel and Peterson (1980) Deferred rewards: frustration ↑ Mischel, Ebbesen, and Zeiss (1972) Mischel and Moore (1973, 1980)
Induced cognitive transformation Threat: anxiety ↓ Johnson et al. (1975) Langer, Janis, and Wolfer (1975) Siegel and Peterson (1980) Visintainer and Wolfer (1975) Wolfer and Visintainer (1975, 1979) Deferred rewards: frustration ↓ Mischel and Baker (1975) Mischel and Moore (1980) Moore, Mischel, and Zeiss (1976)	Induced cognitive attention Threat: anxiety→ Ferguson (1979) Johnson et al. (1975) Deferred rewards: frustration ↑ Mischel and Baker (1975) Mischel and Moore (1980) Moore, Mischel, and Zeiss (1976)

[a] (↑) Arousal increased.
(↓) Arousal decreased.
(→) Arousal unaffected.

harder to divert their attention and may benefit from increased information about the outcome (see Miller, 1981a). This possibility has not yet been explored either with children facing threat or with children attempting to defer gratification. Future research should examine whether varying parameters, such as the intensity of the outcome, affect children's coping preferences in a fashion similar to the way in which they affect adults.

Furthermore, adults apparently exhibit differences that bear on their ability to cope with threat and frustration. However, this issue has been largely overlooked in research with youngsters in both the delay and the threat literatures.[4] Studies should explore whether children, like adults, show information-seeking *styles* that interact with critical situational variables to determine adaptive coping. In addition, future research should take into account the influence of developmental considerations in the coping process. For example, it should examine how these coping styles hold over time and across different phases of development.

Overall, then, there are clear coherences in the cognitive processes underlying adaptive coping with threat and frustration, and there may be coherences between the relevant situational factors and individual differences that moderate these effects. However, there are gaps in both the delay and the threat literatures. Further work should provide a more finely grained analysis of the cognitive mechanisms underlying effective self-regulation, particularly in the domain of children's coping with threat (e.g., what is the differential effectiveness of cognitive avoidance vs. cognitive transformation?). Furthermore, although there is some evidence

[4]Given the importance of cognitive attentional factors in reducing stress and frustration, we have been exploring individual differences in children's ability or inclination to scan for or ignore cues about forthcoming threats and rewards. As a first step in this direction, we have devised a scale for children to measure and assess monitoring–blunting preferences under threat that parallels the already-validated adult scale. We have also devised a scale to identify information preferences during delay of reward (with an adults' as well as a children's version) (Miller & Mischel, 1985). In order to explore whether such information-seeking preferences predict actual coping behaviors, children are faced with the prospect of both an uncontrollable, mildly negative event that parallels the laboratory work already conducted with college student populations (Miller & Green, 1983; Miller, Mischel, Green, & Robinson, 1985), and a standard delay-of-gratification situation (e.g., Mischel, 1974).

One important focus of this research is to investigate the cross-situational links between the processes of coping with negatively and positively valenced events. For example, adults and children who are effective blunters in threat situations may be similarly efficient in their use of cognitive avoidance in the standard delay-of-gratification paradigm. A further consideration bears on the possible origins of these coping patterns, and we have just begun to examine the acquisition of information preferences (Miller & Green, 1983; Miller et al., 1983).

on the importance of situational factors (such as the presence versus the absence of an anticipated reward in promoting delay), the boundaries of these and related factors (e.g., outcome intensity) need to be explored, especially in the case of aversive events. A final empirical void has to do with the role of individual differences and cognitive developmental phase in determining coping competencies.

There are also major differences between the threat and the delay literatures. One such difference concerns the applied versus the conceptual focus of the research. The literature on frustration tolerance has been guided by a cognitive social-learning framework that emphasizes the primacy of cognitive processes in accounting for delay of gratification. Therefore, studies were designed specifically to tap and analyze such processes. In contrast, research on children's responses to threat has been more atheoretical and practically oriented. Hence, studies have used more "shotgun" manipulations to reduce stress, and therefore, crucial comparisons are often lacking (such as the differential effectiveness of external versus cognitive distraction and the differential effectiveness of cognitive avoidance and cognitive transformation). Future work should attempt to fill this void.

The two literatures further differ in the types of measures obtained. The delay literature has been concerned specifically with the role of attentional factors and therefore has devised measures to assess explicitly children's spontaneous ideation when coping with frustration. Research on children's coping with threat would be enhanced by incorporating similar measures for more directly assessing attentional processes. Additionally, studies on deferred reward have focused mainly on actual waiting behavior during the delay interval, and they use waiting time to infer frustration tolerance. In contrast, studies on threat generally use more varied and direct measures of arousal (including self-report, observational, and physiologic indices) obtained during the anticipatory, impact, and postimpact periods. These measures provide a more comprehensive and converging index of arousal. Research on the tolerance of frustration might be enriched by a more global assessment of frustration obtained at various points in the delay cycle.

Lastly, evidence from both the threat and the delay literatures has important and converging implications for understanding maladaptive coping patterns (see, for example, Cole & Kazdin, 1983; Kendall, 1977; Meichenbaum, 1975, 1977; Ross, 1981). A tendency toward the excessive or inflexible use of monitoring in negative situations may underlie a susceptibility to pathologically high levels of anxiety (Miller & Grant, 1979; Miller & Green, 1985). Similarly, excessive or inflexible monitoring in positive situations may produce heightened frustration and self-control problems (Finch & Montgomery, 1975; Meichenbaum & Goodman, 1971). Future research should attempt to identify individuals at risk for such self-regulatory dysfunction.

CONCLUSION

This chapter addresses the nature of and coherences between the processes of coping with threat and frustration. These two affective domains have normally been considered separately. Yet, a review of the literature shows that there is considerable convergence between them, at both the conceptual and the empirical levels.

An adequate analysis of the coping process in both contexts has to take into account the interaction of different cognitive preferences with situational features. The conceptual framework that we outline attempts to do that, by concentrating on two fundamental strategies for dealing with emotional situations. The evidence shows that the main mode for coping with aversive or frustrating events appears to involve cognitive avoidance, blunting, and turning off and tuning down of threat- and reward-relevant information as a means of reducing arousal. When situational considerations make this mode inappropriate or difficult, individuals may switch to a coping mode which involves cognitive sensitization, monitoring, and turning on and tuning in to threat- or reward-relevant cues.

Finally, there may be individual differences in information preferences that interact with situational factors to determine how well individuals cope, with "monitors" possibly benefiting more from information and blunters benefiting more from distraction. Future studies should attempt to identify these dispositional factors in children and to determine their stability over time and their consistency across situations. In particular, it is important to delineate the situational conditions and the developmental phases under which the cognitive avoidance and psychological "blunting" of emotional cues have more adaptive consequences for the coping process than the informational search for and "monitoring" of emotional cues.

ACKNOWLEDGMENTS

The authors would like to thank Dr. Walter Mischel and Dr. Albert Bandura for their invaluable comments on this chapter, as well as Tomas Caballero, Pamela Fawcett, Despi Hadzimichalis, and Renee Robinson for their contributions.

REFERENCES

Anderson, K. O., & Masur, F. T., III. Psychological preparation for invasive medical and dental procedures. *Journal of Behavioral Medicine*, 1983 *6*, 1–40.

Averill, J. R., & Rosenn, M. Vigilant and nonvigilant coping, strategies and psychophysiological stress reactions during the anticipation of an electric shock. *Journal of Personality and Social Psychology*, 1972, *23*, 128–141.

Bandura, A. Self-efficacy: Toward a unifying theory of behavioral change. *Psychological Review*, 1977, *84*, 191–215.

Bandura, A., & Menlove, F. L. Factor determining vicarious extinction of avoidance behavior through symbolic modeling. *Journal of Personality and Social Psychology*, 1968, *8*, 99–108.

Barber, T. X., & Hahn, K. W. Physiological and subjective responses to pain producing stimulation under hypnotically-suggested and waking-imagined "analgesia." *Journal of Abnormal and Social Psychology*, 1962, *65*, 411–418.

Berlyne, D. E. *Conflict arousal and curiosity.* New York: McGraw-Hill, 1960.

Blitz, B., & Dinnerstein, A. J. Role of attentional focus in pain perception: Manipulation of response to noxious stimulation by instructions. *Journal of Abnormal Psychology*, 1971, *77*, 42–45.

Bloom, L.J., Houston, B. K., Holmes, D. S., & Burish, T. G. The effectiveness of attentional diversion and situational redefinition for reducing stress to a nonambiguous threat. *Journal of Research in Personality*, 1977, *11*, 83–96.

Burstein, S., & Meichenbaum, D. The work of worrying in children undergoing surgery. *Journal of Abnormal Child Psychology*, 1979, *7*, 121–132.

Cassell, S. Effects of brief puppet therapy upon the emotional responses of children undergoing cardiac catheterization. *Journal of Consulting Psychology*, 1965, *29*, 1–8.

Chorney, R. L., Efran, J., Ascher, L. M., & Lukens, M. D. *The performance of monitors and blunters during painful stimulation.* Paper presented at the meeting of the Eastern Psychological Association, New York, April 1981.

Cohen, F., & Lazarus, R. S. Active coping processes, coping dispositions, and recovery from surgery. *Psychosomatic Medicine*, 1973, *35*, 375–389.

Cole, P. M., & Kazdin, A. E. Critical issues in self-instruction training with children. *Child Behavior Therapy*, 1983, *2*, 1–23.

Ferguson, B. F. Preparing young children for hospitalization: A comparison of two methods. *Pediatrics*, 1979, *64*, 656–665.

Finch, A. J., Jr., & Montgomery, L. E. Reflection-impulsivity and information seeking in emotionally disturbed children. *Journal of Abnormal Child Psychology*, 1975, *3*, 47–51.

Freud, S. Formulations regarding the two principles in mental functioning. In *Collected papers* (Vol. 4). (Originally published, 1911.) New York: Basic, 1959.

Garber, J., Miller, S. M., & Abramson, L. Y. On the distinction between anxiety and depression: Perceived control, certainty, and probability of goal attainment. In J. Garber and M. Seligman (Eds.), *Human helplessness: Theory and applications*. New York: Academic Press, 1980.

Geer, J. H., & Maisel, E. Evaluating the effects of the prediction-control confound. *Journal of Personality and Social Psychology*, 1972, *13*, 314–319.

Gellert, E. Reducing the emotional stresses of hospitalization for children. *Occupational Therapy*, 1958, *12*, 125–129.

Grim, P. F., Kohlberg, L., & White, S. H. Some relationships between conscience and attentional processes. *Journal of Personality and Social Psychology*, 1968, *8*, 239–252.

Haggerty, R. J. Breaking the link between stress and illness in children: What role can physicians play? *Postgraduate Medicine*, 1983, *74*, 287–295.

Holmes, D. S., & Houston, B. K. Effectiveness of situational redefinition and affective isolation in coping with stress. *Journal of Personality and Social Psychology*, 1974, *29*, 212–218.

Jackson, K., Winkley, R., Faust, O. A., & Cermack, E. The problem of emotional trauma in the hospital treatment of children. *Journal of the American Medical Association*, 1952, *149*, 1536–1538.

Jenkins, J. J. Remember that old theory of memory? Well, forget it! *American Psychologist*, 1974, *29*, 785–795.

Jessner, L., Blom, G. E., & Waldfogel, S. Emotional implications of tonsillectomy and adenoidectomy in children. In R. S. Eisslen (Ed.), *The psychoanalytic study of the child*. New York: International Universities Press, 1952.

Johnson, J. E., Kirchhoff, K. T., & Endress, M. P. Altering children's distress behavior during orthopedic cast removal. *Nursing Research*, 1975, *24*, 404–410.

Johnson, P. A., & Stockdale, D. F. Effects of puppet therapy on palmar sweating of hospitalized children. *The Johns Hopkins Medical Journal*, 1975, *137*, 1–5.

Jones, E., & Gerard, H. B. *Foundations of social psychology*. New York: Wiley, 1967.

Kendall, P. C. On the efficacious use of verbal self-instructional procedures with children. *Cognitive Therapy and Research*, 1977, *1*, 331–341.

Kendall, P. C., & Watson, D. Psychological preparation for stressful medical procedures. In L. A. Bradley & C. K. Proskop (Eds.), *Medical psychology: Contributions to behavioral medicine*. New York: Academic Press, 1981.

Klemp, G. O., & Rodin, J. Effects of uncertainty, delay, and focus of attention on reactions to an aversive situation. *Journal of Experimental Social Psychology*, 1976, *12*, 416–421.

Klineburg, S. L. Future time perspective and the preference for delayed reward. *Journal of Personality and Social Psychology*, 1968, *8*, 253–257.

Klorman, R., Hilpert, P., Michael, R., LaGana, C., & Sveen, O. Effects of coping and mastery modeling on experienced and inexperienced pedodontic patients' disruptiveness. *Behavior Therapy*, 1980, *11*, 156–168.

Lacey, J. L. Somatic response patterning and stress: Some revisions of activation theory. In M. H. Appley & R. Trumbell (Eds.), *Psychological stress: Issues in research*. New York: Appleton-Century-Crofts, 1967.

Landes, H. R. Treatment of anxiety in the families of children undergoing tonsillectomy. (Doctoral dissertation, Northwestern University, 1973). *Dissertation Abstracts International*, 1973, *34*, 2938B-2939B. (University Microfilms No. 73–30, 640.)

Langer, E. J., Janis, I. L., & Wolfer, J. A. Reduction of psychological stress in surgical patients. *Journal of Experimental Social Psychology*, 1975, *11*, 155–165.

Lazarus, R. S. The costs and benefits of denial. In S. Breznitz (Ed.), *The denial of stress*. New York: International Universities Press, 1983.

Lazarus, R. S., & Alfert, E. Short-circuiting of threat by experimentally altering cognitive appraisal. *Journal of Abnormal and Social Psychology*, 1966, *69*, 195–205.

Lazarus, R. S., Opton, E., Nomikos, M., & Rankin, N. The principles of short-circuiting of threat: Further evidence. *Journal of Personality*, 1965, *33*, 622–635.

Lazarus, R. S., Cohen, J. B., Folkman, S., Kanner, A., & Schaefer, C. Psychological stress and adaptation: Some unresolved issues. In H. Selye (Ed.), *Guide to stress research* (Vol. 1). New York: Van Nostrand Reinhold, 1980.

Leonard, R., Skipper, J., & Woolridge, P. Small sample field experiments for evaluating patient care. *Health Services Research*, 1967, *2*, 46–60.

Leventhal, H., Brown, D., Sacham, S., & Engquist, G. Effects of preparatory information about sensations, threat of pain, and attention on cold pressor distress. *Journal of Personality and Social Psychology*, 1979, *37*, 688–714.

Machen, J. B., & Johnson, R. Desensitization, modeling learning, and the dental behavior of children. *Journal of Dental Research*, 1974, *53*, 83–87.

Mead, P. G. The effects of orientation passages on patient stress prior to dentistry. *Psychological Record*, 1970, *20*, 479–480.

Mechanic, D. The experience and reporting of common physical complaints. *Journal of Health and Social Behavior*, 1980, *21*, 146–155.

Meichenbaum, D. H. A self-instructional approach to stress management: A proposal for stress inoculation training. In C. Spielberger & I. Sarason (Eds.), *Stress and anxiety* (Vol. 1). Washington, D.C.: Hemisphere Publishing, 1975.

Meichenbaum, D. H. *Cognitive-behavior modification: An integrative approach.* New York: Plenum Press, 1977.

Meichenbaum, D. H., & Goodman, J. Training impulsive children to talk to themselves: A means of developing self-control. *Journal of Abnormal Psychology*, 1971, *77*, 115–126.

Melamed, B. G. Reduction of medical fears: An information processing analysis. In J. Boulougouris (Ed.), *International symposium on practical applications of learning theories in psychiatry.* New York: Wiley, 1982.

Melamed, B. G., & Siegel, L. J. Reduction of anxiety in children facing hospitalization and surgery by use of filmed modeling. *Journal of Consulting and Clinical Psychology*, 1975, *43*, 511–521.

Melamed, B. G., Hawes, R. R., Heiby, E., & Glick, J. The use of filmed modeling to reduce uncooperative behavior of children during dental treatment. *Journal of Dental Research*, 1975, *54*, 797–801.

Melamed, B. G., Weinstein, D., Hawes, R., & Katin-Borland, M. Reduction of fear-related dental management problems using filmed modeling. *Journal of the American Dental Association*, 1975, *90*, 822–826.

Melamed, B. G., Yurcheson, R., Fleece, E. L., Hutcherson, S., & Hawes, R. Effects of filmed modeling on the reduction of anxiety-related behaviors in individuals varying in level of previous experience in the stress situation. *Journal of Consulting and Clinical Psychology*, 1978, *46*, 1357–1367.

Melamed, B.G., Robbins, R. L., & Graves, S. Preparation for surgery and medical procedures. In D. Russo & J. Varni (Eds.), *Behavioral pediatrics: Research and practice.* New York: Plenum Press, 1981.

Melamed, B.G., Dearborn, M., & Hermecz, D. A. Necessary considerations for surgery preparation: Age and previous experience. *Psychosomatic Medicine*, 1983, *45*, 517–525.

Mellish, P. R. W. Preparation of a child for hospitalization and surgery. *Pediatric Clinic of North America*, 1969, *16*, 543–553.

Miller, S. M. Controllability and human stress: Method, evidence, and theory. *Behavior Research and Therapy*, 1979, *17*, 287–304. (a)

Miller, S. M. Coping with impending stress: Psychophysiological and cognitive correlates of choice. *Psychophysiology*, 1979, *16*, 572–581. (b)

Miller, S. M. *Monitors vs. blunters: Validation of a questionnaire to assess two styles of information-seeking under threat.* Unpublished manuscript, Temple University, 1980. (a)

Miller, S. M. When is a little knowledge a dangerous thing? Coping with stressful life-events by monitoring vs. blunting. In S. Levine & H.Ursin (Eds.), *Coping and health* (Proceedings of a NATO Conference). New York: Plenum Press, 1980. (b)

Miller, S. M. Why having control reduces stress: If I can stop the roller coaster I don't want to get off. In J. Garber & M. Seligman (Eds.), *Human helplessness: Theory and applications.* New York: Academic Press, 1980. (c)

Miller, S. M. *Coping with psychological threat by monitoring vs. blunting.* Unpublished manuscript, Temple University, 1981. (a)

Miller, S. M. Predictability and human stress: Toward a clarification of evidence and theory. In L. Berkowitz (Ed.), *Advances in experimental social psychology* (Vol. 14). New York: Academic Press, 1981. (b)

Miller, S. M., & Grant, R. The blunting hypothesis: A view of predictability and human stress. In P. O. Sjoden, S. Bates, & W. S. Dockens (Eds.), *Trends in behavior therapy.* New York: Academic Press, 1979.

Miller, S. M., & Green, M. *Styles of coping with stress: Origins, nature and development.* Paper presented at the meeting of the Eastern Psychological Association, Philadelphia, April 1983.

Miller, S. M., & Green, M. L. Learned resourcefulness and the development of coping. In M. Rosenbaum (Ed.), *Learned resourcefulness: On coping skills, self-regulation and adaptive behavior.* New York: Springer Press, 1985.

Miller, S. M., & Mangan, C. E. Interacting effects of information and coping style in adopting to gynecologic stress: Should the doctor tell all? *Journal of Personality and Social Psychology*, 1983, *45*, 223–236.

Miller, S. M., & Mischel, W. *A social learning approach to information-seeking styles in the coping process.* Unpublished manuscript, Temple University, 1985.

Miller, S. M., Mangan, C. E., & Wagner, A. *Individual differences in response to information and choice before an aversive gynecological procedure.* Unpublished manuscript, Temple University, 1980.

Miller, S. M., Mischel, W., Green, M., & Robinson, R. *Self-regulatory processes in children: Styles of coping with stress and delayed reward.* Unpublished manuscript, Temple University, 1985.

Mischel, W. A social learning view of sex differences in behavior. In E. E. Maccoby (Ed.), *The development of sex differences.* Stanford, Calif.: Stanford University Press, 1966.

Mischel, W. *Introduction to personality.* New York: Holt, Rinehart and Winston, 1971.

Mischel, W. Toward a cognitive social learning reconceptualization of personality. *Psychological Review*, 1973, *80*, 252–282.

Mischel, W. Processes in delay of gratification. In L. Berkowitz (Ed.), *Advances in experimental social psychology* (Vol. 7). New York: Academic Press, 1974.

Mischel, W. The interaction of person and situation. In D. Magnusson & N. S. Endler (Eds.), *Personality at the crossroads: Current issues in interactional psychology.* Hillsdale, N.J.: Erlbaum, 1977.

Mischel, W. On the interface of cognition and personality: Beyond the person-situation debate. *American Psychologist*, 1979, *34*, 740–754.

Mischel, W. *Introduction to personality* (3rd ed.). New York: Holt, Rinehart, and Winston, 1981.(a)

Mischel, W. Metacognition and the rules of delay. In J. Flavell & L. Ross (Eds.), *Cognitive social development: Frontiers and possible futures.* New York: Cambridge University Press, 1981. (b)

Mischel, W. Delay of gratification as process and as person variable in development. In D. Magnusson & V. P. Allen (Eds.), *Human development: An interactional perspective.* New York: Academic Press, 1983.

Mischel, W., & Baker, N. Cognitive appraisals and transformations in delay behavior. *Journal of Personality and Social Psychology*, 1975, *31*, 254–261.

Mischel, W., & Ebbesen, E. B. Attention in delay gratification. *Journal of Personality and Social Psychology*, 1970, *16*, 329–337.

Mischel, W., & Gilligan, C. F. Delay of gratification, motivation for the prohibited gratification, and responses to temptation. *Journal of Abnormal and Social Psychology*, 1964, 69, 411–417.

Mischel, W., & Moore, B. Effects of attention to symbolically-presented rewards on self-control. *Journal of Personality and Social Psychology*, 1973, 28, 172–179.

Mischel, W., & Moore, B. The role of ideation in voluntary delay for symbolically-presented rewards. *Cognitive Therapy and Research*, 1980, 4, 211–221.

Mischel, W., & Peake, P. K. Beyond déjà vu in the search for cross-situational consistency. *Psychological Review*, 1982, 89, 730–755.

Mischel, W., & Staub, E. Effects of expectancy on waiting and working for larger rewards. *Journal of Personality and Social Psychology*, 1965, 2, 625–633.

Mischel, W., Ebbesen, E. B., & Zeiss, A. M. Cognitive and attentional mechanisms in delay of gratification. *Journal of Personality and Social Psychology*, 1972, 21, 204–218.

Monat, A. Temporal uncertainty, anticipation time, and cognitive coping under threat. *Journal of Human Stress*, 1976, 2, 32–43.

Monat, A., Averill, J. R., & Lazarus, R. S. Anticipatory stress and coping reactions under various conditions of uncertainty. *Journal of Personality and Social Psychology*, 1972, 24, 237–252.

Moore, B., Mischel, W., & Zeiss, Z. Comparative effects of the reward stimulus and its cognitive representation in voluntary delay. *Journal of Personality and Social Psychology*, 1976, 34, 419–424.

Neufeld, R. J. The effect of experimentally altered cognitive appraisal on pain tolerance. *Psychonomic Science*, 1970, 20, 106–107.

Peterson, L., & Shigetomi, C. The use of coping techniques to minimize anxiety in hospitalized children. *Behavior Therapy*, 1981, 12, 1–14.

Prugh, D. G., Staub, E. M., Sands, H. H., Kirschbaum, R. M., & Lenihan, E. A. A study of the emotional reactions of children and families to hospitalization and illness. *American Journal of Orthopsychiatry*, 1953, 23, 70–106.

Ross, A. O. *Child behavior therapy: Principles, procedures, and empirical basis*. New York: Wiley, 1981.

Sawtell, R. O., Simon, J. F., Jr., & Simeonsson, R. J. The effects of five preparatory methods upon child behavior during the first dental visit. *Journal of Dentistry for Children*, 1974, 10, 37–45.

Siegel, L. J., & Peterson, L. Stress reduction in young dental patients through coping skills and sensory information. *Journal of Consulting and Clinical Psychology*, 1980, 48, 785–787.

Singer, J. L. Delayed gratification and ego development: Implications for clinical and experimental research. *Journal of Consulting Psychology*, 1955, 19, 259–266.

Skipper, J. K., & Leonard, R. C. *Social interaction and patient care*. Philadelphia: Lippincott, 1965.

Skipper, J. K., & Leonard, R. C. Children, stress, and hospitalization: A field experiment. *Journal of Health and Social Behavior*, 1968, 9, 275–287.

Speisman, J., Lazarus, R., Mordkoff, A., & Davison, L. Experimental reduction of stress based on ego defense theory. *Journal of Abnormal and Social Psychology*, 1964, 68, 267–380.

Taylor, L. W., Odegaard, V., & Watkins, L. O. Benefits of sensory instruction in preparation for cardiac catheterization: A randomized, controlled trial. *Circulation*, 1983, 68, 111–191.

Vernon, D. T. A. Use of modeling to modify children's responses to a natural, potentially stressful situation. *Journal of Applied Psychology*, 1973, 58, 351–356.

Vernon, D. T. A., & Bailey, W. The use of motion pictures in psychological preparation of children for induction of anesthesia. *Anesthesiology,* 1974, *40,* 68–74.

Visintainer, M. A., & Wolfer, J. A. Psychological preparation for surgical pediatric patients: The effect of children's and parents' stress responses and adjustment. *Pediatrics,* 1975, *56,* 187–202.

Wolfer, J. A., & Visintainer, M. A. Pediatric surgical patients' and parents' stress responses and adjustment. *Nursing Research,* 1975, *24,* 244–255.

Wolfer, J. A., & Visintainer, M. A. Pre-hospital psychological preparation for tonsillectomy patients: Effects on children's and parents' adjustment. *Pediatrics,* 1979, *64,* 646–655.

Author Index

Italic numbers indicate pages where complete reference citations are given.

Abelson, R. P., 23, 26, *36*, 136, *137*
Abound, R. E., 228, 229, *236*
Abramovitch, R., 143, *158*
Abramson, L. Y., 226, 235, 305, *309*
Adamson, L., 149, *160*
Alfert, E., 266, *310*
Alloy, I. B., 226, *235*
Als, H., 149, *160*
Alvarez, M., 42, *52*
Amen, E., 122, *137*
Anderson, K. O., 270, *309*
Anglin, J. M., 147, *157*, 170, 171, *185*
April, C., 244, *259*
Ascher, L. M., 267, *309*
Austin, J., 153, *157*
Averill, J. R., 266, *309*, *313*

Bailey, W., 270, 277, 279, 300, *313*
Baker, N., 293, 297, 298, 301, 303, 305, *312*
Ball, S., 71, 73, *81*
Bandura, A., 65, 66, 71, *81*, 269, 287, *309*
Barahal, R., 144, *157*
Barber, T. X., 266, *309*
Barden, R. C., 194, *208*, 224, *236*
Barenboim, D., 75, *82*
Barnett, M., 233, *235*
Baron, R. A., 70, *82*
Baron, R. M., 246, *259*

Bates, E., 106, *113*, 154, *157*
Bates, J. E., 245, *259*
Bateson, G., 244, *259*
Baumann, D. J., 224, 232, *235*, *236*
Baumeister, R. F., 193, 194, *208*, 246, *259*
Becker, W. C., 242, *259*
Beeghly (-Smith), M., 110, *114*, 166, 182, *184*
Bell, R. Q., 240, *242*, 245, *259*, *260*
Bellow, S., 95, *113*
Benedict, H., 147, *159*
Berenson, J. F., 231, *237*
Berenson, R. J., 231, *237*
Berger, S. M., 71, *81*
Berkowitz, L., 229, *235*
Berlyne, D. E., 291, *309*
Bernfeld, G., 244, *259*
Birch, H. G., 257, *261*
Birdwhistell, R. L., 56, *81*, 141, *157*
Blitz, B., 266, *309*
Block, J., 98, *113*
Blom, G. E., 268, *310*
Bloom, L., 123, *137*
Bloom L. J., 266, *309*
Blurton-Jones, N. G., 150, *157*
Bogatz, G. A., 71, 73, *81*
Borke, H., 119, 120, *137*, 165, 166, *184*
Bouthilet, L., 66, *84*
Bower, G. H., 172, *184*, 235, *235*, *236*
Bowerman, M., 147, *158*

Brazelton, T. B., 101, *114*, 149, *158*
Bretherton, I., 110, *114*, 166, 182, *184*
Brooks (-Gunn), J., 96, *115*, 119, 121, *137*, *138*
Brown, D., 265, *311*
Brown, M., 154, *158*
Bruner, J. S., 106, *114*
Brusa, J., 120
Bryan, J. H., 229, *236*
Bryant, J., 70, *85*
Buck, R. W., 6, *16*, 98, 100, *114*, 143, *158*
Buddin, B., 195, *208*
Bugental, D. B., 216, *235*, 242, 244, 247, 251, 253, *259*
Bullock, M., 182, *184*
Burgess, R., 146, *158*
Burish, T., 266, *309*
Burns, N., 121, *137*
Burstein, S., 276, 277, 286, *309*
Buss, A. M., 200, *208*, 257, *259*
Butkowsky, I., 75, *85*

Camainoni, L., 106, *113*
Campbell, E. Q., 61, *81*
Campbell, S. B., 244, *259*
Campos, J. J., 109, *114*, 167, *185*
Camras, L., 120, 144, 145, 146, 150, 151, 152, 153, 154, 155, 157, *158*
Cantor, J., 70, *81*

315

Cantor, M. G., 67, *82*
Cantor, N., 245, *259*
Caporael, L., 242, *259*
Caron, A. J., 121, *137*
Caron, R. F., 121, *137*
Cassell, S., 269, 277, 278, 300, *309*
Caul, W. F., 6, *16*
Cavey, L., 121, *137*
Cermack, E., 268, *310*
Chaffee, S., 66, *82*
Chance, M. R. A., 56, *82*
Chandler, M., 75, *82*
Chapman, M., 187, *208*
Charlesworth, W. R., 110, *114*, 121, *137*, 142, *159*
Chartier, G. M., 246, *260*
Cheng, K. K., 231, *237*
Chess, S., 257, *261*
Chorney, R. L., 267, *309*
Christie, B., 64, *85*
Cialdini, R. B., 224, 231, 232, *235*, *236*
Clark, H., 154, *158*
Clark, M., 230, *236*
Cline, V. B., 70, *82*
Clyburn, A., 222, *237*
Coates, B., 219, *236*
Cohen, D., 142, *158*
Cohen, F., 265, 277, *309*
Cohen, J. B., 265, 277, *310*
Cohen, L. B., 66, *82*
Cohn, J. F., 105, *114*
Cole, M., 40, *52*
Cole, P. M., 307, *309*
Comstock, G., 66, 68, 72, *82*
Conger, R., 146, *158*
Conner, W. H., 229, *235*
Cooper, J., 193, 194, *208*, 243, *261*
Copitch, P., 245, *261*
Courrier, S., 70, *82*
Cowan, C. L., 232, *237*
Cowan, G., 246, *259*
Croft, R. G., 70, *82*
Cruzcosa, M. M., 250, *260*

Daehler, M. W., 66, *82*
Daly, E., 143, 144, 146, *158*
Darwin, C. R., 117, *137*, 142, 143, 152, *158*
Davidson, R., 143, *158*
Davis, M., 136, *138*
Davison, L., 266, *313*

Davitz, J. R., 122, *137*
Dearborn, M., 276, *311*
DeCharms, R., 245, *260*
DeLoache, J. S., 66, *82*
Demos, V., 105, 106, 108, *114*
DePaulo, B. M., 74, *82*, 247, *261*
Deutsch, F., 65, *82*
Devereaux, G., 40, *52*
Dickes, R., 104, *114*
Dinnerstein, A. J., 266, *309*
Dirks, J., 66, *82*
Dixon, S., 101, 102, *114*
Donovan, W. L., 257, *260*
Dorr, A., 71, 72, 76, 77, *82*, *83*
Dotemoto, S., 244, *261*
Doubleday, C., 71, *82*
Dougherty, L. M., 123, *138*
Doyle, L., 225, *237*
Drabman, R. S., 71, *82*
Dumont, J. P., 40, *52*
Duncan, S. W., 194, *208*
Dunn, J., 167, *184*
Duvall, S., 218, *236*
Dweck, C. S., 246, *260*
Dysinger, W. S., 70, *82*

Ebbesen, E., 223, *236*, 288, 289, 295, 296, 297, 298, 301, 302, 304, 305, *313*
Edwards, C. P., 119, *137*
Efran, J., 266, *309*
Eibl-Eibesfeldt, I., 107, *114*, 141, *158*
Eisenberg, N., 119, *137*
Ekman, P., 6, *16*, 21, *36*, 56, 70, 74, *82*, 92, 93, 105, 107, *114*, 135, *138*, 141, 143, 145, 153, *158*, *159*, 168, 172, *184*, 251, *260*
Ellis, W. C., 225, *236*
Elmer, E., 257, *260*
Emde, R. N., 42, *52*, 136, *138*, 142, *160*, 167, *185*
Endman, M. W., 244, *259*
Endress, M. P., 275, 278, *310*
Engquist, G., 265, *311*
Ervin-Tripp, S., 154, 155, *158*
Eyre-Brook, C., 70, *82*

Fallis, S. F., 72, *84*
Faust, O. A., 268, *310*
Feather, N. T., 219, *236*
Feilitzen, C., 70, *82*
Feinman, S., 11, *16*
Feiring, C., 10, *16*
Ferguson, B. F., 270, 271, 277, 278, 281, 284, 300, 305, *309*
Fernie, D. E., 77, *83*
Feshbach, N., 119, *138*
Field, J., 66, *83*
Field, T. M., 65, *85*, 101, 104, *114*, 142, *158*
Filipson, E., 70, *83*
Finch, A. J., Jr., 308, *309*
Fitzpatrick, M. A., 72, *84*
Flapan, D., 74, *83*
Flavell, J. H., 161, *184*
Fleece, E. L., 271, *311*
Fogel, A., 109, *115*, 149, *159*
Folkman, S., 56, *83*, 265, *310*
Ford, M. E., 224, *236*
Fox, N., 143, *158*
Freud, S., 94, 107, *114*, 229, 287, *309*
Friesen, W. V., 6, *16*, 70, 74, *82*, 93, 105, *114*, 141, 143, 145, *158*, 251, *260*
Frijda, N. H., 74, *83*
Frodi, A. M., 257, *260*
Froming, W. J., 217, 226, 230, *237*
Fry, P. S., 215, *236*
Furman, W., 226, *236*

Ganz, R. L., 246, *259*
Garber, J., 305, *309*
Gardner, H., 14, *16*, 201, 202, *208*
Gardner, K., 192, *208*
Garry, R., 70, *83*
Geer, J. H., 266, 305, *309*
Geertz, C., 40, *52*
Geertz, H., 110, *114*, 173, *184*
Gelfand, D., 245, *259*
Gellert, E., 268, *309*
Gelman, R., 182, *184*
Gerard, H. B., 287, *310*
Gerber, E., 173, *184*
Gianetto, R. M., 251, *259*
Gibson, E., 66, *82*
Gilligan, S. G., 235, *236*, 295, *313*
Glasberg, R., 228, *236*

Glick, J., 270, 300, *311*
Glynn, C. J., 72, *84*
Gnepp, J., 74, *83*, 120, 121, *138*, 171, 172, *184*
Golden, C., 98, *116*
Golinkoff, R. M., 106, *114*
Goodman, J., 308, *311*
Gordon, D., 189, *208*
Gordon, P., 99, *115*
Goslin, D. A., 61, *83*
Gottman, J., 149, *159*
Graham, S., 65, *85*
Grant, E. C., 150, 153, *159*
Grant, R., 265, 266, 286, 305, 307, *312*
Graves, S., 275, *311*
Green, J., 143, 145, *159*
Green, M., 306, 307, *312*
Greenberg, R., 142, *158*
Greenfield, P. M., 23, *36*
Greenspan, S., 75, *82*
Gregg, G. S., 257, *260*
Gregory, W. L., 246, *260*
Greif, E. B., 42, *52*
Grim, P. F., 295, *310*
Grow, G., 144, *158*
Gruendel, J., 147, *159*
Grusec, J. E., 71, *81*
Guttman, D., 202, *208*
Guz, G. R., 179, *184*

Haggard, E. A., 251, *260*
Haggerty, R. J., 268, *310*
Hahn, K. W., 266, *309*
Haley, J., 241, 244, *259*, *260*
Hall, J. A., 98, 104, *114*
Harding, C. G., 106, *114*
Hardman, C. E., 169, 173, *184*
Hargis, K., 232, 233, *237*
Harkness, S., 22, 25, *36*, 39, *52*, 101, *116*
Harris, P. L., 74, *83*, 163, 164, 165, 168, 169, 170, 173, 174, 176, 177, 178, 179, 180, 182, 183, *184*, *185*, 195, *208*
Harrison, R., 70, 74, *82*, *83*
Harter, S., 174, 177, *184*, 195, 196, *208*
Haviland, J. M., 96, 102, 103, 106, *114*, *115*, 119, *138*, 142, 149, *159*

Hawes, R. R., 270, 271, 277, 279, 300, *311*
Hawkins, R. P., 77, *83*
Hay, T. A., 70, *85*
Heberlein, P., 225, *237*
Heiby, E., 270, 300, *311*
Henker, B., 244, *261*
Hermecz, D. A., 276, *311*
Hess, E. H., 56, *83*
Higgins, J. D., 97, *116*
Hilgard, E. R., 192, *208*
Hilpert, P., 276, *310*
Himmelweit, H. T., 70, *83*
Hiroto, D. S., 246, *260*
Hittelman, J. H., 104, *114*
Hochschild, A. R., 2, *16*, 99, 113, *115*, 117, *138*, 188, 192, *208*
Hoffman, H. R., 68, 70, *83*, *84*
Hogg, E., 246, *260*
Hoijer, B., 70, *83*
Hokanson, J. E., 223, 224, *237*
Holmes, C., 246, *260*
Holmes D., 266, *309*, *310*
Holzman, P. S., 251, *260*
Horowitz, F., 121, *139*
Houston, B. K., 266, *309*, *310*
Howard, J. A., 233, *235*
Huebner, R. R., 122, *138*
Hupp, S., 147, *159*
Hutcherson, S., 271, *311*
Hutchins, E., 23, *36*

Ickes, W., 246, *261*
Irvine, A., 74, *82*
Isaacs, K. S., 251, *260*
Isen, A. M., 215, 229, 230, *236*
Izard, C. E., 21, *36*, 56, *83*, 91, 100, 102, 104, 110, *115*, 117, 121, 122, 123, *138*, 141, 142, 143, 144, 149, *159*, 214, 217, 218, 219, *236*

Jackson, D., 244, *259*
Jackson, K., 268, *310*
Jacobson, L., 243, *261*
James, S., 155, *159*
Janis, I. L., 266, 305, *310*
Jenkins, J. J., 287, *310*
Jessner, L., 268, *310*
Jewett, J. L., 182, *185*

Johnson, L. R., 168, *185*
Johnson, J., 201, *208*
Johnson, J. E., 65, *84*, 120, *138*, 275, 278, *310*
Johnson, M., 23, *36*
Johnson, P. A., 269, 280, 283, 284, 305, *310*
Johnson, R., 270, 272, 277, 279, 300, *311*
Johnson, W., 136, *138*
Jones, E., 287, *310*
Jones, G. F., 221, *236*
Jones, J., 193, *208*
Jordan, A., 74, *82*

Kagan, J., 96, 102, *115*
Kanner, A. D., 56, *83*, 265, *310*
Kaplan, A., 40, *52*
Kaplan, B., 33, *36*
Karylowski, J., 233, *237*
Kaswan, J. W., 244, 247, *259*
Katin-Borland, M., 270, 300, *311*
Katzman, N., 66, *82*
Kay, D. A., 170, 171, *185*
Kaye, K., 109, *115*, 149, *159*
Kazdin, A. E., 229, *236*, 307, *309*
Keeler, C., 101, *114*
Keller, B. B., 245, *260*
Kendall, P. C., 268, 307, *310*
Kendrick, C., 167, *184*
Kenrick, D. T., 224, 231, 232, *235*, *236*
King, L. M., 233, *235*
King, M., 122, *138*, *139*
King, R., 122, *139*
Kinzie, D., 99, *115*
Kippax, S., 72, *84*
Kirchoff, K. T., 275, 278, *310*
Kirschbaum, R. M., 268, *313*
Klein, M., 257, *260*
Klemp, G. O., 266, *310*
Klineberg, O., 141, *159*
Klineberg, S. L., 295, *310*
Klinnert, M. D., 142, 148, *159*, 160, 167, *185*
Klorman, R., 276, *310*
Kohlberg, L., 295, 310
Koswolski, B., 149, *158*
Kovaric, P., 71, 77, *82*, *83*
Kraus, R., 33, *36*

Kreutzer, M. A., 110, *114*, 121, *137*, 142, *159*
Krug, R. S., 242, *259*
Kulik, J., 231, *237*

LaBarbera, J. D., 121, *138*
LaBarre, W., 141, *159*
Lacey, B. C., 96, *115*
Lacey, J., 96, *115*, 272, *310*
LaGana, C., 276, *310*
Lahey, M., 123, *137*
Laird, J. D., 121, *138*
Lakoff, G., 23, *36*
Lakoff, R., 154, *159*
Lamb, M. E., 257, *260*
Landes, H. R., 268, *310*
Langer, E. J., 266, 305, *310*
Laosa, L. M., 70, *83*
Laser, P. S., 74, *82*
Lazar, J., 66, *84*
Lazarus, R. S., 56, *70*, 265, 266, 277, 304, *309, 310, 313*
Leavitt, L. A., 257, *260*
Lefcourt, H. M., 246, 258, *260*
Leiderman, P. H., 101, *114*
Leifer, A. D., 79, *83*
Leight, K. E., 225, *236*
Lelwica, M., 142, *159*
Lemond, C., 143, *159*
Lenihan, E. A., 268, *313*
Leonard, R., 268, *310, 313*
Lesser, G. S., 70, *83*
Levenson, R. W., 6, *16*
Leventhal, H., 56, *83*, 91, 99, 112, *115*, 265, *311*
Levin, P. F., 215, 230, *236*
Levy, R. I., 110, 111, *115*
Lewis, M., 3, 8, 10, 11, 14, 15, *16, 17*, 31, *36*, 96, 112, *115*, 119, 121, 126, 132, 134, 135, *137*, *138*, 141, 153, *159*, 213
Lewis, N. L., 97, *116*
Lewis, W. C., 122, *138, 139*
Liebert, R. M., 70, *82*
Ling, A. H., 108, *115*
Ling, D., 108, *115*
Linne, O., 70, *82, 83*
Lipian, M. S., 179, *184*
Litzie, K., 225, 233, *237*
Love, L. R., 244, 247, 251, *259*

Lueptow, L., 187, 202, *208*
Lukens, M. D., 266, *309*
Lundholm, H., 33, *36*
Lutz, C., 23, *36*, 41, 51, *52*, 102, 110, *115*, 169, 170, *185*
Lyle, J., 68, 70, *83, 84*
Lyons, J., 33, *36*

Machen, J. B., 270, 272, 277, 279, 300, *311*
Macnamara, J., 147, *159*
Main, M., 149, *158*
Maisel, E., 266, 305, *309*
Malatesta, C. Z., 102, 103, 104, 106, 108, 109, *114*, *115*, 119, *138*, 142, 149, *159*
Malmstrom, E. J., 70, *83*
Mandler, G., 56, *84*, 214, *236*
Mangan, C. E., 266, 267, 277, 285, *312*
Man-Shu, Z., 179, *184*
Marsella, A. J., 98, 99, *115, 116*
Martin, H., 144, *157*
Masters, J. C., 194, *208*, 224, *236*
Masters, J. W., 226, *236*
Masur, F. T., III, 270, *309*
Maynard, J., 66, *82*
McCandless, B. R., 61, *84*
McCombs, M., 66, *82*
McDonald, M., 246, *259*
McGhee, P. E., 70, *84*
McGillicuddy-Delisi, A., 201, *208*
McGillis, D., 193, *208*
McGinnes, G. C., 123, *138*
McLeod, J. M., 72, *84*
McMillen, D. S., 231, *236*
McNew, S., 110, *114*
Mead, P. G., 266, *311*
Means, B., 40, *52*
Mechanic, D., 275, *311*
Medlin, D. L., 171, *185*
Meerum Terwogt, M., 74, *83*, 163, 168, 174, 176, *184, 185*
Mehrabian, A., 247, 248, *260*
Meichenbaum, D. H., 270, 276, 277, 286, 307, 308, *309, 311*
Melamed, B. G., 270, 271, 272, 275, 276, 277,

Melamed, B. G. (*cont.*)
279, 282, 284, 286, 300, *311*
Mellish, P. R. W., 268, *311*
Menlove, F. I., 244, *260*
Menlove, F. L., 71, *81*, 269, *309*
Mervis, C., 147, *159*
Michael, R., 276, *310*
Michalson, L., 3, 8, 14, 15, *17*, 112, *115*, 126, 132, 134, 135, *138*, 141, 153, *159*
Midlarsky, E., 230, *236*
Midlarsky, M., 230, *236*
Miller, R. E., 6, *16*
Miller, P., 37, *52*
Miller, R. S., 258, *260*
Miller, S. M., 265, 266, 267, 277, 285, 304, 305, 306, 307, *309*, *311, 312*
Minuchin, S., 241, *260*
Mischel, W., 219, 223, *236*, 264, 267, 286, 287, 288, 289, 291, 292, 293, 294, 295, 296, 297, 298, 299, 300, 301, 302, 303, 304, 305, 306, *312*, *313*
Mishler, E. G., 241, *260*
Monat, A., 266, 305, *313*
Montgomery, L. E., 308, *309*
Mood, D. W., 65, *84*, 120, *138*
Moore, B. S., 215, 216, 217, 220, 221, 222, 225, 226, 230, 231, 233, 234, *235, 236*, *237*, 291, 292, 293, 294, 297, 298, 299, 301, 302, 305, *313*
Moos, R., 197, 198, *208*
Mordkoff, A., 266, *313*
Munroe, R. H., 23, *36*
Munroe, R. L., 25, *36*
Murray, J. P., 72, *84*
Murray, M. D., 98, *116*
Mussen, P. H., 61, *84*
Myers, N. A., 66, *82*
Myers, R. S., 121, *137*

Natale, M., 226, *237*
Neff, C. N., 257, *260*
Nelson, K., 147, *159*
Neufeld, R. J., 266, *313*

Nicol, X., 77, 83
Nomikos, M., 266, 310

Odom, R., 143, 159
Olness, G., 192, 208
Olthof, T., 74, 83, 163,
  164, 165, 168, 176,
  177, 178, 179, 182,
  183, 184, 185
Oosterhoff, T., 174, 185
Oppenheim, A. N., 70,
  83
Opton, E., 266, 310
Orne, M. T., 136, 138
Oster, H., 138, 142, 159
Oviatt, S., 147, 160

Pani, J., 147, 159
Panksepp, J., 100, 116
Pannabecker, B. J., 136,
  138
Parisi, S. A., 121, 138
Parker, E. B., 68, 84
Patterson, G. R., 241,
  244, 260
Pawlby, J. S., 149, 160
Peake, P. K., 287, 313
Pearl, R. A., 66, 82, 84
Perlmutter, M., 66, 82
Peterson, L., 272, 273,
  274, 279, 280, 282,
  283, 284, 300, 302,
  303, 305, 313
Phares, E. J., 246, 261
Piaget, J., 168, 185
Pittman, N. L., 246, 261
Pittman, T. S., 246, 261
Pliner, P., 143, 158
Plomin, R. A., 257, 259
Polivy, J., 217, 237
Pristo, T. M., 154, 158
Prugh, D. G., 268, 313

Quinn, N., 23, 36

Radke-Yarrow, M., 122,
  139
Rajecki, D. W., 246, 261
Raleigh, M. J., 92, 116
Rankin, N., 266, 310
Raskoff, A., 219, 236
Reilly, S., 70, 81
Repucci, D., 246, 260
Rescorla, L., 147, 159
Ribordy, S. C., 144, 158
Ridgeway, D., 122, 139
Ringland, J., 149, 159
Risser, D., 123, 138
Robbins, R. L., 275, 311

Roberts, D., 66, 82
Robinson, R., 306, 312
Rodin, J., 266, 310
Roe, K., 120, 138
Rosaldo, M. Z., 173, 185
Rosch, E., 171, 185
Rosenblum, L., 31, 36
Rosenfeld, H. M., 121,
  139
Rosenhan, D. L., 215,
  220, 232, 233, 234,
  236, 237
Rosenn, M., 266, 309
Rosenthal, R., 243, 247,
  261
Rosenthal, T. L., 65, 84
Ross, A. O., 270, 307, 313
Rotter, J. B., 226, 237,
  245, 261
Rousey, C., 251, 260
Ruckmick, C. A., 70, 82
Rushton, J. P., 65, 71, 84
Russell, J. A., 122, 139

Saarni, 74, 84, 89, 116,
  153, 160, 165, 185,
  192, 194, 196, 197,
  198, 204, 208, 209
Sacco, W. P., 223, 224,
  237
Sacham, S., 265, 311
Salomon, G., 68, 84
Salovey, P., 232, 233, 237
Sanders, D. Y., 231, 236
Sands, H. H., 268, 313
Sapolsky, B. S., 70, 85
Sawtell, R. O., 272, 313
Schachter, S., 56, 84, 172,
  185
Schaefer, C., 265, 310
Schank, R. C., 23, 26, 36
Scheerer, M., 33, 36
Schieffelin, B. B., 23, 36
Schramm, W., 68, 70, 84
Schultz, T. R., 75, 85
Schunk, D., 154, 158
Schwartz, G. E., 171, 185
Schwartz, J. C., 223, 237
Schwartz, M. F., 230, 236
Schyller, I., 70, 83
Searle, J., 153, 160
Seeman, G., 223, 237
Selye, H., 95, 116
Shantz, C. U., 65, 84,
  120, 121, 138, 139
Shaw, C., 243, 261
Shennum, W. A., 242,
  253, 259
Sheras, P., 243, 261

Sherk, D., 258, 260
Sherry, D., 257, 260
Shields, S. A., 96, 97, 116
Shigetomi, C., 272, 273,
  282, 283, 284, 300,
  302, 305, 313
Short, J. G., 64, 68, 71, 85
Siegel, L. J., 270, 274,
  277, 279, 280, 283,
  284, 300, 302,
  303, 305, 311, 313
Silvern, L., 154, 157
Simon, J. F., Jr., 272, 313
Simeonsson, R. J., 272,
  313
Singer, J., 172, 185, 287,
  313
Skipper, J., 268, 310, 313
Smith, E. E., 171, 185
Smith, W. J., 152, 153,
  160
Snyder, M., 197, 198, 209
Solomon, G. S., 231, 236
Solomon, T., 244, 261
Sorce, J. F., 142, 148, 160,
  167, 185
Sostek, A. M., 101, 114
Speisman, J., 266, 313
Sproull, N., 70, 85
Staub, E., 268, 288, 313
Stein, N. L., 168, 182, 185
Steklis, H. D., 92, 116
Stenberg, C. R., 109, 114,
  116, 136, 138
Stern, L., 257, 260
Stern, R. M., 96, 97, 116
Stockdale, D. F., 269, 277,
  278, 300, 310
Strauss, M. S., 66, 82
Struthers, S., 246, 260
Super, C. M., 22, 25, 36,
  39, 52, 101, 116
Surgeon General's Scien-
  tific Advisory Com-
  mittee, 66, 85
Sveen, O., 276, 310
Svejda, M., 167, 185

Tagiuri, R., 121, 139
Tanford, S., 246, 261
Taylor, D. A., 180, 185
Tennes, K., 96, 116
Thelen, M. H., 221, 236
Thomas, A., 257, 261
Thomas, M. H., 71, 82
Thompson, W. C., 232,
  237
Tomkins, S. S., 89, 91,
  94, 102, 107, 116, 117,

Tomkins, S. S. (*cont.*)
139, 144, *160*, 218,
237
Trabasso, T., 168, 169,
185
Tronick E., 101, *114*, 149,
160

Ulman, K., 42, *52*
Underwood, B., 215, 217,
220, 221, 222, 225,
226, 227, 230, 231,
233, 234, *236*, 237

van Eck, O., 176, *185*
Vasta, R., 245, *261*
Velten, E., 215, 237
Venn, J. R., 71, *85*
Vernon, D. T. A., 270,
277, 279, 300, *313*
Vietze, P., 101, *114*, 121,
138
Vince, P., 70, *83*
Viscusi, D., 226, 235
Visintainer, M. A., 273,
280, 281, 284, 300,
303, 305, *314*
Volterra, V., 106, *113*

Wack, D., 97, *116*
Wagner, A., 267, *312*

Walden, T. A., 65, *85*
Waldfogel, S., 268, *310*
Ware, E. E., 258, *260*
Waterman, J., 144, *157*
Watson, D., 268, *310*
Watson, J. B., 10, *17*
Waxler, N. E., 241, *260*
Weakland, J., 244, *259*
Weinberger, D. A., 171,
185
Weiner, B., 65, *85*, 245,
261
Weiner, M., 247, *260*
Weinraub, M., 10, *17*
Weinstein, D., 270, 277,
279, 300, *311*
Weitz, S., 202, *209*
Wellman, H. M., 161, *184*
Wells, A., 149, *159*
Wenzel, G., 231, *237*
Werner, H., 33, *36*
Weyant, J. M., 232, *237*
Whalen, C. K., 244, *261*
White, S. H., 295, *310*
Whiting, B. B., 26, *36*, 38,
47, 52, *52*, *53*
Whiting, J. W. M., 38, 52,
53
Wicklund, R. A., 218, *236*
Williams, E., 64, *85*
Wilson, D., 231, *237*

Winkley, R., 268, *310*
Wittgenstein, L., 167, *185*
Wolfer, J. A., 266, 273,
280, 281, 284, 300,
303, 305, *310*, *314*
Wolman, R. N., 122, *138*,
139
Wolpe, J., 66, *85*
Woodson, R., 142, *158*
Woolridge, P., 268, *310*
Wright, M. H., 246, *260*

Yates, L., 228, *237*
Young-Browne, G., 121,
139
Yurcheson, R., 271, *311*

Zahn-Waxler, C., 122, *139*
Zanna, M. P., 243, *261*
Zeiss, A., 223, *236*, 288,
293, 296, 297, 305,
313
Zelditch, M., Jr., 202, *209*
Zelko, F., 194, *208*
Zillmann, D., 70, 71, *85*
Zimmerman, B. J., 65, *84*
Zivin, G., 92, 93, 100,
106, *116*
Zlatchin, C., 70, *82*
Zuckerman, M., 247, *261*

Subject Index

Abused children, 7, 144, 147
Adoption, 49–50
Affect blends. *See* Mixed emotions
Affect displays, 92–94
Affect transformation, 94–95
Age differences, 48, 103, 107, 108–110,
    113, 123–132, 163–165, 178, 179–
    181, 182–183
Altruism, 5, 229–235
Anthropological approach, 51
Attributions, 242–243

Biological model, 2, 12, 92–94, 117–118,
    133–136
Blunting, 265–308

Cognition
    and coping, 273–275
    effect of emotion on, 218–219
    See also Attribution; Cognitive-affective
        structure; Cognitive learning;
        Cognitive styles; Concept forma-
        tion; Self
Cognitive-Affective structure, 33–35, 61–
    62
    See also Cognitive styles; Expectancy
        formation; Internalization
Cognitive learning, 72–74, 80
    See also Cognitive-affective structure
Cognitive styles, 4, 13, 265–308
Concept formation, 147–148
Contagion, 12, 89
Contexts
    of emotion experience, 55–66
    and interpretation, 152–153
    typology of, 56–66
    See also Niche; Situations; Television
Contingency patterns, 108–110

Control of emotion, 161, 163–165
    See also Contagion
Coping, 286–308
Crying, 7, 25–32
    See also Emotional expression; Facial
        expression
Cultural differences, 14
    See also Gusii; Ifaluk atoll; Kenya
Culture
    definitions of, 38–39
    methodology in study of, 39–41, 51

Delay of gratification, 286–299
Developmental theories, 2–10, 95, 100–
    113
    See also Age differences
Direct effects, 10, 57–59, 65–66
Display behavior, 92–94, 99–100
    See also Emotional expression; Facial
        expression
Display rules, 7, 73–74

Emblems, 106
Emotion
    cognitive consequences of, 218–219
    duration of, 178–182, 183
    effect on behavior, 213–235
    manipulation of, 214–217
    mixed, 105–106, 132–133, 170–178, 182
    nature of, 2–10, 90–94
    and response to others, 229–235
    and response to self, 218–235
Emotional elicitor, 3, 4–5
Emotional experience, 3, 8–9, 98–99
    contexts of, 55–56
    and expectancies, 173–203
    and television, 70–72
    transformations in, 106

Emotional expression, 3, 7–8, 99–100
   children's knowledge of, 119, 121–122
   transformations in, 105–106
   See also Facial expression
Emotional meaning, 51–52
   See also Emotional experience
Emotional receptor, 3, 5–6
Emotional state, 3, 6–7, 95–98, 213–235
Emotion labels. *See* Vocabulary
Emotion models, 2–10
Empathy, 148–149, 162, 166
Expectancies, 11–12, 187–189, 196–203
   formation of, 189–191, 193–196
   of the self, 191–193

Facial expression
   conditioning of, 7, 105–108
   recognition of, 7, 142–149
   universality of, 21–22, 134–136, 141
Family Environment Scale, 197–198, 202
Feeling rules, 192
Framed experience, 5, 59–61, 66–69
Frustration, coping with, 286–301

Gusii, 101–102

Identification, 11
   See also Indirect effects
Ifaluk atoll, 9, 41–50
Imitation, 11, 104–105, 149
   See also Indirect effects
Indirect effects, 11, 59–61, 65–66, 69–81
Individual differences, 4, 9, 12–16, 134–
      136, 241
   and abused children, 7, 144–147
   in arousal, 6, 244–245
   in cognitive styles, 13, 265–308
   in coping, 275–286, 295
   in cultural scripts, 31–32, 35, 47–50, 52
   See also Age differences; Cultural dif-
      ferences; Sex differences; Social
      class differences
Instrumental learning, 105–108
Internalization
   of cultural scripts, 32, 33–35, 44–50,
      107–108
   of expectations, 187–191

Kenya, 7, 23–32

Language. *See* Scripts; Vocabulary
Locus of control, 226, 246–247

Maternal behavior, 101–110
Methodology, 39–41, 51
Mixed emotions, 105–106, 132–133, 170–
      178, 182
Monitor-Blunter Style Scale, 167
Monitoring, 265–308
Mood. *See* Emotion
Mood Adjective Checklist, 227

Nguch, 43–50
Niche, developmental, 22, 35
   in Ifaluk atoll, 41–50
   in Kenya, 23–25

PACES, 197–198, 202, 203–207
Parent Attribution Test, 247–248
Peers, 149–153
Phenomenology, 98–99
   See also Emotional experience
Physiology, 95–98
   See also Emotional receptors; Emo-
      tional states
Prosocial behavior, 229–235

Recognition, 74–75, 142–144
   by abused children, 144–147
   cognitive processes in, 147–149
   role of peers in, 151–153
Reminiscence procedure, 216

Scripts, cultural, 8, 23, 26–32, 35
   individual differences in, 31–32, 35,
      47–50, 52
   internalization of, 32, 33–35, 44–50
Self concept, 5, 218–229
Self-generated suggestions, 191–193
Self-Monitoring Scale, 197–198, 202
Self-regulation, 264
Self-reward, 219–224
Sex differences, 14, 49, 103–104
Situations
   children's understanding of, 4, 8, 120–
      121, 128–132, 154–156, 165–178,
      182–183
   and concept *nguch*, 45–47
   evocative power of, 133–136
   See also Contexts
Smiling, 105
   See also Expression; Facial expression
Social class differences, 14–15
Socialization
   anthropological approach to, 51

Socialization (*cont.*)
 anthropological approach to (*cont.*)
  See also Cultural scripts;
   Methodology
 of emotional elicitors, 4–5
 of emotional experiences, 8–9, 98–99
 of emotional expressions, 7–8, 99–100
 of emotional receptors, 5–6
 of emotional states, 6–7, 95–98, 213–235
 through language, 156–157
 through television, 69–81
Socialization model, 2, 118–119, 134–136
Socialization rules, 15–16
Social communications. *See* Scripts
Social learning, 11
 See also Indirect effects

Social referencing, 109
Speech act theory, 153–154
Stress. *See* Frustration; Threat
Structural model of emotion, 3–10
Success-or-failure experience, 216

Television, 5, 69–81
Threat, 265–286, 300
Transactional model, 240–258

Universality of expression, 21–22, 134–136, 141
Unresponsive children, 243–258

Velten technique, 215–216
Vocabulary of emotion, 72–74, 110–113, 122–128, 214–215